Non-Representation

CU00764869

Non-Representational Theory presents a distinctive approach to the politics of everyday life. Ranging across a variety of the spaces in which politics and the political unfold, it questions what is meant by perception, representation and practice, with the aim of valuing the fugitive practices that exist on the margins of the known. This book questions the orientation of the social sciences and humanities and makes essential reading for researchers and postgraduates. It revolves around three key functions:

- it introduces the rather dispersed discussion of non-representational theory to a wider audience,
- it provides the basis for an experimental rather than a representational approach to the social sciences and humanities,
- it begins the task of constructing a different kind of political genre.

Nigel Thrift brings together further writings from a body of work that has come to be known as non-representational theory. Thrift's noteworthy book makes a significant contribution to the literature in this area and provides a groundbreaking and comprehensive introduction to this key topic making *Non-Representational Theory* an incredibly useful text for students of social theory, sociology, geography, anthropology and cultural studies.

Nigel Thrift, Professor at the University of Warwick, is also a Visiting Professor at the University of Oxford and an Emeritus Professor at the University of Bristol. He has authored, co-authored and co-edited more than 35 books and over 200 journal articles. His research includes work on international finance, new forms of capitalism, cities, social and cultural theory and the history of time

International Library of Sociology

Founded by Karl Mannheim
Editor: John Urry
Lancaster University

Recent publications in this series include:

Non-Representational Theory

Space | politics | affect

Nigel Thrift

Routledge
Taylor & Francis Group

LONDON AND NEW YORK

First published 2008
by Routledge
2 Park Square, Milton Park, Abingdon, Oxon OX14 4RN

Simultaneously published in the USA and Canada
by Routledge
270 Madison Ave, New York, NY 10016

Transferred to Digital Printing 2008

Routledge is an imprint of the Taylor & Francis Group, an informa business

© 2007 Nigel Thrift

Typeset in Galliard by
Keystroke, 28 High Street, Tettenhall, Wolverhampton
Printed and bound in Great Britain by
CPI Antony Rowe, Chippenham, Wiltshire

All rights reserved. No part of this book may be reprinted or reproduced
or utilised in any form or by any electronic, mechanical, or other means,
now known or hereafter invented, including photocopying and recording,
or in any information storage or retrieval system, without permission in
writing from the publishers.

British Library Cataloguing in Publication Data
A catalogue record for this book is available from the British Library

Library of Congress Cataloging in Publication Data
A catalog record for this book has been requested

ISBN10: 0–415–39320–5 (hbk)
ISBN10: 0–415–39321–3 (pbk)
ISBN10: 0–203–94656–1 (ebk)

ISBN13: 978–0–415–39320–1 (hbk)
ISBN13: 978–0–415–39321–8 (pbk)
ISBN13: 978–0–203–94656–5 (ebk)

Contents

Preface

This book summarizes and extends a batch of work carried out since the late 1990s concerned with what I call non-representational theory. On one level this is a book about the dynamics of susceptibility and about how we are being made susceptible in new ways. Of course, we are continually being made into new creatures by all kinds of forces, but it is surely the case that as the world is forced to face up to the damage done, so we can no longer move along the same cul-de-sacs of practical-cum-conceptual possibilities. Other possibilities need to be alighted upon for thinking about the world. That requires boosting inventive attitude so as to produce more contrary motion.

Then, on another level, this is a book about apathy. Given what has to be faced, it seems important to find a way of expanding the capacity for action in a world in which action is severely circumscribed. But it is not the heroic, individualized and autonomous action of a certain kind of activist – 'self-confident and free of worry, capable of vigorous, wilful activity' (Walzer 1988: 313) – that I want to concentrate on in this book. Rather, rediscovering, at least to an extent, seventeenth-century notions of agency and selfhood, it is an action that can be associated with passivity, but a passivity that is demanding, that is called forth by another (Gross 2006).

In days when the Iraq War, Afghanistan, 9/11, 7/7 and other such events often seem to have claimed total occupation of the Western academic psyche, and many academics have reacted accordingly with mammoth statements about warfare, imperialism, capitalism, global warming, and numerous other waypoints on the road to perdition, it is difficult to remember that other kinds of political impulse might also have something to say, something smaller and larger, something which is in danger of being drowned out. Instead this book keeps faith with the small but growing number of determined experimentalists who think that too often we have been asking the wrong questions in the wrong way: those who want to re-materialize democracy, those who want to think about the exercise of association, those who want to make performances in the interstices of everyday life, those who are intent on producing new and more challenging environments, those who want to redesign everyday things, those who, in other words, want to generate more space to be unprecedented, to love what aids fantasy, and so to gradually break down imaginative resistance. Rather like Darwin's restless earthworms, slowly going about the work of tilling the soil (Graham and Thrift 2007), they are attempting to make progress in reworking the background by producing new and more productive entanglements. The intent is to produce a political genre in much the same manner that, in the history of painting, the work of the assistants who carried out the painting of the background gradually comes into the light. What was formerly understood as the cheap stuff to be inserted by the apprentices is gradually foregrounded as the genre of landscape painting. The side panels take to centre stage.

Of course, all of this is very easy to misread, especially if you want – even need – to do so. Surely we should all be concentrating our attention on the millions without food or water, the terrible wars, the multiple oppressions that characterize so many people's lives. But this kind of linearization of intent, classically associated with those who want to configure a centre that thinks radical practices (Colectivo Situaciones 2005), too often elides the complex, emergent world in which we live, in which it is by no means clear that everyone could or should suddenly reach a point of clarity and unanimity about means and ends, yet alone a state of compassion. This is a world that is simultaneously monstrous and wonderful, banal and bizarre, ordered and chaotic, a world that is continually adding new hybrid inhabitants, and a world in which the human is consequently up for grabs as 'human nature (the phrase already innocent, nostalgically distant) is melting, running off in unpredictable directions' (Rotman 2000: 59).[1]

Those involved in the kinds of projects that I have mentioned certainly see the imprints of power but they do not believe that everything enters the machine: for example, there can be moments of relation of which no residue remains upon which therefore we may not easily be able to reflect but which can still have grip. Nor do they believe that everyone enters into a contract as an 'individual' with her own body and can therefore easily manifest intention. Rather there are flows of what is and is not subjectivity (Wall 1999) making their ways across fields of flesh, touching some parts and not others, and it has become clear that these flows of subjectivity need to and do involve more and more actors – various kinds of things, various other biological beings, even the heft of a particular landscape – in a continuous undertow of matterings that cannot be reduced to simple transactions but can become part of new capacities to empower.[2]

Acknowledgements

One of the banal but still important principles of non-representational theory is that all work is joint: the idea that such a thing as a single author is there to be named is faintly ludicrous. Rather, all books seem to me to be in the nature of treated novels like Tom Phillips's wonderful (2005 [1980]) *A Humument*, full to the brim with the thoughts of a host of others, alive and dead. I would like to name and thank some of these others who have commented on one or more of the chapters in this book: Jeremy Ahearne, Ash Amin, Jakob Arnoldi, Andrew Barry, Ryan Bishop, Virginia Blum, Dede Boden, Søren Buhl, Geof Bowker, Chris Castiglia, Tom Conley, Verena Andermatt Conley, Gail Davies, J-D Dewsbury, Stuart Elden, Chris Gosden, Steve Graham, Paul Harrison, Kevin Hetherington, Ben Highmore, Alex Kacelnik, Baz Kershaw, Barbara Kirshenblatt-Gimblett, Steen Nepper Larsen, Bruno Latour, John Law, Beverly Lear, Celia Lury, Derek McCormack, Gregor Maclennan, Bill Maurer, David Midgley, Brian Morris, Meaghan Morris, Dana Nelson, Melissa Orlie, Tom Osborne, David Parkin, Claire Pearson, Victoria Perks, Dag Petersson, John Phillips, Chris Philo, Paul Rabinow, Alan Read, Nikolas Rose, Richard Sennett, Michael Sheringham, Peter Slojterdijk, Bent Sørenson, David Stark, Helen Thomas, Grahame Thompson, Frederik Tygstrup, John Urry, Deb Verhoeven, Valerie Walkerdine, Sarah Whatmore, Martin White, Steve Woolgar, and Katharine Young.

Chapter 1: for this book

PART I

Chapter 2: first published in 2006 in *Economy and Society* (reproduced courtesy of Routledge)

Chapter 3: first published in 2001 in *Body and Society* (reproduced courtesy of Sage (© Sage Publications, 2000) by permission of Sage Publications)

Chapter 4: first published in 2004 in *Theory Culture and Society* (reproduced courtesy of Sage (© Sage Publications, 2000) by permission of Sage Publications)

Chapter 5: first published in 2005 in *Economy and Society* (reproduced courtesy of Routledge)

PART II

Chapter 6: first published in *Environment and Planning D: Society and Space* (reproduced courtesy of Pion)

PART III

Chapter 7: first published in 2004 in *Transactions of the Institute of British Geographers* (reproduced courtesy of the Royal Geographical Society, courtesy of Blackwell Publishing)

Chapter 8: first published in 2004 in *Geografiska Annaler* (reproduced courtesy of Blackwell Publishing)

Chapter 9: first published in 2005 in *Transactions of the Institute of British Geographers* (reproduced courtesy of the Royal Geographical Society, courtesy of Blackwell Publishing)

Chapter 10: for this book.

1 Life, but not as we know it

When it was enthusiastically pointed out within memory of our present Academy that race or gender or nation . . . were so many social constructions, inventions, and representations, a window was opened, an invitation to begin the critical process of analysis and cultural reconstruction was offered. . . . The brilliance of the pronouncement was blinding. Nobody was asking what's the next step? What do we do with this old insight? If life is constructed, how come it appears so immutable? How come culture appears so natural?

(Taussig 1993: xvi)

'production,' then, is used according to the meaning of its etymological root (i.e. Latin *producere*) that refers to the act of 'bringing forth' an object in space.

(Gumbrecht 2004: xiii)

a knowledge of arrangement or disposition is, of all others, the most useful.

(Humphrey Repton 1803, cited in Wall 2006: 6)

But can we really assume that the reading of such texts is a reading exclusively concentrated on meaning? Do we not sing these texts? Should the process by which a poem speaks be only carried by a meaning intention? Is there not, at the same time, a truth that lies in its performance? This, I think, is the task with which the poem confronts us.

(Gadamer 2000, cited in Gumbrecht 2004: 64)

we can and we may, as it were, jump with both feet off the ground into or towards a world of which we trust the other parts to meet our jump.

(James 1999 [1911]: 230)

Introduction

Since the early 1990s I have been engaged in an attempt to develop what I call non-representational theory. The chapters in this book are some of the later results of that project, following on in a direct line from *Spatial Formations* (Thrift 1996) and *Knowing Capitalism* (Thrift 2005a). Indeed, the three books should be considered together: they are all part and parcel of the same economic-cum-cultural-cum-political venture.

How to characterize this particular book's contents, then? Stripped to its bare essentials, this is a book about *the geography of what happens*. In large part, it is therefore a work of description of the bare bones of actual occasions but it does not, I hope, adopt a passive stance to its object of enquiry: what is present in experience. And not just because – as I have tried to make clear here and elsewhere – the content of what is present in experience has changed radically. For this is also a book about how these actual occasions, howsoever they may have been altered, might be enlivened – made more responsive and more active – by the application of a series of procedures and techniques of expression. In other words, it is intended as the beginning of an outline of the art of producing a permanent supplement to the ordinary, a sacrament for the everyday, a hymn to the superfluous.[1]

If that sounds too tentative, a little bit tortuous, or even rather portentous, then I am afraid that that is how it will have to be. This is a tentative book because it is not entirely clear what a politics of what happens might look like – indeed, given that so much of what I want to outline is avowedly experimental, perhaps too much in the way of clarity should not necessarily be counted as a good thing[2] (although straightaway I can hear the criticisms from those who believe that theory should slide home like a bolt). It is a little bit tortuous because there is a lot of ground-clearing to do, a lot of hacking back of the theoretical undergrowth in order to get to the nub of the matter. And it is portentous because it involves taking some of the small signs of everyday life for wonders and this involves all manner of risks, and not least pretentiousness. All I can say is that I think that the risk is worth it in order to achieve a diagnosis of the present which is simultaneously a carrier wave for new ways of doing things.

Certainly, in order to achieve its goals, this book has to be three things at once. First, it has to be a work of social and cultural theory.[3] The book builds on a series of cognate traditions in order to construct what I hope is a convincing account of how the worlds[4] are, given that encounters are all there is, and their results cannot be pre-given (although they can, of course, be pre-treated). Complex trajectories rather than blurred genres, as Strathern (1999: 25) puts it. But, second, the book also has to be a diagnostic tool. It is intended to be a work that takes some of the specificities of the present moment and weaves them into what might be called a speculative topography. The contours and content of what happens constantly change: for example, there is no stable 'human' experience because the human sensorium is constantly being re-invented as the body continually adds parts in to itself; therefore how and what is experienced as experience is itself variable.[5] Then, third and finally, the book is intended as a political contribution to the task of reconsidering our hopes for ourselves. This is, after all, a time in which the invention of new 'everyday' forms of democracy has become a part of the political ambition of many people, in which the 'local' and the 'global' have become increasingly awkward political terms but no satisfactory alternative to the connected separation they imply seems to exist, and in which 'what each of us feels capable of' (Ginsborg 2005: 7) is perceived as a vital political issue. The small offering that this book attempts to make to these three debates, and especially to the last one, is an opening up of new political domains which it is then possible to make a corresponding political rumpus about. The book is, most especially then, an attempt to produce an art of the invention of political invention by putting hard questions to the given in experience, the overall intent being to call new publics into existence who will pose questions to politics which are not yet of politics (Rajchman 1998) – whilst recognizing that this questioning can never be more than an inexact science[6] (Stengers 2002a). Bloch (2000 [1923]) called this 'building into the blue'. That is not a bad description for the kind of resource I am trying to construct.

But I need to severely qualify each of these goals. To qualify the first, like many, I think that, in certain senses at least, the social sciences and humanities suffer from a certain kind of over-theoretization at present. There are too many theories, all of them seemingly speaking on behalf of those whose lives have been damaged by the official structures of power.[7] A cynic might think that the profusion of 'fast' theories created by academics is simply a mirror of the rise of brainy classes, who are able to live a life of permanent theoretical revolution whilst everyone else does the dirty work. That would be too harsh. But the criticism is not therefore without any force at all (Rabinow 2006). It seems to me, to qualify the second goal, that this task is a necessary one in a time in which a globalized capitalism based on the rise of the brainy classes has become ever more pervasive, and democracy is in danger of becoming something of a sham, enacted as part of what Sloterdijk (2005c) calls an authoritarian capitalism.

> The mass of the population is periodically doused with the rhetoric of democracy and assured that it lives in a democratic society and that democracy is the condition to which all progressive-minded societies should aspire. Yet that democracy is not meant to realise the demos but to constrain and neutralize it by the arts of electoral engineering and opinion management. It is, necessarily, regressive. Democracy is embalmed in public rhetoric precisely in order to memorialize its loss of substance. Substantive democracy – equalizing, participatory, commonalizing – is antithetical to everything that a high reward meritocratic society stands for. At the same moment that advanced societies have identified their progressive character with perpetual technological innovation they have defined themselves through policies that are regressive in many of their effects. Democracy is where these effects are registered. By virtually every important official norm – efficiency, incentives to unequal rewards, hierarchical principles of authority, expertise – it appears anachronistic, dysynchronous. The crux of the problem is that high-technology, globalized capitalism is radically incongruent with democracy.
>
> (Wolin 2000: 20)

What seems to me more valuable, to qualify the third goal, would be to try to construct *practices* of vocation[8] that can begin to address the deficit of felt powerlessness and to chip away at 'our capacity to interiorize power relations, to delimit by ourselves the realm of the possible' (Ginsborg 2005: 20). These practices would not be permanent solutions. Rather, they would be oriented to escape attempts, some of which would take root: a series of fireworks inserted into everyday life which could confront or sidestep the 'behavioural codes that are not unilateral or totalitarian or especially disciplinarian, and which furthermore appear to offer great freedom of choice, but which none the less convey us effortlessly into a life of normalcy and convention' (Ginsborg 2005: 20). At this point, I am often stuck for words to describe what I mean, so let me take someone else's instead – Greil Marcus's homily on Robert Johnson as a force, and not just a mirror:

> At the highest point of his music each note that is played implies another that isn't, each emotion expressed hints at what can't be said. For all of its elegance and craft the music is unstable at its core – each song is at once an attempt to escape from the world as everyone around the singer believes it to be, and a dream that the world is not a prison but a homecoming. . . . Johnson is momentarily in the air, flying just as one does in a dream, looking down in wonder at where you are, then soaring as if it's the most natural thing in the world.
>
> (Marcus 2005: 103)

Now I am well aware that the cultivation of this form of knowledge may be interpreted as an irredeemably middle-class pre-occupation, the equivalent in theory of Bromell's (2000) characterization of white middle-class teenagers as insiders who long to be outsiders, the kind of consciousness of the world that too quickly falls into a call for 'a quick revolutionary fix that will please everyone and just reinforce a cosy feeling of powerlessness' (Lotringer 2004: 18).[9] But I think there is more to it than that, much more. For it suggests that there may be a more general means of opening up an allusive field in which 'the listener's attention is seized and dropped and held and released by possibilities of meaning that amuse and interest but do not quite come into being' (Bromell 2000: 133). This is what I mean by a politics of hope,[10] the prospect of constructing a machine for 'sustaining affirmation' (White 2000), of launching an additional source of political nourishment and responsiveness and imagination in a time when so many forces militate against it, of locating and warming up the technology of questioning and non-questioning 'by which attention forms and experience crystallizes' (Connolly 2005: 166). In other words, I want to try and add a distinct co-operative-cum-experimental sensibility in to the mix of the world that will help us 'engage the strangeness of the late modern world more receptively' (White 2000: 153). In turn, we could perhaps live in a less 'stingy' (as Connolly (2005) puts it) and more playful way, overcoming or at least bypassing some of the cringes that have been sewn into the fibres of our being as we have learnt how to be embodied. The net outcome would be that the texture of the feel and outcome of the everyday could be reworked as traditional forms of expression were slowly but surely breathed differently (Abrahams 2005).

What is then at issue is what form these practices would take. There is nothing that automatically leads them towards such forms of generosity, after all. In a sense, answering this quest/question about questioning is precisely what the rest of this book attempts to do.

In the remaining pages of this introductory chapter, I will introduce some of the main themes that will be taken up in the chapters of this book. I will begin by briefly outlining some of the main characteristics of non-representational theory and some of the key contemporary issues that non-representational theory highlights. Next, I will consider some of the theoretical and practical issues that the book throws up. Then, finally, I will parse each of the individual chapters, bringing out some of their common problematics.

Non-representational theory

This is a book based on the leitmotif of movement in its many forms. Thus, to begin with, it would be possible to argue that human life is based on and in movement. Indeed, it might be argued that it is the human capacity for such complex movements and the accompanying evolution of movement as an enhanced attractor[11] that has produced the reason for much of our rhizomatic, acentred brain. Then, movement captures the animic flux of life and especially an ontogenesis[12] which undoes a dependence on the preformed subject; 'every creature, as it "issues forth" and trails behind, moves in its characteristic way' (Ingold 2006: 15). Then again, movement captures the joy – I will not say simple – of living as a succession of luminous or mundane instants. Though it is possible, even easy, to get carried away by an emphasis on presence, closeness, and tangibility, and by a corresponding desire to do more than simply squeeze meaning from the world, still we can think of the leitmotif of movement as a desire for a presence which escapes a consciousness-centred core of self-reference;[13] 'Rather than have to think, always and endlessly, what else there could be, we sometimes seem to connect with a layer in our existence that simply wants the things of the world close to our skin' (Gumbrecht 2004: 106). And, finally and relatedly, movement captures a certain attitude to life as potential; 'to pose the problem is to invent and not only to dis-cover; it is to create, in the same movement, both the problem and its solution' (Alliez 2004b: 113).

Non-representational theory takes the leitmotif of movement and works with it as a means of going beyond constructivism. As a way of summarizing its now increasingly diverse character,[14] I will point to seven of its main tenets. First, non-representational theory tries to capture the 'onflow',[15] as Ralph Pred (2005) calls it, of everyday life. It therefore follows the anti-substantialist ambition of philosophies of becoming and philosophies of vitalist intuition equally – and their constant war on frozen states.[16] That means that it has a lot of forebears, of course. These forebears hardly agreed on everything, to put it but mildly, and not least on the status of intention and intentionality. So I will need to take a little time to more carefully specify what I mean. I think that this can be boiled down to three propositions. One is that the most effective approach will be one that is faithful to a radical empiricism that differs – radically – from a sense-perception or observation-based empiricism. As must be clear, that means that although I respect

Humean models of empiricism, I find them too austere. I prefer the lineage of inter-relation that runs from James through Whitehead which is not willing to completely jettison the phenomenological (the lived immediacy of actual experience, before any reflection on it)[17] and the consequent neglect of the transitive. At the same time, I want to temper what seem to me to be the more extreme manifestations of this lineage, which can end up by positing a continuity of and to experience about which I am sceptical, by employing an ethological notion of the pre-individual field in which the event holds sway and which leads to 'buds' or 'pulses' of thought-formation/perception in which 'thought is never an object in its own hands' (James 1960 [1890]: 522). This approach seems to me to be very much in line with Whitehead's monistic way of thinking about the world. As Pred puts it:

> Whitehead extends the scope of radical empiricism and, in effect, points to a way to overcome the limitations inherent in the spatiotemporal and sensory (visual, aural, tactile) metaphor of the stream [of consciousness]. Instead of merely taking a 'general view of the wonderful stream of our consciousness', Whitehead goes 'into' the moment. He refuses to abstract from the moment, any moment, understood as an act of experience issuing from and into other experiences, as an act occurring within the constraints of inheritance from all that is encompassed within the experient's past and with the onflow of experiences. By bringing philosophical analysis into the bud, Whitehead secures access to a post-Cartesian/Humean basis for ontology, and can charac-terize momentary consciousness as it arises from pre-conscious moments of synthesis within a broader stream . . . of activity.
>
> Whitehead applies the notion of buds not only to human moments of experience but also, more broadly, to actual entities or occasions – 'the final real things of which the world is made up'. He elaborates the notions of actual entities and concrescence with rigor and thoroughness, 'with the purpose of obtaining a one-substance cosmology'.
>
> (Pred 2005: 11)

Another proposition, which follows on naturally from these thoughts, is that the most effective approach values the pre-cognitive as something more than an addendum to the cognitive. What is called consciousness is such a narrow window of perception that it could be argued that it could not be otherwise. As Donald (2001) makes clear, defined in a narrow way, consciousness seems to be a very poor thing indeed, a window of time – fifteen seconds at most – in which just a few things (normally no more than six or seven) can be addressed, which is opaque to introspection and which is easily distracted. Indeed, consciousness can be depicted as though it hardly existed, as an emergent derivative of an unconscious. Yet it is clearly dangerous to make too little of cognition, as I perhaps did in some of my early papers. Because it is so weak (though hardly as weak as some commentators have depicted it), it has enrolled powerful allies which can focus and extend conscious awareness – various configurations of bodies and things which, knitted together as routinized environments, enable a range of different technologies for more thinking to be constructed. But, at the same time, the logical corollary of these thoughts is that we should also pay more attention to the pre-cognitive. This roiling mass of nerve volleys prepare the body for action in such a way that intentions or decisions are made before the conscious self is even aware of them. In turn, the many automatisms[18] of 'bare life' or 'creaturely life' mark out not only eminent biopolitical domains[19] but also a series of key theoretical conundrums about what constitutes life itself, such as the nature of 'the open' and motility, animality and undeadness, instinct and drive, poverty in world and what it means to be captivated by an environment in a world marked by all kinds of literal and metaphorical dislocations (Agamben 2004; Santner 2006).

The last proposition follows on again. It is that it is important to specify what unit is being addressed. Nearly all action is reaction to joint action, to being-as-a-pair, to the digestion[20] of the intricacies of talk, body language, even an ambient sense of the situation to hand, and this unremitting work of active reaction imposes enormous evaluative demands, equally enormous demands on intermediate memory, and similarly large demands on the general management of attention. Indeed, many now conclude that the idea of cognition as simply a minor place-holder is an artefact of tests carried out in a highly restricted environment – the laboratory (Despret 2004) – in which consciousness shows up as short-term because of the artificiality of the situation demanded by the researcher. Rather, cognition should be seen as an emergent outcome of strategic joint action for which it acts as a guidance function, monitoring and interpreting the situation as found, and, in particular, as a key ability to theorize others' states, as a kind of 'mindreading' that is the result of the human ability to theorize others' states without having full-blown beliefs about those states (Levinson 2003; Sterelny 2003).[21] And, most of the time, this social awareness – involving high-level cognitive abilities like imitation, learning about learning, and an ability to carry meaning in a whole series of registers (not only language but also gesture) (McNeill 2005) and the manipulation of time and space – predominates over sensory awareness: 'our normal focus is social and social awareness is highly conscious, that is; it heavily engages our conscious activity' (Donald 2001: 68). In other words, cognition has not only a performative aspect but a 'theoretical' aspect too (the two being related) and these aspects are a key to what is often called 'imagi-nation'.[22] This is why non-representational theory privileges play: play is understood as a perpetual human activity with immense affective significance, by no means confined to just early childhood, in which many basic ethical dilemmas (such as fairness) are worked through in ways which are both performative and theoretical.

Second, as must by now be clear, non-representational theory is resolutely anti-biographical and pre-individual. It trades in modes of perception which are not subject-based. Like Freud, I am deeply suspicious of, even inimical to, auto-biography or biography as modes of proceeding. One seems to me to provide a spurious sense of oneness. The other seems to me to provide a suspect intimacy with the dead. As Phillips (1999: 74) puts it, 'Biography, for Freud, was a monu-ment to the belief that lives were there to be known and understood, rather than endlessly redescribed. Biography did to the dead what Freud feared that psycho-analysis might do to the living'. Instead I want to substitute a *material schematism* in which the world is made up of all kinds of things brought in to relation with one another by many and various spaces through a continuous and largely involuntary process of encounter, and the violent training that such encounter forces. This is an approach that has had some forebears in the social sciences. I think of Gabriel Tarde's micrometaphysics, Pitirim Sorokin's forays into socio-cultural causality, Torsten Hägerstrand's time-geography, or Anthony Giddens's expeditions around social theory in the late 1970s and early 1980s, as well as my own hesitant attempts to time space and space time dating from the late 1970s (Parkes and Thrift 1980). It has achieved more grip of late because of theoretical developments like actor-network theory, and the consequent rediscovery of authors like Tarde and Whitehead, as well as the influence of the writings of authors like Deleuze and Guattari on assemblages. As, and probably more importantly, a whole series of fields have been constructed out of the resurgence of what Paul Carter (2004) calls 'material thinking', the 'performative' working methods and procedures of writings (and, very importantly, other methods of exposition) that emphasize how the whole business of praxis and poiesis is wrapped up in the stubborn plainness of a field of things. These fields must necessarily emphasize the materiality of thinking, and include the study of material culture, the sociology of science, performance studies, from dance to poetry, installation and site-based art, elements of architecture, some of the excursions in to interaction design (such as trying to formulate living information), various aspects of archaeology and museum studies, and the range of developments taking place in parts of cultural geography.

Third, non-representational theory concentrates, therefore, on *practices*, under-stood as material bodies of work or styles that have gained enough stability over time, through, for example, the establishment of corporeal routines and specialized devices, to reproduce themselves (Vendler 1995). In particular, these bodies' stability is a result of schooling in these practices, of each actor holding the others to them, and of the brute 'natural' fact that the default is to continue on in most situations.[23] These material bodies are continually being rewritten as unusual circumstances arise, and new bodies are continually making an entrance but, if we are looking for something that approximates to a stable feature of a world that is continually in meltdown, that is continually bringing forth new hybrids, then I take the practice to be it. Practices are productive concatenations that have been constructed out of all manner of resources and which provide the basic intelligibility of the world: they are not therefore the properties of actors but of the practices themselves (Schatzki 2002). Actions presuppose practices and not vice versa.

However, what I am espousing is no naïve practice theory. For example, as practices lose their place in a historical form of life, they may leave abandoned wreckage behind them which can then take on new life, generating new hybrids or simply leavings which still have resonance. Take the example of things. These may have been vital parts of particular networks of practice, only to fall out of use as these networks metamorphose. Consequently their meanings may become hollowed out but may still retain a presence as enigmatic signifiers (Santner 2006). Or they may find new uses in other networks. Or they may linger on as denaturalized reminders of past events and practices, purposely memorialized in various ways or simply present as ruins, as melancholy rem(a)inders. In other words, things can have a potent afterlife.

The mention of things brings us to the fourth tenet. The constitution of non-representational theory has always given equal weight to the vast spillage of *things*. In particular, it takes the energy of the sense-catching forms of things seriously (Critchley 2005) – rather than seeing things as mere cladding.[24] Things answer back; 'not only does our existence articulate that of an object through the language of our perceptions, the object calls out that language from us, and with it our own sense of embodied experience' (Schwenger 2006: 3). But how to describe what Walter Benjamin called the 'petrified unrest' of things? Three main moves seem particularly apposite. To begin with, things become part of hybrid assemblages: concretions, settings and flows. In this approach, things are given *equal* weight, and I do mean equal.[25] Thus things are not just bound by their brute efficacy to the visible termini of humans in some form of latent subjectivism such as 'concern' or 'care', however comforting their presence may sometimes be as mundane familiars. That would be to smuggle 'from the realm of common sense the notion that humans are very different from knives or paper' (Harman 2002: 30). Rather,

> the tool itself is bound up in a specific empire of functions, a system that takes its meaning from some particular projection, some final reference. Admittedly, the meaning of equipment is determined by that for the sake of which it acts. But I flatly contest the view that this *Worumwillen* is necessarily human. Tools execute their being 'for the sake of' a reference, not because people run across them but because they are utterly determinate in their referential function – that is, because they already stand at the mercy of innumerable points of meaning.
>
> (Harman 2002: 29)

Then, it is important to understand the way in which things have another genetic disposition that needs to be mentioned at this point. That is what Simondon (1989) calls their 'technicity', their actual collective character as a 'technology' (the word being placed in scare quotes precisely because we cannot be sure exactly what constitutes a technology). The technicity of something like a hand tool which forms a relatively isolated technical element[26] can be isolated from its context. Indeed, it may have sufficient material character to be given a proper name: Toledo steel or Murano glass, for example (Mackenzie 2002). But the more effective and ubiquitous a technology becomes, the less likely this is to be the case. Portability comes about because of the ramification of a larger and larger infrastructure which means that the technology becomes increasingly a part of an empire of functions encumbered by a network of supportive elements, each of which relies on the other. 'A mobile phone or wireless appliance could be understood from this perspective as a massively encumbered object. Its physical portability comes at the expense of an increased ramification and layering of communication infrastructure' (Mackenzie 2002: 12).

To summarize the argument so far, things form not so much a technological unconscious as a technological anteconscious; a 'spreading so extensive that it can come to the surface in lives entirely different from the one beneath which it is currently sensed' (Schwenger 2006: 4), a warp and weft of inhuman traffic with its own indifferent geographies. But I want to see things as having one more disposition. That is, the way in which the human *body* interacts with other things. I do not want to count the body as separate from the thing world. Indeed, I think it could be argued that the human body is what it is because of its unparalleled ability to co-evolve with things, taking them in and adding them to different parts of the biological body to produce something which, if we could but see it, would resemble a constantly evolving distribution of different hybrids with different reaches. Indeed, the evidence suggests that organs like the hand, the gut, and various other muscle and nerve complexes which have evolved in part in response to the requirements of tools have subsequently produced changes in the brain. The human body is a tool-being. This is, I think, an important point. Of late, there has been a large literature generated on corporeality, most particularly by feminist theorists, which often seems to want to endow the flesh with some form of primordial distinction: goo is good, so to speak.[27] But, whilst it would be profoundly unwise to ignore the special characteristics of flesh,[28] it would be equally unwise to think that the make-up of the human body stopped there, or that it produced an ineffable perceptual membrane. It does not. There is a sense of touch in all parts of the extended physiognomy of the material body.[29] At the same time, it is important to enter a note of caution which has been generated, at least in part, by feminist theorists. Too often, the recent turn to corporeality has also allowed a series of assumptions to be smuggled in about the active, synthetic and purposive role of embodiment which need closer examination. In particular, it is assumed that bodies are bodies-in-action, able to exhibit a kind of continuous intentionality, able to be constantly enrolled into activity.[30] Every occasion seems to be willed, cultivated or at least honed. My own work has been periodically guilty of this sin, I am sure. But the experience of embodiment is not like that at all; not everything is focused intensity. Embodiment includes tripping, falling over, and a whole host of other such mistakes. It includes vulnerability, passivity, suffering, even simple hunger. It includes episodes of insomnia, weariness and exhaustion, a sense of insignificance and even sheer indifference to the world. In other words, bodies can and do become overwhelmed. The unchosen and unforeseen exceed the ability of the body to contain or absorb. And this is not an abnormal condition: it is a part of being as flesh. It may be that it is only 'because the self is sensible, open to the pangs of hunger and eros, that it is worthy of ethics' (Critchley 2002: 21).[31]

All that said, this emphasis on things questions the solidity of the world, since so much of it is ultimately mutable, working according to a spectrum of different time scales (Grosz 2005). Increasingly, many human activities seem to realize this. Indeed, it is a point that has been brilliantly made by Kwinter (2001). Thus

Kwinter points to the rise of a whole series of sports that depend on an artful shaping of the different time scales of the environment for sustenance, tracking and tracing flows and perturbations in order to produce e/affects. Kwinter mentions paragliding, surfing, snowboarding and rock-climbing as sports of falling[32] that extend a streaming ethos to landscapes, understood as 'motorfields of solids' (2001: 29). In their current manifestation, these sports have increasingly understood the environment as exemplifying fluidity of movement, intuition and invention. Take the case of rock-climbing:[33]

> [Climbers] must flow up the mountain, flow or tack against the downward gradient of gravity – but also must become hypersensitive tamers and channelers of the gravitational sink, masters at storing it in their muscles or making it flow through certain parts of the pelvis, thighs, palms, and this only at certain times; they must know how to accelerate the flow into a quick transfer that could mean the difference between triumph and disaster, to mix and remix dynamic and static elements in endless variation – for it is not enough to prevail against gravity but rather to be able to make it stream continuously through one, and especially to be able to generalize this knowledge to every part of the body without allowing it to regroup at any time – transcendant and unitary – as a spatialized figure in the head.
>
> (Kwinter 2001: 29–30)

But note here how the mountain also plays its part:

> The mineral shelf represents a flow whose timescale is nearly unfathomable from the scale of duration represented by the electrolytic and metabolic processes of muscle and nerves – but even at this timescale – nanometric in relation to the millennia that measure geological flows – singularities abound: a three millimeter-wide fissure just wide enough to allow the placement of one finger, and anchored by sufficiently solid earth to permit but eighty pounds of pressure for, say, three seconds but no longer; an infinitesimally graded basin of sedimentary tock whose erratically ribbed surface (weathered unevenly by flows of wind and rain) offers enough friction to a spread palm to allow strategic placement of the other palm on an igneous ledge half a meter above. This very rock face, until recently considered virtually slick and featureless – an uninflected glacis even to classical pick and patio climbers – now swarms with individualized points, inhomogeneities, trajectories, complex relations . . . the climber's task is less to 'master' in the macho, form-imposing sense than to forge a morphogenetic figure in time, it insert himself into a seamless, streaming space and to become soft and fluid himself, which means momentarily to recover real time, and to engage the universe's wild and free unfolding through the morphogenetic capacities of the singularity.
>
> (Kwinter 2001: 31)

Thus we arrive at a notion of 'site', as an active and always incomplete incarnation of events, an actualization of times and spaces that uses the fluctuating conditions to assemble itself (Kwon 2004). Site is not so much a result of punctual, external causes, therefore, as it is an insertion in to one or more flows.[34]

Fifth, non-representational theory is experimental. I make no apologies for this. After all, 'no battle has ever been won without resorting to new combinations and surprising events' (Latour 2005: 252). In particular, I want to pull the energy of the performing arts into the social sciences in order to make it easier to 'crawl out to the edge of the cliff of the conceptual' (Vendler 1995: 79). To see what will happen. To let the event sing you. To some this will appear a retrograde step: hasn't the history of the social sciences been about attaining the kind of rigour that the performing arts supposedly lack? My answers are fourfold. First, I believe that the performing arts can have as much rigour as any other experimental set-up, once it is understood that the laboratory, and all the models that have resulted from it, provide much too narrow a metaphor to be able to capture the richness of the worlds (Despret 2004). Consider just the rehearsal: would anyone seriously say that it is not a rigorous entity? Second, because once it is understood how many entities there are in the world, of which we are able to name but a few, then capturing the traces of these entities, even for a brief moment, will clearly involve unconventional means, a kind of poetics of the release of energy that might be thought to resemble play. After all, who knows what entities and processes lurk in the under- (or should it be over-) growth, just getting on with it? Third, because the performing arts may help us to inject a note of wonder back into a social science which, too often, assumes that it must explain everything. I am often bemused by the degree to which scientific and artistic works are allowed to evince wonder (Fisher 2002). Yet it often seems as if the extraordinary emergences of the 'social' world have to be treated in a different register, as stumbling, inertial and 'mundane' (Abrahams 2005). But any glance at the kinds of columns that tend to appear in newspapers and magazines under bylines such as 'odd world', 'strange world', 'this world', 'funny old world', and so on, show the essential ebullience of that world and the way in which it can never be truly kept within theoretical tramlines. Social imaginaries are just that: they cannot be contained. Thus 'retracing the iron ties of necessity is not sufficient to explore what is possible' (Latour 2005: 261). Instead, social science needs to take on the quality of renewal that it can see all around it as new collectives constantly come into existence: 'for a social science to become relevant, it has to have the capacity to renew itself – a quality impossible if a society is supposed to be "behind" political action' (Latour 2005: 261). Finally, because it is imperative to understand the virtual as multiple registers of sensation operating beyond the reach of the reading techniques on which the social sciences are founded. Culture is, in this sense, an 'involuntary adventure' (Toscano 2004) in which, in a Whiteheadian vein, thought is the operation that constitutes the thinker (who is constituted in the occasion), rather than vice versa (Alliez 2004a). This brings me directly to the topic of affect.

Thus, sixth, I want to get in touch with the full range of registers of thought by stressing affect and sensation. These are concept-percepts that are fully as important as signs and significations but that only recently have begun to receive their due. Recently, like a number of authors, I have taken an affective turn with this work, drawing on a combination of Spinoza, Freud, Tomkins, Ekman, Massumi, and a host of feminist theorists, as well as biological traditions including evolutionary theory and ethology, in order to understand affect as the way in which each 'thing' in acting, living, and striving to preserve its own being is 'nothing but the actual essence of the thing' (Spinosa *et al.* 1997).Thus,

> There is no longer a subject, but only individuating affective states of an anonymous force. The plane is concerned only with movements and rests, with dynamic affective charges: the plane will be perceived with whatever it makes us perceive, and then only bit by bit. Our ways of living, thinking or writing change according to the plane upon which we find ourselves.
> (Spinoza, cited in Alliez 2004b: 27)

All of this said, I do want to retain a certain minimal humanism. Whilst refusing to grant reflexive consciousness and its pretensions to invariance the privilege of occupying the centre of the stage, dropping the human subject entirely seems to me to be a step too far. I have done much to rid myself of an object that often seems to me to be a user-illusion – in my writings, there is 'no longer such a thing as a relatively fixed and consistent person – a person with a recognizable identity – confronting a potentially predictable world but rather two turbulences enmeshed with each other' (Phillips 1999: 20). Still, I am uncomfortably aware that, taken to extremes, a resolutely anti-humanist position parodies the degenerative path taken in the nineteenth century from Rousseau through Balzac to Bergson, from 'an ideal of an immanent community, the subsequent emergence of a strictly codified bourgeois subject capable of constructing and manifesting itself "aes-thetically" through gesture and the eventual somatization of that individual body to a condition of mere potentiality' (Hewitt 2005: 103). This degeneration can be seen equally as a movement from intention to automation as the industrial systems of that century took hold. Whatever the case, I want to keep hold of a humanist ledge on the machinic cliff face. I hold to a sense of *personal authorship*,[35] no matter that the trace is very faint and no matter that the brain is a society, different parts of which are dynamically and differentially connected to all manner of environments. And the reason? Because how things seem is often more important than what they are.

> The fact is that it seems to each of us that we have conscious will. It seems we have selves. It seems we have minds. It seems we are agents. It seems we cause what we do. Although it is sobering and ultimately accurate to call this an illusion, it is a mistake to think the illusory is trivial.
> (Wegner 2002: 341–342)

Further, this conscious will is bolstered in at least three ways. To begin with there is the special constitutional significance of joint action and its particular way of understanding the worlds (Levinson 2003). Then there is the consequent ability of joint action periodically to work across different social fields, refusing to respect boundaries. And finally there is the 'adaptive unconscious' (Wilson 2002) working ceaselessly and nonconsciously to interpolate/interpellate the world. These are not insignificant qualities and they give a significant role to style, a particular way of practising joint action that can be equated to agency in this book.

My stamping ground for these kinds of thoughts has often been dance, but it could just as well have been building or music, two other baseline human activities which, so far as I am aware, are found in all societies, including those of the greatest antiquity. For my purposes, dance is important: it engages the whole of the senses in bending time and space into new kinaesthetic shapes, taps into the long and variegated history of the unleashing of performance,[36] leads us to understand movement as a potential,[37] challenges the privileging of meaning (especially by understanding the body as being expressive without being a signifier; see Langer 2005; Dunagan 2005; Gumbrecht 2004), gives weight to intuition as thinking-in-movement, foregrounds the 'underlanguage' of gesture[38] and kinetic semantics in general (Sheets-Johnstone 2005), teaches us anew about evolution (for example by demonstrating the crucial role of bipedality), and is able to point to key cognitive processes like imitation and suggestion which are now understood to be pivotal to any understanding of understanding (Hurley and Chater 2005) and, indeed, desire.[39]

The aforegoing paragraphs allow me to say something, finally, about ethics.[40] I have been painting a very faint view of human agency, to put it mildly. The classical human subject which is transparent, rational and continuous no longer pertains. Classical ethical questions like 'What have I done?' and 'What ought I to do?' become much more difficult when the 'I' in these questions is so faint, when self-transparency and narratability are such transient features. Similarly, more modern ethical questions like what it means to be genuinely open to another human being or culture take on added layers of complexity. Clearly, becoming ethical now means becoming critical of norms under which we are asked to act but which we cannot fully choose (Butler 2005) and taking responsibility – in a sense to be specified – for the dilemmas that subsequently arise. But this hardly counts as a revelation.

What I will want to argue for, in concert with Santner (2001: 6), is a generalized ethic of out-of-jointness within which 'every familiar is ultimately strange and . . . , indeed, I am even in a crucial sense a stranger to myself'. But, rather than see this form of answerability as a problem, it can as well be thought of as an opportunity to build new forms of life in which 'strangeness itself [is] the locus of new forms of neighborliness and community' (Santner 2001: 6). In turn, this ethic of novelty can be connected to the general theme of 'more life', for it suggests a particular form of boosting aliveness, one that opens us to our being in the midst of life through a thoroughly ontological involvement.[41] For, what is clear is that all too often in our everyday life we are *not* open to that pressure and do not inhabit the midst of life, and thus live everyday life as, well, everyday life, clipping our own wings because we inhabit cringes that limit our field of action.

Everyday life includes possibilities for withdrawing from, defending against, its own aliveness to the world, possibilities of, as it were, not really being there, of dying to the other's presence. The energies that constitute our aliveness to the world are, in other words, subject to multiple modifications and transformations.

(Santner 2001: 9)

Some commentators would, I think, like to understand boosting this out-of-jointness as part of a more general rediscovery of piety – or even epiphany – often heralded as part of a move to a 'post-secular spirituality' (e.g. Goodchild 2002; Gumbrecht 2004; Braidotti 2006). Sometimes following on from Deleuze's thoughts on 'becoming-imperceptible' in which extinguishing the self allows all kinds of unexpected futures to be opened up and drawn strength from. This is 'reversing the subject to face the outside' (Braidotti 2006: 262), thus boosting *potentia*: in Jamesian terms it is the jump towards another world. Whilst, hardly surprisingly, I am sympathetic to the general direction of travel, this is too grand and seductive a vision for me. I would prefer to see a multiple set of projects concerned with the construction of an orientation to the future, the development of 'an anxiety about the future which is analogous to Orwell's anxiety about the loss of the past and of memory and childhood' (Jameson 2005: 23), which is, at the same time, the development of a method of hope (Miyazaki 2004, 2006). In more conventional philosophical terms, this might, I suppose, be thought of as a flourishing of potential in act,[42] not in the sense of the realization of some proper form, but rather as a departure from what is – a potentiality that is brought into being only as it acts or exists in the interstices of interaction. But I would also prefer to see it in another way, as an attempt to re-gather the ethic of *craftsmanship*, a means of composition and channelling which involves bringing together discipline and concentration, understanding and inspiration, in order to bring out potential: a different model of *homo faber*, if you like, working both for its own sake and as part of a community of ability.[43] At the same time, this ethic, following on from a long line of thinking which has tried to overcome nihilism and determine the conditions for an affirmation of life, can be seen as a means of celebrating the joyous, even transcendent, confusion of life itself (Reginster 2006).

Isn't this something to have faith in? The stuff of life, the astonishing, resilient, inventiveness of it all? The extravagant iridescence in the wings of butter-flies. The minute convolutions of Henle's loop in the human kidney, 'like the meanders in a creek'. The song of the Albert's lyrebird, which takes it six years to learn and segues the phrasing of every other bird in the Queensland bush. At times, the gratuitousness of creation, its sheer wild playfulness, can only be understood as a kind of unscripted comedy.

(Mabey 2006: 197)

Finally, I want to broach the topic of space again. For substantive rather than narrow disciplinary reasons, space looms large in what follows. That said, I start from an 'instinctive' understanding of space shared by all the 'field' disciplines – anthropology, archaeology, architecture, geography and large parts of performance studies. This is a sense of the concreteness and materiality of the situation which is hard to put into words, a need to capture being there which is not just a report back – a finding which is also a leaving. Straightaway, I hasten to add that this is not just an excuse for the random empiricism of which such disciplines are sometimes accused. But it has certainly complicated the use of categories which are often assumed to in some way motivate social change (society, class, gender, ethnicity, and so on) because it places variation on an equal footing. And it also complicates what is assumed to be a simple empirical fact, not just because all of these disciplines try to deepen those facts by drawing on all kinds of representational and non-representational registers (digs, ethnographies, various maps and diagrams, buildings, software, performances) but also because they simultaneously explore how particular spaces resonate, obtain their particular 'atmosphere' (Brennan 2004; Sloterdijk 2005a, 2005b), so that the whole is more than the sum of the parts.

I hope that this makes it clear that space is not a metaphorics, nor is it a transcendental principle of space in general (the phenomenological idea of consciousness as the fount of all space, produced by a finite being who constitutes 'his' world), nor is it simply a series of local determinations of a repeating theme. In each of these cases, we can see that the very style of thought is 'oriented by spatial relations, the way in which we imagine what to think' (Colebrook 2005a: 190).[44] Rather, it is three different qualities in one. First, it is a practical set of configurations that mix in a variety of assemblages thereby producing new senses of space[45] and:

> By confronting all those events from which thought emerges, by thinking how there can be perceptions of spaces, we no longer presuppose an infinity to be represented; nor a finite being who constitutes 'his' human world (as in phenomenology) but an 'unlimited infinity'. Each located observer is the opening of a fold, a world folded around its contemplations and rhythms. There are as many space and folds as there are styles of perception. If a fold is the way perceptions 'curve around' or are oriented according to an active body, the thought of these curves produces a life that can think not just its own human world – the space of man – but the sense of space as such.
>
> (Colebrook 2005a: 190)

Second, it also forms, therefore, a poetics of the unthought, of what Vesely (2004) calls the latent world, a well-structured pre-reflective world which, just because it lacks explicit articulation, is not therefore without grip. Third, it is indicative of the substance of the new era of the inhabitable map in which space has more active qualities designed into its becoming – a tracery of cognitive and pre-cognitive assists threading their way through each and every moment of the being-at-work of presentation – which make it into a very different ground from the one that Heidegger imagined as presence.

So far as space is concerned, what I have been most concerned with is banishing nearness as the measure of all things (Thrift 2006b). It is a staple of the literature that a drive towards nearness is regarded as having an intrinsic value. For example, think of all the terms that imply nearness in the philosophical tradition: present-at-hand, flesh, thrownness. In part, this terminological profusion arises from the idea that closeness to the body is the main geometer of the world (Ginzburg 2001b). But this is to take the biological body as an interpellated centre (Gil 1998) with a definable fleshy inside. But even an organ like the gut can as well be thought of as an outside as an inside (Probyn 2005), as a logistics of the movement of things which can be mapped on to the world.[46] And this is without going into the obvious political dangers of identifying the body as a preformed entity. At the same time I do not want to stray into the ambient pieties of some parts of the phenomenological tradition or their collapse into an absolute alterity[47] or a spiritualist immanence[48] (Toscano 2004). Instead I want to substitute *distribution* for nearness or ambience. Why? Well, to begin with, because the paradox of space is that we all know that space is something lived in and through in the most mundane of ways – from the bordering provided by the womb, through the location of the coffee cup on our desk that is just out of reach, through the memories of buildings and landscapes which intertwine with our bodies and provide a kind of poetics of space, through the ways in which vast political and commercial empires – and the resultant wealth and misery – can be fashioned from the mundane comings and goings of ships and trains and now planes, through to the invisible messages that inhabit the radio spectrum in their billions and etch another dimension to life. Then, because there is no need to reduce such complexity to a problematic of 'scale', a still too common move. Actors continually change size. A multiplicity of 'scales' is always present in interactions; the putatively large is of the same kind as the small, but amplified to generate a different order of effects (Strathern 1999; Tarde 2000). Then, because we now understand that the spaces and rhythms of the everyday, everydayness and everyday life (Seigworth 2000) are not just a filigree bolstering an underlying social machine but a series of pre-individual ethologies that incessantly rehearse a materialism in which matter turns into a sensed-sensing energy with multiple centres. Then, again, because increasingly what counts as a 'we' is being redefined by a range of transhuman approaches. These approaches have not just, in what has now become an increasingly hackneyed move, undone the dependence of the point of view on a preformed subject. They have also increased the number of actors' spaces that can be recognized and worked with. Consequently, they have begun to redefine what counts as an actor, most especially through an understanding of the actor as an artefact of different territories of 'thought', conceived as the operations that constitute the thinker.[49] This 'onto-ethological' move can be made precisely because actors can now be seen to not just occupy but to be made up of all kinds of intermediary spaces which cannot be tied down to just one and simultaneously participate with each other. The world, in other words, is jam-packed with entities. Finally, because more and more of the sensory registers in which spaces make their marks as spaces seem to be being recognized,[50] no doubt in part because these registers are continuously expanding but also in part because the sheer cultural diversity of how space appears is increasingly being recognized as more than culture or body (e.g. Levinson 2004; Wilson 2004).

The book

Having outlined some of the main tenets of non-representational theory, let me now move to the book itself. This book is motivated by a heterogeneous series of inspirations, rather than just one. I will point to a theoretical agenda first. I do not subscribe to the spirit guide approach to social science. Thus, for example, though I take Deleuze's work on topics like the gap between sensation and perception, the difference between possibility and virtuality, the heterogenesis of both material density and subjective action from a pre-individual field, and the different time-images of repetition and recurrence, to be important, I am afraid that this has not produced a total makeover of my work in a way that has now become quite common in some quarters, a makeover that sometimes seems to resemble a religious conversion. There are elements of Deleuze's work that I remain out of sorts with[51] and, in any case, I do not think that it is the function of a social scientist to simply apply the work of philosophers (as in a Deleuzian approach, a Foucauldian approach, an Agambenian approach, and so on). It seems to me to be a highly questionable assumption that modern social science stands in this kind of subordinate relationship to a set of themes from Western philosophy[52] or should see its task as simply echoing the assumptions those themes may make. So far as I am concerned, social scientists are there to hear the world and to make sure that it can speak back just as much as they are there to produce wild ideas – and then out of this interaction they may be able to produce something that is itself equally new. But they must share with philosophers like Deleuze one ambition at least and that is to render the world problematic by elaborating questions. To simply offer solutions is not enough.[53]

At the same time, in recent years, there has been an equal tendency to argue that social science must be more practical, policy-oriented, and so on, a tendency which risks losing touch with wild ideas completely; it is the kind of social science that does not understand the basic point that it is producing a form of intelligibility which 'can only confirm the prevailing views within those institutions that generated the data' (Rawls 2002: 54) and in fetishizing the values of methodological rigour seems to me to miss a large part of the point of social science by purposefully going about deadening itself (Law 2005) when that is both pointless and unnecessary.[54]

Instead of all that, this book is about new kinds of practice which are compelled by their own demonstrations and therefore leave room for values like messiness, and operators like the mistake, the stumble and the stutter (Law 2004). To some these practices will appear to be just idle chatter but I prefer to see them as vehicles for bringing into view the conditions of meaning, not so much a means of going further as a technology for tackling inconceivability (Fenves 1993). After all, and this point is crucial, it seems to me to be of the greatest methodological importance to acknowledge that this is a world which we can only partially understand. Not only is it the case that many things are inherently unknowable but also, as Latour (2005) has pointed out, there is every reason to believe that we are surrounded by innumerable hybrids, only a few of which we have named and even fewer of which we can claim to understand. For example, who can truly say that they fully understand the forces we tag as 'affect'? The fact that we (itself a difficult category) must live surrounded by an ocean of hybrids whose nature we do not know or at best imperfectly understand because we bleed into them in so many odd ways means that all kinds of things just seem to show up because we are unable to trace their genealogy or all the forces that trigger how they participate in an event. Some see this as a problem. But I see it as an opportunity, and as a demonstration that there will always be more to do – which brings me to my next point.

Practically, the book arises from a number of political imperatives. The first is the growing realization that there are landscapes of space, time and experience that have been ceded too readily to powerful naturalizing forces which erase the prospect of political action even before it starts by producing *backgrounds*, latent worlds that, by virtue of their routinized, 'unrememberable but unforgettable' (Gerhardt 2004) natures, make certain aspects of the events we constantly come across not so much hard to question as hard to even think of as containing questions at all. In the past, there have, of course, been various politics of ordinary moments which have attempted to show that what might seem like supposedly trivial everyday affairs can have import once the misplaced concreteness of social categories is factored out; wilful acts of political mis-perception and re-perception, if you like. I think here of aspects of surrealism, the fall-out from situationism, some forms of psychoanalytic and psychological therapy, the kinds of political theory that have recently grouped around the banner of a politics of the ordinary, the concrete empirical details of interaction to be found in ethnomethodology, certain kinds of architecture and site-specific installation, and so on. It also draws on those considerable parts of the arts and humanities, and especially art and poetry and dance, that call to the practices of everyday life. What I have tried to do here is to show that these traditions form a living whole with many of the same goals and projects in mind, a poetics of mundane space and time which can teach us to ourselves in better ways, that is ways which will allow peoples to survive their own environing (Wagner 2001) by creating more rather than fewer worlds. Such a poetics of the ways in which witnessable coherence is continually produced requires four things. First it requires a better sense of the future (Bloch 1986 [1959]) built up out of a forward-looking ethics of the moment which is not concerned with outright adjudication but instead tries to work with the affects/percepts/concepts of 'stance' or 'style'. Second it requires serious attention to the spaces of the empirical moment that is built up out of examining the ways in which the spaces of situations are extruded. That may result in a poetics of the spaces of dreams and improvisations, of what Vesely (2004) calls 'rich articulations', that arise out of a deep respect for situations and which manifests itself in continually attempting to go beyond them. Third it requires attempting to let loose a certain kind of wild conceptuality which is attuned to the moment but always goes beyond it, which always works against cultural gravity, so to speak. This improvisatory virtuality provides an opportunity for an unsettled politics of advocacy which 'watch[es] the world, listening for what escapes explanation by science, law, and other established discourses. Accounting for what established systems discounted as noise' (Fortun 2001: 351). Fourth it requires a much better sense of the ways in which practices need objects against which to react and from which to learn, but these objects may have many versions (Despret 2004), many 'offers of appropriateness', to use a Latourian phrase. To summarize, what is being sought for is what might be described as an ethological ethic which is *gratuitously* benign. What I am aiming for is to produce a supplement to the ordinary labour of everyday life which is both a valediction and a sacrament, though I am sure that sounds entirely too grand. If I had to choose an analogy, it might be with Darwin's furtive earthworms which, through continuous ingestion, work a good part of the world into existence. In Darwin's later thought they stand for a lowly kind of secular creation myth; 'something [is being said] about resilience and beneficial accidents; that it may be more marvellous when the world happens to work for us, than to believe it was designed to do so' (Phillips 1999: 58).

Lest I be misunderstood (and this is a point on which there is a lot of misunderstanding, most of it wilful, it has to be said), I am *not* arguing that the back and forth of what we currently call politics should be shut down. I do not think that the constant testing of the limits of what counts as the political implied by this project means that it is either a substitute for other forms of politics of the governed or even the invention of a determinate new political form (Amin and Thrift 2005; Chatterjee 2004). Rather, it is a halting means of producing more interest, identifying swells and overflows, and generating new forms of energy. 'Modest' has become an overused word, of late. But non-representational theory is genuinely intended to be a modest supplement.

Finally, this book is therefore self-consciously interdisciplinary. I have tried to avoid any particular disciplinary tradition in the arts and humanities and social sciences and to take inspiration from them all – or at least a good many of them. There is an important sense in which any politics of ordinary moments is bound to transgress these disciplinary boundaries since it involves so many different elements of discipline and indiscipline, imagination and narrative, sense and nonsense. . . . But each of these disciplines can be bent towards my overall goal: to produce a politics of opening the event to more, more; more action, more imagination, more light, more fun, even. This is not, I should hasten to add, meant to be a romantic or quixotic quest. It is meant to be in-your-face politics. Currently, many people are forced to live their lives in cramped worlds which offer them little or no imaginative relief because of the crushing weight of economic circumstance, the narrow margins of what they are allowed to think by what they have been taught and what lies bleeding around them and the consequently almost routine harrowing of their confidence that the world can ever be for them (Chakrabarty 2002; Chatterjee 2004). Yet, all that said, very many struggle to express something more than just resignation and inconsolability, often against themselves. They may value a certain conviviality, demonstrate hope, resolution, and a kind of dignity, even in the midst of melancholy. That is surely something remarkable, given most people's restricted circumstances and prospects – and it must surely be something worth nurturing. Indeed, some do go further still. And in that process, they may strike out on to new practical-imaginative territories. Of course, these continuous rites of spring hardly mean that all is well in the world. But they do show that life pretty well always exceeds its own terms and conditions: it is not always captured by the small print of the social contract. There is hope that, in amongst the poisons of prejudice and general paranoia, some small beginnings can be made, summonings of what is not that can leap up and hear themselves, that are able to 'seek the true, the real where the merely factual disappears' (Bloch 2000 [1923]: 3).

The chapters

The rest of this book consists of a set of chapters which come from the project that I have been pursuing in various guises since the early 1980s under the banner of 'non-representational theory'. The project was originally an attempt to take practices seriously against the background of a (thoroughly modernist, I should add) emphasis on unknowing (Weinstein 2005) but it has moved on from there, I like to think. For in studying practices in detail, it became clear to me that what was missing from too many accounts was a sense of mutability; of the moments of inspired improvisation, conflicting but still fertile mimesis, rivalrous desires, creative forms of symbiosis, and simple transcription errors which make each moment a new starting point. Whether studying the history of clocks, which is scattered with the unknown foot soldiers of innovation – tinkerers making myriad small adjustments which lead on to 'bigger' things (Glennie and Thrift 2007) – or the way in which styles of financial dealing transmute into new financial instruments (Leyshon and Thrift 1997), or the vagaries of all kinds of artistic performance (Thrift 2001), or the remorseless work of repair and maintenance (Graham and Thrift 2007), what I was increasingly concerned to underline was the ceaseless work of transmutation which drives the 'social'. The social is in scare quotes here because I want to emphasize a set of associationist working assumptions that are in contradistinction to the views of 'sociologists of the social', by drawing (selectively) on the work of Tarde (2000) to produce a means of associating entities. First assumption: everything can be regarded as a society. Consequently, at a minimum, 'there are many other ways to retrace the entire social world than the narrow definition provided by standardized social ties' or, more generally, 'social is not a place, a thing, a domain or a kind of stuff but a provisional movement of new associations' (Latour 2005: 238). Thus, as Latour (2005: 239) nicely puts it, space can be made for 'landing strips for other entities' that have never been followed before, for emergent forms of life (Fischer 2003), or simply forms of life that have never come to notice before. Second assumption: always be suspicious that the difference between 'large' and 'small', 'macro' and 'micro', 'general' and 'specific' is necessarily significant. I am particularly sceptical of any explanation that appeals to scale. Third assumption: keep difference at the core of explanation.

To summarize my summary, non-representational theory asks three main questions. First it questions the divide between theoretical and practical work by ceding certain theoretical conundrums to practice. Second, by questioning what is in the world, it exposes a whole new frontier of inhuman endeavour, what might be called the construction of new matterings, along with their typical attachments, their passions, strengths and weaknesses, their differences and indifferences. Third, by intensifying the intensity of being, it is able to question the load of precognitive conditionings that make up most of what it is to be human. In other words, or so I will argue, it is possible to boost the content of bare life, making it more responsive, more inventive and more open to ethical interventions.

Insofar as it has a political agenda, then, this book is about the construction of new counterpublics through the assembling of more performative political ecologies. At its heart, in other words, is a pressing task of political experiment and invention, a work of 'ensoulment'[55] (Santner 2006), aimed at making more room in the world for new political forms, which, at the same time, produces new excitations of power; 'those enigmatic bits of address and interpellation that disturb the social space – and bodies – of . . . protagonists' (Santner 2006: 24). This is a task that seems vital in an age when politics too often ends up in declarative cul-de-sacs.[56] Further, this politics of effective togethernesses (Stengers 2006) is, so I believe, currently breaking out all over. The numbers of experiments currently taking place with new political forms of effective togetherness are legion, and I cannot list them all here. But, for example, there are the many attempts to forge a new urban politics which can comprehend and work with belonging-in-transience (Amin and Thrift 2005a and b). Then there are all the experiments aimed at disrupting given spatial and temporal arrangements in an age when 'the speed at which new products appear and reconfigurations of technological systems take place precludes the possibility of ever becoming familiar with a given arrangement' (Crary 2004: 9). How is it possible, in other words, to group around states that are neither dependent on lasting objects nor on fixed locations? Then, there are the myriad experiments that set out to invent flexible models of imagination and narrative outside the enforced routines of consumption. And, finally, there are all the experiments that want to understand and work with the 'animality' of bare life, both as a means of understanding what elements of being are included but do not count and as a means of tapping that vital force.

The subsequent chapters in this book are inter-connected. They were often written with one another in mind. Sometimes they purposely follow on one from the other. They make their way as follows. The first four chapters of the book, which form its first section, act as an extended prologue by offering a tentative description of how the world is now. The first chapter attempts to give a description of some of the main contours of experience that currently exist in the West by concentrating on the business of commodity production. My intention is to show how the forces of business are reshaping the world we live in, reworking what we call experience along the way. I do not want to claim any particular power of insight here. The tendencies that I will describe have been extant in prototype form for a number of years now, and in some cases their origins can be traced even earlier. It would also be possible to argue that they have been prefigured in a number of places, by authors who want to give up on the kind of remorselessly monopolist accounts of capitalism that act as a kind of intellectual and political bulldozer (Amin and Thrift 2005).[57] I think of Michel Callon's work on an economy of qualities, Luc Boltanski and Eve Chiapello's work on new forms of economic justification, Edward Lipuma and Benjamin Lee's work on circulating capitalism, Celia Lury's work on brands, Lev Manovich's work on new media, the work of Paolo Virno and Maurizio Lazzarato on intellectual labour and 'immaterial' capitalism, the allied work of Moulier Boutang and others on cognitive capitalism, or even, to travel farther back in time, Alvin Toffler's coining of the term 'prosumerism'. Put baldly, I want to point to three formative tendencies that now structure – and rule – experience in capitalist economic formations: prospecting across the whole of bodily experience, but most especially in the 'anteconscious', thus reworking what is regarded as labour, class, invention and, indeed, much of what was traditionally regarded as political economy; attempting to produce instant communities, worlds gathered around products and production processes which themselves become a vital part of what is regarded as product and production process;[58] reworking space and time so that they fit this new kind of life, most especially by producing new prostheses which are also additions to cognition and precognition.

Most importantly I want to zero in on this latter process. It is possible to argue that the most important reworking of experience that is currently taking place is the production of new kinds of not just attentive and responsive but formative spaces which act as a generalized form of writing on to and in to the world, working especially at the level of bare life. This mass 'production of worlds', as Lazzarato (2004) would put it, consists not just of a multiplication of saleable ways of living, but also the symbolic indexing of these spaces so that they can continually generate what would have been thought of as 'decisive moments' with the result that these spaces can be constantly refreshed and so remain absorbing (see Thrift 2006b). If one of the most important cognitive leaps of the last few hundred years was the growth of writing in its many forms, now, or so I argue, a similar change in the structure of cognition is occurring but as a general process of the purposeful production of semiosis, in which space is both template and font. This is, in other words, the age of the inhabitable map (Fawcett-Tang 2005; Abrams and Hall 2006), an age intent on producing various new kinds of captivation through the cultivation of *atmosphere* or *presence* or *touch* (see Sloterdik 2005a, 2005b; Zumthor 2006).[59] So, for example, when Wheeler (2006) points to a world perfused with signs, privileges emergence, and underlines the importance of responsiveness, I take this stance to be not just an outline of the lineaments of a new kind of political project but also a symptomatic observation concerning a world in which spaces are taking on many of the characteristics of life. The trick, or so it seems to me, is to work with this emerging spatial grain, in the full understanding that it is both a part of a series of means of opening up new opportunities for the exercise of power and profit *and* a new palette of possibilities.

The three subsequent chapters fill out how the background of experience is changing in response to these three insistent imperatives. In essence, they are an attempt to move on from Deleuze and Guattari's famous aphorism from *Anti-Oedipus*, 'The unconscious is not a theatre, but a factory', by documenting how the unconscious has become both together, as the factory and the theatre have blended into each other. Thus 'Still life in nearly present time' considers the ways in which modern societies are experimenting with 'neutral' material backgrounds for commercial gain, burrowing into bare life in order to come up with the goods. I associate bare life with that small space of time between action and cognition and show the way firms have become ever more expert in operating on this new territory for commercial gain. It was one of my first attempts to show up how the backgrounds through which we live are changing as new disciplines have their say. '*Driving* in the city' is intended to demonstrate just how radically bodies are changing as they are augmented and extended by these backgrounds, as they subtly redefine what counts as experience. The chapter argues that de Certeau's understanding of walking as the archetypal transhuman practice of making the city habitable cannot hold in a post-human world. By concentrating on the practices of driving, I argue that other experiences of the city now have an equal validity. In other words, de Certeau's work on everyday life in the city needs to be reworked in order to take into account the rise of automobility. The bulk of the chapter is devoted to exploring how that goal might be achieved, concentrating in particular on how new knowledges like software and ergonomics have become responsible for a large-scale spatial reordering of the city which presages an important change in what counts as making the city habitable. 'Movement-space' takes a slightly different tack by arguing that the background of experience is being changed irrevocably by means of mass calculation which is, perhaps, better described as 'qualculation' with the result that every event turns up digitally pre-disposed, so to speak. The chapter then moves on to consider how this qualculative background is producing new apprehensions of space and time before ending by considering how new kinds of sensorium may now be becoming possible. I illustrate this argument by considering the changing presence of the hand, co-ordinate systems, and language, thereby attempting to conjure up the lineaments of a new kind of movement-space.

The second section attempts to articulate some of the political stakes that arise from non-representational theory. Written in the late 1990s the single chapter in this section forms a kind of pivot. 'Afterwords', was an attempt to make a definitive statement about non-representational theory by focusing particularly on the motif of performance as the key to a politics of experiment. It is intended as a message of hope, of a longing for a future of stutter and clutter that can produce new places within which more interesting practices are able to produce more habitable worlds (Miyazaki 2006).

Having sketched in a background, I can then move on to some more recent work. Non-representational theory has been interpreted by some as being simply a political message of unbridled optimism. That is not the case. As if to prove it, the book ends on a darker note, emphasizing that the quest for a new kind of political that I want to follow may try to multiply positive prehensions, but that it is not therefore a quixotic quest for the new moral styles we so desperately need

(Appadurai 2006). Indeed, I hold to a tragic view of human life insofar as I believe that history is one long stumble into the unknown, and it cannot be tied down and ordered in the way that too many social theorists imply with their too neat theories. Most particularly, it would be foolish to deny some of the more unsavoury facts of existence. Nature is both astonishingly prolific, able to produce infinite variation and exquisite adaptation, and abundantly and unremittingly cruel. Nature does not take sides. The cost of what Nietzsche called 'more life' is depredation on a scale we can hardly comprehend: who could sum the number of violent deaths that casually occur around the world every second or claim to understand this sublime destructiveness?

Human being does not stand outside nature. It is full of all kinds of impulses which are outside its comprehension and are the other (I will not say negative) side of this equation, impulses that can be likened to Freud's death instinct in their capacity to undo connections and destroy life. In the last section of the book, I start to address some of these issues, and, most particularly, the issues of anger, rage and humiliation, by concentrating on the issue of affect, for what it seems important to underline is that a clarion call for 'more life' is disingenuous, even misleading, without some understanding of the surpluses of anger, rage and humiliation that have been unleashed as a result of the 'predatory narcissisms' (Appadurai 2006) that characterize too much of the modern world.

The last four chapters in the book which form its final section point to the need to think about affect as a key element of a politics that will supplement the ordinary. What is certain is that understanding affect requires some sense of the role of biology, howsoever understood. The first chapter, 'From born to made', is an attempt to come to terms with that legacy of thought and practice by taking up some of the themes from the first part of the book and pulling them into the third. It is particularly concerned with forging new links between biology and technology by delivering a set of shocks to the meaning of accepted categories like 'nature' and 'technology', especially by relying on the Whiteheadian dictum that 'nature is a theatre for the interrelation of activities' (Whitehead 1978: 140). To achieve these dual aims, the chapter double clicks on the icon 'intelligence'. 'Intelligence' prioritizes the *active shaping of environments*. It thereby allows space for the spaces of the world to themselves become a part of intelligibility and intellect as elements of distributed cognition *and* distributed pre-cognition. The chapter argues that such a conception of sentience can provide a series of new perspectives, as well as a pressing ethical challenge. I then move to a consideration of the political stakes that the deployment of affect entails against the background of the active engineering of pre-cognition. In the chapter 'Spatialities of feeling' I outline what a politics of affect might look like and especially the more explicit politics of hope that is currently struggling to be born out of an analysis of the affective swirl that characterizes modern societies. However, I take seriously the criticism of this kind of work, that it has tended to neglect the many forms of violence and repression that infest the worlds and knock it around. Thus I try to counterbalance the politics of hope that I espouse with some sober reflections on the affective substrate in which it is embedded and from which it cannot be simply divided. Thus the chapter

'But malice aforethought' considers the affective life that is to be found in modern cities, concentrating on the idea that sociality does not have to mean that citizens automatically like each other. Indeed, modern cities are drenched in dislike and even hatred, and I argue that this misanthropic fact needs to be taken fully into account in any narrative and politics of affect. Finally, 'Turbulent passions' considers how we might better understand the realm of political feeling by concentrating on the affective technologies through which masses of people become primed to act. I argue that this is a pressing political task, given that the systematic manipulation of 'motivational propensity' has become a key political technology. But in order to arrive at a diagnosis of the affective swash of the present, I argue that social science needs to draw on approaches that are willing to countenance a formative role for the biological. I therefore turn to two strands of work, one that directly revalues the biological, the other that calls on ethological models and analogies. Using these different but connected strands of work, I am able to move to such a diagnosis. My argument is that a series of affective technologies that were previously used mainly in the corporate sphere to work on consumer anxiety, obsession and compulsion are now being moved over into the political sphere with mainly deleterious consequences. However, this process of transmission also suggests some interesting counter-politics based on the cultivation of contrary affective motion, not what Appadurai (2006) calls the 'runaway acts of mutual stimulation' which are so prevalent in a media-saturated age but something much more interesting.

Part I

2 Re-inventing invention

New tendencies in capitalist commodification

> The functioning of the economy of qualities involves the establishment of forms of organization that facilitate the intensification of collaboration of supply and demand in a way that enables consumers to participate actively in the qualification of products. The establishment of distributed cognition devices, intended to organize real life experiments as preferences, tends to blur habitual distinctions between production, distribution and consumption. Design, as an activity that crosses through the entire organization, becomes central: the firm organizes itself to make the dynamic process of qualification and requalification of products possible and manageable.
>
> (Callon *et al.* 2002: 197)

> In the long procession of history, capitalism is the late-comer. It arrives when everything is ready.
>
> (Braudel 1977: 75)

Introduction

It is always difficult to tell where capitalism will go next as it continues to seek out new sources of profit. After all, capitalism is not a fixed and unforgiving force. Rather, it is a heterogeneous and continually dynamic process of increasingly global connection – often made through awkward and makeshift links – and those links can be surprising, not least because they often produce unexpected spatial formations which can themselves have force (Amin 2004; Bayart 2001; Moore 2004; Tsing 2005). In this chapter, I therefore want to take some really quite specific links in an increasingly globally connected capitalism, links to do with what might still be considered to be its beating heart – the system of production of commodities and the process of commodification – and to attempt to weave them into a general story about what might be happening currently at its leading edge. Conforming to the premise that there is an urgent necessity to anticipate the transformation and command strategies of capital,[1] I want to argue that it is possible to detect a series of novel practices emerging which are likely to have interesting consequences over the long term, both economically and culturally. Indeed by constantly putting these two descriptors into play, these practices once again reinforce the argument that political economy can no longer claim an '*isolement splendide, majestueux et décevant*' (Tarde 1902: 97).

I will begin the chapter by arguing that these new practices are being forced by a certain kind of desperation which is the result of a long-term profits squeeze (Brenner 2003a, 2003b), a squeeze that points capitalism in two entirely opposed and closely linked directions which combine something that is often very close to barbarism with an increasingly sophisticated corporate vanguard which seems to be attempting to invent a vitalist capitalism. The juxtaposition is increasingly bizarre.

Thus, one direction is towards increasing exploitation of large parts of the world through what Marx called primitive accumulation (Harvey 2003; Retort 2005). It is clear that a considerable area of the globe is being ravaged by force, dispossession and enclosure as part of a search for mass commodities like oil, gas, gems and timber, using all of the usual suspects: guns, barbed wire and the law. This primitive accumulation lies close to but is not always coincident with the vast global shadow economy dependent on illegal activities like smuggling, drug and people trafficking and money-laundering through which trillions of dollars circulate around the globe outside of formal legal reckoning (Nordstrom 2004) and produces a stentorian backdrop to this chapter, one which should be kept in mind throughout what follows.

The other direction, which I will be concentrating on in this chapter, is to try to squeeze every last drop of value out of the system by *increasing the rate of innovation and invention through the acceleration of connective mutation*. A new kind of productive commotion is being achieved through an active refiguring of space and time which has the effect of making knowledge in to a direct agent of the technical-artistic transformation of life: knowledge and life become inextricable. In other words, instead of being thought of as a passive store, knowledge is thought of as a set of continuously operating machines for 'activating competences, risk taking and readiness to innovate' (Soete 2005: 9). These machines act as interfaces that can change perception. At the same time, they function as a means of boosting difference and inserting that difference into the cycles of production and reproduction of capitalism.

This full-on or *full palette capitalism* relies on a series of practices of intensification which can just as well be read as practices of extensification, since they involve attempts to produce the commodity and commodification in registers hitherto ignored or downplayed by using the entirety of available faculties[2] in a wholesale redefinition of productive labour, taking in the collective intelligence (what Virno (2004) calls the 'public disposition') of what counts as the intellect and intellectual labour.

> The politicization of work (that is the subsumption into the sphere of labor of what had hitherto belonged to political action) occurs precisely when thought becomes the primary source of the production of wealth. Thought

ceases to be an invisible activity and becomes something exterior, 'public', as it breaks into the productive process.

(Virno 2004: 64)

These sets of practices of intensification/extensification have not existed before as coherent and systematic entities and they are currently in the middle of things, so they may work – or they may not. But they have at least the potential to redefine what count as the horizons of capitalism by changing how *encounter* with the commodity is thought of and practised by the consumer (by trying to not so much control as to modulate vicissitude by boosting what is brought to the encounter), especially by incorporating the collective agency of the intellectual labour of the consumer into the business of innovation (Berardi 2005). In other words, *value* increasingly arises not from what is but from what is not yet but can potentially become, that is from the *pull of the future*, and from the new distributions of the sensible that can arise from that change. This is hardly a novel stance. After all, labour-power incorporates potential, that which is not current, not present, and this has a pragmatic dimension:

> Where something which exists only as possibility is sold, this something is not separable from the living person of the seller. The living body of the worker is the substratum of that labour-power which, in itself, has no independent existence. 'Life', pure and simple *bios*, acquires a specific importance in as much as it is the tabernacle of *dynamis*, of mere potential.

(Virno 2004: 82)

What, I think, is startling currently is the rate of onset of these different but related tendencies and the way that they are now bearing out many of what may have considered to have been premature general theoretical claims and prognostications. In particular, what I will be presenting could be interpreted as historicizing Tarde's account of an animated economy in which the entities being dealt with are not people but innovations that are constantly trying to multiply themselves, 'quanta of change with a life of their own' (Latour 2005: 15).[3] Thus, what seems to be being produced is a world dependent upon and activated by germs of talent, which are driven by sentiments and knowledge and are able to circulate easily through a semiconscious process of imitation which generates difference from within itself (Leys 1993). The world becomes a continuous and inexhaustible process of emergence of inventions which goes beyond slavish accumulation. In other words, Tarde's analysis in *Psychologie Économique* is becoming true.

In ending this extended introduction, I want to make two main points. First, it can be objected that I am caught up in practices instituted in the corporate aeries of the world by the cultural circuit of capital which ignore the vast bulk of global capitalism and most especially the workaday world. They are the practices of ideologues and visionaries which are, in many cases, not far removed from simple hucksterism. My response is that what the new capitalist practices are about are making their way into this workaday world and refiguring it, so that capitalism can play much closer to the skin, so to speak. But it is also that these practices, like many others, contain within them contradictory impulses which provide the ground for new forms of political formation, a point I will return to briefly in the concluding section of the chapter.

Second, it may be objected that these are arguments without much in the way of empirical foundation. It is true that this chapter is in part speculative, both in its object and in how it proceeds, but that is not to say that it has no evidence base. Spotting a process of the 'redistribution of the sensible' (Rancière 1999), of the production of a new form of consumer divination and appropriation, involves some concentrated gleaning, which depends upon being able to pull together diverse sources and indicators. The chapter is therefore based on three main stimuli. One is 'observant participant' fieldwork in business and in bioscience over a two year period. Another is the mining of a very large range of secondary sources that have proved appropriate. The sheer range of sources able to be drawn on reflects the difficulty of tracking an inchoate ambition that is being constructed in its making, and a consequent tendency to bricolage which is at the heart of new forms of capitalism. The third is an Economic and Social Research Council grant on e-commerce carried out jointly with Andrew Leyshon, Louise Crewe, Shaun French and Peter Webb which pointed to many of the developments I will discuss. Finally, then, this chapter is a work of synthesis, but it is one based on close observation of some particular key arenas of practice.

The chapter is therefore in three parts. In the first part, I will describe three closely related conceptual-cum-practical developments that, though they have been present in embryonic form for varying amounts of time, came together at the end of the twentieth century. They are now being taken on, in lock step, as new ways to squeeze value by amplifying the rate of innovation through a general exteriorization of intelligence out from the corporation, in turn redefining what counts as value. These developments should not be seen as extending everywhere but they are, I think, indicative.

Taken together, this 'second round' of concept-practices describe a new distribution of the sensible. The first of these developments has been an obsession with knowledge and creativity and especially an obsession with fostering tacit knowledge and aptitudes through devices like the community of practice and metaphors like performance. However, this stream of thought and practice has now transmuted into a more general redefinition of intellectual labour arising out of the mobilization of the resource of *forethought,* or rather the possibilities of plumbing the non-cognitive realm and 'fast' thinking in general, a search typified by a book like Malcolm Gladwell's recent business bestseller, *Blink* (2003). Then, second, there was a desire to rework consumption so as to draw consumers much more fully into the process, leaching out their knowledge of commodities and adding it back into the system as an added performative edge through an 'experience economy'(Pine and Gilmore 1999). This stream of thought and practice has now blossomed into a set of fully fledged models of 'co-creation' which are changing corporate perceptions of what constitutes 'production', 'consumption', 'commodity', 'the market' and indeed 'innovation'. The third development has involved the active engineering of the space of innovation, the result especially of an emphasis on communities of knowledge. Informed by the profusion of information technology and by attempts to construct more intellectually productive environments, especially through the construction of built forms that would hasten and concentrate interaction, this stream of thought and practice has transmuted into a more general concern with social engineering of groups, thereby learning how to combine information technology, built form and group formation in ways that really will deliver the goods. Taken together, these three developments have also foregrounded the absolute importance of design.

Throughout the chapter, the reader will notice the difficulty that I have with keeping production and consumption separate: producers try to put themselves in the place of consumers, consumers contribute their intellectual labour and all kinds of work to production in the cause of making better goods, in a kind of *generalized outsourcing*, migrations regularly occur between production and consumption, and vice versa. Innovation can turn up anywhere and is no longer necessarily restricted to particular niches in the division of labour.[4] It has, of course, been a standard component of a number of recent new left accounts that consumption has become, in some sense or another, productive: consumption is no longer a passive terminus but a complicit and creative relay in the production of capitalism. But it seems to me that these accounts, which were almost certainly premature and which were allowed much too great a generality, are now starting to take on real weight.

But what is this weight? In the second part of the chapter, I will argue that these new sets of practices foretell a reworking of *value* as a new form of *efficacy*, one that will change the background of the western world by producing new interactive senses of causality which are, I suspect, likely to be more effective than the scientific and literary metaphors which are usually assumed to be at the root of changes in perception of causality (e.g. Kern 2004). 'Efficacy' may not seem to be an obvious phrase to use in a discussion of globalized capitalism – it sounds a bit old-fashioned perhaps, a word that has seen better days. But I hope to be able to convince the reader that it is not only relevant but has genuine analytical grip.

I want to argue that some notion of efficacy is crucial to any understanding of modern economies for which innovation is such a crucial engine and value, for what I want to broach is what counts as our understanding of the operativity of the economy – including how it goes about the business of innovation – and I want to argue that increasingly this is dependent upon representing and tapping in to a certain kind of value, one that is different from what has come before. Notice here that I am not using keywords like 'knowledge' or 'creativity' to signal this change. They do not seem quite right to me in that they imply a kind of trawling for the new rather than the continuous process of interaction that now seems to be becoming characteristic. At least in the forums that I will want to examine, words like these seem to me to conceal as much as they reveal and, in any case, they are artefacts of a first round of thinking about the issues, now being superseded.

Thus, I will want to argue that a new kind of efficacy is making its mark, one in which the process of satisfactory encounter with the commodity is central. This constructed sense of 'rightness' increasingly figures both as an understanding of the understanding of how modern economies prosper, as an index of what it is to be a successful agent, and as a form of labour resource in its own right, albeit one that it is hard to touch and unlock, through its ability to extend or even redefine *value* in a period when marginal returns are becoming ever harder to make, in the core at least, in the face of generally heightened competition and a homogenization of business models as a result of the parallel spread of narrow concepts of business efficiency. I will offer three models of this new kind of efficacy, three different takes on how it might be characterized.

In the third and concluding part of the chapter, I draw some brief conclusions. These are concerned with the procedural, political and theoretical implications of these developments. I will argue that they are producing a different kind of capitalist world, one in which a new epistemic ecology of encounter will dwell and have its effects, a world of *indirect but continuous expression*, which is also a world in which that expression can backfire on its makers.

To summarize, my intention in this chapter is to try to tease out some of the underlying elements of a forthcoming processed world as it becomes operational[5] and then to consider some of the consequences that are arising from its inception. Inevitably I feel a certain amount of guilt at what I will have to miss out, not least because this necessitates omitting some of the most important elements of that heterogeneous set of linked processes that go under the name of 'globalization'. I have already signalled the grotesquery of a world in which the kind of continuous, 'vitalist' co-creation that I will describe is coming about alongside concerted attempts at primitive accumulation which often seem to hark back to an imperialism that had been written off but, in the conclusion, I will argue that this juxtaposition has more links than might be supposed and that these can constitute a fertile political resource.

A forthcoming epistemic ecology

For some time, Western capitalism has been suffering from a crisis of profits. Although the addition into the world economy of new economic powerhouses like parts of China and parts of India certainly muddies the waters. What evidence there is suggests that, over a considerable period of time, Western capitalism has been in a long-term downturn following on from the post-war boom, based on overcapacity and overproduction. Episodes like the stock-market Keynesianism of the telecommunications, media and information technology boom from 1995 to 2000 did nothing to dispel this secular tendency, while investment in information and communications technology – one mooted saviour – has until recently produced at least questionable returns.

But, against this dour background, there have been numerous efforts to alight on new business models that will soak up overproduction and overcapacity, most especially by either engaging more closely with consumers or boosting the rate of innovation. Most of these models have ended up producing ambiguous results in aggregate, partly for minor but important reasons (for example, managers can have very different understandings of what constitutes innovation (Storey and Salaman 2005)) and partly because this kind of cultural engineering is not easy to do and has required constant experimentation to be made effective. But I think that this is now changing. What might be regarded as a set of new fuel sources for capitalism are coming together as a powerful system, new sources of energy that capitalism can tap (Mitchell 2002).

In this first section, I want to outline what these fuel sources are. Taken as a whole, I argue that they add up to a different kind of encounter with the commodity, as an experimental ecology based on continuous interaction sufficiently imposing to resemble an aspect of time itself, a different set of crystallizations of time (Lazzarato 2000, 2002). This cultural model of economic change is, not surprisingly, based on and in the continuous interactivity of the media (Manovich 2001). The effect of this *streaming ethos* is, or so I will argue, to begin to restructure what counts as production and consumption and market and innovation so as to bring consumption closer to hand. If this epistemic ecology has an overall goal, then it seems to me to be to make the commodity even more empathetic by enabling it to lie ever closer to the concerns of the consumer, thus echoing Benjamin's (1977 [1938]: 63) pregnant remarks on the soul of the commodity; 'if the soul of the commodity which Marx occasionally mentions in jest existed, it would be the most empathetic ever encountered in the realm of souls, for it would have to see in everyone the buyer in whose hand and house it wants to nestle'.

Activating forethought

> It is by logic that we prove. It is by intuition that we discover.
> (Poincaré, cited in Myers 2002: 63)

Let me start my consideration of the reworking of encounter with the commodity by considering the mobilization of forethought as part of a more general broadening of what capitalism counts as intellect and intellectual labour. Cognition is, of course, a vital aspect of human practice but research over many years has shown that it is at best a fragile and temporary coalition, a tunnel which is always close to collapse:

> During the past forty years, in countless laboratories around the world, human consciousness has been put under the microscope, and exposed mercilessly for the poor thing it is: a transitory and fleeting phenomenon. The ephemeral nature of consciousness is especially obvious in experiments on the temporal minima of memory – that is the length of time we can hold on to a clear sensory image of something. Even under the best circumstances, we cannot keep more than a few seconds of perceptual experience in short-term memory. The

window of consciousness, defined in this way, is barely ten or fifteen seconds wide. Under some conditions, the width of our conscious window on the world may be no more than two seconds wide.

(Donald 2001: 15)

But the message gets worse: the average person can only grasp a few things at a time. And worse: the average person is prevented from becoming aware of most of their thought processes, they are simply not available for conscious reflection. And worse again: consciousness is notoriously vulnerable to distraction; the conscious mind finds it very difficult to maintain a sharp focus in the presence of other attractions. In other words, conscious awareness is fragmented and volatile; 'our intellectual home, the cradle of our humanity, appears to be the most limited part of our mind' (Donald 2001: 25). This description is something of an exaggeration[6] – it derives from laboratory experiments and glosses over the richness of joint action in which subjects do much better – but it also points to the way in which this minimal conscious perception is constantly backed up by other systems, two of which are particularly important. One is all the non-cognitive relays that hold it in place and do much of what we count as thinking:

a huge reservoir of unconscious or automatic cognitive processes that pro-vide a background setting within which we can find meaning in experience. By relying on these deep automaticities, we can achieve great things intel-lectually. We can even carry out several parallel lines of cognition at the same time, provided they are kept out of consciousness. Musicians know this. When professional pianists play, they cannot afford to become overly conscious of their fingering or the specific notes of the passage they are playing, particularly the more rapid ones. That kind of self-consciousness is paralyzing. They have to automatize these difficult passages, or they will make major mistakes. The same rule applies to speaking.

(Donald 2001: 26)

The other is that this minimal conscious perception is boosted and held in place by all manner of systems and environments and sites that extend awareness, systems and environments and sites that are increasingly artificial and increasingly made up of commodities. For example, the system of reading and writing[7] trains people to apply a highly detailed set of eye and other corporeal movements to a set of systematic practices that allow the environment to act as a prosthetic for think-ing (and allow resultant ideas to hold still long enough to be worked on and developed). The facts of ethology cut in.

What is new about the current conjuncture is the way in which capitalism is attempting to use the huge reservoir of non-cognitive processes, of *forethought*, for its own industrial ends in a much more open-ended way.[8] In the past, capitalism usually drew on non-cognitive processes by training managers and workers and consumers to conform to set routines grooved into forethought by various kinds of training such that the body could not master its own movements, or by trying to elicit conformist reactions to a brand. But, more recently, much thought has been given to understanding forethought as not just a substrate but as a vital performative element of situations, one which cannot only produce its own intelligibilities but which can be trained to produce ideas. In other domains, this ambition has a long history. One thinks of, for example, a nineteenth-century phenomenon like Delsartism which was a new way of reading minute body signs from gesture. But now the intention is to read and exploit signs of invention by regarding the body as a mine of potentiality and to generate and harness unpredictable interactions as a source of value by regarding space as more than a map. The automaticity of intuition can then be enrolled to produce better outcomes: it becomes a fund of expertise. For example, in the 1980s and 1990s managerial capitalism turned to various performative methods which were meant to be simultaneously forms of team-building and effective means of producing innovation (Thrift 2005a), often based on that famous slogan from Michael Polanyi: 'we know more than we can tell'. Not unreasonably, it was assumed that placing people in new combinations which were simultaneously re-arrangements of bodies and environments would produce new and reproducible tacit knowledges arising out of shifts in the practical intelligence needed to be successful at practical problem-solving (Sternberg *et al.* 2000).[9] Of late, however, this kind of emphasis on a more effective everyday creativity has been added to, most particularly through the application of models drawn from writings from neuroscience which attempt to mobilize the momentary processes that go to make up much of what counts as human.[10]

Persons are to be trained to 'unthinkingly' conjure up more and better things, both at work and as consumers, by drawing on a certain kind of *neuro-aesthetic* which works on the myriad small periods of time that are relevant to the structure of forethought and the ways that human bodies routinely mobilize them to obtain results (Donald 2001; Myers 2002) to produce more of the kind of ideas that seem to just turn up, which, in reality, are thoughts that we are forever prevented from becoming directly aware of. Intuitive expertise can be learned, for example by paying attention to the smallest corporeal detail, by so-called 'thin-slicing' (Gladwell 2005).

Inevitably, this emphasis on a kind of hastening of the undertow of thought and decision, an open training of intuition, has led workers in this field to pay much more attention to *affect*, because waves of affect are often born in these small spaces of time out of a series of deep expressive habits and out of different emotional 'intelligences'. Further, it has become clear that affectively binding consumers through their own passions and enthusiasms sells more goods. Consumption is itself a series of affective fields[11] and more and more of the industry that investigates consumer wants and desires is given over to identifying possible emotional pressure points.[12] It has also led them to consider the design composition of things in more detail to see if it is possible to provide more in the way of momentary 'thing-power', as well as the associated construction of circumstances rich enough in calculative prostheses to allow the neuro-aesthetic to function more forcefully, via the construction of a disposition that can produce a spatial appropriateness in the moment regularly and reproducibly, thereby not so much taming as harnessing chanciness to produce 'small miracles'. In other words, the aim is to produce a certain anticipatory readiness about the world, a rapid perceptual style which can move easily between interchangeable opportunities, thus adding to the sum total of intellect that can be drawn on. This is a style which is congenial to capitalism, arising out of new senses of kinds and collections of matter (Bennett 2004) which will do more, an extended set of sense organs, if you like, that will sense the right things, and the right things to do and, more to the point, will mobilize new structures of forethought out of which can arise new ideas (Thrift 2005a).

Activating consumer ingenuity

> The market as a forum challenges the basic tenet of traditional economic theory, that the firm and consumers are separate, with distinct, predetermined roles, and consequently that supply and demand are distinct, but mirrored processes oriented around the exchange of products and services between firms and consumers.
>
> (Prahalad and Ramaswamy 2004: 135)

For some time now, there have been attempts to extend the signature of the commodity, both by enlarging its footprint in time and by reinforcing its content, most especially by loading it with more affective features. A series of different strategies have been involved, which are only now becoming related. Three such strategies are worth noting. One is well known: the advent of project-working around what might be termed 'value proposals' which necessitate a structured flow of work that allows a product to be continuously developed. More and more companies are becoming like project co-ordinators, outsourcing the 'business-as-usual' parts of their operations so that they can be left free to design and orchestrate new ideas, aided by new devices like product life-cycle software which allow product designs to be rapidly changed.

> Nike, for instance, does not make shoes any more; it manages footwear projects. Coca-Cola, which hands most of the bottling and marketing of its drinks to others, is little more than a collection of projects, run by people it calls 'orchestrators'. . . . BMW treats each new car 'platform', which is the basis of new vehicle ranges, as a separate project. Meanwhile Capital One, a fast-growing American financial services group, has a special team to handle its M&A 'projects'. For all these firms, project-management has become an important competitive tool. Some of them call it a core competence.
>
> (*The Economist* 2005c: 66)

What is striking is that, in certain senses, these commodity projects never end, or are certainly extended in time by slight but significant transformations of performance, because of the need to continuously interact with consumers. And, as the response time of interactivity has speeded up, so different imaginations of the consumer and commodity have been able to come into play (Lury 2004).

Another means of extending the commodity has proved to be through finding means of aggregating so-called 'long tails' so as to make more goods more saleable. In this model, information technology makes it possible to sell more goods but this is not just a logistical exercise. It involves the active fostering of various consumer communities and their aggregation into critical masses with the result that commodities that would have had only faint sales records in the past because of their isolated 'audience' come to have substantive sales records which, when aggregated with those of other audiences, produce a substantial new market segment (Brynjolfsson *et al.* 2003). In turn, these new audiences can be worked on: their enthusiasm can be played to, for example through the medium of websites which act as 'honey traps'. So, for example, Amazon.com now sell more books from the backlist outside their top 130,000 bestsellers than they do from within them, in part through all manner of devices that are intended to capture and foster enthusiasms and automate 'word of mouth'.

One other strategy has been to think of commodities as 'resonating' in many sensory registers at once, increasing the commodity's stickiness (or at least making it more recognizable in amongst the commodity cacophony of modern capitalism): 'today the value proposition is more intimate and intuitive' (Hill 2003: 20). The aim is to add in more feeling by appealing to registers of the senses formerly neglected, thus stimulating the emotions connected with things, and so generally producing more affective grip for those things – and thus more engaging artefacts that produce more commitment and so sell more. This tendency, which in the 1990s gathered around slogans like the 'experience economy', has been most obvious in areas like commodity design. Thus, increasingly, commodities are thought of as interfaces that can be actively engineered across a series of sensory registers in order to produce positive affective responses in consumers. Aided by a set of new material surfaces, commodities must appeal across all the senses, reminding us that the original meaning of the word 'aesthetics' was the study of the senses. Sensory design and marketing has become key (Hill 2003). Thus, car doors are designed to give a satisfyingly solid clunk as they shut. New cars are given distinct smells. Breakfast cereals are designed to give a distinct crunch.[13] Travel experiences are given distinctive aromas.[14] And so on. In turn, this deepening of the sensory range of commodities is related to distinct market segments. For example, there is currently a thriving area of consultancy that is based on advising on how to make products supposedly more appealing to women (see, for example, Molotch 2003; Barletta 2002). Nearly all of these products involve various supposedly distinctive forms of 'sensorizing'.[15]

However, the most significant means of squeezing value out of the commodity's signature has been achieved by reworking production and consumption, questioning both categories in the process, so leading to the perception of the commodity as consisting of an iterative process of experiment, rather than as a fixed and frozen thing, on the understanding that 'an organization's capacity to innovate relies on a process of experimentation whereby new products and services are created and existing ones improved' (Thomke 2003: 274). In other words, what is at issue is 'a particular mode of innovating . . . linked to constructions of the market framed by information about the consumer' (Lury 2004: 62) which, in turn, depends upon *a reworking of what is meant by the commodity from simply the invention of new commodities to the capture or configuration of new worlds*[16] into which these commodities are inserted.

In the sphere of production, this reworking has been achieved by giving much greater emphasis to the process of rapid experimentation, especially early in the production process, resulting, in particular, from the integration of new information technologies into the product development process, thus allowing a much greater spectrum of possibilities to be tested, thereby speeding up the experimentation-failure cycle and making it possible to produce a process of continuous redevelopment. Specifically, this reworking has drawn on four ongoing developments: using the resources provided by computer simulation, re-organizing production processes so that they can cope with preliminary conclusions and rough data,[17] putting in place systems that explicitly learn from the experience of products and, lastly, shifting the locus of experimentation to customers because all the evidence shows that users' intellectual labour can itself be a powerful source of innovation (Thomke 2003). The distinctions between exploratory and exploitative innovation therefore become much more difficult to maintain (Roberts 2004) since lots of ideas are being generated at relatively low cost through organizations that are 'permanently beta' (Neff and Stark 2003).

This latter strategy of moving innovation beyond the organization by tapping into the commodity involvements of consumers and others, under the general slogan 'not all the smart people work for you' (Chesborough 2003), has proved particularly important, and I will therefore concentrate more attention on it. It is important to note that consumer inputs into innovation have a long historical record. For example, Franz (2005) has shown the way in which early automobiles were the subject of all kinds of consumer innovations – what she calls 'tinkering' was one of the main motors of technical improvement. Then, in the late 1920s and 1930s, the rise of large corporations with specialized research and development facilities and the ambition to manage consumer desire, combined with designs that made automobiles easier to drive but harder to modify, put a stop to tinkering as a major source of innovation. But that is now changing and consumers are able to take back some measure of technological authority. A change in the technical background, most notably the mass codification of all kinds of knowledge and the associated democratization of the learning process that has been encouraged by information technology (Foray 2004), has allowed ingenuity to flourish again. In particular, information technology has reduced the transaction costs of sharing information about commodities and has, simultaneously, made it much easier to construct communities around this sharing. The result has been a flowering of so-called open or user-centred innovation, which may even be comparable to the diffusion of innovations noted by Mokyr (2003) in the nineteenth century which resulted from massive cuts in the transaction costs of innovation.

In open or user-centred innovation, consumers are a vital force in research and experimentation:[18]

Users of products and services – both firms and individual consumers – are increasingly able to innovate for themselves. User-centred innovation processes offer great advantages over the manufacturer-centric development systems that have been the mainstay of commerce over hundreds of years. Users that innovate can develop exactly what they want, rather than rely on manufacturers to act as their (very often imperfect) agents. Moreover, users do not have to develop everything they need on their own: they can benefit from innovations developed and freely shared by others.

(von Hippel 2005: 1)

Companies are increasingly likely to 'free reveal' in order to increase incentives to innovate, giving away ownership rights in order to obtain other benefits. Though the example often given is open source programming, the democratizing of innovation goes far beyond this particular practice (von Hippel 2005), by recognizing the enthusiasms and pleasures of consumers' involvements with numerous commodities and entering into a relation with those involvements, thus producing 'experience innovation' (Prahalad and Ramaswamy 2004) through shifting the boundary between private and collective.

But it is important to note that not all or even most consumer communities are active innovators. Rather, they are likely to be involved in something much closer to what Barry (2000) and Lazzarato (2002a), following Tarde, call 'invention', as a means of distinguishing the practice of iterative improvements resulting from particular modes of interaction from innovation. Invention may multiply the possibilities for technical change but is rather a form of imitative change that opens up the possibilities for further action: 'the amplification of slight transformations in the design, styling, promotion and delivery of a particular product (or service) has the potential consequence of non-linear returns as it is exploited in the multiple relations between products' (Lury 2004: 60). In invention, mere use[19] is superseded by pleasure in the activity itself, of which the commodity is an active partner. When a commodity produces a sufficiently compelling experience environment, *consumer communities* will evolve beyond a company's control, thus directly co-creating value and providing the firm with a new terrain of profit – generalized outsourcing – if it is nimble enough to adapt to the new conditions. These communities gather round particular obsessions, which cover an enormous spectrum although many of the prototypes were in music, fashion and information technology. Sometimes these communities resemble mere interest groups, sometimes groups of fickle fans, sometimes hobbyists, and sometimes cults. What is clear is that their existence is not predictable, in part because they are engaged in activities which find their own fulfilment in themselves, without necessarily objectifying these activities into 'finished' products or into objects which survive their performance (Virno 2004). The quality of interactivity therefore becomes a major part of the commodity, not only because that interactivity assumes the presence of others but also because a number of products have become more complex and require more consumer investment, in part playing to this social tendency.[20]

This emphasis on open innovation achieved through much closer involvement with consumer experimentation clearly blurs the distinction between production and consumption by drawing the powers of consumers in to production and by drawing producers into the worlds of consumers to a much greater degree than heretofore. Company-consumer interaction becomes crucial. The information asymmetries that characterized the boundaries between producers and consumers are thus being redrawn. Because this is proving to be a particularly important new practice, I propose to spend more time on it.

Consumers have become involved in the production of communities around particular commodities which themselves generate value, by fostering allegiance, by offering instant feedback and by providing active interventions in the commodity itself. Thus markets become less simple means of selling products composed at the terminus of a value chain whose only forms of interactivity are sales figures and the diverse forms of market research and more forums in which interchange takes place around a co-created commodity experience: 'products and services are *not* the basis of value. Rather, value is embedded in the experiences co-created by the individual in an experience environment that the company co-develops with consumers' (Prahalad and Ramaswamy 2004: 121). In turn, producers increasingly become the equivalent of agents, acting as links back to a disaggregated commodity chain and forward into current consumer obsessions. This new view necessarily challenges dominant conceptions of what constitutes a market. The market becomes a forum where dialogue between firms and consumer communities takes place, this dialogue being much more heterogeneous than formerly. The market is no longer outside the value chain, acting as a point of interchange between producer and consumer. Greater interactivity means that 'the market pervades the entire system' (Prahalad and Ramaswamy 2004: 125).

Activating space

A further crucial element in the development of a full palette capitalism is the more active use of space to boost innovation and invention. In line with the increasing tendency to want to gather invention in wherever it may be found, new time-space arrangements have to be designed that can act as traps for innovation and invention. In other words, attempts are being made to extend the environment in which ideas circulate by producing 'thinking spaces' that can continuously pick up, transmit and boost ideas. But, crucially, these spaces are not sealed. They are insertions within already present flows (Kwinter 2001). They are designed to allow continuous interaction both within and across boundaries by maximizing 'buzz' (Storper and Venables 2004). They are spaces of circulation, then, but, more than that, they are clearly also meant to be, in some (usually poorly specified) way that is related to their dynamic and porous nature, spaces of inspiration incorporating many possible worlds (Lazzarato 2005a).

It is clear that the construction of these thinking spaces could not have become possible without the concerted application of large doses of information technology which have made many more environments highly equipped and thus 'ready-to-think' (Steventon and Wright 2005). Information technology acts as a means of propagation which is also a means of structuring perception (Liu 2004). It acts as a means of singularization which is also a means of aggregating a multiplicity of voices. It acts as a system of distributed cognition which is also a means of capturing new potential.[21] And it acts to radically increase the general availability of consumer goods and services.

Indeed, information technology forces five features which, taken together, constitute a spatial extension of intelligence. One is simply the sheer amount of information becoming available to consumers all but instantly, especially through software like Google. The second is the greater access to information that has accompanied this trend, both by consumers about products and by companies about products. Access costs have plummeted. The third is that linkages and associations are automatically generated for the consumer. Information is continuously linked providing shortcuts that can arrest time for a moment and make more of an encounter by providing backup, connectivity and inspiration. The fourth is that a certain kind of transparency therefore develops. This should not be overdone but it is quite clear that consumers can now find the means to be better informed and to find the means to more easily *learn* about products. Finally, the process of acquisition of information becomes, in principle at least, continuous. It is not fixed but is something that is akin to a never-ending walk. In other words, information technology, through continuous interactivity, offers more reflexivity but a very particular kind of reflexivity that both promotes and inhibits exchange between producers and consumers by instigating performances of its own at the interface which are more than simple mediations (Latour 2005) as it tries to not simply approximate being-in-the-world but boost it by constructing new kinds of in-formed affinity and participation, new communities of all kinds (Dourish 2001).

This settling-in of information and communications technology can be interpreted as the product of a further step in what Callon famously calls 'the economy of qualities' which is now producing a new 'post-phenomenological' commodity architecture, a frame that can combine interactive systems (most of which rely on software in one form or another) and commodities with the spaces and times of everyday life, thereby producing an environment filled with applied and firmly embedded intelligence that is involved in constant iteration and feedback (Thrift 2005a, 2005c). Thus, authors in many of the literatures on information technology constantly resort to quasi-phenomenological models to write about producing a new ground or place or repository, one in which commodification would nestle as an unassuming and thereby even more powerful presence – remember Benjamin's remarks about the soul of the commodity – but, because of the actively seeking efforts of individual consumers and consumer communities, would be even more profitable. These new grounds would constitute a streaming space in which the circuits of value and culture would be fused through a redefinition of the nature of materiality, through what is, in effect, a redistribution of the sensible.

But the settling-in of information technology is only half the story. If space now comes loaded with information, still the question of how individuals and groups interact in order to actually generate learning and innovations is hardly closed off. Thus, again usually in a poorly specified way, it is reckoned that space needs to be designed to boost these capacities by maximizing social interaction. In the 1990s, in particular, this form of reasoning was boosted by a general belief that context was crucial because 'knowledge workers do not follow procedures so much as expertly play their contexts. Without an ability to improvise in context, people who are merely following official prescriptions are utterly lost as soon as they stray from known conditions, which of course happens all the time' (McCullough 2004: 150–151). Thus contexts needed to be actively designed as an extension of intelligence. The first of these contextualizations of expert play was achieved through explicit design of group interaction. Building on a long tradition of management thinking about issues like tacit knowledge, this was chiefly embodied in the notion of community of practice. The second contextualization was the construction of physical spaces that would fit with and boost such formations. Again, this built on a long tradition of trying to design teamwork into buildings, a tradition which had passed through an industrial phase and was becoming interested in buildings which could encompass many modes of social interaction by encouraging both concentration and dispersion simultaneously. So, for example, an office building might contain decloistered spaces of semi-public interaction and all kinds of dens in which individuals or smaller groups could make their way (Duffy 1997).

However, the early twenty-first century has seen further developments, born particularly out of the domain of production of intensive knowledge like various forms of science, which try to blend action and perception by building spaces of potential movement (Massumi 2004). A new round of buildings are beginning to provide a more general model for how spaces of invention should be built and managed. What do these spaces look like?

A good example of the kinds of spatial prototypes that are now being constructed which can confidently be expected to become more general models of innovation incubators is provided by the new generation of biosciences buildings, built as a result of the massive private and public funding that the biosciences have been able to attract through their rhetorical capabilities, and most especially the new generation of therapies that they hopefully prefigure. Concurrent with the rise of the biosciences to such a level of prominence has been a radical redesign of scientific space, reflected in the construction of numerous new 'performative' buildings. For example, every University campus worth its salt is now expected to have its own gleaming temples to interdisciplinary bioscience. These buildings are clearly meant to manipulate time and space in order to produce intensified social interaction so that all manner of crossovers of ideas can be achieved. In other words, the aim is to make architecture more effective by making it more performative.

Through the 1990s and into the twenty-first century, these buildings have been being routinely constructed. For example, just in the UK, the science buildings in the Centre for Life at the University of Newcastle (opened in Newcastle in 2000), the Wellcome Trust Biocentre and the Centre for Inter-Disciplinary Research, both in Life Sciences at the University of Dundee (opened in 1997 and

2006 respectively)[22] or the Manchester Interdisciplinary Biocentre (opened at the University of Manchester in 2006) are typical. Similarly, around the world, a series of elite scientific spaces are being constructed which are intended to produce performative, interdisciplinary machines (cf. Livingstone 2003). The most well-known model for these spaces is to be found at Stanford University in the shape of Bio-X. However, a series of other such buildings have either just been completed or are under construction, including the QB3 consortium buildings at UCSF in Mission Bay, San Francisco, the Institute for Systems Biology in Seattle, and the Howard Hughes Medical Institute research campus at Janelia Park in Virginia.

These buildings usually have a number of features in common. First, they will often include an explicit attempt to represent 'life', whether that be swooping architecture, some forms of public display of science, and similar devices. Second, they are meant to be highly interdisciplinary. As a matter of routine, they usually include not only biologists but also physicists, chemists, computing engineers and so on, all clustered around root technologies like genomics, proteomics, imaging, and the like. Very often, they will place apparently unlike activities (such as computer laboratories and wet laboratories) side by side, or have unorthodox office allocation schedules, all intended to stimulate interdisciplinarity. Third, they are porous. Personnel (for example, scientists arriving and departing on a permanent basis) and information constantly flows through them: as Galison and Thompson (1999) note, the emphasis on co-dependence and co-extension makes it difficult to decide where the experiment begins and ends; rather, there is a global network of software and hardware with no single object or author which the building may only capture fleeting aspects of. The experiment, like the building, is partially dispersed, occurring at a number of locations at once. Fourth, in keeping with an architectural rhetoric about changing ways of working which arose in the mid-1980s and is now an established convention, they are meant to encourage creative sociability arising out of and fuelling further unpredictable interactions. From cafés to temporary dens to informal meeting rooms to walkways that force their denizens to interact (Duffy 1997), the idea is clearly to encourage a 'buzz' of continuous conversation oriented to 'transactional knowledge' and, it is assumed, innovation. Fifth, they are meant to be transparent: there are numerous vantage points from which to spot and track activity, both to add to the general ambience and to point to the values/value of the scientific activity that is going on. In other words, these buildings are meant to encourage a certain kind of notion of interactive knowledge.

But, though these buildings place a clear premium on interdisciplinary discovery, it is often not clear how that process of discovery is being maximized (Rhoten 2003). Often, it is simply assumed that these buildings must generate better results. Only very recently have most of the managers of these buildings even countenanced installing knowledge management and data mining[23] systems that could tell them whether the work going on within their bounds is somehow better than the average and what difference the new environment itself may be making. It is interesting to note the way in which, very gradually, new working practices are growing within them based upon an art of flexible and temporary agglomeration in order (supposedly) to guarantee maximum innovation. In particular, I want to point to three developments that are becoming clear. One is a move to agglomerate in a quasi-organic fashion around key individuals who are good at brokerage across structural holes in the organization. Thus, one requirement may be to 'leverage the likeable' so that groups form naturally and so that linkages between groups are maximized: then the concern is to find individuals who form 'affective hubs' (Casciaro and Lobo 2005) as people who are liked by a disproportionate number of other people. But in the organizations I have looked at, such individuals may just as likely be those who have a certain scientific charisma and are not necessarily likable. Whatever the case may be, it is clear that these organizations are searching for people who can act as brokers around which new groups can constantly form. These people will routinely cross the spaces between existing groups and so maximize between group thinking that might otherwise not exist, very much in line with Burt's finding that people whose networks span structural holes 'are at higher risk of having good ideas' (2005: 349): they are more likely to express ideas, less likely to have ideas dismissed, more likely to have ideas evaluated as valuable, and more likely to be relied on to keep on proposing ideas. But the second development in these organizations is to keep the groups on the move so as to avoid group decay and organizational inertia. They are not allowed to coalesce for anything other than a limited period of time (usually six to twelve months) before they are split up and new groups are formed. This is akin to project working but project working that is self-selecting. In other words, what we see coming into existence is an attempt to socially engineer the process of scientific discovery, using the physical environment as a resource but not as a determining factor. Then, the third development is that in some of these buildings a new position in the formal division of labour has started to grow up, crystallizing out these kinds of skills. Thus a number of buildings now employ 'pathfinders', selected staff that function on either a full-time or fractional basis,[24] whose function is to make sure that the hopper of ideas is constantly kept topped up through formal job descriptions that give them the freedom to 'find and bind'.

Summary: the role of design

> Design is how we can be dominated by instrumental rationality and love it, too.
> (Liu 2004: 236)

How can we summarize these three tendencies? What seems certain is that their net result has been to show the degree to which design is becoming ever more central to the whole production/consumption process (Molotch 2003):

> Until recently, most businesses held little regard for design, . . . because they saw it as something applied after the fact. When it merely dealt with packaging (including front-end interfaces) design seemed superficial. When it was thought of as applied decoration, which may still be the most widespread connotation of the word, design implied cost rather than income. Industrial

design's origins in corporate identity, in which a brand is applied to something that has already been produced, only reproduced that perception. This is a vicious circle. When design is applied to productions that have long since been analytically conceived, the self-fulfilling unimpressive results can be used to demonstrate the superficiality of design.

Now that circle is breaking. Widespread computation makes business strategies based on reductive numerical models more or less available to everyone. Because efficiency models become more of a prerequisite but less of a competitive advantage, strategic emphasis shifts to design. The design of industrial products such as shoes and automobiles has advanced considerably as a result.

(McCullough 2004: 150)

Design has increasingly therefore become interaction design: the design of commodities that behave, communicate, or inform, if even in the most marginal way, in part by making them into processes of variation and difference that can allow for the unforeseen activities that they may become involved in or used for which they may then act as clues to further incarnations. In other words, 'the success of a design is arrived at socially' (McCullough 2004: 167), that is through structured processes of cultural deliberation which massage form (Molotch 2003). In a sense, the goal is to produce commodities that are as 'natural' as longstanding commodities like books but to do so in an accelerated way by dint of various collective design processes that spill outside the organizational boundary, including not just the full spectrum of qualitative methods now routinely used by corporations (or at least by the consultancies that they hire) such as focus groups, ethnography of various kinds, style boards, means-end chains, clinics, pre-launches, information acceleration, conjoint analysis, and so on, but also fan websites, open innovation, and so on.

Thought of in this way, more and more design activity is not defined in relation to a final endpoint. Rather, the 'production process has no final goals, no natural target or final user, but rather continuously feeds on itself. Another way of putting this is that through the activity of design the process of production provides information for itself about itself' (Lury 2004: 52). This is another means of understanding co-creation of course, as a continual process of tuning arrived at by distributed aspiration.

Thus, these three tendencies increasingly mean that commodities have become extended architectures of onflow, designed as a process in order to capture process. The commodity becomes like a Whiteheadian process micrometaphysics whose aim is to generate and maximize involvement, however temporary that may be, for example by placing the commodity in the context of an often heterogeneous experience that has itself been designed as part of what constitutes the commodity, and which has the power to redefine what the commodity is.

Of poetry and profit

> In a genuinely new economy, what constitutes value itself must change.
>
> (McCullough 2004: 261)

It is obviously difficult to find a common denominator for all these different developments but in this section I will argue that what they signify is a more general change in how and what constitutes the *value* form. No longer can the value form be restricted to labour at work. It encompasses life, with consumers trained from an early age to participate in the invention of more invention by using all their capabilities, and producers increasingly able to find means of harvesting their potential.

> Capitalists are interested in the life of the worker, in the body of the worker, only for an indirect reason: this life, this body, are what contains the faculty, the potential, the *dynamis*. The living body becomes an object to be governed not for its intrinsic value, but because it is the substratum of what really matters: labor-power as the aggregate of the most diverse human faculties (the potential for speaking, for thinking, for remembering, for acting, etc.). Life lies at the center of politics when the prize to be won is immaterial (and in itself non-present) labor-power.
>
> (Virno 2004: 82–83)

Thus, capitalism increasingly uses the whole bio-political field as labour is redefined as what Marx in the *Grundrisse* called the 'general intellect' (1973: 706), or general social knowledge acting as a direct force of production organizing social practice (Negri 1991; Lazzarato 2002a). Whether this reserve of virtuosity, 'the subjective, affective, volitional aspects of production and reproduction which tend to become the main sources for the extraction of surplus value' (Toscano 2004b: 211), should go under the heading of immaterial labour, as some Italian Marxist writers would have it, is a moot point[25] but it seems important to signal in some way the degree to which capitalism increasingly attempts to draw on the whole of the intellect. The extent to which this intellect stands apart from capitalism is again debateable. For example, Lazzarato (2002b: 138) argues that 'social labour power is independent and able to organize both its own work and its relations with business entities. Industry does not form or create this new labour power but simply takes it on board and adapts it'. But this seems unlikely. As we have already seen, capitalist firms are intimately bound up with organizing and harvesting this labour, though it would be an exaggeration to say that they control it. Finally, what it means for the value form is, to say the least, unclear. Perhaps the best solution may be to go back to the discussions of value by Tarde in *Psychologie Économique* and use them to renew inspiration, as Lazzarato (2002, 2005) has done. Notably, Tarde wanted to bring together three kinds of value: valeur-utilité (economic activity conventionally understood), valeur-verité (the activity of knowing) and valeur-beauté (aesthetic activity) and I will try to operationalize these categories in a contemporary setting.

What does seem certain is that the developments I have outlined in the previous section add up to more than the sum of their parts. They have begun to form a new distribution of the sensible which simultaneously constitutes a living means of generating more and more invention. It is as if someone had found a way to form and then mine a new phenomenological substrate.[26] In particular, another kind of model of causality (cf. Kern 2004) is gradually starting to evolve, one which has been coded by words like network or creativity or complexity but which I will want to describe rather differently by making an argument about the quality of '*efficacy*'.

Efficacy is variously defined by dictionaries – as the 'ability, especially of a medicine or a method of achieving something, to produce the intended result', as 'the capacity or power to produce an effect' or as 'the ability to produce desired results'. In other words, efficacy constitutes a certain kind of capability, a force. Efficacy can take on a number of different forms, of course. For example, anthropology is chock full of examples of efficacy which Western cultures find odd, even outlandish, centred on practices like magic, witchcraft, divination and sorcery (Peek 1991). In the past, these kinds of practices would have been interpreted as evidence of a comprehensive cosmology. Nowadays, they are more likely to be seen as moments in a habitus of structured improvisations, fixations if you like. But whatever the case, they are seen as expressing the lines that trace out how a culture is conceptually determined,[27] the beliefs a culture holds in what works and what doesn't which are enshrined in all manner of bodily dispositions, objects and ecologies.[28]

I want to argue that, of late, as a result of the conjuring up of a particular sensory configuration of time and space in which commodities can unassumingly nestle and which I examined in the previous section, a different kind of efficacy is gradually being foregrounded. It is a form of efficacy that I will call '*rightness*' in that it is an attempt to capture and work into successful moments, often described as an attunement or a sense of being at ease in a situation, although it is both more and less than that; more in that it is now being constructed as a reproducible technology for harnessing potential; less in that the necessarily formulaic nature of this technology is bound to mean that certain sensings of potential are diminished or even go missing. This search after a certain sense of rightness has always been an intrinsic feature of the operations of capitalism, of course. One only has to think about the importance ascribed to reading financial markets of various kinds which, in large part, is about knowing when to buy and sell various financial instruments and which has been described in books and primers that date back to the nineteenth century and before. And it is not that it has never been noticed or commented on. For example, in an address to the Harvard Business School in 1932 John Dewey identified one of the key skills of business to be a quality of foresight which was also a sense of timing. But I want to argue that it has become a more highly sought-after quality which it is now thought can be actively engineered on a mass scale.

What seems certain is that the implementation of this new version of efficacy demands that capitalism becomes '*both a business and a liberal art*' (McCullough 2004: 206), in that what is being attempted is to continuously conjure up experiences which can draw consumers to commodities by engaging their own passions and enthusiasms, set within a frame that can deliver on those passions and enthusiasms, both by producing goods that resonate and by making those goods open to potential recasting. It is a Latourian sense of the world made incarnate by a co-shaping which is neither an intrinsic property of the human being nor of the artefact:

> For the thing we are looking for is not a human thing, nor is it an inhuman thing. It offers, rather, a continuous passage, a commerce, an interchange between what humans inscribe in it and what it prescribes to humans. It translates the one into the other. The thing is the nonhuman version of the people, it is the human version of things, twice displaced. What should it be called? Neither object nor subject. An instituted object, quasi-object, quasi-subject, a thing that possesses body and soul indissolubly.
>
> (Latour 1996: 23)

If one wished to specify this tendency more concretely, it would be as an attempt to mass produce commodities as so many experiences of a sense of rightness through a series of new practices of innovation that draw directly on consumers' collective intelligence.

How might we understand this new form of efficacy that lies somewhere between business and art? Are there models of value which might shine a light on it? I will end this section very speculatively by noting just three possible models which might act as sources of inspiration for further thinking about what is currently happening to value and how it will be rendered sensible and, in certain senses, calculable in new ways:[29] an instrumental model, a characterological model, and an aesthetic model, each echoing Tarde's three kinds of value. In the first model, rightness is understood as a general cultural model of how to attain ends, in the second as a model of correct epistemological deportment, and in the third as an aesthetic quality. In each model, a certain kind of belief in the world is manifested, which is effective in exerting influence in certain ways.

Rightness as a general cultural model of instrumentality

Let me turn first to a general cultural model of how the world is conceived of as turning up next. This is a model of consuming the world that presumes a different carpet of expectation, one based on a form of opportunism that rewards the skill of manoeuvre amongst interchangeable opportunities.[30] Perhaps the best analogy that can be drawn is with the Chinese concept-practice of 'shi'. That concept-practice (which is indeed an attempt to collapse that distinction) originally derived from warfare but soon moved into many other domains including everyday life. It tries to capture and work with the propensity of things by cultivating a potential born of disposition (Jullien 1995). A person is expected to exploit the potential of the conditions she encounters. She must organize circumstances so as to derive profit from them. She must find the line of force that exploits the configuration she finds to hand. This is not a personal capacity: 'human virtues are not intrinsic, since the individual neither initiates nor controls them, but are the "product" (even in the materialistic sense of the word) of an external conditioning that is, for its part, totally manipulable' (Jullien 1995: 30). The tactical disposition of things is more important than moral qualities: manipulation not persuasion is what counts. The tactic must be devised to evolve along with the situation, and must therefore be constantly revised according to the propensity at work. Thus a disposition is effective by virtue of its renewability and does not have to be decisive and direct. There is no finality. Rather, 'the fundamental objective of all tactics is to ensure that dynamism continues to operate to one's advantage' (Jullien 1995: 34) and that the hands of an opponent are tied by the situation. All reality is a deployment, a continuous deployment.

> Reality was not regarded as a problem but presented itself from the beginning as a credible process. It did not need to be deciphered like a mystery but simply to be understood in its *functioning*. There was no need to project a meaning onto the world or to satisfy the expectations of a subject/individual, for its meaning stemmed in its entirety, without requiring any act of faith, from the propensity of things.
>
> (Jullien 1995: 264–265)

This sense of rightness as a continuous deployment seems to me to encapsulate much of what is now happening in the world, a disposition to and for change that regulates itself as it goes along in a kind of hyper-instrumentality.

Rightness as a mode of governance of knowledge

Tapping into consumer capacities also relies on a model of government of knowledge that will produce a background for new practices of innovation. The second model of value may be understood as a dislocated liberalism which performs power-knowledge in novel ways based on the practices of character formation (Joyce 2003). Above all, this form of power-knowledge is motivated by a fear of stagnation, and is reminiscent of largely forgotten practices of government that individualize personal character and totalize it, practices that were especially popular in Britain and North America from the late eighteenth to the early twentieth century that aimed to govern through the ethical possibilities and constraints of improving 'character' by imposing 'good habits'.

It seems to me that we are seeing something like this form of 'ethological governance' (White 2005), based on a form of power-knowledge that analyses human character and its formation, recurring through the galvanizing of the consumer realm as commodities increasingly use characterological means to communicate themselves. Liu (2004) shows how modern commodities increasingly assume such characterization as a means of providing dramatic unity to an experience. Commodities become directors to and of character and are committed to the goal of self-transformation as part of a more general mimetic model of culture based on the prevalence of media, using example rather than discipline and imitation rather than coercion; 'the paradigmatic body of our societies is no longer the mute body moulded by discipline, but rather it is the bodies and souls marked by the signs, words and images (company logos) that are inscribed in us' (Lazzarato 2005a: 8).

Rightness as an aesthetic

And so to the final model of value, a model which I want to approach through the figure of Wallace Stevens. By all accounts, Wallace Stevens (1879–1955) was a man who enjoyed life. He was a lawyer, admitted to the New York bar in 1904, who worked in New York until 1916. In that year he left New York and moved to Hartford, Connecticut to join the Hartford Accident and Indemnity Company, where he worked in its fidelity and surety claims department. He became a Vice-President of the company in 1934 but refused all advancement after that date. He was proud of his work and was seemingly very good at it. He even published a couple of short papers on insurance.

Stevens was also undoubtedly one of the twentieth century's greatest poets. By most counts, a late bloomer – he was 36 before he published his first work, did not publish his first book until 1923, and is widely regarded as having written some of his finest work in his sixties and seventies – Stevens is now judged by many writers to be the quintessential modernist poet.

One of Stevens's key tasks was to resonate with the moments of sudden rightness in an ultimately bewildering world, those moments of everyday life when 'mere' things seem to light up, seem to become 'precious portents of our powers' (Stevens 1960: 174):

> The dark metaphysical activity of the poet is described in musical terms, where rightness would be a kind of harmony between mind and world. In this sense, our being-in-the-world would be experienced as emotional attunement, which is one rendering of Heidegger's *Stimmung*, which is otherwise rather flatly rendered as 'mood'. Metaphysics in the dark is a kind of music where rightness means sounding right.
>
> (Critchley 2005: 39)

Such a determined pursuit of rightness can be interpreted as presaging one aspect of the new model of efficacy, one with many forebears, of course, but one which heralds a different kind of belief in the *causation* of the object. If the word 'belief' has a quasi-religious tone, that is as it should be, for this form of efficacy, a 'metaphysics in the dark' (Critchley 2005), consists of enlarging the powers of objects through a series of procedures and technologies for building their capacities, including working on the appropriate spaces and times in which they are to be found (Mitchell 2005). But this is not a revelatory or edifying belief. Rather it is a boost to what we regard as mundane certainties about how the world will turn up next, about what *is*, with all the imperfections we often see kept in, confirmed by a combination of vivid sensory stimuli, new forms of narrative, and a controlled element of surprise. In a sense, the aim is simply to see the thing itself, to see things as they 'merely' are, through a material aesthetics (Verbeek 2005) that allows objects to be turned into 'poetics'. Things as portents of our powers remain remote from our intentions but not necessarily from us.

Conclusions: 'Always sell hope'[31]

In these conclusions, I want to make three points, one procedural, one political and one theoretical. The procedural point has been made many times now but it still bears repeating. That is the increasingly bizarre and bitter disjuncture between a fluid core of producer-consumer practices that mark time and an impoverished periphery in which something close to anarchy often reigns in what is often an extended battlefield (Nordstrom 2004) of uncivil wars conducted by, sanctioned by decentralized powers – warlords, gangsters, sects – that the modern state was meant to banish. As Keane puts it:

> For citizens living in the so-called democratic zone of peace, alas, the world is not so neatly subdivided into peaceful and violent zones. Nor can it become so, thanks in part to the links between the two worlds forged by global arms production and the violence-ridden drug trades. Mass migrations, pauperization and prejudice also ensure that rootlessness, ethnic tensions, and violent lawlessness are features of nearly every city of the developed world.
>
> (Keane 1996: 4)

The disjuncture is only underlined by the fact that some of the same companies are involved in both worlds, participating in both a new kind of capitalism and in primitive accumulation through their activities in finance, engineering and construction, and the extraction of primary commodities.

And, then there is a political point. At times in this chapter, I have come close to depicting a world in which capitalism is a force so strong that what it wishes simply comes in to existence. But that is simply incorrect. There are two ways of reading the developments I have outlined. Certainly, one of these is of capitalism as a leviathan not only making its way in the world largely unimpeded, but using all manner of consumers' own passions to stoke the engines a bit more. In other words, what we have here is simply a further depressing episode in what Sheldon Wolin (2000: 20) has called 'inverted totalitarianism', in which economic rather than political power is dominant, in which change and movement has been appropriated for the care and feeding of the brainy classes, and in which what was the political has become pure tactics: 'democracy is embalmed in public rhetoric precisely to memorialize its loss of substance' (Wolin 2000: 20). This case seems to me to be unarguable.

But I have also stressed another side to these developments. In order to generate more invention and innovation, situations have to be designed that are more open-ended and less predictable. For example, to engage more fully with consumers in the ways outlined above requires an acceptance that they will not always do what the producer wants. Since they are often engaged in activities that are their own fulfilment, they may import all manner of other factors, they make unexpected judgements, they may decide that they are in charge, they may even turn on the producer.[32] Consumer passions do not just run to fan websites. They also run to ethical consumption (Barnett *et al.* 2004), to websites and blogs that can be openly and even savagely critical of their object, and to all manner of other fractious communities that want to object to particular commodity associations – or even to the commodity system itself. For example, they may point to the profligate and almost certainly unsustainable expenditures of energy that have arisen with the turn to information and communications technology, and suggest design alternatives (Thackara 2005). There is, in other words, an uncomfortable status quo in a world in which, if 'marketers only real choice is to become more dependent on emotional ties or face ever-dwindling profits' (Atkin 2004: 199), there is a real danger that emotions do not just buttress a brand but overwhelm it, and that co-operation between consumers means working on new forms of co-operation that use commodities in ways that avoid the profit nexus. This explains much of the concern recently with building brand relationships which, in part at least, is defensive, a desperate attempt to build long-term associations by means of symbolic integration and experiential nexus.

Similarly, 'open innovation' cannot only be seen as one of the next big management fads but also as a means of challenging current property regimes by building new kinds of creative commons through a wider culture of knowledge. In other words, some commentators argue that a democratization of innovation is occurring which enhances overall and not just corporate welfare (von Hippel 2005; Lessig 2005). I suspect that, overall, the amount of ambiguity and unexpectedness in the system will increase, and make the system appear to both producers and consumers as more 'alive' than ever before.

The theoretical point follows on. It is interesting to consider the main currents of thought that are currently prevalent in social theory, and appropriate to register a certain amount of discomfort. One current consists of a reconsideration and reworking of vitalism. Another is a growing interest in the intermingling of human and material and most especially the increasing power of the scaffolding provided by a legion of objects. Still another is a revival of systems thinking but flattened and made communicative. I do not believe that this emphasis on onflow (Pred 2005) is a coincidence.

While it would be going too far to say that social theory simply runs in lockstep with what is happening in the world, neither, by definition, can it just ignore it. I would claim that much of modern social theory is, in fact, a meditation on the kind of world – and the increasingly problematic nature of human experience (in the sense of both 'human' and 'experience') of that world – that I have sketched out in this chapter.

Increasingly, that world is being constructed by business, and furthermore by a business that uses theory as an instrumental *method*, as a source of *expertise* and as an *affective register* to inform an everyday life that is increasingly built from that theory.[33] Yet, still, too few social theorists seem willing to recognize that fact or to consider what it might mean for the practice of social theory. They prefer bracketing off business as an other which is to be deplored and then largely ignored. This must surely be dangerous when it can be argued that theory, in its attempt to be fast-moving and productive, is increasingly trying to mimic the very forces that may endanger it.

This chapter argues, in contrast, that what is now going on in business is intended to populate nearly every event with content that has some commercial resonance and, understood in a broad sense, gain through a general redefinition of what counts as value. Capitalism is carpeting expectation and capturing potential. Simple condemnation of this tendency, as if from some putative outside, or, alternatively, embracing it as a part of some continuously fluid overarching vitalist order, will not do. Rather, it seems to me to call for radically new imaginings of exactly how things are, but under a new aspect that we can currently only glimpse; 'a tune beyond us, yet ourselves', as Wallace Stevens (1960: 133) put it.

3 Still life in nearly present time

The object of nature

If winds, currents, glaciers, volcanoes, etc., carry subtle messages that are so difficult to read that it takes us absolutely ages trying to decipher them, wouldn't it be appropriate to call them intelligent? How would it be if it turned out that we were only the slowest and least intelligent beings in the world?

(Serres 1995: 30)

It is not enough to say the subject is constituted in a symbolic system. . . . It is [also] constructed in real practices.

(Foucault 1984: 369)

What happens if the half-second delay is set, not in a super-sensible domain, but in the corporealisation of culture and the culturalisation of corporeality?

(Connolly 1999: 20)

Introduction: towards a genealogy of background

In this chapter, I want to make an argument concerning the importance of nature, the body and time in Western societies. It is not, I think, the usual kind of argument, based upon genealogical accounts of the rise and fall of discourses like romanticism or modernism (which is not to say that elements of these accounts do not adhere). Rather, it is an attempt to strike out towards a new understanding of how nature is apprehended, based upon giving much greater credence to that small but vitally significant period of time in which the body makes the world intelligible by setting up a background of expectation which, I will go on to argue, is much of what we feel as 'nature'.

In a sense, what I want to do is to restate some of the current concerns of the turn to a vitalist conception of the world. But I want to do so in a way which goes beyond the general and sometimes rather portentous philosophical statements about time, the body and becoming, which have now become so familiar (e.g. Grosz 1999), by connecting up with understandings of body practices from the social sciences – and capitalist business.

Using these resources, I want to argue that nature has become a, and perhaps even the, key site of contemplation and mysticism in the modern world as a result of the evolution of a set of body practices which, as they have taken hold, have produced an expanded awareness of present time. My problem in making such an argument is that contemplation and mysticism are not practices much associated with an enhanced grasp of the modern world; they are more usually associated with figures from times of yore like hermits and monks. How can such practices of slowness make sense to an increasingly frantic capitalist world, a ferocious jumble of signals, journeys and screens which has squeezed out or is likely to squeeze out such sedate activity once and for all (see just most recently, Bertman 1998; Brand 1999; Flaherty 1998; Kovach and Rosenstiel 1999; Speak 1999)? Surely it is all quick, quick and no slow.

In order to refute such easy characterization, I will therefore make an argument in six stages, each of which corresponds to a particular part of the article. The first part of the article therefore begins by setting out some theoretical aspirations, aspirations which all attempt to escape the traps of representational thinking of the kind that wants, for example, to understand nature as simply a project of cultural inscription (as in many writings on 'landscape') in favour of the kind of thinking that understands nature as a complex virtuality (Cache 1995; Rajchman 1998). With an account distilled from these thoughts, in the second part of the article I will argue that a go-faster world, in which time takes on an increasingly frenetic future-oriented quality, has been balanced by a series of contemplative practices – many of them to do with a heightened awareness of movement – which have, in fact, produced an expansion of awareness of the present. The third part of the article follows on. It concerns the classical idea that the world has been disenchanted. My argument here is to the contrary. In fact, the mystical qualities of the world remain in place. Assured by a whole series of body practices, some old and some new, these practices have produced an expansion of awareness of present time. The fourth part of the article then argues that the experience of these two sets of immersive body practices accounts for a large part of what we attend to as 'nature'; they define much of what we cleave to as a 'natural' experience by setting up a background of expectation. The fifth part of the article suggests that these body practices can be seen as part of a larger biopolitical project which is an attempt to renovate and value 'bare life'. But 'bare life' is not bare. It is most of what there is. Then, the sixth part of the article offers some words of warning. Another such project of renovation of bare life is already in motion, but it is being undertaken by business and its goal is a narrow one. The article concludes with some further clarifications.

Becoming there

My thinking on nature, the body and time in this article is based upon four different but quite clearly associated sources of inspiration which, when taken together, make it possible to construct an emergent account of emergent body practice which is the base of the rest of the article. The first of these is the work of biological philosophers and philosophical biologists like A. Clark (1997), Deleuze (1988), Margulis (1998), Margulis *et al.* (1999) and Ansell Pearson (1997, 1999) who want to argue for a reconfigured ethology in which bodies become means of transporting 'instincts'[1] which are best thought of as particular territories of becoming, maps mapping out 'populations' of identities and forces, zones and gradients, through differentiation, divergence and creation.

> Behaviour can no longer be localized in individuals conceived as preformed homunculi; but has to be treated epigenetically as a function of complex material systems which cut across individuals (assemblages) and which transverse phyletic lineages and organismic boundaries (rhizomes). This requires the articulation of a distributed conception of agency. The challenge is to show that nature consists of a field of multiplicities, assemblages of heterogeneous components (human, animal, viral, molecular, etc.) in which 'creative evolution' can be shown to involve blocks of becoming.
>
> (Ansell Pearson 1999: 171)

Maps are their own practitioners, in other words

The second source of inspiration is the revival of interest in the non-cognitive dimensions of embodiment. Probably 95 per cent of embodied thought is non-cognitive, yet probably 95 per cent of academic thought has concentrated on the cognitive dimension of the conscious 'I'. Without in any way diminishing the importance of cognitive thought (though certainly questioning its exact nature), we can conceive of non-cognitive thought as a set of embodied dispositions ('instincts' if you like) which have been biologically wired in or culturally sedimented (the exact difference between the two being a fascinating question in itself), action-oriented 'representations' which simultaneously describe aspects of the world and prescribe possible actions. There has, of course, been a considerable amount of work on body practices stemming from the work of authors as different as Mauss, Benjamin, Wittgenstein, Merleau-Ponty and Bourdieu (e.g. Taussig 1994), which recognizes that much of human life is lived in a non-cognitive world. But I think it is fair to say that its implications are only now being worked through, most especially in areas like performance studies, feminist theory and non-representational geographies. In particular, when we say that human beings act to think or that they learn by doing, we need to refigure what we count as thought and knowledge. In particular, much cognitive thought and knowledge may, indeed, be only a kind of post-hoc rumination; 'to be aware of an experience means that it has passed' (Norretranders 1998: 128). For example, most of the time, an action is in motion before we decide to perform it; our average 'readiness potential' is about 0.8 seconds, although cases of up to 1.5 seconds have been recorded.[2]

As McCrone (1999: 135) makes clear, none of this means that conscious awareness is just along for the ride. Rather, we can say that the non-conscious comes to be more highly valued – the 'not properly conscious impulses, inklings, automatisms and reflexive action' can no longer be regarded as trivial. And, at the same time, conscious awareness is repositioned as a means of scrutinizing and focusing these actions. To put it another way, what has been found is that the body has a number of ways of conjuring with time that work through structures of anticipation, the something to be known which is very often the result of the body's own movements, which leave 'some aspect of the movement standing proud' (McCrone 1999: 158). Why? Because:

> the brain was never really designed for contemplating images. Our ability to imagine and fantasize is something that has to piggyback on a processing hierarchy designed first and foremost for the business of perception. And to do perception well, the brain needs a machinery that comes up with a fresh wave of prediction at least a couple of times a second, or about as fast as we can make a substantial shift in our conscious point of view . . . it would be unnatural for the brain to linger and not move on.
>
> (McCrone 1999: 158)

In turn, such work points to the pivotal importance of emotions as the key means the body has of sorting the non-cognitive realm through a range of different sensory registers, including the interoceptive (including not only the viscera but also the skin), the proprioceptive (based on musculo-skeletal investments) and fine touch which involves the conduct of the whole body and not just the brain.

> Note that, depending on the object, there may be different proportions of musculoskeletal and emotional accompaniment, but both are always present. The presence of all these signals describes both the object as it looms towards the organism and part of the reaction of the organism towards the object.
>
> (Damasio 1999: 147)

Which brings us to the third source of inspiration – the much greater emphasis that is being placed on the object. To begin with, the body is objectified as a composite of biological – cultural 'instincts' which enable and in many ways constitute thought as a result of the development of particular organs. For example, the development of the hand, with all the possibilities it presents, was an impetus to the redesign, or re-allocation of the brain's circuitry so that the hand speaks to the brain just as much as the brain speaks to the hand (E.R. Wilson 1998).

Then, these organs are closely linked with particular objects (Sudnow 1993). Organs like the hand become as one with tools they relate to,

> The idea of 'becoming one' with a [mechanical] back hoe is no more exotic than the idea of a rider becoming one with a horse or a carpenter becoming one with a hammer and this phenomenon may itself take its origin from count-less monkeys who spent countless eons becoming one with tree branches. The mystical feel comes from the combination of a good mechanical marriage and something in the nervous system that can make an object external to the body feel as if it had sprouted from the hand, foot, or (rarely) some other place on the body where your skin makes contact with it.
>
> (E.R. Wilson 1998: 63)

Then again, objects do not just constitute an extension of bodily capacities; they themselves are a vital element in distributed ecology of thought, so that 'what used to look like internalisation (of thought and subjectivity) now appears as a gradual propagation of organised functional properties across a set of malleable media' (Hutchins 1995: 312); 'the true engine of reason . . . is bounded neither by skin nor skull' (Clark 1997: 69). Thus, as Hayles puts it:

> no longer is human will seen as the source from which emanates the mystery necessary to dominate and control the environment. Rather, the distributed cognition of the emergent human subject correlates with – in Bateson's phase, becomes a metaphor for – the distributed cognitive system as a whole, in which thinking is done by both human and nonhuman actors.
>
> (Hayles 1999: 290)

Not only do objects make thought do-able (e.g. Latour and Hermant 1998) but they also very often make thought possible. In a sense, then, as parts of networks of effectivity, objects think. We might even go still further, by arguing that 'everything that is resounds' (Lingis 1998: 99):

> It is not that things barely show themselves, behind illusory appearances fabricated by our subjectivity; it is that things are exorbitantly exhibitionist. The landscape resounds; facades, caricatures, halos, shadows, dance across it. Under the sunlight extends the pageantry of things. The twilight does not put an end to their histrionics. In the heart of the night the pulse of the night summons still their ghosts.
>
> (Lingis 1998: 100)

The fourth source of inspiration is the genealogy of the body practices which must be a large part of an ethology of 'instincts' – these are now, finally, coming under intense scrutiny. Grouped around terms like 'performance', and around theorists like Bourdieu and Foucault, researchers in the social sciences and humanities have, over the last 20 years, begun to produce a history of particular organs (e.g. Hillman and Massio 1997; Jordanova 1994) and particular body practices – from drill to dance. But it is true to say that we still understand very little of how the body practices that comprise 'us' have come down to and inhabit us, passing into our being, passing our being back and forth between bodies and passing our being on (Hayles 1999).[3]

These four sources of inspiration allow us to begin to sense, through this combination of work in areas as diverse as biology, philosophy and performance studies, what an understanding of that little space of time that is much of what we are, a space not so much at the edge of action as lighting the world. I will call this domain 'bare life' after Aristotle's notion of *Zoé*, a 'simple natural sweetness' (Agamben 1998). Of course, it is not really bare; bare life pulses with action. And it is not simple. And it is not preternatural. But what such a notion allows us to do is to point beyond the grand notions of bodily hexis like habitus towards something more specific and more open to description. And it does two more things. One is to begin to understand qualities like anticipation and intuition as not just spirits but material orientations. And the other is to understand that this little space of time is a vast biopolitical domain, that blink between action and performance in which the world is pre-set by biological and cultural instincts which bear both extraordinary genealogical freight – and a potential for potentiality.

How might we begin to understand the structure of this domain of flourishing? One manageable and useable account has been offered by Gil (1998). Gil argues, as I would (see Thrift 1996, 1997, 1998, 2000a), that we need to escape the constructionist notion of the body as simply an inscribed surface, in which the body is reduced to what Gil (1998) calls a 'body image', an individual unitary, organismic body which can act as a surface upon which society can construct itself. This interpretation is mistaken in at least three ways. First, the body becomes a static signified to be filled with signs of society. Second, the body is divorced from other things, from the object world. Third, the body is located in space, it does not produce space. But, there is another, non-representational view (Thrift 1997, 2000a). In this view, the body is 'not about signs and meanings but about a mechanics of space' (Gil 1998: 126) brought about by the relation between bodies and things. Thus:

> the space of the body has limits that are not those of the body image, if we understand by that the limits of the body lived in a unitary fashion. The limits of the space of the body are in things. In movement, for example, the body places changing limits on these things. To the extent that they are 'subjective', these limits constitute the end result of the integration into the body of the relations (of distance, form, and so on) that it holds with things in objective space. To the extent that they can be pinned down topologically, these limits are no longer 'lived' but are properties of space itself.
>
> (Gil 1998: 125)

In turn, and following a Deleuzian interpretation:

> the body 'lives' in space, but not like a sphere with a closed continuous surface. On the contrary, its movements, limbs and organs determine that it has regular relations with things in space, relations that are individually integrated for the decoder. These relations imply exfoliations of the space of the body that can be treated separately. Relations to a tree, a prey, a star, an enemy, a loved object or desired nourishment set into motion certain privileged organs including precise spaces of the body. Exfoliation is the essential way the body 'turns on to' things, onto objective space, onto living things. Here there is a type of communication that is always present, but only makes itself really visible in pathological or marginal experiences. Nevertheless the ordinary experience of relations to things also implies this mode of communication. Being in space means to establish diverse relationships with the things that surround our bodies. Each set of relations is determined by the action of the body that accompanies an investment of desire in a particular being or particular object. Between the body (and the organs in use) and the things is

established a connection that immediately affects the form and space of the body; between the one and the other a privileged spatial relation emerges that defines the space uniting them as 'near' or 'far', resistant, thick, wavy, vertiginous, smooth, prickly.

(Gil 1998: 127)[4]

In other words, the space of the body consists of a series of 'leaves', each of which 'contains' the relations of the body to things and each of which is more or less related to other spaces. Correspondences are not, at least initially, conceptual but result 'from the work done by the body spatialising space' (Gil 1998: 130). Thus:

Analogy, similitude, opposition, and dissimilitude are given in the forms of the space of the body before being thought of as concepts. In the same ways as the 'concrete science' which establishes classification on the basis of sensorial differences found in 'primitive thought', the recording-body gathers up, brings together, unites, dislocates, spreads, and separates things to the spatial forms that contain in themselves (because they bring them about) the properties of unification and division.

(Gil 1998: 130)

It follows that in what follows body practices are not to be thought of, at least in the first instance, as cognitive. This would be a first-order mistake. For, to reiterate, we know that 'consciousness is a measure of but a very small part of what our senses perceive' (Norretranders 1998: 127).

Conscious thought is the tip of an enormous iceberg. It is the rule of thumb among cognitive scientists that unconscious thought is 95 per cent of all thought – and that may be a serious underestimate. Moreover the 95 per cent below the surface of conscious awareness shapes and structures all conscious thought. If the cognitive unconscious were not doing this shaping, there could be no conscious thought.

The cognitive unconscious is vast and intricately structured. It includes not only all our automatic cognitive operations, but also all our implicit knowledge. All of our knowledge and beliefs are formed in terms of a conceptual system that resides mostly in the cognitive unconscious.

Our unconscious cognitive system functions like 'a hidden hand' that shapes how we conceptualize all aspects of our experience. This hidden hand gives form to the metamorphosis that is built into our ordinary conceptual system. It creates the entities that inhabit the cognitive unconscious – abstract entities like friendships, bargains, failures and lies – that we use in ordinary unconscious reasoning. It thus shapes how we automatically and unconsciously comprehend what we experience. It constitutes our unreflective common sense.

(Lakoff and Johnson 1998: 13)

And this cognitive unconscious rises out of the layerings and interleavings of body practices and things which we might frame as 'instincts' or, more accurately, ride on the back of the cognitive unconscious. Rather, every moment is processed as a prior intent, style or tone which arises from perception-in-movement, every moment is the fleeting edge of a sensory forecast (McCrone 1999), quite literally a stance to the world.

With these 'thoughts in mind' (how easily we use these questionable phrases), we can now move to a consideration of how body practices show up in the modern world and how the modern world shows up in them. To do this, we first need to clear away some tired old pictures of the world.

The go-faster world

Elsewhere (Thrift 1995, 1996, 1997), I have criticized the notion that we live in a speeded-up world in which friction has been lost and everyday life skids along on the plane of velocity. Much of the literature which enforces this notion is based upon a simple technological determinism which unproblematically maps the apparent powers of things on to subjects. While it is undeniable that people and messages now move faster than they did, old practices have been adjusted, and new practices have been invented, which make it impossible to simply read off this physical fact on to culture. Further, it is possible to argue that speed is itself in part a cultural creation, a classical modernist trope now in general cultural circulation (see Kern 1983) as a series of metaphors and analogies and as a rhetoric of 'speedy' things.[5] This cultural creation of speed itself depends upon the depiction of certain places, things and people as slow-moving, most particularly those places, things and people connected with nature, the countryside and so on.

This is, of course, a very strange opposition since one might just as well argue – precisely through the instruments which have become available to measure speed – that nature is actually very fast. The speed of light is, well, the speed of light. Chemical reactions can work at astounding speeds. Even that slow old thing, the human body, works reasonably fast. Though in our brains, nerve impulses only tend to crawl along – at between 2 and 20 miles per hour – along the heavily myelinated nerves (such as muscle and the sensory nerves) nerve impulses travel at up to 240 miles per hour (McCrone 1999; Norretranders 1998).

But, more than this, the opposition ignores a general reconstruction of time which has taken place (quite literally) over the last 150 years, a sense of body practices which constitute and value the present moment, rather than spearing into the future. Ironically, these body practices have all taken shape around the increasing awareness of kinaesthesia, a sixth sense based on the interactive movement and subsequent awareness of body parts:

> we obtain a sense of our own movement not only from specialised receptors in the inner ear, joints, tendons and muscles but also from what we can see hear and feel . . . vision, 'for instance', is kinaesthetic in that it registers

movements of the body, just as much as do the vestibular receptors and those in the muscles, joints and skin.

(Reason 1982: 233)

Contrary to Sherrington's direct correlation of sensory experience with the activation of specific receptors and their nerves of different cellular levels, the kinaesthetic sense is a gestalt emerging from the interaction of all the other senses. After Gibson we can speak of kinaesthesia in terms of its muscular, articular, vestibular, cutaneous, auditory and visual modalities (J.T.Gibson 1966: 36–38). In this view kinaesthesia is the ground to our consciousness (Stewart 1998: 44).

I think it can be argued that greater awareness of movement has in turn produced a set of resources that enable us to separate out and value a present-orientated stillness, thus promoting a 'politics' based in intensified attention to the present and unqualified affectivity. Where might this present-orientation have come from? I would argue that its history is born out of a number of developments which, taken together, constitute a genealogy of the present.

The first of these developments is practices of contemplation. Foucault and others have highlighted the significance of confession as a model for recent practices of the technology of the self. I think an argument can be made for a similar kind of history based in practices of contemplation understood as 'aptitudes of performance' (Asad 1993), rather than explicit belief. This history might touch upon certain forms of prayer, the practices of some rituals and other religious technologies which concentrate time.

Whatever the case, there seems no doubt that extant practices of contemplation were gradually transmuted by a whole series of developments in the nineteenth century and thereafter (Segel 1998). The first of these was the development of a series of body practices which stressed sensory appreciation through a more complete control of the body in order to provide more harmonious relations with the environment. A good example of these developments is the rise of various body techniques like the Alexander Technique, the Feldenkrais technique, Bioenergetics and Body–Mind Centring, which teach movement awareness and the reorganization of movement sensation (Feldenkrais 1972; Hartley 1995; Lowen 1975; MacDonald 1998; McGowan 1997a, 1997b). Feldenkrais (1972), for example, argued that cultivation of certain bodily practices could enhance our ability to 'know' the world through systematic correction of what he called the 'body image'.

The second development is the rise of systematic knowledge of body measurement, based on increasing the efficiency of the body. From Marey's and Muybridge's study of the physiology of movement through to Gilbreth and Taylor's time-and-motion studies and modern ergonomics and sports science, the study and articulation of minute human movement have become a key to producing human comportment (Dagognet 1992; Mattelart 1996). In turn, it can be argued that the increasingly fine grain of the many bodily movements built out of this study has made its mark on how time is constructed by the body.[6]

The third development is the fixing of a still, contemplative gaze, which is able to capture transience. Such a gaze is found in art from the eighteenth century on but reaches a kind of technological fulfilment in the photograph, especially with the growth of popular photography from the end of the nineteenth century onwards. Crawshaw and Urry (1997) argue that popular photography consists of a set of socially organized rituals which fix a place, a 'language' of material objects through which we understand and appreciate the environment (and the material objects themselves) and a means of organizing time itself. In each case, what are being described are a set of practices which momentarily fix the body and other things in spaces and times by producing spaces and times in which they can be fixed.[7]

The fourth development is the forging of a body of knowledge about social interaction as the distillation of detailed body practices. Such knowledge can already be found in the nineteenth century and early twentieth century (for example, in the development of various movement notations) but it reaches a peak in the twentieth century with the rise of various knowledge of body practice from work on the psychology of body language and gesture, though work on bodily intonations of space, as in Hall's 'proxemics' (Hall 1990), through to the detailed conversational analysis of symbolic interactionism, ethno-methodology and the like to be found in the work of Goffman, Garfinkel, Sacks and so on (e.g. Burns 1992). In turn, this knowledge, much of which was developed in academia and other relatively formal arenas, has gradually seeped out into everyday life as a whole new corporeal curriculum of expressive competence, for example through courses on body language (now being given, for example, to checkout operators in some supermarket chains), cultural awareness training and all manner of training in self-presentation (cf. Giddens 1991; Thrift 1997). Thus, what was quite specific knowledge has become general and routine.

Each and every one of these four developments of body practice stretches out the moment, most especially by paying detailed attention to it. They expand, if you like, the 'size' of consciousness, allowing each moment to be more carefully attended to and invested with more of its context. Taken together, they may be seen as constructing a slow-down of perception, as much as a speed-up.

Re-enchantment

These developments have to be taken in concert with others to complete my argument. One of the most damaging ideas that has swept the social sciences and humanities has been the idea of a disenchanting modernity (Thrift 1996). This act of purification has radically depopulated thinking about Western societies as whole sets of delegates and intermediaries have been consigned to oblivion as extinct impulses, those delegates and intermediaries which might appear to be associated with forces of magic, the sacred, ritual, affect, trance and so on. Now, however, the contemporary turn towards vitalist ways of thinking (cf. Watson 1998b) has made it much easier to see that the magic has not gone away. Western societies, like all others, are full of these forces (Dening 1996; Muecke 1999).

They can be seen as concentrating, in particular, in a set of practices which can be described as 'mystical'. Like practices of contemplation, with which they are intimately linked, they can be seen as the result of a number of overlapping processes of animation and play which allow forces and intensities to be focused and channelled: it is stimulation that produces tranquility and it is stimulation that produces trance.

First, then, there is the importance of various forms of mystical communication, mental and physical techniques that 'fix the conditions of possibility of an encounter or dialogue with the other (method of prayer, meditation, concentration)' (de Certeau 1992: 5). Current forms of practice have a long genealogy in Western cultures and stem from traditions as different as the Christian (both Anglican and Catholic), the nature mysticisms of Romanticism as found in various forms of the sublime, the numerous forms of Eastern thinking which have been imported into the West, especially in the nineteenth century, and the cathartic elements of many types of performance. More recently, there has been the growth of New Age religions, nearly all of which contain an explicitly mystical component (for example, following on from sources as diverse as the writings of Gurdjieff or Hopi Indian practices). Not least, in all these traditions can be found, to a greater or lesser degree, an approach to nature as both the focus and the object of mystical energies. For example, New Age thinking often stresses grids of power like ley lines, nature goddesses and the like, as well as the importance of particular sites as magical territories able to conjure up communication with the other.

This brings us to the second process, the importance of ritual, understood as practices which offer a heightened sense of involvement in our involvements through various performative technologies (Hughes-Freeland 1998; Schechner 1993). There may actually have been a multiplication of these performative spaces of affirmation, in which mystical experiences can be brought forth and animated through the power of body postures, repetitive movements, schedules of recall and spatial juxtapositions. Western societies have evolved more and more bodily practices which are a means of amplifying passions and producing 'oceanic' experiences: music, dance, theatre, mime, art and so on, which very large numbers of the population participate in; rather more than is often thought (see, for example, Finnegan 1989). These practices have at least the potential to provide mystical experiences[8] – the trance state of some kinds of dance (Malbon 1999), the 'high' of listening to a piece of music, and so on.[9]

Last, but not least, there has been the rise of varying forms of body therapy, which, though they often rest on various psychological and psychiatric principles, have quite clear links not only to contemplative but to mystical body practice. These are the various forms of dance therapy (e.g. Roth 1998), music therapy, massage therapy, variants of bioenergetics (e.g. Lowen 1975), autogenic therapy, body–mind centring, and so on, which try to harness and work with emotional energy on the grounds that movement causes emotion, rather than vice versa.

These body practices again allow the present to be intensified since they produce both an intensified sense of body movement and, at the same time, focus and enhance that movement. They are tempos of involvement without any necessary intention or initiative. They 'flow' time through the minute particulars of body movements that both have effects and yield experiences. They are 'performed dreams' (Schechner 1993), 'virtual actualizations' of time which allow consciousness to become acute without necessarily being directed by drawing on the non-cognitive.

Nature as background

What I want to argue next is that these contemplative and mystical developments which, taken as a whole, are widespread in modern Western societies, constitute a background within which nature is apprehended and which provides quite particular experiences of what nature is. They form, if you like, an 'embodied unconscious', a set of basic exfoliations of the body through which nature is constructed, planes of affect attuned to particular body parts (and senses) and corresponding elements of nature (from trees and grass, to river and sky) (Massumi 1997b), 'the sense and recognisability of things . . . do not lie in conceptual categories in which we mentally place them but in their positions and orientations which our postures address' (Lingis 1998: 59).

Following on from this point, I want to argue, very tentatively, that these immersive practices are producing a new form of vitalism (Watson 1998a, 1998b), a stance to *feeling* life (in the doubled sense of both a grasp of life, and emotional attunement to it) which explain many of the strong, sometimes even fanatical, investments that are placed on the 'natural'. The very ways in which, through these practices of contemplation and mysticism, embodiment is reproduced in the West, have produced an increasing bias towards framing life as a moving force, as push. In other words, the forms of embodiment I have set out in this article constitute a biopolitical domain arising out of a heightened awareness of particular forms of embodiment which, in turn, allow certain forms of signification to be grasped 'instinctively'.

This biopolitical domain has been strengthened by three developments. The first of these is the turning of certain body practices into privileged kinaesthetic spaces, and the privileged kinaesthetic spaces into body practices. I am thinking here especially of walking, which since the nineteenth century, precisely in association with greater mobility (Wallace 1993), has produced a new experience of nature. This is not walking as travel, but walking for itself. As walking becomes a natural practice to be indulged in for its own sake, so, against the background I have outlined, it can become a means to contact the Earth, to be at one with 'nature', even to be deemed therapeutic. It becomes a means of gathering stillness, without having to stay still, a means of contemplation and mystical communion to be found within the body. Lingis captures what I take to be a culturally particular investment particularly well:

> when we go out for a walk, our look is not continually interested, surveying the environment for landmarks and objectives. Even when we are on our way

somewhere, for something, once launched we shift into just enjoying – or ending – the walk or the ride. Our gaze that prises beyond things is not situating on coordinates. It surveys across things, drawn to the distance when it fuses into the tone and mists of space. . . . The perception of things, the apprehension of their content and of their forms, is not an appropriation of them, but an expropriation of our forces into them, and ends in engagement.

(Lingis 1998: 70)

Of course, none of this is to deny the cultural industry that has grown up around the practice of walking – the vast literature of books and guides, the special clothing and so on, all of which enhance or expand the range of affordances that inhere in any setting – but it is to suggest that the power of the meanings circulated by this industry is founded in the intensification of present experience coded in the body practices set out above. The background has allowed this foreground of symbolic delegates to develop.

The second development is, as the example of walking shows, the style of the body's location in space. What has developed has been both overall body stance and the formation of certain sequences of bodily experiences which, in their virtualized nature, produce an expectation, an anticipation, of a 'natural' experience: 'it is the way in which the body sits in space that allows signification to be grasped' (Gil 1998: 109). For example, travel to a 'natural' place sets up the body to fall into a 'natural' stance to the world. There is, if you like, a genetics of movement which the body slips into through constant practice. There are 'dance floors of nature' (Lingis 1998: 87).

The third development is similar but different. The body attends to configurations of objects which are in line with its expectations and which produce particular exfoliations/spaces and times. The body produces spaces and times through the things of nature which, in turn, inhabit the body through that production. Thus, for example, trees do not so much mean nature (Rival 1998) as they are present as evidence of a natural configuration that embodiment itself has produced: our bodies know themselves in such thinking. Thus trees become flesh by being bound up in a practical field. And, in the intensified present time I have described, that presence becomes its own justification. There *is*. Nature, in a sense, becomes more natural.

In turn, of course, nature, understood as body practices like walking, expectations and configurations of objects, pushes back in confirmation. For example, our experience of walking is validated by its effects on the body – from sweat to heart rate to muscles stretching – which are a function of a resistance on certain planes which confirms the existence of other planes. So nature speaks in us as 'an infralanguage' (Gil 1998) of movement which, through the articulations and micro-articulations of the body-in-encounter, fixes 'symbolic' thought as affect, mood, emotions and feelings[10] (thus as self-evidently present and numinous). Nature observes and writes us, bumping intensities into our thought[11] (understood especially as unconscious thought), rather as Deleuze would have it:

[Deleuze's] projection of virtual elements too fast and multiple for conscious inspection or close third-person explanation meshes with his exploration of how differential degrees of intensity in thought moves it in some directions rather than others, open up lines of flight through which new concepts are introduced into being, and render thinking too layered and unpredictable to be captured by a juridical model in the Kantian tradition. He translates the story of juridical recognition in which Kant encloses thought in the last instance into one in which thinking is periodically nudged, frightened or terrorised into action by strange encounters. Recognition is a secondary formation often taken by consciousness in its innocence to be primary or apodictic, but thinking sometimes disturbs or modifies an established pattern of thought.

(Connolly 1999: 24)

'May I not be separated from thee'[12]

In an important book, Giorgio Agamben (1998) manages to conjure up a depiction of 'bare life' (zoé) immured. Through the development of a whole set of governmental templates in a manner familiar to those who read Foucault or study the totalitarian state, bare life has become 'a life that has been deadened and mortified into juridical role' (Agamben 1998: 187), a life 'naturalized' (to use a bitterly ironic term) from birth. Thus:

the Foucauldian thesis will have to be corrected or, at least, completed, in the sense that what characterizes modern politics is not so much the illusion of *zoé* in the polis – which is, in itself, absolutely ancient – not simply the fact that life as such becomes a principal object of the projections and calculations of state power. Instead the decisive fact is that, together with the process by which the exception everywhere becomes the rule, the realm of bare life – which is originally situated at the margins of the political order – gradually begins to coincide with the political realm, and exclusion and inclusion, outside and inside, *bios* and *zoé*, right and fact, enter into a zone of incredible indistinction. At once excluding bare life from and capturing it within the political order, the state of exception actually constituted, in its very separateness, the hidden foundation on which the entire political system rested. When its borders began to be blurred, the bare life that dwelt there frees itself in the city and becomes both subject and object of the political order, the one place for both the organization of state power and emancipation from it. Everything happens as if, along with the disciplinary process by which state power makes man as a living being into its own specific object, another process is set in motion that in large measure corresponds to the birth of modern democracy, in which man as a living being presents himself no longer as an object but as the subject of political power. These processes which in many ways oppose and (at least apparently) bitterly conflict with each other –

nevertheless converge insofar as both concern the bare life of the citizen, the new biopolitical body of humanity.

(Agamben 1998: 8–9)

For Agamben, one of the questions is how to produce a notion of bare life that constitutes a politics but does not weigh it down with state imperatives. But his answer is pessimistic. Such a revitalization of bare life cannot be born.

Bare life remains included in politics in the form of an exception, that is, as something that is included solely through an exclusion. How is it possible to 'politicize' the 'natural sweetness of rot'? And first of all does *zoé* really need to be politicized, or is politics not already contained in zoe as its most priceless centre? The biopolitics of both modern totalitarianism and the society of mass hedonism and consumerism certainly constitute answers to these questions. Nevertheless, until a completely new politics – that is, a politics no longer founded on the exception of bare life – is at hand, every theory and every praxis will remain improvised and immobile and the 'beautiful day' of life will be given citizenship only either through blood and death or in the perfect senselessness to which the society of the spectacle condemns it (Agamben 1998: 8–9).

What Agamben seems to argue for, in part, is a revitalization of the body, in new forms of life: 'we are not only, in Foucault's words, animals whose life as living beings is at issue in their politics, but also – inversely – citizens whose very politics is at issue in their natural body' (Agamben 1998: 188). What this article has argued is that such an emancipatory politics of bare life, founded in practices such as contemplation and mysticism, both already exists – and continues to come into existence which is a 'product of the double investment of the body by space (the information coming from the physical world) and the investment of space by the body (as a certain kind of receiver-encoder of information)' (Gil 1998: 28). This is a politics of enhancement of the anticipation and conduct of certain bodily skills which, at the same time, contains its own premises though the effects of those skills.

This 'politics of the half-second delay' has the potential to expand the bio-political domain, to make it more than just the site of investment by the state or investments by transnational capitalism. It may well explain the deep affective investments that are made by so many in a politics of nature, investments which move far beyond the cognitive and which are often figured as a restitution of all that has been lost. Perhaps, though, as this article has argued, the outcome might be figured more accurately as new appreciations and anticipations of spaces of embodiment, best understood as a form of magic dependent upon new musics of stillness and silence able to be discovered in a world of movement.

But: 'Step inside the great outdoors'[13]

Let's not overdo this. There are powerful contra-forces. For there is another politics of bare life which I have so far only touched on. This is the politics that arises out of the enormous efforts currently being made to foreground the background of bare life – to make it comprehensible and therefore able to be apprehended and so made more of – across a range of different interests and arenas. And of these interests and arenas the most powerful and, in many ways, the most advanced is capitalist business: Agamben's mass consumerism.

Capitalist firms are drawing on the various knowledges of bare life they are producing to produce new products, products which animate – 'turn on' – the body by producing an engaging and compelling ethology of the senses. This is the rise of an 'experience economy' (Pine and Gilmore 1999), a new genre of economic output which can construct experiences in order to produce added value. What have been the chief knowledges of bare life from which this experience economy has grown? There are four. The first has been tourism. Since the 1960s a new kind of tourism has emerged based upon the theming of spaces. Relying on the experience of running museums, heritage centres, theme parks and certain kinds of themed retailing (Gottdiener 1997) it has gradually constructed knowledge of how to produce spaces which can grip the senses. Of late, the kinaesthetic element of tourism has accordingly been amplified. For example, there are all the postcolonial forms of adventure set out by Guttman: houseboating, portaging, mountain-biking, cattle-driving, bob-sledding, tall-ship sailing, tornado-chasing, canyon orienteering, wagon training, seal viewing, iceberg tracking, racing car driving, hot-air ballooning, rock climbing, spelunking, white water rafting, canoeing, heli-hiking, hut-to-hut hiking, whale kissing, llama trekking, barn-storming, land yachting, historic battle re-enactments, iceboating, polar bearing and dog-sledding. The second knowledge, one clearly linked to the former, is sport and exercise. Sport and exercise have become key elements in modern experience economies, through their ability to influence bodily comportment (including specialized precision knowledges) through the specialized spaces that are constructed to serve them, and through the connections to the mass media (Abercrombie and Longhurst 1998).

A third knowledge has been of performance. Since the 1960s again, knowledge of performance – which is, after all, extensive – has moved out from the stage to fill all manner of venues – from corporate presentations to the street. Buoyed up by mass media which have, in all probability, made the population at large more performative (Abercrombie and Longhurst 1998), the art of performance has become a general art which concentrates especially on the conduct of the now and which can be appropriated. The fourth knowledge has been from education. Pedagogy has become a more and more active affair. Bolstered by findings from fields like cognition and consciousness, learning is now universally practised as active, even sensuous.

Capitalist firms have taken these knowledges and produced a series of purchases on the world. The first of these has been advertising. Advertising companies have become alive to an approach that takes in all the senses. Companies like the London advertising agency St Lukes have led the way towards advertising which is meant to tug at bare life by emphasizing kinaesthetic qualities. Another purchase is through sensorializing goods – producing goods that will richly engage the senses.

Doing so requires awareness of which senses most affect customers, focuses on those senses and the sensations they experience, and the corporate redesign of the good to make it more appealing. Automakers, for example, now spend millions of dollars on every model to make sure that car doors sound just so when they close. Publishers greatly enhance the covers and interiors of books, and magazines with a number of tactile innovations (embossed lettering. scratching, bumpy or ultrasmooth surfaces) and sight sensations (translucent covers, funky fonts, clear photographs, three-dimensional graphics). Even presentation markers aren't just coloured anymore; Sanford scents them as well (liquorice for black, cherry for red, etc.).

(Pine and Gilmore 1999: 18)

Even quite simple goods are being designed that can feed back to the senses. For example, 'radar' baseballs make it possible to know how fast a ball was thrown, and generate social interaction since the catcher has to relay the speed back to the thrower.

The third purchase is the growth of packaged experiences which rely on theming contexts, so as to produce enhanced sensory experiences. This packaging can range all the way from the increasing outsourcing of children's parties from the home to companies, to the most elaborate virtual environments, which are virtually self-contained ethologies.

Companies that want to stage compelling capacities should . . . determine the theme of the experience as well as the impressions that will convey the theme to guests. Many times, experienced stagers develop a list of impressions they wish guests to store away and then think creatively about different themes and storylines that will bring the impressions together in the cohesive narrative. Then they winnow the impressions down to a manageable number – only and exactly those which truly devote the chosen theme. Next they focus on the animate and inanimate cues that could connote each impression, following the simple guidelines of accentuating the positive and eliminating the negative. They then must meticulously map out the effect each cue will have on the five senses – sight, sound, taste and smell – taking care not to overwhelm guests with too much sensory input. Finally; they add memorabilia to the total mix, extending the experience in the customers' mind over time. Of course, embracing these principles remains, for now, an art form. But those companies which figure out how to design experiences that are compelling, engaging, memorable – and rich – will be the ones leading the way into the emerging Experience Economy.

(Pine and Gilmore 1999: 61)

The fourth purchase is on objects that will produce kinaesthetic experiences, on the grounds that these experiences are usually the most compelling and the most memorable. What is fascinating is the speed with which this kinaesthetic purchase on the world is now expanding its grip, as knowledge of movement becomes engineered in institutions as different as film animation and special effects houses, virtual reality games, exponents of light shows, producers of extreme sports, and those who construct theme park rides. Increasingly, in particular, this knowledge is projected through objects which are based on maximizing movement experiences through the application of particular sequences of movement which engage the visceral sense as well as the proprioceptive and fine touch, rather like hieroglyphs of the kind found in dance and other performing arts (Thrift 2000a). For example, roller coasters are now often described in specifically choreographic terms.

> Then a final purchase is, as already prefaced, memorabilia. Memorabilia both encapsulate and string out experiences. Most experience businesses mix memorabilia into what they offer. Memorabilia are becoming more sophisticated as objects can increasingly be customized. For example, guests' credit card signatures can be digitized and transferred to objects like clothing, sports equipment and photographs, often next to the signatures of appropriate celebrities. And, increasingly, memorabilia are being played for affective capacity. For example:
>
> Hillenbrand Industries of Butestaffe, Indiana, developed a new memorabilia capacity for the funeral industry. The concept emerged from the practice in many funeral homes of producing memory books for display at viewing and memorial services. Hillenbrand sought to bring greater efficiencies to the process but also to preserve the kind of one-of-a-kind collages families now put together to commemorate the lives of lost loved ones. Hillenbrand does this by developing a proprietary system to digitize, merge and print mass customized collages to both paper and video output media.
>
> But these life space collages serve merely as a prop for the experience Hillenbrand really offers, A self-guided kit that walks a family, group of friends or co-workers through a series of steps to create their own memories. 'What we sell', says Gary Bonnie, who handled the initiative, 'is the life scaping experience of gathering with others, rummaging through old photographs and other mementos, and recalling fond memories. The collage gift happens to be the outcome; the value is experienced in going through the process we've helped script.' Accordingly, Hillenbrand charges for the kit experience, whether or not people actually buy the collage.
>
> (Pine and Gilmore 1999: 58)

So, what we see is bare life laid bare and anatomized, and put together again as saleable, immersive experiences. Through history, of course, landscapes have been constructed and experiences have been put up for sale but I think the new developments which, by engaging all the senses, produce new realms of experience to exchange should give us pause. It may be that 'the history of economic progress consists of charging a fee for what once was free' (Pine and Gilmore 1999: 67). Alternatively, this maxim can be seen as simply another rationalization of the neoliberal order, one which entails a significant broadening and deepening of economic relations through much more sophisticated means of interpellation.[14]

In particular, of course, it involves a stance to nature, one which by re-embodying natural ethologies, using the examples gleaned from museums, theatre and theme parks, sets aside the immersive practices of contemplation and mysticism based on make-believe for immersion of a different kind based on make-us-believe (Walton 1990). This is play without play, if you like[15] – play without the kind of anticipations that make live – that can produce an enhanced nature.

> In 1996 Ogden [Corporation] committed $100 million to create eight attractions called the American Wilderness Experience. There it immerses guests in nature scenes that feature the live animals, foliage, scents, and climates indigenous to various locales. The company's first American Wilderness Experience opened in late 1997 in the Ontario Mills Mall in San Bernadine, California. The company charges an admission fee of $9.95 for adults to take in live 'biomes' depicting various aspects of California's natural environment: Redwoods, sierras, deserts, coasts and valleys. These exhibits are inhabited by 160 wild animals, across 60 distinct species, including snakes, bobcats, scorpions, jelly fish and porcupines. Guests begin their journey with a motion-based attraction, called the Wild Ride Theater, that lets them experience the world through the eyes of various animals – moving like a mountain lion, buzzing like a bee – and then tour live animal exhibits and enjoy nature discussions with costumed Wilderness rangers. Of course, once guests pay to participate in the American Wilderness Experience, Ogden also makes money on the food service at its Wilderness Grill and the memorabilia at its Nature Untamed retail store.
>
> (Pine and Gilmore 1999: 23–24)

Conclusion

The stakes are high. Should we move towards a capitalist super-nature, tuning our bodies to an economy of naturalized experiences, or to something more modest, more fluid and less market-driven? Unlike Agamben, I think there is hope, precisely born out of the heightened participations in bare life, shown up by movement, that I have tried to show up in this article. To begin with, there are the myriad activities which exist at the edge of the economic system which travel all the way from those who are simply looking for simple forms of exercise to those who are trying to sense something different. Then, there is the realm of the performance studies and arts, which, since at least the 1960s, have, through techniques as different as dance and performance art, been attempting to stimulate new corporeal sensibilities (e.g. Jones and Stephenson 1999). And, last, there is the more general move towards a philosophy which can incorporate the body and so think thought differently (Shusterman 1999).

Taken together, these alternative forms of biopolitics continue to allow a different time to inhabit the moment and even to flourish. Though they may be a small thing, they are not insignificant: sometimes a little can be a lot.

4   *Driving* in the city

Introduction

Perhaps the most famous and most reproduced piece of writing from Michel de Certeau's many works – anthologized or extracted almost to distraction – is the seventh chapter from *The Practice of Everyday Life* called 'Walking in the city'. In this chapter, I want to use that chapter as a jumping-off point, as a means of indexing and interrogating the nature of some (and only some) of the practices of the modern city. In particular, I want to lay the practice of walking, that de Certeau uses as a sign of the human, alongside the practice of driving. I want to argue that one hundred years or so after the birth of automobility, the experience of driving is sinking in to our 'technological unconscious' and producing a phenomenology which we increasingly take for granted but which in fact is historically novel. This new and very public sense of possession (de Certeau 2000) which is also a possession of sense constitutes a radically different set of spatial practicings of the city which do not easily conform to de Certeau's strictures on space and place, and should at least give us pause.

The chapter is therefore in three main parts. In the first part, I will do no more than outline some of de Certeau's thoughts on spatial practices in the city. In the second part, I will then argue that de Certeau's work on everyday life needs to be reworked to take into account the rise of automobility and the consequent changes in how space is ordered, changes which cannot easily be subsumed into his account of the city. The third part of the chapter will argue that these changes have been even more far-reaching than might at first be imagined, as developments like software and ergonomics rework how automobility is practised, and that these developments presage an important change in the nature of this particular form of habitability. The chapter then concludes by returning to de Certeau's vision of everyday life in the city in order to take up some of the challenges he bequeathed to us again.

Walking in the city

As Ian Buchanan (2000) has rightly indicated, de Certeau's project in *The Practice of Everyday Life* was a tentative and searching one which cannot and should not be read as a set of fixed theoretical conclusions about the nature of the world but rather should be seen as a means whereby it becomes possible to open up more spaces within which the operational logic of culture can be addressed. And we can see the ways in which this project both foreshadowed and produced a set of distinctively modern concerns – with practices rather than subjects or discourses, with moving beyond a model of culture based purely on reading, with creativity as well as discipline, with new ways of articulating otherness, with the presence of capability on the margins as well as subservience (Terdiman 2001), and so on. These concerns are now so well established, not least in large parts of cultural studies, that they are becoming a taken-for-granted background: not so much common end points as common starting points.

'Walking in the city'[1] starts atop of one of the towers of the World Trade Center which for de Certeau constituted 'the tallest letters in the world', a gigantic set of capital letters, a kind of sky writing if you like. For de Certeau, to be lifted to the summit of one of the Towers and to look out was to feel a violent delight. Distanced from the roar of the 'frantic New York traffic' and the location of the body in a criss-cross of streets, it is possible to think of the city as one vast and static panoramic text, able to be read because it is 'removed from the obscure interlacings of everyday behaviour'.

But down below, millions of walking bodies are engaged in a different kind of activity. Here I make no apology for quoting de Certeau at length, for the following passages from early on in the chapter seem to me to get to the nub of what he has to say.

> [I]t is below – 'down' – on the threshold where visibility ends that the city's common practitioners dwell. The raw material of this experiment are the walkers, *Wandersmänner* [*sic*], whose bodies follow the cursives and strokes of an urban 'text' they write without reading. These practitioners employ spaces that are not self-aware; their knowledge of them is as blind as that of one body for another, beloved, body. The paths that interconnect in this network, strange poems of which each body is an element down by and among many others, elude being read. Everything happens as though some blindness were the hallmark of the processes by which the inhabited city is organized. The networks of these forward-moving, intercrossed writings form a multiple history, are without creator or spectator, made up of fragments of trajectories and alteration of spaces: with regard to representations, it remains daily, indefinitely, something other.
>
> Eliding the imaginary totalizations of the eye, there is a strangeness in the commonplace that creates no surface, or whose surface is only an advanced limit, an edge cut out of the visible. In this totality, I should like to indicate the processes that are foreign to the 'geometric' or 'geographic' space of visual, panoptic or theoretical constructions. Such spatial practices refer to a specific form of *operations* (ways of doing); they reflect 'another spatiality' (an anthropological, *poietik* and mystical spatial experiment); they send us to an opaque, blind domain of the inhabited city, or to a *transhuman city*, one that insinuates itself into the clear text of the planned, readable city.
>
> (de Certeau 1987)

In such passages, de Certeau shows some quite remarkable powers of theoretical foresight as he works towards other forms of habitability. In particular, he fore-shadows the current strong turn to so-called 'non-representational' aspects of the city (e.g. Amin and Thrift 2002) in his emphasis on the diachronic succession of now-moments of practice which emphasize perambulatory qualities such as 'tactile apprehension and kinesic appropriation' (de Certeau 1987: 105), moments which are to some extent their own affirmation since they are an 'innumerable collec-tion of singularities' (de Certeau 1984: 97). He values a sense of invention[2] as a means of opening out sites to other agendas, so producing some degree of free play in apparently rigid social systems, and thereby foreshadowing the current demonstrative emphasis on performance. He also begins to think through the quite different spatial dynamics that such a theoretical-practical stance entails, a stance in which other kinds of spatial knowings are possible.

But, at the same time, I think we also have to see that de Certeau cleaves to some old themes, all based on the familiar model of (and desire for) what Meaghan Morris (1998) nicely calls 'evasive everdayness', and I want to concentrate on three of these. One such theme, highlighted by numerous commentators, is that he never really leaves behind the operations of reading and speech and the sometimes explicit, sometimes implicit claim that these operations can be extended to other practices. In turn, this claim that 'there is a correspondence or homology between certain enunciative procedures that regulate action in both the field of language and the wider network of social practices' (Gardiner 2000: 176) sets up another obvious tension, between a practice-based model of often illicit 'behaviour' founded on enunciative speech-acts and a text-based model of 'representation' which fuels functional social systems. I am uneasy with this depiction because of its tendency to assume that language is the main resource of social life (cf. Thrift 1996, 2000a, 2003b) and the obvious consequence; close readings can quite easily become closed reading. Another is that he insists that much of the practice of everyday life is in some sense 'hidden' away, obscured, silenced, and able to be recovered only by tapping the narrative harmonics of particular sites which 'are fragmentary and convoluted histories, pasts stolen by others from readability, folded up ages that can be unfolded but are there more as narratives in suspense' (p. 115). Each site has a kind of unconscious, then, an 'infancy' which is bound up with the movements of its inhabitants and which can be pulled back into memory – but only partially. I am similarly uneasy with this kind of depiction precisely because of its psychoanalytic echoes, for they seem to me to rely on a familiar representational metaphysics of presence and absence of the kind exten-sively criticized by Michel Henry (1993) and others in relation to certain kinds of Freudianism. A final questionable theme is de Certeau's implicit romanticism which comes, I think, from a residual humanism.[3] Now I should say straightaway that I am not convinced that a residual humanism is necessarily a bad thing (cf. Thrift 2000b) but in this case it leads de Certeau in the direction of a subterranean world of evasive urban tactics produced by the weak as typified by practices like walking 'as a model of popular practice – and critical process' (Morris 1998: 110) which I believe to be profoundly misleading for several reasons. For one, as

Meaghan Morris (1998) has so persuasively argued, de Certeau's pursuit of the apotheosis of the ordinary in the ordinary arising from his equation of enunciation with evasion, creates all manner of problems. Not only does it produce a sense of a beleaguered, localized (though not necessarily local) 'anthropological' everyday of poetry, legend and memory[4] being squeezed by larger forces, thus embedding a distinction between small and large, practice and system and mobility and grid which is surely suspect (Latour 2002) but it also chooses an activity as an archetype of the everyday which is far more ambiguous than it is often made out to be: for example, it is possible to argue not only that much walking, both historically and contemporarily, is derived from car travel[5] (and is not therefore a separate and, by implication, more authentic sphere) but also that the very notion of walking as a deliberately selected mode of travel and its accompanying peripatetic aesthetic of being somehow closer to nature – or the city – has itself been carefully culturally constructed in representation itself in concert with the evolution of automobility (Wallace 1990; Solnit 2000).[6] Thus, when Solnit (2000: 213) declares that de Certeau 'suggests a frightening possibility: that if the city is a language spoken by walkers, then a postpedestrian city not only has fallen silent but risks becoming a dead language, one whose colloquial phrases, jokes, and curses will vanish, even if its formal grammar survives' she may be missing other languages which also have something to say.

In the next section, I want to argue that if these three themes were thought to contain suspect assumptions in the 1970s then they are now even more problematic. I want to illustrate these contentions via a consideration of contemporary automobility[7] because I believe that the knot of practices that constitute that automobility provide a real challenge to elements of de Certeau's thought, especially as these practices are now evolving. Neither in *The Practice of Everyday Life* nor elsewhere in de Certeau's writings on the city have I been able to find any sustained discussion of the millions of automobile 'bodies' that clog up the roads:[8] de Certeau's cities echo with the roar of traffic but this is the noise of an alien invader.[9] However, in the short interlude following 'Walking in the city' – Chapter 8, 'Railway navigation and incarceration' – there are some clues to this absence, at least. For de Certeau, the train (and the bus), it turns out, is a 'travelling incarceration' in which human bodies are able to be ordered because, though the carriage is mobile, the passengers are immobile.

> Only a rationalized cell travels. A bubble of panoptic and classifying power, a module of imprisonment that makes possible the production of an order, a closed and autonomous insularity – that is what can traverse space and make itself independent of local roots.
>
> (de Certeau 1984: 111)

Continuing in this Foucauldian vein, de Certeau tells us that inside the carriage:

> There is the immobility of an order. Here rest and dreams reign supreme. There is nothing to do, one is in the state of reason. Everything is in its place,

as in Hegel's *Philosophy of Right*. Every being is placed there like a piece of printer's type on a page arranged in military order. This order, an organizational system, the quietude of a certain reason, is the condition of both a railway car's and a text's movement from one place to another.

(de Certeau 1984: 111)

De Certeau then switches from a panoptic to a panoramic (Schivelsbuch 1986) mode:

> Outside, there is another immobility, that of things, towering mountains, stretches of green field and forest, arrested villages, colonnades of buildings, black urban silhouettes against the pink evening sky, the twinkling of nocturnal lights on a sea that precedes or succeeds our histories. The train generalizes Dürer's *Melancholia*, a speculative experience of the world: being outside of these things that stay there, detached and absolute, that leaves us without having anything to do this departure themselves: being deprived of them, surprised by their ephemeral and quiet strangeness. . . . However, these things do not move. They have only the movement that is brought about from moment to moment by changes in perspective among their bulky figures. They have only *trompe-l'oeil* movements. They do not change their place any more than I do; vision alone continually undoes and remakes these relationships.

(de Certeau 1984: 111–112)

Leaving aside the evidence that de Certeau had clearly never travelled on the Dickensian British rail system, what we see here is the classic account of machine travel as distanciated and, well, machine-like. We can assume that de Certeau might have thought of cars, though of a less spectatorial nature (at least for their drivers), as having some of the same abstracted characteristics. But, if that is the case, it would be a signal error. For research on automobility shows the world of driving to be as rich and convoluted as that of walking. It is to telling this world that I now turn.

Driving in the city

The automobile has been with Euro-American societies for well over a century and since about the 1960s (not coincidentally, the time of de Certeau's observations on the city) the car has become a common feature of everyday life itself (Brandon 2002; Thrift 1990), almost a background to the background. Take as an example only the utter familiarity of automobile-related urban lighting from the orange glow of streetlights and their counterpoint of gaudy lit signs through the constant flash of car headlights to the intermittent flicker of the indicator. As Jakle (2001: 255) observes 'by 1970, the influence of the automobile on night-time lighting was felt in its entirety. . . . Cities were lit primarily to facilitate the movement of motor vehicles'. Around a relatively simple mechanical entity, then, a whole new civilization has been built; for example, the layout of the largest part of the Euro-American city space assumes the presence of the complicated logistics of the car, the van and the truck (Beckmann 2001; Sheller and Urry 2000). We can go farther than this; whole parts of the built environment are now a mute but still eloquent testimony to automobility. As Urry (2000: 59) puts it, 'the car's significance is that it reconfigures civil society involving distinct ways of dwelling, travelling and socialising in and through an automobilized time-space'. For example, most recently, large parts of the landscape near roads are being actively moulded by formal techniques like viewshed analysis so that they make visual sense to the occupants of cars as they speed by[10] or by more generalized developments like so-called time-space geodemographics which conceptualize the commuting system as a whole and are trying to produce continuously changing advertising on the multitude of signs scattered along the sides of roads, signs which will adjust their content and/or message to appeal to the relevant consumer populations that inhabit the highways at each time of day.[11] And then there is a whole infrastructure of specialized buildings that service cars and car passengers, from the grandest service stations to the humblest of garages (e.g. Jakle and Sculle 2002). We can go farther again. Automobiles have themselves transmuted into homes: for example, by one reckoning 1 in 14 US Americans now live in 'mobile homes' of one form or another (Hart *et al.* 2002).[12]

Until recently, however, this remarkable complex has been largely analysed in purely representational terms by cultural commentators as, for example, the symbolic manifestation of various desires (see, for example, most recently, Sachs 2002). But, as de Certeau would have surely underlined, this system of automobility has also produced its own embodied practices of driving and 'passengering', each with their own distinctive histories often still waiting to be written. Though we should not of course forget that how the car is put together, how it works and how and where it can travel are outwith the control of the driver, yet it is still possible to write of a rich phenomenology of automobility, one often filled to bursting with embodied cues and gestures which work over many communicative registers and which cannot be reduced simply to cultural codes.[13] That is particularly the case if we are willing to travel off the path of language as the only form of communication (or at least models of language as the only means of framing that communication) and understand driving (and passengering) as both profoundly embodied and sensuous experiences, though of a particular kind, which 'requires and occasions a metaphysical merger, an intertwining of the identities of the driver and car that generates a distinctive ontology in the form of a person-thing, a humanized car or, alternatively, an automobilized person' (Katz 2000: 33) in which the identity of person and car kinaesthetically intertwine.[14] Thus driving, for example, involves the capacity to

> embody and be embodied by the car. The sensual vehicle of the driver's action is fundamentally different from that of the passenger's, because the driver, as part of the praxis of driving, dwells in the car, feeling the bumps on the road as contacts with his or her body not as assaults on the tires, swaying around

curves as if the shifting of his or her weight will make a difference in the car's trajectory, loosening and tightening the grip on the steering wheel as a way of interacting with other cars.

(Katz 2000: 32)

Perhaps the best way to show this sensuality is through the work of Jack Katz (2000) and his students. Through detailed study of driving behaviour in Los Angeles, Katz shows that driving is a rich, indeed driven, stew of emotions which is constantly on the boil, even though cars prevent many routine forms of inter-subjective expression from taking shape – indeed the relative dumbness of driving and especially its lack of opportunity for symmetrical interaction may be the key aggravating factor. Katz is able to demonstrate four main findings. First, that drivers experience cars as extensions of their bodies. Hence their outrage on becoming the subject of adverse driving manoeuvres by other drivers: their tacit automobilized embodiment is cut away from them and they are left 'without any persona with which one can relate respectably to others' (Katz 2000: 46). Second, that, as a result of this and the fact that drivers attach all manner of meanings to their manoeuvres that other drivers cannot access (what Katz calls 'life metaphors'), driving can often be a highly emotional experience in which the petty realities of everyday situations are impressed on an unwilling recipient causing anger and distress precisely because they are so petty or in which a carefully nurtured identity is forcefully undermined causing real fury. Third, that the repertoire of reciprocal communication that a car allows is highly attenuated – the sounding of horns, the flashing of headlights, the aggressive use of brake lights, and hand gestures – within a situation which is already one in which there are limited cues available, occasioned by the largely tail-to-tail nature of interaction. Drivers cannot therefore communicate their concerns as fully as they would want and there is therefore a consistently high level of ambiguity in driver-to-driver interaction. As a result, a considerable level of frustration and anger (and frustration and anger about being frustrated and angered) can be generated.[15] But, at the same time, driving, and this is the fourth finding, is

a prime field for the study of what Michel de Certeau called the 'tactics' of contemporary everyday life. Many people develop what they regard as particularly shrewd ways of moving around society. These include carefully choosing streets that one knows carry little traffic, sneakily cutting across corner gas stations to beat traffic lights, discreetly using another car as a 'screen' in order to merge onto a highway, passing through an intersection, and brazenly doubling back to avoid the queue in a left-turn lane, and such triumphs of motoring chutzpah as following in the smooth-flowing wake of an ambulance as it cuts through bottled traffic.

(Katz 2000: 36)

At the same time, such tactics are very often read as violations of moral codes by other drivers, leading to all manner of sensual/driving expressions which are attempts to take the moral high ground and so bring to an end episodes of anger and frustration.

What Katz's work reveals, then, is an extraordinarily complex everyday ecology of driving. It makes very little sense to think of such express moments of auto-mobility as just cogs in a vaulting mechanical system (though I am certainly not arguing that they are not that too) or simply an assertion of driver independence. Rather, they are a complex of complex re-attributions which very often consists of interesting denials of precisely the interconnections that they are intent on pursuing (Dant and Martin 2001).

But, there is one more point to make, and that is that the nature of automobility is itself changing. The car cum driving of the twenty-first century is no longer the same knot of steely practices that it was in the twentieth century. It has been joined by new and very active intermediaries and it is this change that is the subject of the next section.

The changing nature of driving

Katz (2000: 44) points to the way in which cars are beginning to change and, in the process, are producing a new kind of phenomenology when he writes that

> The marketing of cars has long offered the potential of publicly display-ing oneself to others in an enviable form but also the promise of a private daily metamorphosis affording hands-on, real world, sensual verification that one fits naturally into a peaceful, immortal, or transcendent form. Cars are increasingly designed in elaboration of this message. The button that will automatically lower the window happens to be just where the driver's hand naturally falls. His key is a bit different than hers, and when he begins to work it into the ignition, the driver's chair 'knows' to adjust itself to a position that is tailored to his dimensions and sense of comfort. Cars have replaced watches . . . as the microengineered personal possession that, like a miniature world's fair exhibit, displays the latest technological achievements to the masses. Also, like watches, cars can be readily consulted as a reassuring touchstone for the assessment of messier segments of one's life.
>
> (Katz 2000: 44)

I want to approach the way that what was thought to be a mature technology is currently changing and transmuting into something quite different by an oblique route whose relevance will, I hope, become clear. For I want to argue that cars are one of the key moments in the re-design of modern urban environments in that they bring together a series of reflexive knowledges of 50 or so years' vintage now which are both technical and also – through their attention to 'human factors' – close to embodied practice and can be considered as some of the first out-posts of what might be called, following the work of the late Francisco Varela and his colleagues, the 'naturalization of phenomenology'. Of course, scientific knowledges have been routinely applied to the urban environment for a long time but I believe that the sheer scale and sophistication of what is happening now amounts to something quite different: a studied extension of the spatial practices of the human which consists of the production of quite new material surfaces which are akin to life, not objects, and thereby new means of bodying forth: new forms of material intelligence producing a new, more fluid transubstantiation.[16]

This transubstantiation is taking place in four ways. First, as Stivers (1999) has noted, it is foreshadowed in language itself: what were specifically human qualities have been externalized onto machines so that computers, for example, now have 'memories' and 'languages' and 'intelligence'. Concomitantly, human relationships have taken on machine-like qualities: we create 'networks' and 'interface' with others. But it goes deeper than that. So, second, it is arising from a continuous process of critique, as knowledges about technological and human embodied practices circle around and interact with each other, producing new knowledges which are then applied and become the subject of even newer knowledges in a never-ending reflexive loop. Then, third, as a result of the previous cumulative process of critique, automobiles become more and more like hybrid entities in which intelligence and intentionality is distributed between human and non-human in ways which are increasingly inseparable: the governance of the car is no longer in the hands of the driver but is assisted by more and more technological add-ons to the point where it becomes something akin to a Latourian delegate; 'first, it has been made by humans; second, it substitutes for the actions of people and is a delegate that permanently occupies the position of a human; and, third, it shapes human action by prescribing back' (Latour 1992: 235). Thus, increasingly, 'cars' are not just machines whose meanings are stamped out by 'culture' (Miller 2001) but have their own qualities which increasingly approximate the anthropological spaces that de Certeau is so concerned to foster and protect. And, fourth, as already foreshadowed, this transubstantiation is the result of explicitly operating on the phenomenological space of habitability that is focused on the car, consisting of both the space of the flesh and the space surrounding the body, in order to produce new bodily horizons and orientations (Changeux and Ricoeur 2002). In this transubstantiation objects are increasingly allowed their own place in the solicitations of a meaningful world.[17] They become parts of new kinds of authority.

If we take a tour around the modern car we can see two main ways in which this extension of extension through the systematic application of knowledge about embodied human practice – and the interaction between technology and embodied human practice – is taking place. One is through computer software (Thrift and French 2002). Software is a comparatively recent historical development – the term itself has only existed since 1958 – and though recognizable computer software has existed in cars since the 1970s, it is only in the last ten years or so that software, in its many manifestations, has become an integral element of the mechanics of cars, moving down from being only the province of luxury cars to becoming a norm in the mass market. Now software controls engine management, brakes, suspension, wipers and lights, cruising and other speeds,[18] parking manoeuvres, speech recognition systems,[19] communication and entertainment, sound systems, security, heating and cooling, in-car navigation, and last but not least, a large number of crash protection systems. Almost every element of the modern automobile is becoming either shadowed by software or software has become (or right from the start, as in the case of in-car navigation systems, has been) the pivotal component. The situation is now of such an order of magnitude greater than in the past that manufacturers and industry experts are quite seriously discussing the point at which the software platform of a car will have become so extensive that it will become one of the chief competitive edges; customers will be loath to change to different makes because of the investment of time needed to become familiar with a new software environment and style.[20] Such an allegiance might be strengthened by the increasing tendency for automobiles to become locations of activity other than driving; places for carrying out work, communicating, being entertained, and so on, via a legion of remote services.

Increasingly, automobile software also reaches beyond the vehicle itself. So, for example, 'intelligent vehicles' drive on 'intelligent streets' loaded up with software that surveys and manages traffic, from the humblest traffic light phasing to the grand visions of integrated transport management systems which will increasingly control traffic flow whilst giving an illusion of driver freedom. Each hybrid will become simultaneously a moment in a continuously updated databank of movement.

The other extension is through the application of ergonomics. Ergonomics (or 'human factors'[21]), like software, originated in the Second World War and has existed as a formal discipline since the late 1940s (Meister 1999). However, its widespread application has only come about since the 1980s, most especially with the advent of automated systems (Sheridan 2002). It is an amalgam of anatomy, physiology and psychology with engineering dedicated to the careful study of human-technology interactions and mostly concerned with creating new and more 'friendly' interfaces in which arrays of different objects act as one smooth process by reworking system complexity.[22] Though it argues that it is attempting to increase the cognitive fit between people and things, it might just as well be thought of as an exercise in hybridization, producing new forms of 'humanization', rather than simply discrete sets of interactions, by producing new kinds of authority.

The application of these two knowledges can be seen as simply a way of compensating for human error or it can be seen as a symptom of something much more far-reaching; a practical working-through of a more abstract project, namely the grounding of phenomenology in scientific, naturalistic principles. Now this, of course, might seem an odd project, given Husserl's consistent opposition of naturalistic methods to the sciences of 'man' but, grouped around an alliance of workers in AI, cognitive science and the like who have valorized embodied action, what we can see is a concerted project to represent the non-representational through scientific principles, mainly by working on the very small spaces and times of movement that can now be apprehended and worked with in order to produce a 'structural description of becoming aware'. Through such a project of the scientific renewal of phenomenology, in which intentionality is naturalized, objects like cars can then become very exactly computed environments in which, to use a famous phrase, 'the world is its own best model' (Brooks 1991: 142), both in the sense of cleaving to a particular scientific approach and in the engaged sense that what works works. In other words, cars become examples of 'geometrical descriptive eidetics' based on differential geometry and topology and designed for 'inexact morphological essences', essences which do not conform to a fundamental classical physical account but which are still amenable to a naturalized description, especially since the advent of complex system models (Petitot *et al.* 1999). Such forms can only come into the world because of the advent of large-scale computing and software, thereby demonstrating a pleasingly circular generativity.

What we can see as a result of these developments is something very interesting. First, driving the car becomes much more closely wrapped up with the body (or, at least, a naturalized view of embodiment) via the active intermediaries of software and ergonomics. Senses of weight and road resistance are reconfigured. What the driver 'listens' to and works on is altered. Relatedly, much more of the judgement involved in driving is now being either imposed or managed by software (for example, through innovations like traction control and ABS). In the process, almost certainly – even given hysteresis effects – this new kind of coded govern-mentality is producing safer road conditions. As a result, it is now commonly argued that software-based innovations like those mentioned, when combined with the better ergonomic design of controls, seating and steering, combine to produce 'better' driving experiences by giving more exact (in fact, more heavily intermediated) embodied contact with the road.[23] Second, the car becomes a world in itself. Sound and even video systems, climate control, better sound insulation, ergonomically designed interiors, easy recall of certain memories, and the like, all conspire to make the car into a kind of monad which increasingly refers to the world outside itself via heavily intermediated representations. Third, the car increasingly becomes locatable to itself and to others in a burgeoning artificial ethology.[24] The advent of a mixture of geographical information systems, global positioning and wireless communications means that getting lost will no longer be an option and, equally, that increasingly it will be possible to track all cars, wherever they may be. The result is that both surveying and being surveyed will increasingly become a norm: it is even possible that through the new informational and communicational conduits that are now being opened up, some of the social cues that have been missing from the experience of driving will be re-inserted (for example, who is driving a particular car), making the whole process more akin to walking again, but with a new informationally boosted hybrid body, a new incarnation.

We therefore arrive in a world in which knowledge about embodied knowledge is being used to produce new forms of embodiment-cum-spatial practice which are sufficiently subtle and extensive to have every chance of becoming a new background to everyday life. No doubt, a fellow *traversiste* of de Certeau like Virilio would be inclined to make such developments into a part of a humanist melt-down, a window onto a brave new informational world which is frighteningly sterile, a further chapter in the 'data coup d'état' which arrives from relying on informational models which model people as machines.

> The horsepowered car was motorized with the aid of the synthetic energy of the combustion engine in the course of the transport revolution is now gearing up to *motorize the reality of space*, thanks to the digital imagery of the computer motor, perceptual faith letting itself be abused, it would seem, by the virtuality generator. Dynamized by the artifice of continuous speed, the real-space perspective of the painters of the Quattrocento then gives way to the real-time perspective of the computer cognoscenti of the Novocento, thereby illustrating surrealist writings of the 1930s: 'One day science will travel by bringing the country we want to visit to us. It will be the country that visits us, the way a crowd visits some animal in a cage; then the country will leave again, miffed at having stirred itself for so little'.[25]
>
> (Virilio 1995: 151, author's emphasis)

In part, as we have seen from de Certeau's musings on rail travel, I think that de Certeau might have subscribed to this kind of line. But I think his positive sense of the mundane, combined with a realization that more and more software and ergonomics is derived from models of embodied knowledge which arise precisely out of the critique of informational models put forward by authors like Merleau-Ponty upon which he drew (which is now, ironically, being written into the software that surrounds us), would have made him pull back and head for a more nuanced interpretation. At least, I like to think so.

Conclusions

Such auto-mobile developments as I have laid out in the previous section lay down a set of challenges to de Certeau's work which I want to use to fashion a conclusion to this chapter. Given that de Certeau's project was a tentative and developing one, and embedded in a particular historical conjuncture, none of these criticisms need to be seen as necessarily disabling, but they are at least interestingly problematic. In order to bring some structure to these challenges, I will backtrack to the three criticisms of de Certeau made in the second section of this chapter and use these criticisms to sketch a rather different sense of the everyday in the city.

I want to begin by returning to de Certeau's continued reduction of practices to a generally cursive model. I have described this practice as problematic. But I think that it can be read more sympathetically in another way – as prefiguring a real historical change in which large parts of what were considered as non-representational embodied practice begin to be represented as they are brought into a kind of writing, the writing of software. It has, of course, been a constant in history to produce systems for describing human embodied movement of which conventional writing was only ever one: other systems of notation have abounded (cf. Finnegan 2002). But what we can see in the current prevalence of software

are embodied spatial and temporal practices being minutely described and written down using this new form of mechanical writing; to use another theoretical vocabulary, bare life is being laid bare – and then cursively extended (Thrift 2003a). Interestingly, de Certeau himself begins to provide the beginnings of a vocabulary for describing this change later in *The Practice of Everyday Life* (though admittedly in a different context) when he writes in his brief history of writing in Chapter 10 about a new form of scriptural practice which is not married to a reality of meaning but is a writing given over to its own mechanisms. This is 'a model of language furnished by the machine, which is made of differentiated and combined parts (like every enunciation) and develops, through the interplay of its mechanisms, the logic of a celibate narcissism' (de Certeau 1984: 152). And we can interpret automobile hybrids as made up of flesh, various mechanical components – and such a form of writing (de Certeau's body, tool and text), gradually taking in the other two. As I have already pointed out, such a development can be seen in wholly negative terms as existing alongside what de Certeau (1984: 153) calls a 'galloping technocratization' but I prefer to think of it as also offering new possibilities for the extension of physical extension and thought.

The second challenge arises from the use of adjectives like 'hidden'. I think that such a description of large parts of everyday life has become an increasingly mistaken one. The sheer amount of locationally referenced information about everyday life that is available or is coming on stream, and which by using wireless, GIS, GPS and other technologies will be constantly updated, suggests that most of the spaces of everyday life will no longer be hidden at all. Indeed, they are likely to be continually catalogued on a real-time basis using categorizations and geometries that are themselves constitutive of subjectivity.[26] But, I would argue that much of what actually characterizes everyday life – the creative moments arising out of artful improvisation on the spur of the moment – will still continue to be opaque to systematic surveillance: there will still be 'strangeness in the commonplace'. It is these performative moments of narrative dissonance that we should be concentrating on. It may therefore be that, in contemporary social systems, it is not so much hiding as trying to fashion different modes of visibility which is crucial.

The third challenge arises from de Certeau's weak humanism. The problem, of course, as Deleuze, Latour and many others have continually emphasized, is 'what is human?' The answer is rather less clear now than it was twenty or so years ago but, equally, the possibilities of what counts as 'humanity' have expanded. What seems clear to me is that it is not necessary to equate the human with the near and local, the slow and the small, as Gabriel Tarde pointed out well over one hundred years ago (see Latour 2002a): though de Certeau's humanism comes with a heavy dose of the scriptural, it is difficult to escape the conclusion that when it comes to the kind of liberatory spatial practices he is willing to envisage, that writing is still handwriting. In an age when electronic signatures are becoming the norm, this is, in a quite literal sense, anachronistic – and whatever the spatial equivalent of that term might be.[27] But, equally, de Certeau's appeal to a 'transhuman' city surely still retains its force.

Which brings me to a final point. As the example of driving shows, new modes of embodiment are being invented by the grand experimental forces of capitalism, science and war. One very popular reaction to such developments is to fall back on a narrative of beleaguerement, in which everyday life is gradually being crushed by forces without its control. But another reaction is to argue that such models are at root too simple to be adequate to a situation in which new capacities are continually being formed as well as new modes of control. This might be seen as a Panglossian response: I prefer to see it as a re-affirmation of a Certeauian politics of 'opening the possible' (Giard 1997) which realizes that new spaces for action are continually being opened up as old ones are closed down. New and friendly habitabilities are therefore constantly on the horizon, some of which may still be able to be realized. Escape, no. Work with and on, yes.

5 Movement-space

The changing domain of thinking resulting from the development of new kinds of spatial awareness

> Civilization advances by extending the number of operations which we can perform without thinking about them.
>
> (A.N. Whitehead 1911, cited in Myers 2002: 17)

Introduction

What is an idea? In this chapter, I want to argue that, whatever an idea's exact content might be, it is also important to be able to understand the way in which an idea is framed because that framing has consequences. Yet, it is remarkable how few papers on knowledge actually consider the mundane frameworks in which ideas come wrapped and from which they must spring. This chapter is a first attempt to suggest another way of looking at the world of 'pre'-ideas, one that is meant to be both destabilizing and, at the same time, productive. It arises out of a theoretical shift that does now seem to be gathering momentum, one that allows new things to be seen and handled by concentrating on the utterly mundane frameworks that move 'subjects' and 'objects' about.

The chapter therefore follows on from some of my other recent work which has attempted to understand the new kinds of electronic background time-spaces that are making their way into the world, and their capacity for changing what we might be (see Thrift 2003a, 2003b, 2004d, 2004g; Thrift and French 2002). In particular, I have looked at how, as a result of the intervention of software and new forms of address, these background time-spaces are changing their character, producing novel kinds of behaviours that would not have been possible before and new types of object which presage more active environments. In this chapter, I want to extend these thoughts in various directions, hoping to capture the outlines of a world just coming into existence,[1] one which is based on continuous calculation at each and every point along each and every line of movement.

In conventional accounts of the modern world, this 'figured materiality' (Verran 2001) would be regarded as cause for concern. It would be taken as yet another sign of a more rationalized, calculative world, one increasingly bereft of humanity (see, for example, Ritzer 2003); a sign taken for a portent of doom rather than wonders. I am sceptical of such accounts and want to suggest something rather different; a move towards a world in which new qualities are being constructed, which are based on assumptions about how time-space can turn up, which would have been impossible before, spaces which are naturalistic in the sense that they are probably best represented as fluid forces that have no beginning or end and which are generating new cultural conventions, techniques, forms, genres, concepts, even (or so I will argue) senses. This is the rise of what I call 'qualculation'.

The chapter is therefore in four main parts. The first and briefest part considers the issue of the growth of artificial paratextual forces, invisible forms which constitute the bare bones of the world, concentrating especially on structures of repetition. The second part of the chapter is concerned with the extent to which these forces are dependent upon and operationalized through all manner of forms of quantitative calculation, from the very simplest operations like listing and numbering and counting through to various kinds of analytical and transformative operations. But, more to the point, I argue that in recent years the activity of calculation has become so ubiquitous that it has entered a new phase, which I call 'qualculation', an activity arising out of the construction of new generative microworlds which allow many millions of calculations to continually be made in the background of any encounter. I argue that it is no longer possible to think of calculation as necessarily being precise. Rather, because of massive increases in computing power, it has become a means of making qualitative judgements and working with ambiguity. In other words, what we are seeing is a new form of seeing, one which tracks and can cope with uncertainty in ways previously unknown.

The problem then becomes how to frame and represent this new kind of space of thinking thinking. This is the subject of the third main part of the chapter. I will argue that this is best achieved by aligning my arguments with the literature on ethnomathematics which not only demonstrates the wide variety of different kinds of calculation which can be shown to exist, or to have existed, in the world, but also, in its emphasis on the transition from calculation as practised in oral cultures to calculation as practised in literate cultures, provides a kind of model for the transition from a calculative world to a qualculative world.

The fourth and final part of the chapter is an attempt to show how these developments are producing a new sense of space as folded and animate, one that assumes a moving point of view, a 'nomadologic' rather than a monadologic (Vidler 2000), which may, for example, be showing up in new forms of anxiety and phobia which are representative of new stresses and strains, or in new forms of intuition. However, too often discussions of these senses end with this point or are so abstract that they leave the reader to do all the interpretation. Instead, I want to begin to discuss what this might mean concretely. This I will do by considering the way in which the human sensorium is changing, specifically by considering changes in the way the body 'talks' and is addressed.

I also append some brief conclusions.

The world of paratexts

All human activity depends upon an imputed background whose content is rarely questioned: it is there because it is there. It is the surface on which life floats. At one time, the bulk of this background would have consisted of entities which existed in a 'natural order', all the way from the vagaries of the surface of the earth through to the touch of currents of air or the itch of various forms of clothing through to the changes in the sky. But over time, this background has been filled with more and more 'artificial' components until, at the present conjuncture, much of the background of life is 'second nature'; the artificial equivalent of breathing. Roads, lighting, pipes, paper, screws and similar constituted the first wave of artificiality. Now a second wave of second nature is appearing, extending its fugitive presence through object frames as different as cables, formulae, wireless signals, screens, software, artificial fibres, and so on. It is possible to think of these object frameworks in a number of ways. First, and most obviously, they can be considered as the technological equivalent of the Heideggerian background, but presumably involving a new kind of dwelling. However, there is a problem with such a narrative. The notion of background still clings to its roots in a Greek notion of a bordered and enclosed topos, and therefore might be thought of as an inappropriate fit to contemporary developments (Irigaray 1999; Perniola 2004).[2] Second, they can be thought of as like paratexts (Genette 1999; Jackson 1999), 'invisible' forms which structure how we write the world but which generally no longer receive attention because of their utter familiarity. Like the set-up of the page, indexes, footnotes and the rest of the paraphernalia of written thinking, they have become a kind of epistemic wallpaper. Third, they can be interpreted as new kinetic surfaces to the world, along and across which things run (Parks 2003; Thrift 2004a), surfaces like screens which are becoming ubiquitous interfaces and which demand certain kinds of structured engagement which are both geophysical and also phenomenological in that they may alter our understandings of space, time and movement. Fourth, they can be understood as a new 'technological unconscious' whose content is the bending of bodies-with-environments to a specific set of addresses without the benefit of any cognitive inputs. The technological unconscious is therefore a prepersonal substrate of guaranteed correlations, assured encounters, and therefore unconsidered anticipations (Clough 2000; Thrift 2004a). Finally, they can be understood as a methodological challenge. Most notable here is the paraethnographic movement instigated by writers like George Marcus and Annelise Riles which has attempted to instigate a new kind of aesthetic practice of 'hearing' in order to be able to locate and understand the 'known unfamiliar' and the 'unknown familiar'. The avowed intent is to find a way of discussing subjects that cannot not be apprehended as distant analogues to anthropologists' own knowledge, and are not therefore open to metaphorical interpretation. Many of these subjects are not instrumental but are based on shared appreciations at levels which are often 'on the surface, in plain view, and yet precisely for this reason, unseen' (Riles 2003: 22).

What each of these interpretations share in common is a focus on (1) the utter mundanity of this second nature which is also an inescapability: these items act as natural primitives which through their recursivity guarantee the recursivity of the world; (2) the fact that they therefore exist outside of the realm of meanings, being known only in their performance; (3) the importance that is consequently attached to the persuasiveness of form; (4) the observation of a kind of fugitive materiality which lives in the interstices of life, the materiality of a ground which only receives attention if its workings are interrupted; but (5) the parallel observation that these items require continuous effort to keep going, in the shape of service and repair, effort which is nevertheless almost never commented upon.

Establishing these frameworks so that they are reliably recursive means imposing four different but closely related frames which will allow formal self-description and therefore some measure of control, self-description which nowadays will almost always be numerical. First, it requires the imposition of metrics. As the historical record shows, this is an enormous task in itself. Second it requires the imposition of standards which allow what are often different local frames to be crafted into a secure global assemblage. Third, it requires the imposition of a system of addresses so that all parts of the system are able to be located by all other parts. Fourth, it requires the imposition of modularity so that reliable 'objects' can be identified and described. If these frames can be imposed then four further achievements become possible (Manovich 2001). First, variability can be constructed and dealt with. Second, transcoding can occur on a regular basis: lists, records and arrays can be generated and they will mean roughly the same thing at all points in a network. They can also be translated into other formats. Third, it becomes possible to build archives of various kinds which provide a kind of memory and possibilities of re-use (Bowker 2003). And, fourth, automation of many operations can occur, a characteristic which has been much enhanced in the present by programmability.

If all these characteristics can be imposed, then the logic of the system, as it becomes both necessary and general, will gradually become the logic of the world. As this ontogenetic process occurs, so the system will fade from human perception, becoming a part of the landscape which the body 'naturally' adjusts to and which it regards as a normal part of its movement. In the next section I want to start to assemble the components which will allow me to understand this process as it pertains to the construction of quantitative calculation as a norm.

From quantification to qualculation: the growth of calculation

The growth of quantitative calculation in the world, by which I understand the growth of ideas and procedures concerned with number, counting, logic, and consequent forms of spatial and temporal configuration, and the combination and organization of these operations into systems which are clearly 'secular, time-bound, and empirically tainted' (Rotman 1993: 49) is a long and complicated story which can take in all kinds of milestones, from the invention of mathematics in fifth century BC Greece to the current rise of quantum computing. But what seems certain is that the sheer amount of calculation going on in the world has undergone a major shift of late as a result of the widespread application of computing power through the medium of software to the extent that many quite mundane human activities are now shadowed by numerous, often quite complex, calculations. Calculation, in other words, is becoming a ubiquitous element of human life. Three facts can illustrate this point. First, there is the sheer growth in computing power, as represented not just by processing power but also by developments like grid computing which represent distributed means of solving very large problem sets. On one reckoning, the upper bound of human brainpower has been calculated to be 2×10^{16} calculations per second. If computational power continues to conform to Moore's Law then by 2030 just an ordinary PC should compute at around 10^{16} instructions per second (Sharpe 2003). Second, and relatedly, there is the increasing ubiquity of hardware and software which means that computing can take place in many locations (Thrift and French 2002). Small bits of hardware and software are now part of the hum of everyday life, working away silently on their calculations in all manner of unexpected locations. Third, forms of calculation are changing. Increasingly, analytic solutions are being replaced by brute computing force engendered by mass recursivity with the result that what is regarded as mathematics is spreading far beyond its original kernel of knowledge.[3] The problem then becomes how to represent this increase in calculation and its consequences.

I will argue that we are in a situation which has a number of historical parallels which have manifested themselves again under the new conditions of computability and which form a kind of cognitive history told through practices of number. One is with the discovery of mathematical deduction itself. The second is with the identification of population as a thinkable entity. The third is with the exact gridding of time and space in the eighteenth and nineteenth centuries. The fourth is with the invention of various filing and listing systems at the turn of the nineteenth century. The fifth is the invention of logistics in the mid-twentieth century. It would be possible to argue that thinking in the modern world is founded on the powering up of these abstractions and extensions of movement and that developments like the growth of surveillance in the twentieth century are but logical outgrowths of them. I want to argue that, just as these developments produced a new sense of the world and new forms of representation of it, so we can see something similar happening now. These developments have, if you like, produced new figured ontologies by decomposing and recomposing the world in their own image: they have been the real winners of the ontological wars, defining not so much what is to be done in any situation but how the situation turns up in the first place. It is a messy kind of purity that is being produced, of course, one which has to work hard to keep itself in place: we simply do not see the work going on.

First, then, the discovery of mathematics. Netz (1999) argues convincingly that this discovery resulted from the transition from a visually based pre-literate society to a verbally based literate culture and especially from the material implementation of the lettered diagram, a limited lexicon, and the formula which was the hallmark of Greek mathematical activity. Thinking in and through the tangible tool of the diagram, a limited range of letters, and formulae,[4] Greek mathematicians were led towards a cognitive style which allowed for new kinds of argumentation, and a universe of discourse with high degrees of implicitness which acted as a new ontology:

> It is the essence of cognitive tools to carve a more specialised niche within general cognitive processes. Within that niche, much is automatised, much is elided. The lettered diagram, specifically, contributed to both elision (of the semiotic problems involved with mathematical discourse) and automatisation (of the obtaining of a model through which problems are processed).
>
> (Netz 1999: 57)

In particular, the cognitive method called mathematics allowed the world to be seen as concise, transferable and thus manageable, shaping a new kind of necessity. In particular, this method relied on being able to establish repeatability, most especially by reducing the scope for variability in both diagram and text and therefore producing 'controlled' results.

Second, the discovery of population (or, more accurately, 'multitude') as a thinkable entity, an entity which can be characterized and summed in different ways. There are many possible dates from which such a cognitive style can be argued to have come into existence. For example, just in English history the date can be placed as early as the twelfth or thirteenth centuries, as a result of the Church's further extension of control over marriage, increasingly close grappling with issues of marriage and procreation amongst the faithful, the extraordinary development of pastoral expertise and observation, and more general issues of inhabitation brought about by an expanding notion of geography (Biller 2000; Clanchy 1992). Or it can be understood as occurring much later, in the sixteenth and seventeenth centuries, as a result of the rising domestic administrative demands of the state, as opposed to the already familiar demands of raising money and waging war. Similar variations in judgement can be found in many other cultures (for example, see Goody 1986 on list-making and its relation to the move from oral to literate cultures). Perhaps the most obvious observation to make is that the notion of population is caught up with the rise of states and their need to both circumscribe and enlarge their capacities through synoptic facts. It is a part of what J. Scott (1998: 80) calls an 'ongoing project of legibility'. Whatever the case, it is clear that a notion of population of the kind that subsequently became common in the nineteenth century has been crucial to the quantification of the world, allowing many modern statistical ideas to come into existence and be applied in the background as a kind of background (Porter 1992).

Third, there is the gridding of time and space in the eighteenth and nineteenth centuries. The story of the standardization of space and time has been told many times but it is no less remarkable for that. For, as various metrics were generalized and standardized, so making different parts of the world locatable and transposable within a global architecture of address, so each and every part of the world could in theory be given an address. The process of achieving this goal had to wait until the late twentieth century to achieve fruition, especially with the advent of GIS and GPS, but the trajectory was clear long before this. For example, Burnett (2003) shows how in the nineteenth century a number of authors dreamed of a 'chronometrical sea', a sea that behaved like a clock, a sky-like entity which would yield to metrical and mathematical analysis. Such a vision demanded a means of holding the sea in place which could only truly be achieved late in the twentieth century as satellites, computers and lasers provided means of orientation which had hitherto been lacking (cf. Galison 2003). In turn, the technology of address produced genuine locatability in an absolute space and, with it, the possibility of making calculations which had been difficult or long-winded before. In particular, objects could be followed from location to location as a continuous series so simulating movement in a way that was, for all intents and purposes, indistinguishable from movement itself.

Fourth, there is the growth of means of making mass lists and registers. Yates (1994, 2001) has argued that the end of the nineteenth century saw a seismic shift in the technology of list-making as a result of the invention of technologies which not only recorded, copied, duplicated and stored information but also, in effect, created the modern idea of what information consists of. These technologies included: the typewriter, prepared forms, new means of duplication (such as carbon paper, hectographs and stencils), filing systems, card files, and new means of indexing. Much of the content and style of these technologies was subsequently translated into modern computers with minimal change, from keyboard layout to various procedures, codes and algorithms.

Fifth, there is the rise of logistics, a set of knowledges synonymous with movement, effectively the science of moving objects in an optimal fashion. This science, which originated with the military in the eighteenth and nineteenth centuries but found its 'ground' in the business world after the Second World War as the realm of thinking about linkages and how to make them as efficient as possible, has gradually become associated with the technology of address. That association has produced a background host of calculations of object movement which have made statistics a part of the normal functioning of the world, and not just a set of summary descriptions (Desrosieres 1998). Most recently, the rise of continuously computed environments has made logistics perhaps the central discipline of the contemporary world – though one curiously unsung – as it has pursued the goal of 'intelligent logistics processes' which

> have the ability to bring together the right information and materials, spatially and electronically, to the right place at the right time no matter where in the world they originate. In short, this new set of logistical processes requires a logistical environment that is time-based, collaborative and intelligent.
>
> (Greis 2004: 41)

In each of these five practices/apprehensions of number, number does not just describe, it constructs. Numbers take on virtual properties (D. Miller 1998) in that they produce an impetus towards the construction of 'a terrain and a population with precisely those standardized characteristics that will be easiest to monitor, count, assess and manage' (J. Scott 1998: 81-82). In other words, number tends to cast the world reciprocally in its image as entities are increasingly made in forms that are countable. Number performs number. As importantly, in Euro-American cultures at least, it also performs a notion of a terrain and population existing in a 'similar and immovable'[5] abstract space which has had to be slowly and laboriously built up, one which assumes that there are fixed reference points, cardinal dimensions, and the like (Hatfield 1990).

It could be argued that by the middle of the twentieth century most of the building blocks of contemporary developments had already been put in place. All that was left was to implement them – thereby producing a tightly constrained and ordered world of calculation in which potentially every thing and every location (the two increasingly becoming interchangeable) could be given a number and become the subject of calculation, and in which each calculation could potentially be redone several times a minute. This task was able to be achieved because of a number of contributory factors but principally because of the spread of the interfaces and defaults of computer software which both encapsulated the new possibilities and acted as a vehicle for them (Thrift and French 2002). Whatever the cause, the world has become increasingly one in which a numerical flux becomes central to activities, rather than incidental, giving rise to more and more 'flow architectures', to use Knorr Cetina's felicitous phrase.

> In a timeworld or flow-world . . . the content itself is processual – a 'melt' of material that is continually in flux, and that exists only as it is being projected forward and calls forth participants' reactions to the flux. Only 'frames', it would seem, for example, the frames that computer screens represent in a financial market, are pre-supposed in this flow-world. The content, the entire constellation of things that pass as the referential context wherein some action takes place, is not separate from the totality of ongoing activities.
>
> (Knorr Cetina 2003: 4)

In other words, in a world in which numerical calculations are being done and redone continuously, so that static representation becomes subordinated to flow (not least because 'the image, in a traditional sense, no longer exists' (Manovich 2001: 100)), the nomadologic of movement becomes the natural order of thought. The world is reconfigured as a global trading zone in which network forms, which strive for co-ordination, are replaced by flow forms which strive for observation and projection.

> Like an array of crystals acting as lenses that collect light, focussing it on one point, such mechanisms collect and focus activities, interests, and events on one surface, from whence the result may then be projected again in different directions. When such a mechanism is in place, co-ordination and activities respond to the projected reality to which participants become oriented. The system acts as a centering and mediating device through which things pass and from which they flow forward.
>
> (Knorr Cetina 2003: 4)

Treatises from the mid-twentieth century onwards had attempted to understand precisely the large amount of numerical information that was becoming available and, more importantly, how to specify such a situation, work with it and shape it. In other words, it had been realized that the plethora of tightly packed grids of numbers would produce opportunities to frame movement in different ways as the sheer amount of calculative power that was becoming available became apparent and as a world of continuously flickering rotations and transformations and projections hoved into view.

An example of this process in action is the rise of cybernetics. Originally conceived as the science of a certain class of machines, cybernetics has, in its various later hybrid forms such as found in parts of computer science, become a part of the way in which number is routinely handled (Mirowski 2002). Thus, forces of recursivity moved from being models on the page to something approaching forces of nature: in Manovich's (2001) terms, the loop – the repetition of a set number of steps – becomes the key figure producing a new form of temporality and spatiality. In contrast to the temporality and spatiality of the narrative, playing out once and for all, we find a progression based on a shuffling between loops which are all active simultaneously, which are constantly changing their character in response to new events, and which can communicate with each other in a kind of continuously diffracting spatial montage. There are no longer calculations with definite beginnings and ends. Rather there is a plane of endless calculation and recalculation, across which intensities continually build and fade.

In turn, this process of shaping numerical flow such that it seems to shape us has produced not just new quantities but new qualities, based in and around new kinds of perceptual labour and expertise which, or so I claim, are producing a shift in understanding the world similar to that which attaches to the move from oral to literate cultures. These qualities are the subject of the next section.

As a parting shot, I want to emphasize that these developments are producing not only shifts in what is understood as 'human' but also shifts in what is understood as 'environment' since, increasingly, the 'artificial' environment is sentient and has the feel of a set of 'natural' forces blowing this way and that. It is possible to argue that, as a result, the world is becoming re-naturalized and resembles nothing so much as a Spinozan universe of geometrical laws but one that has been constructed rather than one that is necessarily extant.

New apprehensions of space and time

Much has been written of late about new sensings of space and time. In particular, three related characterizations seem to have become dominant, each of which triangulates with the others. First, there is the issue of relative space: it is reckoned that a more plastic sense of space and time has come into existence, one that recognizes space as folded and animate because everything can be framed as in perpetual movement: 'the shape of this space is that of a river: not the surveyor's river which is simply a gap on the map, a frozen interval, but the river as serpentine motion, as an evolving pattern of vortices, expanding and collapsing' (Carter 1992: 92).

Second, this perpetually mobile space is seen as one in which joint action arising out of several causes brings new things into the world. The realm of the virtual or quasi-causal is recognized as having an existence, one which continually marks up the world. Third, spacetime is seen as arising out of multiple encounters which, though structured, do not have to add up: as myriad adjustments and improvisations are made, so new lines of flight can emerge. The fabric of space is open-ended rather than enclosing.

However, it must be noted that these sensings would be impossible without the fine grid of calculation which enables them: they are not, as many writers would have it, in opposition to the grid of calculation but an outgrowth of the new capacities that it brings into existence. A carefully constructed absolute space begets this relative space.

Most importantly, I will argue that the sheer amount of calculation that is now becoming possible at all points of so many spaces is producing a new calculative sense, which I will call 'qualculation' (Callon and Law 2004). That sense has the following characteristics. First, speed. Calculations are done all but instantaneously, to the point where many calculations become part of a background whose presence is assumed. Second, faith in number. We might say that the kind of obsessive faith in number exhibited by luminaries like Galton in the nineteenth century has become generalized (cf. Gillham 2002). Almost anything is thought susceptible to counting, ranking, and the like, as evidenced by the current mania for ranking just about anything, often in what might seem completely inappropriate ways (Kimbell 2002). Third, and at the same time, only limited numerical facility is available in the bodies of the population. Though much of the population is innumerate, this no longer necessarily matters because the environment acts as a prosthesis which offers cognitive assistance on a routine basis. Fourth, some degree of memory. This memory will be based upon producing symbols (e.g. personal surnames, stable national languages, currencies, fingerprints, barcodes and other addresses) that can be used as stable identifiers and, increasingly, these have taken on numerical form (J. Scott 1998). Again, the general population seems to be in the grip of a mania for 'remembering forwards' by recording their lives which, in part, seems to be an echo of this desire to identify, as well as a new way of dreaming (Carter 1992).

In turn, we might argue that qualculation demands certain kinds of perceptual labour which involve forms of reflexivity which position the subject as an instrument for seeing, rather than as an observer, in which a number of the mechanisms that we take for granted have been integrated into larger systems or into specialized feedback processes. Increasingly, subjects do not encounter finished, pre-existing objects but rather 'clearings' that disclose opportunities to intervene in the flow (Knorr Cetina 2003).

How to characterize this qualculative sense more generally? I want to argue that the best way of thinking about this characterization is to take a leaf from the book of ethnomathematics and to thereby think about transitions to new cognitive modes occasioned by adding new features to physical matter (and especially all manner of pervasive infrastructures) which, arguably, alter the sense of what matter is about. In particular, the new qualculative sense involves a different sense of number and counting and series,[6] a sense which relies on (1) a series of prostheses which routinely offer cognitive assistance and which do much of the work of navigation automatically; (2) a highly provisional sense of spatial co-ordination which is based in the continual spatial and temporal revisions made possible by track and trace systems (the so-called 'elasticity of synchronicity'); (3) a sense of continual access to information (so-called 'ambient information') arising out of connectivity being embedded in all manner of objects, which means that the effort involved in foraging is much less than was the case; (4) a more flexible sense of metric; (5) much less sense of locations as places of return or permanent gathering of the kind constructed around the institution of the domestic house in Euro-American societies from the fourteenth century onwards (D.V. Smith 2003).

Ethnomathematics argues that 'there is no single, universal path . . . that . . . mathematical ideas follow' (Ascher 2002: 2). Ethnomathematics is therefore concerned to value systems of number and calculation which do not conform to the base ten numeration system of modern mathematics and which do not regard this system as necessarily at the apex of numerical perfection. Different numerical systems are treated as akin to different languages (suggesting the need for 'bilingual' forms of mathematical teaching in many parts of the world, for example) and are not, as they were in the past, interpreted as indices of differential degrees of civilization or as found entities complete unto themselves. Indeed, part of the attraction of ethnomathematics is that it easily makes space for the complexity of mucking about with numbers that typifies much of everyday life, a complexity which cannot easily be reduced to a 'culture', not least because numbers are figured in multiple ways – usually as little rituals of gesture, utterance and the use of appropriate prostheses – and are not easily reduced to a singular activity called 'calculation' (Lave 1996). This is to say more than that the use of numbers varies with context. It is also to say that the use of numbers is inevitably partial, performative, distributed, and often integrated into other activities (for example, navigation, decoration, calendrics, religion) rather than understood as a discrete activity carried out for itself. Another part of the attraction of ethnomathematics is its understanding of how number interpellates subjectivity by producing particular forms of link. Thus subjects may increasingly understand themselves as the subject and object of number and numerical calculation (cf. Eglash 1999; Mimica 1992).

But what ethnomathematics, in its understandable desire to show up difference, is perhaps less effective at seeing is how the spread of various prostheses is producing an allegiance to base ten means of ordering almost by default. More and more of the world is brought into this means of ordering through the operations of various forms of code and the ordering microworlds that they generate.

What is the cognitive style of the figured materiality in which the North and increasing parts of the South now participate? I have already begun to argue that this is best described as 'qualculation', a style arising out of the sheer amount of calculation now taking place. This style of calculation arises out of the generality of the numbered fields against which and with which so much activity now takes place, the increasing amount of calculation done via machinic prostheses – often to the point where 'human' intervention is distant or even non-existent for long periods of time – and an increasing tendency to frame number as quality, in the sense that calculations are so numerous and so pervasive that they show up as forces rather than discrete operations. Number both frames movement and is framed by it: the two reciprocally confirm each other and provide a window onto a perception of a world which sways and shimmies with the force of qualculation, which folds and flows in numerous ways as different architectures of flow meld and then melt away because of the increased elasticity of synchronicity (and 'synchoricity') that has been made possible.

One word of caution is in order, however. The idea of spaces that fold and flow is hardly a new one. As Carter and many others have pointed out, such a depiction was the stock in trade of a certain kind of modernism and has circulated since at least the beginning of the twentieth century in forms as differently similar as Bergson's philosophy, various art forms (T.J. Clark 1999), and numerous works of literature. What is different, however, is that the means to realize this world have now come into being as a result of much enhanced calculation, allowing all kinds of entities which could be imagined but not actualized to finally make their way into the world.[7]

How might we understand how this qualculative world shows (or will show) up? How will it be experienced? In the next section, I want to begin the task of working through how a new sensorium based on qualculation – which assumes a world of movement – might look and feel.

It is important to note right from the start that we already have considerable evidence that what counts as the senses varies cross-culturally. There is no reason to believe that what we count as 'senses' has to be static in character. The sensory orders of cultures can vary radically and so, therefore, can the expectations of what counts as perception and experience. For example, Geurts (2002) outlines a sensorium connected with a number of West African cultures which is quite different from the Euro-American folk model of five senses which inhabit habitual bodily practice, not least in the fact that there seems to be no articulated sensorium and therefore one has to be imputed. With that caveat in mind, Geurts is able to build up a model of a sensorium which is less attuned to a standard Euro-American depiction of a strong divide between physical sensation and mental process and between external environment and internal state[8] and which, furthermore, seems to map over into judgements of moral character (Table 5.1).

The point of Geurts's work is that it shows that there is no need to think that what we name as the senses has a predetermined or stable character. In all likelihood, the constellation of senses and what we may consequently regard as sensations goes through periods of regular redefinition and re-embedding (Howes 2003).[9] Using this insight, the next section takes up the challenge of understanding the qualculative world.

Table 5.1 The indigenous Anlo sensorium

Aural perception or hearing
A vestibular sense, balancing, equilibrium from the inner ear
Kinaesthesia, walking, or a movement sense
A complex of tactility, contact, touch
Visuality or sight
Terms used to describe the experience of tasting
Olfactory action or smell
Orality, vocality, and talking
Feeling in the body; also synaesthesia and a specific skin sense

Source: Geurts (2002: 46–47)

A new sensorium?

How might we expect qualculative developments to make themselves known in the sensorium? It is possible to make a loose analogy with what happened when the material form of the Euro-American city changed in the nineteenth century. Then, a whole set of new habits and their accompanying anxieties had to be learnt: new ways of walking and talking were developed as new addresses for the body were laid down by the new spatial orders (Joyce 2003).What kinds of indices might suggest a similar reshaping of experience?

One of the ways that qualculative developments are most likely to surface is as so-called mental conditions in which what is generally a part of the technological unconscious is able to make itself known again as various anxieties and phobias. In the past, there have been a number of examples of such manifestations, including the phenomenon of so-called 'mad travellers' (Hacking 1998). What are the corresponding anxieties and phobias which might become apparent under the new regime of movement-space? Carter (2002) has argued that the range of symptoms known as agoraphobia (which, by some estimates, affects up to 5 per cent of Euro-American populations) should be understood as a movement inhibition arising out of an 'environmental unconscious' which has been generated by specific spatial arrangements and the kinds of 'body talk' that these arrangements make possible. But Carter's discussion remains frustratingly oblique about many aspects of these symptoms and other ambulatory conditions: too often in his account the allusive becomes the elusive. That said, his book lays down a challenge to think about how, as spatial arrangements and their consequential modes of body talk are changing, so a different kind of environmental unconscious may be coming about, one in which space is reworked, providing new kinds of locational fantasies and fears, new ambulatory tropisms and tendencies.

Another way in which qualculative developments might make themselves known is through the rise of new forms of intuition (Myers 2002). Such forms of rapid reasoning might be expected to alter as the new qualculative background makes itself felt, especially by enhancing intuitive expertise and teaching new forms of intuition. For example, it has been hypothesized that our ability to frame and read 'thin slices' of behaviour may have increased because we live in a world where all kinds of mechanical additions demand (and reveal) fast responses (Thrift 2004d). Again, there is a challenge to think about new kinds of locational knowledge and how they sink into and condition normal social interchange.

In the final major part of this chapter, though, I want to try to work through what the experience of a qualculative world might be in a somewhat more systematic fashion. I can only begin this task, however, not least because few accounts have tended to work out in any detail what the space-time signatures of a lifeworld that was heavily calculated (or, as I would have it, qualculated) would look like, even though it could be argued that this is the world that we are increasingly living in, without resorting to the crudest kinds of technological determinism. Often, it is assumed that such worlds would somehow be less human because more 'rational' and 'flowsy'. But perhaps something quite different would happen: new qualities might become possible which assumed this enhanced calculativity as a space-time background through an array of new co-ordinate systems, different kinds of metric and new cardinal points, backed up by much enhanced memory and a certain limited predictive capacity. This background would enable new kinds of movement to occur, against which all kinds of experiments in perception might become possible, which might in turn engender new senses, new intelligences of the world, and new forms of 'human'. Necessarily, at this point, I must move to the very limits of conjecture, and perhaps beyond them. But, in order to get some form of grip on these issues this seems to me to be a worthwhile risk to take.

Perhaps it is possible to get at least some sense of the new sensorium that might become possible by considering the reworking of space and time that is being written into the human body and language which, in turn, is instilling a different sense of how things turn up. For what is clear straightaway is that there are and have been considerable shifts in the way in which space and time have been perceived, shifts which work at a very basic level and which call to the body in different ways. I want to suggest just a few of these, each of them related to the others. The first is the body itself. I will argue that the hand is changing its expectations. Second, the address. I will argue that, because things are now instantly locatable, space is changing its character. Third, language. I will argue that the basic cardinals of what we regard as space are subsequently shifting. In other words, I want to argue that we are increasingly a part of a 'movement-space' which is relative rather than absolute – but which, as I have already pointed out, relies on an absolute space for its existence – in which 'matter or mind, reality has appeared to us as a perpetual becoming. It makes itself or it unmakes itself but it is never something made' (Bergson 1998 [1911]: 272). This making has retreated into the background from where it directs more and more operations. We sense it as a different kind of awareness of the world, one in which space itself seems to perform.

Let me begin with the body. It has become increasingly apparent that to understand the body it is vital to take in the world in which the body finds itself. For example, recent research shows that the body schema extends well beyond the body's apparent physical limit, taking in items like the body's shadow as explicit means of gauging where the body is and how it is moving in relation to other objects. Certain parts of the body are particularly important in acting as bridges to the world and here I concentrate on one of the most important of these – the hand. The sensory system of the hand is complex and capable of exquisite fine-tuning. It is not just an 'external' organ: it is so vital to human evolution that it seems quite likely that parts of the brain have developed in order to cope with its complexities rather than vice versa, thereby providing a sense of the world deep in the supposedly enclosed human body as new kinds of distance have opened up between organism and environment which need to be crossed. A convincing case can be made that the development of the hand has driven human intelligence by being the first, 'ur-tool' (Tallis 2003), a tool able to precisely localize objects in space and apply muscular force to them (Vogel 2001), thereby also, incidentally, giving the body a much greater sense of its own self and existence by labelling actions as 'mine'.[10]

The hand is particularly important in providing not just active manipulation of the world but also a sense of touch (Field 2001). As Tallis puts it:

> In the cerebral cortex, different components of touch are integrated into more complex tactile awareness. The movement of the fingers over a surface creates a sense of texture. The overall pressure detected by a large number of displaced sensory endings gives an idea of weight and size. Active manipulation gives a sense of the malleability of the object. The combination of weight and size (and inferred from that, density) of the texture, gives a notion of the material of which the item is made and, indeed, its general identity. This is . . . far from dim groping: it is a highly cerebral matter, as is demonstrated by the huge expansion of the cortical representation of the relevant fingers in individuals who use their hands for skilled tasks – violinists, Braille readers.
>
> (Tallis 2003: 29–30)

I want to argue that in a qualculative world the hand will take on some different styles of haptic inquiry: it will reach out and touch in different ways. In particular, the sense of touch will be redefined in three ways as haptic engineering moves beyond today's primitive keyboard, keypad, mouse and data glove. First, from being conceived as a heavily localized sensation, touch will increasingly be thought of as a sense that can stretch over large spaces, as a 'being of movement from here to there, from one to the other' (Virilio 1997: 24). In addition, through multilinking, more than one site will be able to be touched at a time (Goon 2003). Second, entities that are able to be touched will correspondingly expand; all manner of entities will be produced with an expanded sensory range. Third, paramount amongst these newly touchable entities will be data of various kinds which, through haptic engineering, will take on new kinds of presence in the world as something closer to what we conventionally regard as 'physical' objects. In other words, the hand will extend, be able to touch more entities and will encounter entities which are more 'touchable'. The set of experiences gathered under 'touch' will therefore become a more important sense, taking in and naming experiences which heretofore have not been considered as tactile and generating haptic experiences which have hitherto been unknown. Equally, we might expect that descriptions of tactile sensations like 'soft', 'hard', 'rub', 'stroke' and 'caress', 'hold', 'shove', 'push', 'grasp', 'hit', 'strike' and 'seize' will change their meanings. Whether, as in the Anlo world that Geurts studied, a distinctive sense called touch will no longer be encountered as the spectrum of haptic experiences expands is a moot point.[11]

Let me move now to the nature of the co-ordinate system itself. The environment can be laid out in a large number of ways. But what seems certain is that, increasingly, the world will come loaded up with addresses. It will become normal to know where one is at any point, a mechanically induced version of the sense of direction which is similar to that of the cultures that have this facility that were discussed in the previous section. As importantly, the ability to tag addresses to moving objects, which started with barcodes and credit cards and is now expanding and becoming more information-rich with the rapidly expanding use of radio frequency identifier chips, will mean that over a grid of fixed co-ordinates will be laid a series of moving addresses specific to particular entities. This move is already having consequences which call up an analogy with the kinematics of the reach of the hand. Hands which are reaching out will hover over a moving set of co-ordinates (which Tallis (2003) likens to a flickering flame rather than a single spot), thereby maximizing degrees of freedom until the last possible moment. Similarly, it is possible to see a new locational background appearing in which most of the difficulties of spatial co-ordination will be solved in the same way, by large numbers of calculations, many of which will be just-in-time. In turn, this should allow new kinds of exploration which we are only just beginning to show up (see Parks 2003).

Then, finally, I want to consider the matter of language. Here I want to consider some findings from the anthropology of cognition. For what this anthropology has shown is that thinking about space can vary quite radically from culture to culture, down to and including the most basic frames of reference such as what counts as the characteristic shape of an object, sense of direction, the spatial relation of bodies as they are pointed to, and the sense of where a body is in its relation to larger surroundings. In turn, these frames of reference define basic spatial competences such as shape recognition, navigation, sense of where parts of the body are, and control of the arm and hand in reaching for something, competences which are regarded as central to most cultures, to the point where not having one of them can be regarded as a sign of madness. Perhaps the most studied of these frames of reference and their corresponding competences is the ability to specify where things are and wayfind by using various co-ordinate systems. This is convenient since I wish to argue that it is these co-ordinate systems which are most being changed by the numbered materiality in which we now live. It is also convenient because it is clear that cultures vary, and sometimes vary quite radically, in the way that they name and operate cognitively on space in terms of memory, inference, navigation, gesture, and so on. For example, Levinson (2003) shows that a number of languages do not operate with the kind of egocentric co-ordinate system which is implied by the English expression 'left of'. In one Mayan area of Mexico there is an absolute co-ordinate system consisting of 'uphill', 'downhill' and 'across' but although 'there are body-part terms for left and right hands and a few speakers find it acceptable to talk about, for example, left and right breasts during breast-feeding . . . there is certainly no way to use these terms to indicate left and right visual fields' (Levinson 2003: 149).

As another example, Levinson shows that a number of cultures have what might be considered an uncanny sense of direction in Western eyes, seemingly having something like a mental compass, a learned ability to maintain fixed bearings at all times arising out of the co-production of brain and gesture, which enables them to point to known locations with very high levels of accuracy.

As one more example, Levinson shows that a number of cultures have massively extended vocabularies for describing spatial configuration, in part apparently developed out of a plethora of material possessions which require fine description (e.g. types of vessel). Other cultures do not, at least in part because they have few material possessions, but rely on intimate descriptions of the environment instead which use other spatial anchors (e.g. place names, topological and topographical correlates).

This discussion makes it possible to speculate about how vocabularies for describing spatial configuration will change in a qualculated world in which much greater cognitive assistance is routinely available. First, sense of direction will become a given. It will no longer be something that has to be considered. Second, and similarly, wayfinding will become a much easier matter, with much of the effort of search moving into the background.[12] Third, space will increasingly be perceived as relative, strengthening Poincaré's dictum that 'absolute space is nonsense, and it is necessary for us to begin by referring space to a series of axes invariably bound to the body' (cited in Levinson 2003: 9) but this will be a normal means of perception because an absolute space has been established which allows how bodies are moving in relation to one another to be established. It may be that egocentric co-ordinate systems will be strengthened, precisely because that movement is able to be more fully registered. Finally, vocabularies of spatial configuration will multiply. The critical importance of spatial distribution in flow architectures will produce an extended spatial vocabulary which will provide new opportunities for thinking the world, opportunities which will themselves be constitutive of that world. We can already see something of this going on in the practical aesthetics of fields like architecture, performance and film where an emphasis on flow and plasticity has been able to arise out of the numerical weave occasioned by the use of common software packages which, in a certain sense, allow objects to remain in the process of conception and outwith standard perspectival norms (Vidler 2000: 253–254).

Conclusions

What I have tried to do in this chapter is to begin the work of trying to demonstrate how exactly a qualculated world will show up, and especially the kinds of movement awareness/cognitive assistance that will be promoted by it. Such a world assumes a certain kind of relative space (though, as I have underlined, riding on the back of the most absolute of absolute spaces) and the migration of a good many spatial skills and competences into the technical background where they are neither seen nor heard but still exert an influence through the agency of software and other recursive entities, calculating each move down to the last instant, so to speak.

What I have been particularly intent on showing is that the realm of ideas exists within a shifting framework which dictates not just how ideas will show up but also a good part of their content. None of this is meant to suggest that ideas cannot have emergent properties and cannot throw themselves forward into new domains. But it is to suggest that it would be foolish to ignore the presuppositions imposed by the generally unremarked backgrounds I have tried to set out here.

Throughout the chapter, I have been acutely aware that I am walking a tightrope between the kind of techno-hyperbole which is all too common in this area of work and my desire to start thinking about how the background hum of thinking will be changed by developments like flow architectures. I am sure that I have overbalanced several times but it seems to me that it is only through instigating this kind of sometimes fevered projection and coupling it with an attention to the basic basics of everyday life that it is possible to obtain some measure of what is going on and what is falling away as new kinds of subjectivity are forced into existence by spaces and times that, through the power of what I have called qualculation, exceed and transform existing spaces and times as they apply a new set of arts of distribution which bring with them new problems and new solutions (Batchen 2001). This is surely how the history of the present will have to be written.

Part II

6   Afterwords

Positivism holds – and this is its essence – that what we can speak about is all that matters in life. Whereas Wittgenstein passionately believes that all that really matters in human life is what, in his view, we must be silent about. . . . When he nevertheless takes immense pains to delimit the unimportant [that is, the scope and limits of ordinary language], it is not the coastline of the island which he is bent on surveying with such meticulous accuracy, but the boundary of the ocean.

(Englemann 1967: 97)[1]

Why does many a man write? Because he does not possess enough character not to write.

(Kraus 1966: 124, cited in Janik and Toulmin 1973: 201)

Post-script

This chapter is connected with a particular event, the death of my father. I feel a need to write the event and yet, as I make clear in this chapter, I am not at all sure that this is what I want to do. In a sense, I believe that this writing down is a part of the problem. I do not want to take over my father's being by making him into fodder for yet more interpretation, by colonizing his traces.

Why? Because my father was a good man who did a lot of good; more than most, I suspect. Almost nothing that he ever did was written down and whereas I once would have seen this as a problem I now think that putting his life in order through text, in order to rescue him from the enormous condescension of posterity, may, in certain senses, be just another form of condescension. I am not sure, in other words, that he needs writing down, or, put in another way, we need a form of writing that can disclose and value his legacy – the somatic currency of body stances he passed on, the small sayings and large generosities, and, in general, his stance to the world – in such a way as to make it less important for him to be written.

As I work up a non-representationalist style of work that I hope can describe and value this legacy, this thought lies constantly at the back of my mind. 'Sometimes, we go into a man's study and find his books and papers all over the place, and say without hesitation: "What a mess! we really must clear this room up". Yet, at other times, we may go into a room which looks very like the first;

but after looking around we decide that we must leave it just as it is, recognising that, in this case, even the dust has its place' (Wittgenstein, cited in Janik and Toulmin 1973: 207).

Ghosts

How, then, might we find a space for my father? This is the question I want to ask in this chapter. But to ask it requires a consideration of the politics of what Phelan (1993) calls the 'unmarked', that, is, an attempt to find, value, and retain what is not marked as 'here', yet palpably still reverberates; invisible dust still singing, still dancing. Phelan approaches this question of disappearance through a psychoanalytical perspective.[2] As will become clear, my approach is a rather different one, based upon valuing practices in and for themselves. But I believe that we are searching for the Sonic. As she puts it 'by locating the subject in what cannot be reproduced within the ideology of the visible, I am attempting to revalue a belief in subjectivity and identity which is not visibly representable' (Phelan 1993: 152).

Champagne without fizz

One of the ways in which I have tried to understand the world in which my father lived and, I believe, still has agency is through actor-network (or actant-rhizome) theory. My project has many affinities with actor-network theory, as will become clear in this chapter (see Thrift 1996).[3] Most especially I like its emphasis on the agency (or, rather, actancy) of objects and the rhizomatic multiplicity of space-times formed and maintained by them. Again, I like actor-network theory's emphasis on invention, rather than reflection; 'ANT [actor-network theory] keeps adding to the world and its selection principle is no longer whether there is a link between account and reality – this dual illusion has been dissolved away – but whether or not one travels' (Latour 1997: 178). And I like the corresponding sense of a distributed and always provisional personhood that arises from actor-network theory; an 'envelope' of sideways movements that never add up but arise out of performances whose competence is deduced after the event and so become a part of an institution. However, I also find that, for my purposes, actor-network theory poses some quite severe problems: in certain ways this chapter can be seen both as an elaboration of these problems and as a tentative resolution.

To begin with, for all its commitment to the 'particularities of sites, the unpredictability of circumstances, the uneven patterns of the landscape and the hazardous nature of becoming' (Henalf 1997: 72), there is a sense in which actor-network theory is much more able to describe steely accumulation than lightning strikes, sustained longings and strategies rather than the sharp movements that may also pierce our dreams. Actor-network theory is good at describing certain intermediated kinds of effectivity, but, even though fleet Hermes is one of its avatars, dies a little when confronted with the flash of the unexpected and the unrequited. Then, and I think this problem arises out of the first, actor-network theory still has only an attenuated notion of the event, of the fleeting contexts and predicaments which produce potential. Though in recent years more and more attention has been paid to the event in actor-network theory (see, for example, Law 1998), the fact is that the troubling impasses and breakthroughs, the trajectories and intensities of events 'carried in by different voyagers and beings in becoming' (Deleuze 1997a: 66) are too often caught up and neutralized.

I think these two problems directly lead to a third one. In their surely correct insistence that action is a property of the whole association, actor-network theorists tend to recoil with horror from any accusation of humanism. Quite rightly, they fear the taint of a centred human subject establishing an exact dominion over all. But the result of their fear is that actor-network theory has tended to neglect specifically human capacities of expression, powers of invention, of fabulation, which cannot be simply gainsaid, in favour of a kind of flattened cohabitation of all things.[4] But human expressive powers seem especially important in understanding what is possible to associate, in particular the power of imagination, 'the capacity to posit that which is not, to see in something that which is not there' (Castoriadis 1997: 151), which is the fount of so many non-preexistent relations. Imagination might be thought of as having a number of components: the defunctionalization of physical processes as they relate to biological being, the domination of 'representational' pleasure over organ pleasure, and the defunctionalization and autonomization of affect and desire (Castoriadis 1997). Though these processes are ineluctably linked to the object world, they cannot be reduced to it. Let me give just one example. Gell writes of 'abduction', the mode of inference brought to bear on objects, 'the tentative and hazardous tracing of signification rules which allow the sign to acquire its meaning. . . . [It] occurs with those natural signs which the Stoics call indicative and which are thought to be signs, yet without knowing what they signify' (Eco 1989: 40). As Gell notes:

> The usefulness of the concept of abduction is that it designates a class of semiotic inferences which are, by definition, wholly distinct from the semiotic inferences we bring to bear on the understanding of language, whose internal understanding is a matter of observing semiotic conventions, not entertaining hypotheses derived ad hoc from the case under consideration [Eco, 1989, page 40]. Abduction, though a semiotic concept (actually it belongs to logic rather than semiotics) is useful in that it functions to set limits to linguistic semiosis proper, so that we cease to be tempted to apply linguistic models where they do not apply, while remaining free to posit inferences of a non-linguistic kind.[5]

(Gell 1998: 14–15)

For me, these three all-but-missing elements of actor-network theory have forced me to become interested in how events are shaped as they happen, with how we can understand, if you like, what the possible can do with the possible. This means moving away from the largely genetic outlook of the social sciences, and equally from accounts which assume that a developmental account tells all, towards a'history of the present' (Foucault 1986) in ways only now being dreamed of.

> In philosophy the genetic fallacy is the mistake of allowing the question 'How come?' to preempt the question 'What?' It is the mistake of thinking that the power of knowledge can be justified, explained away, or nullified by an account of its history. For example, a scientist might justify the predictive power of a conclusion by giving an account of the rigorous procedures which led to the conclusion. A social constructionist might call an argument into question because it is the product of particular historical, or cultural circumstances that could have been otherwise. . . . Both arguments commit the genetic fallacy, the fallacy of forgetting that the primary value or meaning of an event has no necessary connection with its genesis in history or its causal explanation.
>
> (Bradley 1998: 71–72)

What gets mislaid in the genetic outlook, in other words, is 'any sense of the many difficulties inherent in *understanding the present in its own right*' (Bradley 1998: 72, my emphasis).

How might we start to understand what is carried in and carried away by different voyagers and beings in becoming? How might we begin to tack away from the vapid certainties of so much current cultural work? In previous books and papers (Thrift 1996, 1997, 1998) I have pointed to the uses of an alternative 'non-representational' style of work. Note that I use the word 'style' deliberately: this is not a new theoretical edifice that is being constructed, but a means of valuing and working with everyday practical activities as they occur. It follows that this style of work is both anti-cognitivist and, by extension, anti-elitist since it is trying to counter the still-prevalent tendency to consider life from the point of view of individual agents who generate action by instead weaving a poetic of the common practices and skills which produce people, selves, and worlds. But 'how hard I find it to see what is right in front of my eyes' (Wittgenstein 1980: 39). For to see what is in front of our eyes requires thinking – and thinking about thinking – in different ways.

Drawing on a number of traditions of work, I will therefore, in the first part of the chapter, offer an account of a style of thinking which I call 'non-representationalist'. I will argue that this style of thinking offers an engaged account of the world which has inevitable practical consequences. Then, in the second part of the chapter, I will argue that the protagonists of this approach all tend to lay stress on 'performance' but have insufficiently investigated what this usage might entail. I will try to correct this imbalance by considering some lessons drawn from the performing arts. In the third part of the chapter I then turn to a particular example of a performing art (dance) as an illustration.

So, throughout the chapter, the emphasis will be on activating powers of invention and, especially, the invention of new means of occupying, usurping, and producing spaces and times. In particular, this emphasis on active contrivance must mean paying attention to the potential of stylistic free variation (Massumi 1997a) and it is to this topic that I therefore turn first.

The push: new styles of thought

> Style . . . is not the dress of thought, but part of its essence.
>
> (Dening 1996: 116)

Too much of social and cultural theory assumes the event, too much of social and cultural theory is fundamentally unprocessual (Massumi 1997a). Non-representational theory aims to compensate for this deficit through the serious consideration of what I call the push that keeps the world rolling over; the energy that fuels change; the work of transformation which ensures that 'the reproduction of the other as the same is not assured' (Phelan 1993: 3). How can we approach the push? I want to start by outlining the 'non-epistemic ontology-activity' (Newman and Holzman 1997: 11) that underlines non-representational theory. As I have already explained elsewhere (see Thrift 1996, 1997, 1998), non-representational theory is an approach to understanding the world in terms of effectivity rather than representation; not the what but the how (Kemp 1996). In order to begin the task of understanding, non-representational theory draws on three traditions of work which, though they are very different in certain respects, share this common concern.

The first is recent developments in feminist theory, and most especially the more recent work of writers such as Bordo, Butler, Grosz, and Threadgold on a rhetorical or performative philosophy, as well as the later writings of Irigaray on space. The second tradition is distributed theories of practices. Taking its cue from writers such as Wittgenstein and Heidegger, Bourdieu and de Certeau, this kind of work reaches all the way from 'discursive' social psychology to human geography. A recent development has been the greater emphasis on spatial distribution imported from actor-network theory. Then, there is a tradition which has fixed on biology for both inspiration and illustration. Drawing on writers as diverse as Von Uexküll, Bateson, and Canguilhem, as well as Heidegger's later work, this tradition has been given renewed impetus by the current strength of the sciences of life as represented by, for example, genetics. Thus, there is now a growing school of 'biological philosophy' to which writers such as Deleuze and Serres might be said to belong (see Ansell Pearson 1997) as well as anthropological work on biosciences as represented by, for example, Rabinow's recent excursions (Rabinow 1995, 1996). Needless to say, each of these three traditions can draw strength from the others.

How can this style of work be summarized? In embryo, it can be said to depend upon an argument which relies on dispelling analogical imaginings of a diagnostic kind, so beloved of certain kinds of intellectuals, in favour of the direct significances of practices. Most importantly, this means that the world is a making (Threadgold 1997): it is processual; it is in action; it is 'all that is present and moving'

(R. Williams 1972: 128). There is no last word, only infinite becoming and constant reactivation.

The surprisingness of the event

But these are little more than a string of slogans. So what can be said in more detail? To begin with, I want to argue that this is a world bowling along, in which decisions have to be made for the moment, by the moment.[6] This is a momentary world. It follows that this is a world which must be acted into. This is not a contemplative world (though some of its practices perhaps more than in past times value contemplative aspects). And as a world which is being acted into it produces effects that must then be accounted for in a never-ending chain of circumstances.

The corollary of such a depiction is that this is a world which is howling into the unknown. But it is not, therefore, a world of despair. As Bernstein (1994) and Morson (1994) make clear, a world which is not 'foreshadowed' (that is, in which the consequences of actions are known and time is therefore closed) is a world of radical possibility, in which each actual event lies amidst many alternatives, in which possibilities exceed actualities. There is, in other words, what Bernstein and Morson call a 'sideshadowed' middle 'realm' of unactualized possibles

> that could have happened even if they did not. Things could have been different from the way they were, there were real alternatives to the present we know, and the future admits of various paths. By focusing on the middle realm of possibility, by exploring its relation to actual events, and by attending to the fact that things could have been different, sideshadowing deepens our sense of the openness of time.
>
> (Morson 1994: 6)

Or, to put it another way:

> in Bakhtin's terms, we might say that events must have eventness, they must not be the utterly predictable outcome of earlier events, but must somehow have something else to them, some 'surplus' that endows them with 'surprisingness'. Otherwise people are turned into 'piano keys or organ stops' as the underground man writes.
>
> (Morson 1994: 9)

In other words, the event can be connected to potential, possibility, experimentation. This is not, however, to proffer a naive vitalism. The potential of events is always constrained. Events must take place within networks of power which have been constructed precisely in order to ensure iterability. But what is being claimed is that the event does not end with these bare facts. The capacity to surprise may be latent, but it is always present because 'in a becoming, one term does not become another, rather, each term encounters the other and the becoming is something between the two, outside the two' (D.W. Smith 1997: xxx).[7]

But if something exceeds the event, what is it? I want to argue that this excess is an expressive 'virtual' dimension which can be summarized as the generation of signs grasped in practice. I want to understand signs in a quasi-Deleuzian way. That is, I want to depart from a consideration of the sign as a result of the arbitrary relation between the signifier and the signified. Instead:

> a sign comes into being when thought is thrown into crisis because the reassuring world of representation has broken down. The signifier and the signified constitute a 'dreary world', whereas signs indicate the deterritorial-isation and reterritorialisation of thought. The sign itself entails heterogeneity in three ways: it 'flashes' between the two realities of the sign itself and the object which carries it; the sign also 'envelops' another object within the object that bears it; and the sign does not produce resemblance in someone per-ceiving the sign, but rather perception as a sort of aparallel evolution. Deleuze uses as an example the process of learning to swim: the movement of the swimmer does not resemble that of the wave, in particular, the movements of the swimming instructor which we reproduce on the sand bear no relation to the movements of the wave, which we learn to deal with only by grasping the former in practice as signs [. . .] Our only teachers are those who tell us 'do with me', and are able to emit signs to be developed in heterogeneity rather than propose gestures for us to reproduce (Deleuze 1994: 23). The sign is an expression of the way in which order has been created rather than discovered.
>
> (Marks 1998: 37)

In order words, 'the sign is an encounter rather than an act of recognition. and it can only be felt or sensed: signs act directly on the nervous system' (Marks 1998: 38).

In turn, this emphasis on the generation of signs leads us to the three chief elements of signification which together form, to borrow a phrase from Bateson, an ecology of mind or consciousness. The first of these elements is embodiment. But quite crucially, this is not the body considered as individual being, but embodi-ment as a field of flesh in which 'the body believes in what it plays at: it weeps if it mimes grief. It does not represent what it performs, it does not memorise the past, it enacts the past, bringing it back to life' (Bourdieu 1991: 23).

In such a conception, embodiment is about the content of social worlds and 'not just those which are material and extant but those which are ephemeral and possible' (Radley 1996: 560). Embodiment, then, concerns 'what is made possible because we are embodied – in brief what we can show about ourselves and our situation'(Radley 1996: 561) because

> embodiment involves a capacity to take up and to transform features of the mundane world in order to portray a 'way of being', an outlook, a style of life that shows itself in what it is. Like the painted pictures in a frame, it has self referential qualities that allude to something not easily specified. This is the

totality . . . which cannot be isolated in a particular movement or word because it transcends these when taken as a fragment of the mundane (e.g. the physical body). At the same time, it does not exist beyond the particulars of the act because it is only through the specific engagements of embodied people together that such symbolic realms are made to appear.

(Radley 1996: 569, emphasis in the original)

This conception of embodiment is one, in other words, in which groups of actors can conjure up virtual 'as-if' worlds, by delineating a space-time in which something significant is to occur and, at the same time, 'the actors are themselves reconfigured in the light of the possibilities that flow from them' (Radley 1996: 570). Thus embodiment both signals beyond the present and reworks the present by exemplifying a totality rather than exactly specifying a class or category.[8] In evoking another bounded world, the actors conjure powers and meanings that they despair of, which yet appear to derive from a location other than their 'ordinary' selves (this is the sense, when watching a dramatic scene, that the actors are invigorated by passions or can draw upon powers that have their source beyond the immediate setting or their physical capacities).

What the actors draw attention to is an ongoing rearrangement of objects and symbols within a field involving the body. An attempt to convey the idea has been set out previously in terms of the concepts of meta-communication (Bateson 1973) and framing (Goffman 1974). However, these concepts do not emphasize sufficiently the crucial point that the ground of the display indicates itself; it is self-referential. It is embodied beings who, by virtue (not by means) of their physical presence, can portray transmutations of the 'here and now' which delineate the immediate as a fragment of some different, or new, totality of meaning. This underlines the point made by Merleau-Ponty (1962) that the 'immediate movement is transcended, or achieves significance, not in spite of our physical form, but because of it' (Radley 1996: 566). Woven into this conception of embodiment is a strong role for affect. Affect is not simply emotion, nor is it reducible to the affections or perceptions of an individual subject. 'Percepts are not perceptions, they are packets of sensations and relations that outlive those who experience them. Affects are not feelings, they are becomings that go beyond those who live through them (they become other)' (Deleuze 1995: 137).

But we can 'dumb down' this notion and think of emotions as coursing through the force fields of flesh and other objects, producing a continually changing distribution of intensities which prefigure encounters, which set up encounters, and which have to be worked on in these encounters (Gil 1998)? As Massumi puts it:

affect is synaesthetic, implying a participation of the senses in each other: the measurement of a living thing's potential interaction is its ability to transform the effects of one sensory mode into those of another. . . . Affects are virtual synaesthetic perspectives anchored in (functionally limited by) the actually existing particular things that embody them. The autonomy of affect is its participation in the virtual. Its autonomy is its openness. Affect is autonomous to the degree to which it escapes confinement in the particular body whose vitality, or potential for interaction, it is. Formed, qualified, situated perceptions and cognition's fulfilling functions of actual connection or blockage are the capture and closure of affect. Emotion is the interest's (most contracted) expression of that capture – and of the fact that something has always and again escaped. Something remains unactualised, inseparable from but unassimilable to any particular, functionally anchored perspective. That is why all emotion is more or less disorienting, and why it is classically described as being outside of oneself, at the very point at which one is most intimately and unshareably in contact with oneself and one's vitality. Actually existing, structured things live in and through that which escapes them. Their autonomy is the autonomy of affect.

(Massumi 1997b: 228)

It follows that:

The escape of affect cannot but be perceived, alongside the perceptions that are its capture. This side-perception may be punctual, localised in an event (such as the sudden realisation that happiness and sadness are something besides what they are). When it is punctual, it is usually described in negative terms, typically as a form of shock. . . . But it is also continuous, like a background perception that accompanies every event, however quotidian.

Simondon notes the connection between self-reflection and affect. He even extends the capacity for self-reflection to all living things although it is hard to see why his own analysis does not constrain him to extend it to all things.

(Massumi 1996: 229)

And this latter point is important, for it leads to the second element of signification, the world of other things, things which have their own resonances, so ably captured by actor-network theory. These resonances are of a number of kinds. To begin with, thought is bound up with things: it is through things that we think. Then, things act back. Latour's famous example of the automatic door closer and the weighted hotel key are both just the simplest of the means by which bodies are guided along particular paths by things.

After all, why is expression not available to things? There are affects of things, the 'edge', this 'blade' or rather the 'point' of Jack the Ripper's knife is no less an affect than the fear which overcomes his features and the resignation which finally seizes hold of the whole of his face. The Stoics showed that things themselves are borne of ideal events which did not exactly coincide with their properties, their actions and reaction.

(Deleuze 1986: 97)

And, of course, encounters in which other things are a part of the interruption are increasing in importance and, as a result, the nature of other things has become increasingly active, providing a further decentring of the 'human' subject and increasing the difficulty of conceiving of 'human' 'agency' at all. And, as the 'ecology of mind' (Bateson 1973) becomes ever richer as intermediaries and mediaries multiply, so the 'human' 'subject' migrates on to many more planes and is mixed with other 'subjects' in increasingly polymorphous combinations. 'The body is nourished by technology in the same way that it is nourished by chemical products' (Marks 1998: 48).

In turn, such thoughts allow us to more easily conceive of a present-oriented (a 'cartographic') notion of a person. Such a notion is quite different from an archaeological conception of the person, as found in psychoanalysis.

> The latter establishes a profound link between the unconscious and memory: it is a memorial, commemorative, or monumental conception that pertains to persons or objects, the milieus being nothing more than terrains capable of conserving, identifying or authorising them. . . . Maps, on the contrary, are superimposed in such a way that each map finds itself modified in the following map, rather than finding its origin in the preceding one: from one map to the next, is it not a matter of searching for an origin but of evaluating displacements.
>
> (Deleuze 1997a: 63)

Thus persons become, in effect, rather ill-defined constellations rattling around the world which are

> not confined to particular spatio-temporal coordinates, but consist of a spread of biographical events and memories of events, and a dispersed category of material objects, traces, and leavings, which can be attributed to a person and which, in aggregate, testify to agency and patienthood during a biographical career which may, indeed, prolong itself well after biological death. The person is thus understood as the sum total of the indexes which testify, in life and subsequently, to the biographical existence of this or that individual. Personal agency, as inherent in the causal milieu, generates one of these 'distributed objects', that is, all the material differences 'in the way things are' from which some particular agency can be abducted.
>
> (Gell 1998: 222–223)[9]

We now have the tools to turn to the third element of signification: creativity. It is remarkable how little effort has been exerted by academic writers upon precisely the element which they would – presumably – most wish to characterize their work. Yet, it is not that such work has not been attended to or that it has no connections to contemporary thought. For example, the expressivism of Herder, the pragmatism of Peirce[10] and Dewey, and some of Simmel's[11] later thoughts all contain pointers to subsequent work by writers such as Deleuze, Castoriadis, and Joas, who all (in their quite different ways) want to emphasize creativity (Thrift 1999), who all (in their quite different ways) want to privilege the power of the imagination.

In turn, this lack of attention to creativity makes it difficult to understand certain kinds of expressive action. In particular, a whole category of social and cultural action, usually termed play, is unable to be grasped. Play is a process of performative experiment: 'The ongoing, underlying process of off-balancing, loosening, bending, twisting, reconfiguring, and transforming the permeating, eruptive/disruptive energy and mood below, behind and to the side of focused attention' (Schechner 1993: 43) which is brought into focus by body-practices such as dance and which 'encourages the discovery of new configurations and twists of ideas and experience' (Schechner 1993: 42). It is the world of the 'enacted subjunctive' (Sutton-Smith 1997), the world where possibilities are acted out. It is, in other words

> a mode, not a distinctive behavioural category. . . . play is viewed as an attitude or frame that can be adopted towards anything. . . . [It] occurs at a logical level different from that it qualifies. . . . play is functional because it teaches about contexts; it teaches about frames not being at the same level as the acts they contain.
>
> (Schwartzman 1978: 169)

Such meta-communication presupposes fantasy produced through intersubjectivity, and is characterized by quirkiness, redundancy, and oddity. It is, in other words, about producing variation.

Re-timing space and re-spacing time

Another element of the non-representational interpretation of the event is the refiguring of space and time. Given the aforegoing account of signification, what we find is that notions of space and time need to be radically refigured. To begin with, it is clear that there are multiple spaces and times, not one Newtonian grid.

> Time and space are not the Newtonian sensoria in which events occur and planets fall along ellipses. But neither are they forms of our perception, the unreal a prioris that our mind has to use in order to have or accommodate the multiplicity of beings and entities. Far from being primitive terms, they are, on the contrary, consequences of the ways in which both relate to one another. We must therefore link our meditation on time to a third tradition, the Leibnizian, which considers space and time as expressing some relation between the entities themselves. But instead of a single space-time, we will generate as many spaces and times as there are types of relations. Thus, progressing along jungle trails will not produce the same space-times as moving along [modern transport] networks . . .

> The difference between [these] trips . . . comes from the number of others
> one has to take into account, and from the nature of these others. Are they
> well-aligned intermediaries making no fuss and no history, and thus allowing
> a smooth passage, or full mediators defining paths and fates on their own
> terms?
>
> (Latour 1997: 174–175)

Then, these space-times – which are themselves complex – are in complex, active,
and only partial relation with one another: scattered, haphazard, plural. Thus, as
Serres outlines it:

> rationality and the real itself are sporadic. They are distributed, not in geo-
> metrically regular patterns, but as archipelagos in a turbulent, disordered sea.
> For the Serres of *L'Interférence*, there is no ruling science, and a pluralistic
> epistemology is urgently required. But it is not only epistemology that must
> be pluralised. Aesthetics must become polymorphic, too, an aesthetics of
> multiple proliferations of spaces. It must turn away from laws and regularities
> to exchanges and interferences, connections and disconnections between
> spaces.
>
> (Gibson 1996: 13)

So, it follows that understanding space-times requires new 'geometric'
metaphors that are able to describe them in their own- heterogeneous – terms and
can take full account of the number and nature of other actual and possible space-
times.

In other words, we need to look for different kinds of topologies based on
communication and connectedness across divides between exclusive and disparate
disparities. This is a *topologie sauvage* which cannot be fixed and frozen, but can
only keep on making encounters: 'a succession of spatial accidents, bifurcations,
catastrophes, loops, crossroads between various spaces that have no common
measure and no boundaries in common' (Gibson 1996: 17), a world of continual
questioning.

In turn, the search for different topologies must produce many new narrative
styles, 'a diversification of models corresponding, not only to the actual absence
of technical variants, but also to the multiplicity of resources made possible by the
proliferation of resources' (Gibson 1996: 15). What this diversification might
then do is to restore a sense of the work and the effort and the force that goes
into producing and linking space-times, which would, precisely, restore Latour's
variegated sense of relation in tension.

But we cannot stop here. For as practice always generates the ghostly correlates
of unactualised possibles, so space-times are always accompanied by their
phantoms, which rehearse 'the active presence of absent things' (Valéry, cited in
Dening 1996: 116), and for at least four reasons. First, because nearly all spaces
bear the freight of their past. As Calvino (1979: 13) puts it in his description of
the City of Zaira, 'The city does not tell its past, but contains it like the lines
of a hand, written in the corners of the streets, the antennae of the lighting rods,

the places of the flags, every segment marked in turn with scratches, indentations, scrolls.'

Second, because as many space-times have become increasingly strung out across the globe, so the sense of the faraway as near has been able to become increasingly prevalent. Phantoms are often, therefore, figures of technological transmigration and metamorphosis (Bayer 1998) which stand for the clandestine spirit of a larger network of practices. Third, because space-times – to return to a point made earlier in the chapter – generate many of the unactualized possibles without which they cannot be sensed and described. The distribution of space-times is complex and the response to this complexity is not theoretical but practical: different things need to be tried out, opened up, which can leave their trace even when they fail. Space-times very often provide the 'stutter' in social relations, the jolt which arises from new encounters, new connections, new ways of proceeding. Then, last, space-times are nearly always approximate and these approximations, close-to but not-quites, can linger as all sorts of clues to a story that never quite happened: the body used for another purpose, the aspect of a bodily stance that looks increasingly at odds with the world, and so on.

So it is no surprise that 'that which appears to be not there is often a steely presence, acting on and often meddling with taken-for-granted realities, the ghost is just the sign, or the empirical evidence if you like, that tells you a haunting is taking place' (Gordon 1997: 8). Or as Gordon (1997: 7) puts it in another way, haunting is 'a paradigmatic way in which life is more complicated than those of us who study it have usually granted'.[12] Haunting is where it's at which is where it's not. Haunting is the place that never is but always was and will be.

Practical knowing

I hope I have already hinted, by using the term 'style', that in non-representational theory what counts as knowledge must take on a radically different sense. It becomes something tentative, something which no longer exhibits an epistemo-logical bias but is a practice and is a part of practice. Most of the writers currently attempting to grapple with this sense of theory have based their thoughts on the work of writers such as Vygotsky and Wittgenstein. Roughly speaking, current non-representationalist writers want to lay epistemology to one side.

> At their most extreme, they might ask 'Can we really give up knowing?' And, you may reasonably (and philosophically) ask 'How would we know?' This may appear to be still another quasi-self-referential paradox. But it isn't for there is an answer – a non-paradoxical answer – to the question 'How would we know?' We wouldn't. Yet the force of modern epistemology is so great that many find it almost inconceivable to accept such an answer. If something is, it must be at least possible to know that it is? This, of course is the voice of epistemological modernism speaking. It is the typical dualistic reduction of ontology to epistemology – the insistence of science and modernism that everything (worthy or not worthy of a name or a description) must be knowable. But if a challenge to that claim is successful, it will still not

be known. . . . It will 'merely' be performed. Still the question 'Can we give up knowing?' remains. This question *can* be answered, even if we do not know the answer. But in answering (or, at a minimum, exploring) it, we recommend doing so in a way which gives up our deep-rooted modernist need to know that we have done so. Such an exploration entails abandoning not simply the troublesome substantive conceptual elements of epistemology (mind, self, truth, and company) but epistemology itself as a form of life. Consequently, we must substantively eliminate the substantive myths of modernism (amongst them the individuated mind, the individual self, and individual cognitions) only as we deconstructively/ reconstructively (socially activistically) eliminate the mythic ancient (Aristotelian) *forms* of modernism (explaining, describing, interpreting, identifying, and knowing).

(Newman and Holzman 1997: 31, emphasis in the original)

We do this by positing a 'third kind' of knowledge which gives up modern assumptions about knowledge, reality, the orderliness of the world, unreal and underlying appearances, in favour of a new stance towards the world-practical-moral knowledge which argues that the world is constructed through activity, and especially the activity of talk [where 'talk is action, not communication' (Edwards 1995: 585)], which includes the expressive powers of embodiment. Yet how we conduct talk tends to make this kind of knowledge invisible. But this need not be the case, if we acknowledge that talk is responsive and rhetorical, not representational; it is there to do things. In other words, this is to reject the cognitive notion that talk is primarily communication (or rule-governed and concerned with exchanging meanings). Instead talk is conceived of as a 'structure of presuppositions and expectations of a non-cognitive, gestural kind that unfolds in the temporal movement of joint action' (Shotter 1995: 66).

This is not just a restatement of speech-act theory, rather it is an attempt to understand knowing from within a situation, a group, social institution, or society. Rather than knowing-what or knowing-how, it is 'knowledge-in-practice' and 'knowledge held in common with others' (Shotter 1993: 19). At the same time, it is an attempt to initiate, along with Wittgenstein, not new theories but new practices which can make us more attuned to sensing other possibilities.

That is, instead of helping us to 'find' or 'discover' something already existing, but supposedly hidden behind appearances, they help us grasp something new, as yet unseen, that can be sensed in the emerging articulation of the appearances unfolding before our very eyes (or ears). And in these instances, the problems facing us 'are solved not by giving new information, but by arranging what we have always known' (Wittgenstein 1953, No. 109). We find in our current ways of 'going on' with each other (as a social group) possibilities for relating ourselves to each other in new ways, possibilities for new social practices. Thus Wittgenstein's methods 'move' us, professionally, towards a new way of 'looking over' the 'play' of appearances unfolding before us, such that, instead of seeing them as related to each other in terms of certain theoretical assumptions, we see them in terms of the connections and relations they might actually make, the roles they might play in our lives.

(Shotter 1998: 46–47)

And such meditations must lead us on to thinking about thinking itself. In many accounts, such an impulse leads naturally to the work of Deleuze and his systematic realignment of concepts and affects, and to Castoriadis and his emphasis on the radical imaginary (see Thrift 1996). What can be written (and what cannot) about these practices of imagining depends, I believe, upon 'the curious collision of the mystical with the close and commensurate study of active language practices' (Perloff 1996: 182) as is found in much modern 'disclosive' poetry which recognizes that

> the most extraordinary things are also the most everyday; the strangest things are often the most trivial. . . . Once separated from its context . . . once presented in all its triviality i.e. in all that makes it trivial, suffocating, oppressive – the trivial becomes extraordinary, and the habitual becomes 'mythical'.
>
> (Lefebvre 1991: 13)

In turn, this leads to an activist politics of disclosure which attempts to make different things significant and worthy of notice, and most particularly through the practices of historical disclosure which force a change of style. Two kinds of skills are required for historical disclosure. 'First, one has to be able to sense and hold on to disharmonies in one's current disclosive activity; second, one has to be able to change one's disclosive space on the basis of the disharmonious practices' (Spinosa *et al.* 1997). According to Spinosa *et al.* (1997) there are at least three ways that it is possible to change a disclosive space in response to the realization that practices are not in harmony: focusing a dispersed practice (articulation); making what was a marginal practice central (reconfiguration); and adopting and activating a neighbouring practice (cross appropriation). Such changes in practice nearly always come about through involved experimentation rather than deliberative thinking (even though, when, subsequently written about, they are often couched in terms of the deliberative model of going on). Thus, for example, such an approach to politics does not conform to the literal model as it does not see the course of people's lives as determined by private judgements:

> a judgement made in private reflection is a judgement that one is not yet ready to follow. Such a judgement grows out of dispassionate ratiocination – the imagining and sifting of ideas and potential consequences. It may tell one that one should change one's heart, but a reflective judgement does not amount to a change of heart. A separate act of heroic will is then required before one can act. A resolution that emerges through group action, conversely, is precisely one that emerged because one's practices have readied one for it. Liberal life is ultimately made desperately voluntarist by the necessity of taking

action; for which one if one follows the liberal model has not yet developed skills. Fortunately almost no one acts according to the liberal model.

(Spinosa *et al.* 1997: 29)

The virtue of this kind of approach to the practice (and definition) of the political is threefold. First, it recognizes that all kinds of disclosing are going on in the skilled responses to the situations in everyday life: we do not live in an alienated void. Second, it recognizes that all manner of activity can be political; small projects and modest enterprises can produce political outcomes. Third, much of this activity will be the result of skilful coping, of intentions concerning how to respond to the solicitations of a situation; 'that receptivity is what makes skilful behaviour as nuanced and feasible as it is. Skilled politicians respond appropriately to small perturbations that rule-followers miss' (Spinosa *et al.* 1997: 179). Further, political activity nearly always involves changing backgrounds and showing how they can make a change. These changes to backgrounds are, broadly speaking, of two related kinds. There is, to begin with, the skill of forming an association. Then, there is the skill of working on 'one' self through all manner of practices – including writing (see Shusterman 1997; Steedman 1998).[13]

In the social sciences and humanities, many of these thoughts concerning the push have now crystallized around one metaphor, the metaphor of performance. What is interesting about performance as a metaphor is its evolution from the notion of 'life is like theatre' to a notion that 'life is like performance' and the corresponding move from an interest restricted to certain areas of the humanities to a full-blown discipline, complete with its own sources and journals. This evolution might well be seen as a filling-out of the meanings of this metaphor.

Yet the metaphor of performance is, more than most of its kind, a vessel still waiting to be filled. In general, the metaphor refers to, and operates through, the enactment of events with what resources are available in creative, imaginative ways which lay hold of and produce the moment; events are, performed more or less effectively as an infralinguistic transduction (Gil 1998). In other words, life is a constant rehearsal, which allows a faint grip on what is to hand (Dening 1996). But the metaphor is often used in a very loose way which provides a specious dynamism to many accounts, a description masquerading as an exploration, a way of making good a processual deficit. In the next section of the chapter I therefore want to examine the metaphor of performance, and the ways in which it is currently being filled out.

Working mystic: the push of performance

In order to understand some of these issues more concretely, I now want to turn to a set of literatures/practices which have been created by their allegiance to a single metaphor, the metaphor of performance. Performance is, at this moment, one of the most pervasive metaphors in the human sciences – Dolan (1993: 430) has called its wholesale appropriation 'promiscuous' – precisely because it provides a way of understanding meaning as not residing in something but as generated through processes, and which does not therefore assume a realm of representation and a realm of the real. Thus, for example:

> anthropologists interested in cultural performance (religious rituals, political pageants, folk entertainments, living ceremonies, spirit seances, and so on) have moved increasingly away from studying them as systems of representation (symbolic transformations, cultural texts) to looking at them as processes of practice and performance. In part this reflects a growing dissatisfaction with purely symbolic approaches to understanding material like rituals, which seem to be curiously robbed of life and power when distanced in discussions concerned largely with meaning. 'Performance' deals with actions more than text: with habits of the body more than structures of symbols, with illocutionary rather than propositional force, with the social construction of reality rather than its representation.
>
> (Schieffelin 1998: 195)

Of the various usages of the metaphor of performance, four seem particularly germane: in symbolic interactionism, in sociological accounts, in contemporary culture theory, and in the performing arts. Although, for reasons of space, this list omits certain writers – most notably Taussig (1992, 1993, 1997) and his performative recasting of Benjamin – it hopefully provides the bare bones of an account.

Symbolic interactionism

The first of these usages, and perhaps the most often cited, is associated with the work of Goffman and, latterly, the symbolic interactionist school. I will consider only Goffman's well-known dramaturgical frame of reference here but it is a frame of reference which casts a strong shadow over much subsequent work in this area (Burns 1992; Thrift 1996). Goffman's turn to a dramaturgical reading of social behaviour owed much to the work of anthropologists such as Mauss and Turner on ritual, and Burke's 'dramatism' – which characterized social production as drama – as well as, perhaps, his own early background in film.[14] Though in later years Goffman was to distance himself from the elaborated dramaturgical metaphor he employed in *The Presentation of Self in Everyday Life* (1971) (with its first chapter on 'performances') his work continued to be based on two root notions: first, that there has to be an audience to which performances are addressed – and that the part played by audiences is important – and, second, that performances of every kind require a 'back-stage', the time and space which allows preparation of 'procedures, disguises or materials essential to the performance, or for the concealment of aspects of the performance which might either discredit it or be somehow discordant with it' (Burns 1992: 112). The book was much criticized for giving a sense of human social interactions as based in individualistic contrivance, in pretence, even deceit – in other words, for overextending the dramaturgical metaphor. In later works on the fleeting enactments of 'talk'

Goffman attempted to counter these criticisms by, in a sense, arguing the case more strongly. Thus, in *Frame Analysis* (Goffman 1974) there is

> in a way, a reversal of the *theatrum mundi* image around which he constituted *The Presentation of Self* . . . So *Frame Analysis* as a whole, as well as the chapters in it devoted to the analysis of staged and scripted performance, is in a separate world of discourse – something more than a new conceptual framework – from that of *The Presentation of Self*. The distinction between the two books is put quite bluntly. 'All the world is not, of course, a stage', he says in the *The Presentation of Self* (p. 72). On page 124 of *Frame Analysis*, on the other hand, we have 'All the world is like a stage . . . ' We know, of course, that they are different. Life is real, whereas theatre . . . is not.
>
> But how real is the life the ordinary individual experiences, or talks about? The immediate answer is that it is both real and make-believe. Any individual's experience is made up of a great deal of action he is engaged in, or intends, of other people's action which involves him. All this is real enough. 'On the other hand, it is known, although perhaps not sufficiently appreciated, that the individual spends a considerable amount of time bathing his wounds in fantasy, imagining the worst things that might befall him, daydreaming about matters sexual, monetary, and so forth. He also rehearses what he will say when the time comes . . . '. And the time comes very frequently. A great deal of the day, after all, is spent in talk.
>
> (Burns 1992: 313–314)

Sociological accounts

The second usage of the metaphor of performance is in a more straightforwardly sociological account which relies on a wider metaphor of performance which starts to go beyond the dramaturgical metaphor in order to argue that we live in performative times:

> derived from the Greek word for seeing and sight, theatre . . . is a . . . term for a certain kind of special participation in a certain kind of event. Performance, by contrast, though it frequently makes reference to theatricality as the most fecund metaphor for the social dimensions of cultural production, embraces a much wider range of human behaviours.
>
> (Roach 1995: 46)[15]

One such variant of this account argues straightforwardly that performances of all kinds have become a key moment in modern societies. For example, performance is a key to the

> development of the heritage and tourist industries, where costume drama – whether in the form of retro-dressing or the contemporary couture of slick uniforms – is increasingly the norm. It can be detected as easily in the associated industries of catering and travel, where the waiter and the air-host are encouraged to add a flick of performative spice to the fire. It appears in

the retail industries, where the name tag on the check-out person confers an identity which has little to do with individual character, everything to do with a quasi-personalised and dramatised conception of service.

(Kershaw 1994: 166)

In turn, some authors have argued that the metaphor of performance is a key to thinking about new embodiments which add value to market-based encounters; the workplace becomes 'a stage', the service centre is 'theatre', the self is 'performed', various kinds of training such as 'role-play' are used to heighten the effect, and so on. Though such practices are often derided as inauthentic, Crang, writing about tourism, rightly argues that this is too easy a move:

For a start, as an explicit manifestation of a more implicit and complex set of ordering discourses that construct just what social practices it is that managers, consumers and employees expect to constitute tourism work, these (drama-turgical) understandings matter despite their conceptual and empirical confusions. They constitute a way into discursive formations that have shaped the cultural understandings of what tourism as a matter of fact involves. More specifically, through the application of managerial theories, they are a powerful tool in managerial constructions of tourism-related jobs and workplaces. Second, . . . they also provide a complementary route to the application and critique of theories established through other work-based situations, such as deskilling and flexibility. They offer an alternative to shoe-horning tourism employment into conceptual moulds cast elsewhere, and raise the possibility of re-focusing theoretical understandings of paid work more generally. Far from marginalising studies of tourism employment, some of the particular concerns reviewed above may actually destabilise the dormant sense of what is theoretically central and marginal about paid work in contemporary capitalist societies in the first place.

(Crang 1997: 142)

On another sociological account, performance becomes the key to under-standing what is distinctive about contemporary societies:

Simultaneously, the mediatisation of developed societies disperses the theatrical by inserting performance into everyday life – every time we switch into the media we are immediately confronted by a performative world of representational styles – and in the process the ideological functions of performance become ever more diverse and, maybe, diluted. Moreover, the globalisation of communications stages the life of other cultures as increasingly performative, as widening realms of human identity become object to the spectators gaze, and the social and political resonances of particular crises, such as the suffering of starving Somalians or the quasi-invasion of Haiti by the United States, are absorbed by the relentless opacity of the spectacle.

(Kershaw 1994: 133)

For example, Abercrombie and Longhurst (1998) argue that because of the growth and general pervasiveness of the media we now live in a performative world, one which is predicated on the redefinition of what the audience is and what the audience does, what they call a diffused audience; 'in contemporary society everyone becomes an audience all the time' (Abercrombie and Longhurst 1998: 83). So pervasive is performance that it has become both constitutive and a general quality of everyday life, embedded in desires, daydreams, and fantasies.[16]

> So deeply infused into everyday life is performance that we are unaware of it in ourselves or in others. Life is a constant performance; we are audience and performer at the same time; everybody is an audience all the time. Performance is not a discrete event.
>
> (Abercrombie and Longhurst 1998: 73)

The diffused audience arises from the interaction of two processes, both of which are modern:

> On the one hand, there is the construction of the world as spectacle and, on the other, the construction of individuals as narcissistic. People simultaneously feel members of an audience and that they are performers, they are simultaneously watchers and being watched. As Rubin (1970) puts it in talking about street political action 'Life is theatre and we are the guerillas attacking the shrines of authority. The street is the stage. You are the star of the show and everything you were once taught is up for grabs' (p. 250, quoted in Schechner 1993: 64). Spectacle and narcissism feed off each other in a virtuous cycle, a cycle fuelled largely by the media and mediated by the critical role of performance. As with the other types of audience, performance is the key, but, unlike the other types, performance is not so linked to events, but has, so to speak, leaked out into everyday life.
>
> (Abercrombie and Longhurst 1998: 75)

In turn, audiences, using the media as a resource, have been able to create new skills and knowledges of various kinds which allow them to both function in and constitute this new kind of everyday life, technical, analytical, and referential skills and knowledges modelled on fan-like and enthusiast-like practices, now made general.

Contemporary cultural theory

The third usage of the metaphor of performance has been by contemporary cultural theorists. Of these theorists, probably the best known is Judith Butler. Butler's work is important for a number of reasons. First, she questions embodiment as a ground. Second, she is clearly attempting to go beyond simple constructionist positions. Third, she questions the distinction between sign and referent, chiefly through adopting the notion that each category is confused with/in the other as a series of spacings. But, it might be best to think of Butler as a transitional figure. For example, Kirby (1997a) argues that, in her allegiance to sign and referent, she holds back from the final step: that language is not first and foremost a system of signification and meaning is not the defining purpose of its expression. Thus:

> matter for Butler may not be a blank or passive surface, but it is still a surface, and one that demands to be interpreted or written upon by something other than itself. It seems that matter is unintelligible to itself, and this lack of intelligibility can only be remedied by thought/language. Although matter possesses the capacity to call upon thought, it is apparently incapable of calling upon itself to interpret itself: matter can only exceed itself in thoughtless activity. However if the nature of matter is generative – if it conceives and construes itself through an involved re-presentation, or differentiation of itself – then why must we presume that thought/language is alien to its identity or this process?
>
> (Kirby 1997a: 115)

Come what may, Butler's influence on the notion of performance has clearly been crucial and I will therefore devote some space to it.

Butler's initial project was to bring discourse theory and performance (especially as found in the work of Turner and Schechner) together (see, for example, Butler 1990a, 1990b). Butler's initial definition of performance was essentially repetitive and the repetition is normative; 'performance mobilises history as and through repetition' (Pollock 1998: 2). As McKenzie (1997) puts it, this is 'command performance'. Thus, according to Butler (1990a: 140), history is 'at once a re-enactment and a re-opening of a set of meanings already socially established; and it is the mundane and ritualised form of their legitimation'. History and performance become 'collaborators in a kind of backward/forward motion' (Pollock 1998: 2) in which history is a constraint on the productive possibilities of performance.

This is, of course, a very conservative notion of both history and performance. It is as if Butler is unable to 'disarticulate performance and history. In her formulation they remain entwined like sad lovers, bound to repeat themselves in slow circling half-steps while, at best, it seems their mutual distress unfolds' (Pollock 1998: 2). It is no surprise, then, that in her most recent work (see, for example, Butler 1997), Butler tends to back away from this conception, laying more stress on the performative side of the equation. Though still enmeshed in textual metaphors, Butler now pays more attention to the effectiveness of speech acts, to the force of the utterance. By concentrating on a notion of speech acts as bodily acts which is boosted by drawing on a Wittgensteinian notion of rule-following (filtered through the work of Taylor and Bourdieu on embodied activity) she is able to rework linguistic agency as performative force. But, for her, writers such as Bourdieu do not go far enough in their attention to performativity. And she uses Derrida to show this performative deficit. Thus:

Bourdieu offers a promising account of the way in which non-intentional and non-deliberate incorporation of norms takes place. What Bourdieu fails to understand, however, is how what is bodily in speech resists and confounds the very norms by which it is regulated. Moreover, he offers an account of the performativity of political discourse that neglects the tacit performativity of bodily 'speech', the performativity of the habitus. His conservative account of the speech act presumes that the conventions that will authorise the performative are already in place, thus failing to account for the Derridean 'break' with context that utterances perform. His view fails to consider the crisis in convention that speaking the unspeakable produces, the insurrectionary 'force' of censored speech as it emerges into official discourse and opens the performative to an unpredictable future.

(Butler 1997: 142)

In other words, for Derrida,

the force of the performative is derived precisely from its decontextualisation, from its break with a prior context and its capacity to assume new contexts. Indeed, he argues that a performative, to the extent that it is conventional, must be repeated in order to work. And this repetition presupposes that the formula itself continues to work in successive contexts, that it is bound to no context in particular, even as, I would add, it is always found in some context or another. The 'illimitability' of context simply means that any delineation of a context that one might perform is itself subject to a further consideration, and that contexts are not given in unitary forms. This does not mean, and never meant, that one should cease any effort to delineate a context; it means only that any such delineation is subject to a potentially infinite revision.

(Butler 1997: 147)

Derrida, in other words, fixes his attention on the utterance that will persist apart from social contexts – and all consideration of semantics – according to the same logic as written models. Thus:

Derrida's account tends to accentuate the relative autonomy of the structural operation of the sign, identifying the 'force' of the performative as a structural feature of any sign that must breed with its prior contexts in order to sustain its iterability as a sign. The force of the performance is thus not inherited from prior usage but issues forth precisely from its break with any and all prior usage. That break, that force of rupture, is the force of the performative, beyond all question of truth or meaning.

(Butler 1997: 148)

But Butler is clearly as unhappy with this structural account as she is with Bourdieu's contextual account. For whereas Bourdieu fails to take account of the way in which a performative can break with and assume new contexts, refiguring the terms of legitimate utterance themselves, Derrida appears to install the break as a structurally necessary feature of every utterance and every codifiable written mark, thus paralysing the social analysis of forceful utterance.

(Butler 1997: 150)

Thus, for Butler, Bourdieu is quite clearly necessary as a means of capturing a bodily stylistics that, in turn, performs 'its own social magic [which] constitutes the fact and corporeal operation of performativity' (Butler 1997: 153) but Bourdieu also constantly misses that 'something [which] always exceeds the speech act the body performs [which] remains uncounted by any of its acts of speech' (Butler 1997: 155). 'What breaks down in the course of interpellation, opening up the possibility of achievement from within, remains unaccounted for' (Butler 1997: 156). Yet Butler offers little to help the reader account for the unaccounted. This is ultimately, I think, because she cannot bear to part entirely with a textual model of performance based upon sign and referent.

The same criticism can, I think be applied to Bhabha, the second significant contemporary cultural theorist with investments in performance. For Bhabha 'performativity' is defined by instability. It represents 'the ever-present potential for language to mean something else, to betray one set of meanings for another, to slip from one context or set of relations into another's arms, taking commercial pleasure with it, laughing all the way' (Pollock 1998: 23). In other words, Bhabha is focusing on the creative moment in meaning-making:

the moment when the story-in-history is in effect caught red-handed, not inventing the facts per se but investing the authority from which they derive their meaning and weight. Like Bakhtin, he finds the ambivalence at the centre of the narrative at its would be 'origins' – less a cause for despair than celebration (even real romance). In fact, Bhabha characterises it as the next best thing to an ongoing moment; it is, for him, a performative moment, redolent with possibility, productivity, and agency.

(Pollock 1998: 24)

In other words, performance, used here in a distinctively theatrical sense, becomes a technology for mining the creative implications of signification. But Bhabha's tendency to stick to textual signification makes it difficult for him to realize the potential of his own thoughts. Not so for Deleuze, the third contemporary cultural theorist I want to consider.

For Deleuze, the performative is an integral part of his conception of thought and life. And the essentially textual model of Derrida and Bhabha, and even the becoming-more-corporeal Butler model, are not sufficient to capture this general generative intelligibility:

For me, a text is merely a small cog in an extra-textual practice. It is not a question of commentating on the text by a method of deconstruction or by a method of textual practice, or by other methods: it is a question of saying what use it has in the extra-textual practice that prolongs the text.

(Deleuze, cited in D.W. Smith 1997: xvi)

Thought, like the process of life itself, is an accretion, an addition to a ceaseless production of variation (and the selection and synthesis of variants) whose chief goal is to create effects through new encounters which beckon and become;[17] 'one term does not become another; rather, each term encounters the other, and the becoming is something between the two, outside the two' (D.W. Smith 1997: 154). This is, if you like, the speech act radicalized, made into a tool of maximum modulation and push through which new modes of existence can be glimpsed, even actualized. It is knowing 'how to leave, how to push the process further, to follow a line of flight, to enter into a becoming that escapes the resentissement of persons and the dominance of established orders' (D.W. Smith 1997: xi). The technology that Deleuze uses in order to produce maximum modulation, the stress on singularities and events, the dissolution of the subject, the intersection of the body, the minorization of politics, the stuttering of language – are well enough known now to require no repetition.[18]

It is no surprise, then, that for Deleuze performance, like literature, is regarded as a key means of reading and creating signs. It is a symptomatology, a diagnostics of signs which isolates a particular possibility of life and which helps to make more modes of existence possible. It is a process that operates by means of experimental and unforeseen becomings, just like Deleuze's own life. Thus, in Deleuze's world, the acts of theatre become more broadly performative.

[Theatre] will surge forward as something representing nothing but what presents and creates a minority consciousness as a universal becoming. It forges alliances here and there according to the circumstances, following the lines of transformation that exceed [theatre] and take on another form, or else that transform themselves back into [theatre] for another leap. It is truly a matter of consciousness-raising, even though it bears no relation to a psychoanalytic consciousness, or a Marxist political consciousness, nor even to a Brechtian one. Consciousness-raising is a tremendous strength but one made neither for solutions nor for interpretations. When consciousness abandons solutions and interpretations, it thus acquires its light, its gestures and its sounds, its decisive transformation. Henry James wrote 'she ended up knowing more than she could ever interpret; there were no more obscurities clouding her clear vision. These remained only a raw light'. The more we attain this form of minority consciousness, the less isolated we feel. Light. We are our own mass, by ourselves, mass of my atoms. Under the ambition of formulas, there is the most modest appreciation of what might be a revolutionary [theatre] a simple loving potentiality, an element for a new becoming of consciousness.

(Deleuze 1995: 243)

Performing arts/arts of performing

The last use of the metaphor of performance is in the performing arts, in the conduct of creative performances. The body of work produced by the performing arts constitutes perhaps the single most sustained treatment of the metaphor of performance. I therefore intend to treat it in greater depth than the previous three usages. But, in providing a survey (which, given the enormous range of work, must be indicative rather than schematic) it is important to note that the metaphor of performance is itself contested in performance studies (see Roach 1996). To begin with, there is the problem of what exactly counts as performance. Certainly, there is no doubt that performance has moved beyond the theatre. For Schechner, for example:

> performance is an inclusive term. Theatre is only one node on a continuum that reaches from the ritualism of animals (including humans) though performances in everyday life – greetings, display of emotion, family scenes, professional roles, and so on – through to play, sports, theatre, dance, ceremonies, rites, and performances of great magnitude.
>
> (Schechner 1988: xii)

Thus:

> any event, action, item or behaviour may be examined 'as' performance. Approaching phenomena as performance has certain advantages. One can consider things as provisional, in-process, existing and changing over time, in rehearsal, as it were. On the other hand, there are events that tradition and convention declare 'are' performances. In western culture, until recently, performances were of theatre, music and dance, the 'aesthetic genres', the performing arts. Recently, since the 1960s at least, aesthetic performances have developed that cannot be located precisely as theatre or dance or music or visual arts. Usually called either 'performance art', mixed media, 'happenings', or 'intermedia', these events blur or break boundaries separating art from life and genres from each other. As performative art grew in range and popularity, theorists began to examine 'performative behaviour' – how people play gender, heightening their constructed identity, performing slightly or radically different selves in different situations. . . . The performative engages performance in places and situations not traditionally marked as performing arts, from dress-up to certain kinds of writing or speaking.
>
> (Schechner 1998: 361–362)

There is, as might only be expected, much argument as to whether performance should therefore be understood as a 'theatre-plus' model, expanding what counts as theatre, or whether such an understanding should be seen as a backward step, a betrayal of the history of performance studies which in many ways has been – and still is – antitheatre, given its genesis in post-war experimental performance and performance art and in the dematerialization of the visual arts which arose out of the convergence of art media, forms, and practices. Then the art of life is the question. In turn, the expansion of notions of performance indicated by the adoption of the performative induces a number of problems. For example, there is the question of 'liveness' (Auslander 1999) in an age of mass media. Some authors, for example, have argued that the immediacy of performance is dulled by its re-presentation in the media which is, quite literally, a means of distancing the event.

> performances form an elongated chain. . . . They travel over a greater distance. Performances from the past, captured in some recording medium, can be replaced in the present. At the same time, performance is not spatially restricted but can be received well away from the context of the original event. As a result, it becomes less clear what set of processes constitute the performance, which is stretched out, for example, from the recording studio at one end to the playing of a record in the home, which is itself a performance of a kind, if a secondary one, at the other.
>
> (Abercrombie and Longhurst 1998: 62)

At the same time, re-presented performances gradually adopt their own styles and conventions which differ from immediate performance. For example in film and television, acting styles, production conventions and audience responses have all changed as a 'constituted aesthetic' (Abercrombie and Longhurst 1998) has taken over from the 'immediate aesthetic' of the theatre. In turn, the signs and cues of the new aesthetic have made their way into immediate performance.

But equally many authors argue that this does not necessarily mean that performance events somehow lose their edge; even a mediated performance cannot be exactly restated:

> The uniqueness of a given performance derives from the combination of forces that gather the various assemblages that will constitute the performance. These forces combine and bring together audience, performers, text, revenues, management, scenic space, costumes, and scenic objects, deriving them out of larger fields – the population of a city, the pool of actors, the money spent elsewhere – in which people had otherwise showed no such immediate connection. This process of gathering or mobilisation is, for any given performance event, momentary and nonrepeatable. Even if the occasions recur, what gathers (at) the scene is a determinate particularisation of what transpires between performers and public. The interface between performers and public can be restated on another occasion, but even that restatement must be collected all over again by means of rites and pathways that meet on the field of play.
>
> (Martin 1997: 188)

Yet what seems clear is that many of those working in performance studies have wanted to keep to a definition of performance which emphasizes the special knowledges that derive from improvisatory immediacy and presence; performance is the art of (and the art of valuing) the now:[19]

> Performance's only life is the present. Performance cannot be used, recorded, documented or otherwise participate in the circulation of representations of representations; once it does so it becomes something other than performance. To the degree that performance attempts to enter the economy of reproduction it betrays and lessens the promise of its own ontology. Performance's being becomes itself through disappearance.
>
> (Phelan 1993: 146)

It follows that performance cannot be seen as (though it may well involve) 'text'.[20]

> Although some scholars have written as though performance could be treated as a form of text . . . its unique strategic properties are destroyed when it is considered as, or reduced to, text. To be sure, performances share some qualities with texts. They have beginnings, middles and ends, they have internal structure, may refer to themselves, etc. But it is precisely the performativity of performances for which there is no analogue in text. Unlike text, performances are ephemeral. They create their effects and then are gone – leaving their reverberations (fresh insights, reconstituted selves, new structures, altered realities) behind them. Performances are a living social activity, by necessity assertive, strategic and not fully predictable. While they refer to the past and plunge towards the future, they exist only in the present.
>
> (Schieffelin 1998: 198)

In other words, performance conjures up the precarious 'emptiness' of the now, and, in so doing, provides a distinctive force opposed to the representational economy in which we live. 'Non-preservable, fluid, full of uncertain architecture and temporary sets, performance honours the idea that a limited number of people in a specific time/space frame can have an experience of value which leaves no visible trace afterward' (Phelan 1993: 178 and 149).

What, then, are the chief characteristics of performance as the art of now? Six come to mind. First, performance is a heightening of everyday behaviour, rather than something standing apart from it. It is thereby a construction of a tension between performance as a more or less continuous presence in the stream of everyday life and performance as something staged in specific spaces and times. In Schechner's (1993) famous phrases it is 'twice-behaved' or 'restored' behaviour, but what is being behaved and restored is precisely the issue. Second, performance is liminal, 'a mode of embodied activity whose spatial, temporal and symbolic "awareness" allows for dominant social norms to be superseded, questioned, played with, transformed' (McKenzie 1997: 218). But 'liminal' means more than this. The term 'liminal' comes, of course, from the anthropologist Turner, who developed it from van Gennep's *The Rites of Passage* (1961) and his own study of Ndembu ritual. In turn, Schechner generalized the notion, spreading it across a much wider range of cultural activities, from rituals to theatre and beyond. More recently, liminality has become the key concept for theorizing the politics of performance:

> as a mode of embodied activity that transgresses, resists, or challenges social structures, immediately has been theorised both in terms of the political demonstrations of the 1960s and 1970s and the political performances of the 1980s and 1990s. Yet the concept has not simply been applied to performances; it has also helped construct objects of study. . . . Performance study has put liminality to such ends: to delimit its field of objects; to situate its own problematic passage into a field, a discipline, a paradigm of research and to circulate its own interdisciplinary, intercultural resistance to the normative forces of institutionalism.
>
> (McKenzie 1997: 218–219)

Third, performance is concerned with constructing unstable times. Thus:

> Part of what performance knows is the impossibility of maintaining the distinction between temporal tenses, between an absolutely singular beginning and ending, between living and dying. What performance studies learns most deeply from performance is the generative force of these 'betweens'.
>
> (Phelan 1998: 8)

This sense of the temporal instability of the event is crucial:

> While we can reify the performance as an event that exceeds the labour that brings it into being, as Herbert Blau has observed, the stability of the event is elusive, given that what specifically makes any performative moment disperses as soon as the event is consummated. Hence what opens in the cause of the performance may be recalled or reinscribed elsewhere, but it leaves no trace of the constellation of forces that mobilise its appearance in the first place.
>
> By means of these unstable conditions, performance brackets an internal and external time off from one another so that the performance appears as the negative of both its past and its future. On the one hand, what is taken as central to performance is narratively laid to rest during that performance; on the other, the momentary combination of forces that make up the performance (the gathering and dispersal of forces that yield the sense of immediate temporal presence) cannot account for itself or its own formation. This arrest of life to make a show of the living is the crisis that brings the performance into being and points to its early demise.
>
> (Martin 1997: 188–189)

Fourth, performance is also concerned with constantly unstable spaces, spaces of possibility, 'as-if' spaces. Such spaces are fleeting, dialogical, and, above all, risky.

It is always possible the performance may fail. This performance is always inherently interactive, and fundamentally risky. 'Amongst the various people involved (who often have different agendas) there is always something theoretically and/ or practically at stake, and something can always go wrong' (Schieffelin 1998: 198). Indeed, even a 'successful performance must be a qualified failure' (Connor 1996: 121).

Fifth, performance is often assumed to be transgressive. But this is not necessarily the case; there is a romance of performance. In truth, much performance is normative;[21] if Butler does nothing else she makes clear that performative transgression must be seen side by side with performative normativity:

> within performance studies, Butler has in effect challenged the sedimented signification of 'performative' as referring only to oppositional cultural practices and sought to queer the term so that it refers to normative practices and discourses. One might protest that such a queering amounts to a misuse of language. 'Surely, Butler's performative refers to something else!' 'It's linguistic rather than embodied!' 'It means normativity as much as subversion.' 'Couldn't we use another term?!' Rather than attempting to justify her use of this term by again citing *Gender Trouble*'s alliance of theatrical performance and discursive performativity, I shall entertain the thought that it is a misuse, and that this misuse is itself a tactic of resignification, of queering.
>
> (McKenzie 1997: 229)

Sixth, writing about performance as the art of the now is a problem since marking the unmarked is likely to alter fundamentally and to devalue precisely what it is about by pulling it into the system of mass reproduction and what Phelan (1993: 14) calls the 'drive of the documentary'. At the same time, there is the problem of describing what performance is about in writing, why we should attend to it, especially when

> in representational arts like dance and music we are, indeed, quite accustomed to deciding whether someone – a critic – has 'understood' a piece in terms not of their formed analysis but of their figurative description, their account not of what the music meant but how it did ('the music rose and hesitated, dropped and rose again, like a kite in flight').
>
> (Kemp 1996: 160)

Of course, performance is irrefutably bound up with the written word.[22] Especially since the 1960s, performance has been boosted by clear theoretical imperatives. Then, many of those working in performance studies have tried to work towards various forms of 'performative writing' which can capture some of the travails of performance such as incursion, permeation, and multiplicity, and can constitute a performance in their own right. Thus, 'performative writing seems one way not only to make meaning but to make writing meaningful' (Pollock

1998: 87). Again, much performance is now being written in different scripts which better capture embodied practice, for example, in dance, by the use of movement scripts such as Labanotation (Farnell 1994). But, fundamentally, much performance cannot be written down. It is unwritable, unsayable, and unstable. And that is its fascination: it is a living demonstration of skills we have but cannot ever articulate fully in the linguistic domain.

Phelan and Blau's emphasis on a traceless effectivity can, of course, be taken entirely too far. In truth, it applies only to certain forms of performance. Many forms of performance leave many kinds of traces dependent upon the time frame that is chosen as a register, what counts as effect, and so on. The break that Phelan and Blau sometimes seem to identify between the immateriality of performance and the materiality of everything else includes within it the danger of reinserting a romantically inclined distinction between the artistic immaterial and the gross material which they are at such pains to deny. In particular, they tend to downplay the power of objects taken not as brute signs but as events that unfold to a different rhythm with which I want to end this chapter (see Phelan 1998).

But whatever the nature of performance, there is no doubt that an extra-ordinarily diverse archive of forms of performance has been built up – especially in the later twentieth century – which now constitutes perhaps the single most important contemplation of the time-spaces of now that exists. It is a contemplation which values improvisation and encourages attunement to emergent form. It ranges from formal and experimental theatre to formal and experimental dance, to all kinds of performance art, as well as to various forms of musical performance (Frith 1997). Then there are all the kinds of events which have tried to get closer to 'everyday life' by performing in its spaces, the 'happenings' of the 1960s and early 1970s (Sandford 1995), the radical street performance that has flourished from the 1970s onwards (Cohen-Cruz 1988), and so on.

What is particularly noticeable about this resonant archive of practice – so little touched on by so many in the social sciences and humanities and yet so important – is the amount of attention paid to practical means of organizing space and time as a means of heightening receptiveness, stimulating involvement, and evaluating and (not least) undermining authority (see, for example, Tufnell and Crickmay 1990). Yet remarkably little of this work has ever made its way into the wider literature on spatiality which now, as a result, presents (or rather pasts) us with a kind of tomb, full of dead, dead, dead geographies.[23] In the next section, I therefore want to start to examine this archive by placing an emphasis on dance.

The shapes of change

> The body is not something I possess to dance with. I do not order my body to bend here and whirl there. I do not think 'move' and then do move. No! I am the dance; its thinking is its doing and its doing is its thinking. I am the bending. I am the whirling. My dance is my body and my body is myself.
>
> (Fraleigh 1987: 32)

Let me now turn to a specific illustration of these thoughts: the medium of dance. It would, of course, have been possible to consider a number of other performing arts as exemplification, for example music, theatre, opera, or performance art. And it is important to remember that most performances do not exist in just one medium of expression; for example, dance nearly always involves music and music very often involves dance (Kemp 1996). Again, bodily skills are often taught across different media of expression: actors may learn some dance skills and dancers some acting skills, for example. But dance suits my purposes well. For a start, since at least the 1960s writers on dance have been attempting to grapple with the issues raised in this chapter (cf. Langer 1953; Sheets-Johnson 1966) and though in the early years they often did so in undifferentiated and abstracted ways, dance studies now provide a substantial and important archive of work which emphasizes social and cultural difference, not least in dance's use of spaces. Then, dance has an extraordinarily rich history which, in part, can be regarded as an attempt to understand what dance is about – by dancing. Thus dance has been the focus of attempts to harness the body to totalitarian regimes, it has been the means of explicit or dissimulated resistance, it has been a focus of high modernism, it is one of the key means of mass acculturation, and so on. This is a history that can tell of medieval dance manias, the 'ring shout' of African-American slave cultures, and the court ballets of the sixteenth and seventeenth centuries, as well as the jitterbug, disco, and raves. Moving on, dance is important for other reasons. In particular, as one of the key means of performance, it is posing the question that many who write about performance want answered; it has become an increasingly central mode of cultural expression, all the way from the street to the boardroom (George 1998), as a contemplation which values improvisation and encourages attunement to emergent form; and it is one of the chief means of knowingly constituting virtual spaces through choreographic and other performance methods, all of which are now routinely taught. And, last, dance has become a crucial political moment in modern feminist thought. Indeed it is often difficult to separate writing on dance and feminist writing.[24]

Dance suits my purposes well for one other reason too. It has proved – and still proves – peculiarly difficult to write about. Three reasons recur in the literature. First, because though dance's chief characteristics are clearly involved with generating embodied expression and affect, they do so in ways which are often non-representational. We might even think of dance as embodying a sixth kinaesthetic, proprioceptive sense, the sensation providing awareness of movement and the position of body parts (Stewart 1998). Second, because dance is, like much other performance, an art of the now: 'we have created and studied a discipline based on that which disappears, and that which cannot be preserved or, posted' (Phelan 1998: 8). Dance is a 'one time only' phenomenon, even when it involves repetition of a number of performances. Third, because dance, as 'meaning' in motion (Desmond 1997), is not easily recorded. For many writers, video and other means of recording lose much of what dance performance is about, rendering it sterile, filtering out exactly the things dance knows that are worth knowing which skid beyond the figure. In any case, until recently, there were few accessible systems for recording dance (but see Franko 1993). Now, of course, there are a number of these systems. Labanotation records the dancing body's changes in position and the timing of these changes (Farnell 1994). Effort-shape analysis documents the effort and flow of movement and the body's shaped configurations in relation to its own parts and other surrounding objects (see, for example, Farnell 1994). Smith has experimented with 'dance hieroglyphs' (Albright 1989; Stewart 1998). These are all systems which both write dance and also make dance into a kind of writing.

> EXERCISE. Imagine a writing instrument is located at the top of your head at the soft spot where the bones of the skull meet. Imagine you can draw with this instrument as a sky-writing plane draws in space. The space around you is a three-dimensional canvas. Allow your writing object to draw pathways on the canvas letting the rest of your body be loose and responsive. Adjust your body to accommodate your drawing pathways, always letting the top of your head lead. Explore different speeds, levels, and degrees of locomotion. Allow your eyes to scan, seeing all but focussing on nothing. Work to the point of disorientation and stop.
>
> (Gamble 1977: 38)

Yet dance has a particularly rich history consisting of experimentation with many genres and styles, which is of immense significance in trying to forge a symptomatology of movement which can help us to both understand and create expressive potential by gesturing to new ground. I will point to just a few of the ways in which dance can aid in this search.

Dancing the body

The first – and most obvious – is through the body. Dance can perform the 'techniques of the body' (Mauss 1993: 19) now and through history in a number of ways which go to show that 'the facts as documented in any recorded discourses . . . do not a body's meaning make. They substitute the casual relationship between a body and these cultural forces that prod, poke and then measure its responsiveness. They substitute only bodily reaction. They lie askew from a body's significance' (Foster 1995: 8). To begin with then, dance can sensitize us to the bodily sensorium of a culture, to touch, force, tension, weight, shape, tempo, phrasing, intervalation, even coalescence, to the serial mimesis of not quite a copy through which we are reconstituted moment by moment. In history, for example, much interesting work has been done on the rise of so-called 'serial' or 'interval' cultures (see, for example, McAloon 1995). Then, dance can help us to realize the bodily theories – performative theories and theoretical performatives – that cultures hold dear and which are often potent sources of power without the need to understand these theories as total systems.

> Any standardised regimen of body training, for example, embodies, in the very organisation of its exercises, the metamorphs used to instruct the body,

and in the criteria specified for physical competence, a coherent (or not so coherent) set of principles that govern the action of the regimen. These principles, reticulated with aesthetic, political and gendered connotations, cast the body which enacts them into larger arenas as of meaning where it moves alongside bodies bearing related signage. Theories of bodily significance likewise exist for any prior historical moment. Circulating around and through the partitions of any established practice and reverberating at the interstices among distinct practices, theories of bodily practices, like images of the natural body, are deduced from acts of comparison between past and present, from rubbing one kind of historical document against others. In the fictional encounters between texts, such as those expressing aesthetic praise, medical insights, proscriptive conduct and recreational pursuits, theories of bodily significance begin to consolidate.

(Foster 1995: 8)

Then again, dance can produce new bodily expressions which turn on the body's power to purposely transgress, play, or dissimulate. The body is not just written upon. It writes as well.

To approach the body as capable of generating ideas, as a bodily writing, is to approach it as a choreographer might. Dance, perhaps, more than any other bodycentred endeavour, cultivates a body that imitates as well as responds. Even those dance-makers who see in the dancer's body a mere vehicle for aesthetic expression must, in their investigation of a new work's choreographic problematics, consult bodies, their own or the dancers'. During this playful probing of physical and semantic potential, choreographers' and dancers' bodies create new images, relationships, concepts and reflections. Here bodies are cast into a discursive framework where they can respond in kind to the moved queries initiated in the process of formulating a dance. Such bodies have, admittedly, been trained so as to accomplish this fluency, a disciplining that strongly shapes the quality of their interaction with dance-making. Nevertheless they sustain a 'conversation' throughout the rehearsal process and sometimes in performance, their imagination invents and then lucidly enunciates their specific corporeal identities.

(Foster 1995: 15)

Dance can, then, be seen as a form of ambulant 'theorizing' (Stewart 1998). Dance has evolved forms which can aid this process. Of these, perhaps the best known is Contact Improvisation (see, for example, Novack 1990) developed in the 1970s but with recognizable roots in the 'performative revolution' of the 1960s. Contact Improvisation is a practice which mixes together the casual, individualistic improvisatory ethos of ordinary social dancing with the kind of task-oriented movement favoured by early postmodern dance groups such as the Judson Church Dance Theater. It focuses on the process of becoming and is therefore an improvisational process of touch with no real end point.

Resisting both the idealised body of ballet and the dramatically expressive body of modern dance, contact seeks to create what Cynthia Novack calls a 'responsive' body, one based in the physical ease of weight. . . . the physical training of Contact emphasises the release of the body's weight into the floor or into a partner's body. In Contact, the experience of internal sensations and the flow of movement between two bodies is more important than specific shapes or formal positions. Dancers learn to move with a consciousness of the physical communication important within the dancing. . . . But human bodies, especially bodies in physical contact with one another, are difficult to see only in terms of physical counterbalance, weight and momentum. . . . On first seeing Contact, people often wonder whether this is, in fact, professional dancing or rather a recreational and therapeutic form. Gone are the formal lines of much classical dance. Gone are the traditional approaches to choreography and the conventions of the professional stage. In their place is an improvisational movement form based on the expressive communi-cation involved when two people begin to share their weight and physical support. Instead of privileging an ideal type of body or movement style, Contact Improvisation privileges a willingness to take physical or emotional risks.

(Albright 1997: 84–85)

In other words, Contact Improvisation cleaves to a non-representational credo emphasizing the 'kinesthetic sensations and physics of weight and momentum rather than the visual picture of bodily shape within the stage space' (Albright 1997: 86).

Dancing identity

The second way in which dance can help us to understand expressive potential is in the ability to forge identity. This identity can be of a number of forms. For example, there is identity which simply consists of evoking a mood. Nonmimetic and non-representational, this kind of identity citation can be powerful. Identity can be constructed by dance at the level of individual experience, or at the level of social assemblages.

What dance is in the case of identity is one of a number of techniques for creating new forms of awareness and persistence. Two examples will suffice. The first is at the level of individual identity and is Pini's (1996) account of her mother's devotion to dance – Irish step dancing and rock and roll – as a young woman (see also McRobbie 1991). For her mother, dance was a way of expressing herself – her private space and her 'real' identity – a way of producing and channelling desire, and a means of making sense of her situation. So that, as she grows older, her declining dance powers become a significant challenge to her sense of self.

I just feel really sad when I can't do it properly. Maybe I hate people to be better than me. I just feel so sad when I see them all doing it; and I hate to go in and feel 'well, I'm just one of the crowd'. It's sad because you don't stand out and nobody knows you. You're just – and this is why I need to practice more and get absolutely back into it – part of the crowd. I'm not the one. And I feel so sad about that. I was always the one who people would look at and say 'oh look, she's the dancer over there. See her.' And now, I just go in and I'm a nobody.

(Pini 1996: 424)

The second example is concerned with the use of dance as a more general instrument of change in identity. Such dance can be found in contemporary examples such as the case of the numerous African-American dance groups which are struggling to embody history and then provide 'biomythographies', tales that elaborate visionary sagas of social and personal survival (Albright 1997). It can be found in the case of dance groups that have disabled members who have had to make the journey from the classical notion of the body – and even more particularly, from classical priorities for dance – towards new syllabuses based on weight and expressive force. For example, in one duet, two dancers are able to gradually rewrite the physical expectations of the classical form, exploring, like Contact Improvisation, 'the kinesthetic sensations and physics of weight and momentum, rather than the visual picture of bodily shape' (Albright 1997: 86). And it is found in a number of projects involving Community Dance, which provide all kinds of ways of investing new forms of presence (Thomas 1998). Nowadays, where dance is involved in general projects to change identity this will often mean a connection to performance art, a motley collection of practices which emerged in the 1960s from dada, experiment with projective verse, happenings (Sandford 1995).

. . . Cage's and Kaprows' Zen-influenced theories of non judgement and present-centredness, politicised art, feminists who insisted that the personal and the political went hand in hand, and even street demonstrations. Thus: performance has been a powerful catalyst in the history of twentieth century art not only because it has subverted the formal conventions and rational premises of modernist art but also because it has heightened our awareness of the social role of art and, at times, has served as a vehicle for such change.... The term 'performance art' first appeared around 1970 to describe the empirical time-based and process-oriented work of conceptual 'body' and feminist artists that was emerging at the time. . . . Over the past thirty-five years many styles and modes of performance have evolved, from private, introspective investigations to ordinary routines of everyday life, cathartic rituals and trials of endurance, site-specific environmental transformations, technically sophisticated multimedia productions, autobiographically based cabaret-style performance, and large-scale, community-based projects designed to serve as a source of social and political empowerment.

(Brentano 1994: 31–32)

Again, it may also mean a connection to community theatre with its undoubted affective investments:

> Such performances are not make-believe enactments, fictions. They are individual or group 'testimony' . . . performances at risk, socially, psychologically and physically. The 'body' as a frail and multivalent vessel of life and meaning is expressed, played with, compromised, celebrated, penetrated, pierced, covered, pressed – done with in innumerable ways. Yet the bodies are also persons, living subjects who are more than the objects of performance. These persons are, to use Bill T. Jones' phrase from his controversial 1994 piece, 'still here'. Persistent in their presence, present as concrete, physical, transphysical and metaphysical beings, these persons are makers and receivers both, doers together.
>
> (Schechner 1998: 91)

Dancing the city

The third way in which dance can help us to understand expressive potentials is in its ability to capture the city (Thomas 1998). Here we can see dance as a means of helping to understand some of those areas of experience which have been so elusive. In particular, dance's qualities of allusion can help us to us.

To begin with, dance can help us to understand urban 'skills'. Day after day, all kinds of skills of expression are constantly deployed in the city, delineating time-spaces in which something significant and worthy of notice is to occur. These 'minor' skills include all the everyday means of negotiating the city – driving the car, walking the pavement, crossing the street – and the knowledge stemming from those encounters (sometimes formalized in City Guides and A–Zs):

> What the relationship is between the published timetable and the real timetable. What the likely effects will be of the visit of a president or a public demonstration. Where to be able to meet people without fear of missing them in crowded parts of the city. How long to hold the line. And Living in the City is also a matter of developing certain psychological capacities. To not take it personally when somebody is late; or cancels an appointment. To have a sense of realism about what may be possible to practice, while only having a partial knowledge of what goes on elsewhere. To develop a quite sophisticated idea of what it might be possible to know, and what it might be possible for others to know.
>
> (Barry 2000: 23)

In turn, these skills produce a city which is in continual flux. According to Lefebvre (1995: 230–231) apprehending the to and fro of these skills of expression itself requires the cultivation of special skills of 'rhythm-analysis', which will apprehend the city as a series of times, polyrhythmically interacting with one another to produce a 'music of the city'.[25] To hear this music you have to be out of it. Externality is necessary. And yet to grasp a rhythm you must yourself have been grabbed by it, given or abandoned yourself inwardly to the time that it rhythmed. Is it not thus in dance or music? . . . If one attentively observes a crowd during peak times and especially if one listens to its rumour, one discovers flows in the apparent disorder and an order which is signalled by rhythms: chance or predetermined encounters, hurried or nonchalant meandering of people going home to withdraw from the outside, or leaving their homes to make contact with the outside, business people and vacant people – so many elements which make up a polyrhythmy. The rhythmanalyst thus knows how to listen to a place, a market, an avenue.

(Lefebvre 1991: 177)

Dance provides us, amongst other things, with an exaggerated example of these urban skills of expression (Schechner's 'restored' or 'twice-behaved' behaviour) and their outcome, which Lefebvre was trying to apprehend, and, at the same time, a medium through which they can be understood. Dance, in other words, enables us to rediscover and rework the plural, performative skills of the city, stimulating both a greater sense of extant situations, and a glimpse of new styles of urban living which might simultaneously produce new senses of how the world is (Spinosa *et al.* 1997). In particular, the backward embodiments of gender and age can be challenged by changing the value placed on particular bodily skills and styles, and by showing just how skilled certain performances are.

Dance can also help in another way to apprehend the city. That is, by conjuring up the imaginary worlds which lie just on or across the border of perception, and which parallel all our urban journeys. This kind of tangential, oblique, dispersed knowledge draws on the body's memory to produce folds in experience, and allows imaginative access from one dimension into others. Movements in one zone allow corresponding exploratory movements in other zones.

Thus, the city can be prompted to 'reveal' itself in Baudelairean fashion through 'a rhythmical prose capable of rendering the innumerable connections that characterize "giant cities", and especially of communicating their impact on the city dweller' (Sheringham 1996: 110). Thus a new category of experience is founded which is the object of Breton, Benjamin, de Certeau, and other urban writers and which can be accessed by cultivating the right stance: 'knowing the city is dependent on attunement to a particular wavelength, a process involving the adoption of an attitude of lyrical expectancy and availability to experience' (Sheringham 1996: 111). In turn, one might see this kind of knowledge of what Lefebvre (1995) called, rather misleadingly, the 'urban unconscious', as opening up the spaces of eventuality of the city, the glimmers of all the possibles that might have but never did come about, each with their own senses of possibility. As Caygill puts it in his study of Walter Benjamin:

The experience of a City is made up of a constant negotiation with the ghosts and residues of previous experiences, most notably in Paris, with the ghosts of insurrection and revolution, but also in Berlin which for Benjamin was above all a City of ghosts. For Benjamin, the field of such negotiations is not exhausted by actual past experiences of the City, but also takes in those experiences which did not ever happen. The experience of the City includes the lost choices and the missed encounters . . . the forfeiture of an experience itself leaves traces which persist and shape the experience of the present. The surrealists were the masters of the experience of the City that might have been, but not for us. Finally, Benjamin insists that the experience of the City is ecstatic and futural, haunted by intimations of the future, whether as the City ecstatically fusing into an epic unity of its past, present and future citizens as in the Paris of Victor Hugo, or in the melancholy of the allegorical City which lives on without us, in repetitive change, as in the Paris of Baudelaire's anti-epic poetry.

(Caygill 1998: 119)

Dance produces many examples of disclosure of urban skills and their employment, producing, at its best, a kind of urban symptomatology which, like the urban, escapes the intent of the makers:

the presentation of these bodies carried meaning regardless of the narrative or conceptual theme of the dance. Are their bodies grounded or do they sustain an image of lightness through the dance? Do they use a lot of space, or is their movement contained, bound to their body by some unknown force?

(Albright 1997: 33)

These dancers provide, to use the title of one such dance group, a kind of 'active graphics'. For example, in *La Tristeza Complice* (The Shared Sorrow) by the Belgian dance group Les Ballets C. de la B., the aggression and empathy of the city are conjured up.

Set in a theoretical huis clos of a public waiting area, *La Tristeza Complice* features the particular neurosis of despair of each vagrant character as they enter the space one by one. We see the crazed man in his underwear careering through space on one roller blade, at times gliding gracefully and at other times limping around the stage. Then there enters the tall lanky drag queen, precariously balanced on his heels as he fights off the taunts and abuses of two adolescent boys. More characters enter the fray, including a bag lady whose compulsive arranging and rearranging of her possessions bespeaks a spiritual searching for her self. . . . In the midst of all the loneliness, however, there are several extraordinary moments of physical communication. Often these moments arise from the kinaesthetic rhythms of the movement itself rather than from a specific dramatic intention. In this public no-man's-land, there is little direct interpersonal contact, but physical energy is contagious, and when one person begins a rhythmic, repetitive stamping combination, others are drawn in to his dance. Sometimes this exchange of energy becomes destructive, but at other times it suggests a kind of curious, almost unconscious communication.

(Albright 1997: xix–xx)

Conclusions

Writing in 1934, Lefebvre commented that

> upon the basis of acts repeated billions of times (practical, technical and social acts, like the acts of buying and selling today), customs, ideological inter-pretations, cultures and lifestyles erect themselves. The materialist analysis of these styles has progressed very little.
>
> (Lefebvre 1934: 72)

Until quite recently, this materialist analysis has been stilled, held back by an undue emphasis on cognition and a lack of technologies which might further our understanding. But now there is no excuse. Non-representational styles of work provide a very different means of 'theorizing' and 'witnessing', which can produce a sense of engagement with the world by emphasizing the push. I want to argue that such styles make three main differences.

The first is in the style of work. Non-representationalist work does not pretend to grand theory (though it is still concerned with 'overviews'). Rather it is an attempt to produce strategic and hopefully 'therapeutic' interventions which stress the disclosive power of performance as recognition of the fact that all solutions are responsive, relational, dialogical. The 'embodied embeddedness' (Shotter 1998: 49) of this flow of responsive activity is ineradicable: 'only in the stream of thought and life do words (and our other activities) have meaning' (Wittgenstein 1980: No. 173). To write as though this were not the case is to produce the kind of distanced account that lets cognitivism in again by the back door, a cardinal error in a project which is, in effect, an attempt to revive phronesis.

The second and related difference is the emphasis non-representational work places on classes of experience which have been too rarely addressed, the produc-tive, the interactive, play; all those responsive activities which are usually involved in 'setting up' situations which, because they are often considered to be always already there, are still too little considered; they are regarded as 'trivial'. This means moving towards a poetics of encounter which both conveys a sense of life in which meaning shows itself only in the living, and which, belatedly, recognizes that the unsayable has genuine value and can be felt 'on our pulses' (Wittgenstein 1969: 23). We can see performance as a metaphor which best expresses this poetics, and which, in its workings out, provides imaginative ways of dealing with juxtaposition, ways which are more than just arrangements and namings (cf. Hetherington 1997).

The third influence is methodological. Current work in cultural studies and cultural geography still draws on a remarkably limited number of methodologies – ethnography, focus groups, and the like – which are nearly always cognitive in origin and effect. Non-representational work, in contrast, is concerned with multiplying performative methodologies which allow their participants equal rights to disclosure, through dialogical actions rather than texts, through relation rather than representation. In particular, therefore, it has tried to enhance 'performance consciousness' (Dening 1996) by turning to examples of the intensification of presence provided by the performing arts – art, sculpture, theatre, dance, poetry, music. It is therefore able to draw on a rich archive of experiments with disclosing and therefore describing and constructing space-times. Much, but not all, of this work has its roots in 1960s experimentation with 'focusing the problematic' through embodied expression and now manifests itself in movements such as systems theatre, legislative theatre (Boal 1998), and so on, which aim to discover the 'tacit performativity of power' (Butler 1997: 159). Others do different things: Shotter's experiments with three-way psychotherapy are one case in point. McNamee and Gergen's (1998) invitation to a 'relational responsibility' is another. Newman and Holzman's (1997) improvisational pedagogy is yet another. Attempts to write and act out studies of intimate partners are one more case (see, for example, Chadwick and de Courtivron 1993).[26] All are involved in creating something together, in jointly constructing ways of seeing other possibilities, in continuously unfolding relations on the principle that there is 'never anything like enough contrivance' (Deleuze 1995: 20).

So, as theory ends, something else takes its place. What that something is I do not know, and I am not sure that it matters. But that it is different, that it is lively, and that it represents a challenge to the still elite practices of the current rather cloying hegemony of the cultural turn, I am sure.

I want to end with the figure of John Dewey, the remarkable pragmatist philosopher who, as if to prove the point, was also active in other worlds (Ryan 1995). What distinguishes Dewey's philosophy from that of many of his contemporaries was its commitment to a 'sensuous scholarship' which recognized nondiscursive somatic practice as crucial to the world (and to philosophy). Such practice could be used to enrich knowledge: 'A better measured sense of breathing could provide a cooler, better measured process of thought; an ineffable flush of energetic excitement could spur one to think beyond habitual limits' (Shusterman 1997: 167).[27]

As if to prove the point, Dewey was a keen exponent of and participant in the Alexander Technique, a system of body therapy. 'Long a devoted student of [F. Matthias] Alexander (not simply of his texts but of his somatic exercises) Dewey wrote encomistic introductions to three of his books' (Shusterman 1997: 167). Though Dewey's commitment to the Technique as demonstrating a new scientific principle now seems of its time, still that involvement has some uncanny echoes with the present. To begin with, the Alexander Technique still flourishes: in Britain and North America; you will still find notices and flyers in community centres, dance studios, and local halls advertising courses as part of a wider turn to body therapies (including, I might add, dance therapies). Then, in trying to link thought to the body and in trying to show that thought was embodied, Dewey's work is redolent of the work of later and currently more influential writers from Bakhtin to Deleuze. And, in his search for a philosophy as an embodied, aesthetically engaging way of life, Dewey was making the same move as many contemporary philosophers, back before the grand legislative experiments of the eighteenth and nineteenth centuries, to the embodied, aesthetically engaging way of life favoured by the Greeks and Romans, so powerfully revived by Foucault.[28] 'The bios philosophicus is the animality of being human, taken up as a challenge, practised as an exercise and thrown in the face of others as a scandal' (Foucault 1984, cited in Shusterman 1997: 176–177).

Perhaps we really should think that thought again. Perhaps 'we have to stop pushing words and start moving limbs: stop talking and start dancing. Perhaps I should say no more' (Shusterman 1997: 129).[29]

How it is

So how to understand a chapter which keeps on saying more when there is nothing more to be said? As a plea. As a signpost. As an attempt to value the immaterial. As a politics of passing. As a remembrance. And how might these ambitions be realized when the whole point of the chapter is to value the unmarked? Perhaps as something like a Malanggan (Küchler 1988, 1992, 2002), the ritual carving used in northern New Ireland to take things on after death, the push briefly incarnated in the performance of the object of social relations as one long last sigh.

> Malanggan only 'exist' as socially salient objects, for a very short period, during the mortuary ceremonies for important persons, during which they are gradually inbued with life by being carved and painted, brought to perfection and displayed for a few hours at the culminating part of the mortuary ritual – only to be 'killed' with gifts of shell-money. Once they have been killed they no longer exist as ritual objects. . . . The Malanggan is an object whose physical existence can thus be measured only in days, or even hours, as an index of agency of an explicitly temporary nature. During the brief duration of the ceremony, the carving objectifies a dense and never-ending network of past and future relationships between members of the land-occupying matrilinial units which constitute northern New Ireland . . .
>
> The purpose of a Malanggan is to provide a body or, more precisely, a 'skin' for a recently deceased person of importance. On death the agency of such a person is in a dispersed state. In our terms, indexes of their agency abound, but are not concentrated anywhere in particular. The gardens and plantations of the deceased, scattered here and there, are still in production, their wealth is held by various exchange partners, their houses are still standing, their wives or husbands are still married to them, and so on. The process of making the carving coincides with the process of reorganisation and adjustment through which local society adjusts to the subtraction of the deceased from active participation in political and productive life. The gardens are harvested, the houses decay and become, in time, particularly productive fields, and so on. That is to say, all this stored 'social effectiveness' of the deceased, the difference

they made to how things were, gradually becomes an objectifiable quantity, something to which a given material index may be attributed, and from which this accumulated effectiveness may be abducted. This is what the Malanggan is; a kind of body which accumulates, like a charged battery, the potential energy of the deceased dispersed in the life world.

(Gell 1998: 224–226)

Forced to be a message but no longer able to mean one, I can only do this once.

My work consists of two parts: the one presented here, plus all that I have not written. And it is precisely this second part that is the important one.

(Wittgenstein 1969: 35)

Part III

7   From born to made

Technology, biology, and space

Three requests for significance

I want to begin this chapter by calling on Justina Robson's (2003) book, *Natural History*. Therein, Robson tries to write a modern science fiction fable about life and technology in which she conjures up a whole series of hybrid human-animal-machine forms of life, ending with an alien form of technology which has evolved into life and vice versa. The irony is, and of course Robson knows this very well, that all of these hybrids exist now, with the single exception that they have not always come together in single bodies easily narrativized but are distributed. Similarly, her most alien form of life, a new material surface generating itself in many dimensions at once and called 'stuff', is a fusion of technology and organic life, which in many ways resembles most what is 'human' now in that it is a technology and it is also people, indivisibly fused. You could not define it one way or another at any particular moment. It has no consciousness as you assume individuals must, nor does it have the insensible responses of a tool – but properties of both and also neither. It is intelligent, responsive, compassionate but it does not have an identity of its own, although it contains the fragments of many identities and is capable of creating individuals who could act and exist as ordinary people (Robson 2003: 251).

Robson purposely makes no real distinction between different forms of matter: they can all have a kind of awareness or attunement and it is this move towards the notion of a world that is becoming more and more like 'stuff' that I want to tackle, by concentrating on forms of knowledge that are only now becoming possible – and their possible effects.

Robson wants to answer a set of questions in her book, and they are the same ones that many others also want to wrestle with, not least in the vibrant debates that currently circulate at the edges between the social sciences and the humanities and the sciences. They are: 'What is life?', 'What is human?', 'What is thing?' and 'What is intelligence?' On the whole, most participants in these debates have concentrated on the first three questions but I want to argue that the last question is in many ways the most interesting, though it clearly cannot even begin to be addressed without straying into the territory of the other three.

In this chapter, I want to argue that the world consists of a series of 'intelligencings', to use a rather clumsy phrase, intelligencings which vary substantially in their reach and understanding and interaction, and which have geographies we can and should map – 'infovorous' geographies that can and do teach us how to be, and that therefore have an important ethical dimension. In building this argument, I want to consciously make links with and continue to build on an ecological-cum-ethological tradition that understood geography and biology as cognate subjects but I want to do this by adding in the porous intertwining of technology, understood not just as an intermediary but as a vital component of understanding life itself. In other words, I want to redefine what is essential nature, and what the pursuit of that nature might be (Hampshire 2005) by understanding ecology as a 'cascade of parasites . . . roiling around inside each other's stomachs, . . . medial organs grab[bing] hold of each other, gain[ing] purchase and insight by means of their particular capacities' (Fuller 2005: 174).

My argument is in four parts. To begin with, I shall address three of the different forms of sentience that can currently be found in the world: animal, human and thing. Then, I will argue that these forms of intelligencing are beginning to have more in common as a result of the efflorescence of a suite of 'understated' technologies which enable environments to become both extended and more active. In the subsequent part of the chapter, I want to consider how we might work through the way in which these intelligencings cross with each other by understanding them as territories of instruction but working in the domain of bare life. I will concentrate, in particular, on how recent developments are producing a potential for new kinds of gathering of informed material by revitalizing a world that is often thought to be in danger of being crushed by abstract forces. In the penultimate part of the chapter, I argue that one productive way of understanding these developments is as a new form of reading/writing the world, but in the precognitive rather than the cognitive domain. In the final part of the chapter, I want to begin to address the vexed question of ethics. Here, in line with my emphasis on intelligence, my argument is that we need to produce a politics of knowledge, based around boosting our ability to teach ourselves to the world (Wagner 2001) by emphasizing 'matters of concern' rather than 'matters of fact' and thereby enacting 'a wide range of transportable realities' (Law 2004: 9).

Throughout the chapter, my main concern will be with how the background of being is changing. How the world is disclosed seems to me to be in a period of radical change. It is being added to. Moreover, this addition involves significant political stakes which in turn demand the formation of an ethics of intelligencing.

But, before I start, I need to make a number of points about intelligence. First, I take it that intelligence is not a property of an organism but of the organism and its environment. I want to move, therefore, beyond obvious organismal boundaries and towards the 'superorganismal' idea that organisms are integral with the world outside them as put forward by writers like Tansley and Whitehead in an earlier time. In J.S. Turner's (2000) phraseology, organisms are extended. They are extended in space as different territorial configurations with different effectivities and in time as different forms of process with different temporal signatures. In particular, Turner argues that there is no real difference between an organism and its environment. Organisms extend beyond the obvious integuments of their 'internal physiology' in persistent and systematic ways and adaptively modify their environment. Environments, in turn, can be thought of as a myriad of 'external physiologies' that have been adapted to act in roles as different as substitute or accessory organs, means of communication, or even microclimates. We now know that this process of constant bioturbation is a key element of evolution. Second, and following on, such a conception of organism has an explicit spatiality. Intelligence is a dynamic map of the way in which particular bodies are constructed. Different entities construct their bodies differently using different means of becoming and different locational anchors: for example, 'animals' can be foraging herds, or migrating flocks, or hunting carnivores, each of which has their own distinctive geographies which are a part of what they are, including at what level of aggregation it becomes sensible to talk about a definable entity (Lulka 2004). Then, third, intelligence is about the capacity to lay out territories of intelligibility, environments which are predictable but which can also compel knowledge, can instruct, can teach, can make all manner of requests for significance. Environments are more than means of testing therefore. They are means of learning, of in-forming, if you like.

Another way of putting this is to turn to Simondon's account of overcoming hylomorphism, the form-matter model so common in Western thinking (Mackenzie 2002) (equally plausibly, recourse could be made to Whitehead's critique of misplaced concreteness, that is Newtonian science's tendency to construct ideally isolated objects as the basis of knowledge). For Simondon, hylomorphism is a 'model of the genesis of form as external to matter, as imposed from the outside like a command on a material which is thought inert and dead' (Simondon, cited in Fuller 2005: 18). In contrast, Simondon counterposes the process of individuation, whereby materials produce their own capacities of formation in relation to the environment around them and the affordances that it offers. This focus on a dynamics of combinatorial production is similar to Deleuze and Guattari's notion of the machinic phylum in which forces, capacities and predispositions intermesh to make something else occur, and to complexity theory's notion of self-organization. Indeed nowadays it has become routine to mesh the two together (cf. De Landa 2002; Parisi 2004), with the threshold into self-organization being crossed when what might be a motley bunch of cells or components becomes something else. Just as in the natural world, so in the technical world, there are a series of more or less temporary settlements driven by what it is possible to combine. These settlements often appear to be standard objects but they too are susceptible to constant change and mutation.

Three requests for significance

In this section, I want to briefly consider three different kinds of sentience, pointing up their qualities and biases and spatial ranges and how they add up, in order to begin to understand the new developments that are now going on. I will want to argue that current technological developments mean that human intelligence is gradually becoming attuned in different ways which mean that we can start talking about what the stuff of stuff consists of.

I will begin with animals because I want to illustrate the sheer range of different kinds of intelligence that currently inhabit the world. The problem, of course, is that, as Derrida (2002) has pointed out at length, 'animal' covers a very large range of different kinds of affects, sufficient to make it possible to question the very category itself. 'Animal' is clearly not a satisfactory descriptor, a judgement only strengthened by its association with all kinds of 'petishism' (L. Marks 2002) – the tendency to 'polish an animal mirror to look for ourselves' (Haraway 1991: 21), perceiving the 'good' qualities of animals as reflections of our ideal selves and projecting the 'best' human attributes onto animals.

Thus it is clear, to begin with, that animals live in what are often radically different umwelten; think only of the sonar of the hunting bat and its prey, the moth, the ultraviolet light seen by birds, the infrared light seen by insects, the acute sense of smell of dogs, the electric and magnetic fields to which some fish and a few other animals are sensitive, the changes in air pressure that birds can pick up (Wynne 2004). And so on. And this is to ignore the way in which some animals have evolved senses that allow them to impinge directly into other umwelten, as, for example, in the case of the owl's auditory system which is specialized to the noises of its prey. Then, animals are bound up with different and diverse spaces, from the enormous territories covered by the whale or the albatross or many migratory animals to the mid-ranges of many carnivores to the micro-spaces inhabited by many insects (Clubb and Mason 2003). They also live in very different times, in terms of metabolic rates, reaction times and forms of foresight, lifespans and memories. Finally, they have widely differing degrees of individuation and social complexity, from herd, hive and swarm forms that are probably best thought of, at least at certain emergent times, as collective organisms, through animals that have proto-social systems (such as dolphins or elephants or many primates) to animals that spend much of their lives alone. Further, it has become clear that at least certain animals display quite high internal degrees of variability; they may even have developed forms of social complexity that have characteristics that are 'cultural', though this is still a matter of very considerable dispute (de Waal and Tyack 2003).

In other words, animals exist in spaces and times which mean that the relation that they have to the things in an environment may be radically different from ours and each others (Hauser 2000). As Jakob von Uexküll showed many years ago, there is no single world in which all living beings are situated. 'The fly, the dragonfly and the bee that we observe flying next to us on a summer day do not move in the same world as the one in which we observe them, nor do they share with us – or with each other – the same time and the same space' (Agamben 2004: 40). Rather, there are a series of 'worlds-for'. But this does not mean that these worlds-for do not relate. Of course they do. Take the spider and the fly. The threads of the spider's web are exactly proportioned to the visual capacity of the fly – the fly cannot see them and flies towards death unawares. Though the two worlds of the spider and fly may not communicate, still they are exactly attuned to one another.

One argument commonly made is that there is not much difference between animals and humans and especially certain kinds of animals and humans. Usually, some form of genetic continuum is posited (for example, that a chimpanzee is genetically closer to a human than to a baboon) or a salient genetic fact is paraded, such as that we share 98.4 per cent of our DNA with chimpanzees (and probably even more with bonobos), or, alternatively, evidence of tool-using, and even secondary tool-using, behaviour or elementary understanding of linguistic cues or even the existence of proto-mathematical skills in at least some animals is mustered. Certainly, one of the key findings of research over the last 20 years or so is that animals are more rational than was formerly thought (that is, they have more cognitive and pre-cognitive capabilities) while humans are less rational than was once thought (that is, they have less unique cognitive and pre-cognitive capabilities that are able to be used as a sign of supremacy over animals). In particular, we now understand that 'instinct' does not equate with non-cognitive: an animal can have a genetic endowment that makes it behave in a particular way but it is also able to reflect on that behaviour.

Equally, however, we are now coming to understand that there are differences between humans and other animals, what those differences are, and how these differences make a startling difference to the human umwelten, to the worlds-for that human beings assume exist. It is these differences that I want to concentrate on in this chapter, though I shall also want to point to some of the new means of attunement of the animal and human world that are currently becoming possible.

The reason that these distinctively human differences are so important is because it becomes possible to 'learn not just from the other but through the other' (Tomasello 1999: 6) with the result that cognitive resources can be pooled and elaborated in ways that other species are not able to achieve. In other words, through a special kind of intelligencing, learning sticks and is able to be projected forwards in time.

I want to note five of these differences. First, and probably most importantly, 'interactional intelligence'. Human beings tend to have an inordinate concern with the implications of others' actions which dates from birth and before and which almost certainly has a biological basis. This innate capacity for 'participatory thought' arising out of expressive-responsive bodily activities (Shotter 2004) can be thought of as a capacity to understand conspecifics as 'beings like themselves who have intentional and mental lives like their own' (Tomasello 1999: 5). It consists of a whole series of complexly linked behaviours including language (and associated sensibilities such as hearing that is acute precisely in the wavelengths that speech is broadcast in), face recognition, and general adaptivity to others that enable multiple simultaneous perspectives on and representations of each and every perceptual situation. In turn, this dialogical capacity allows us to do a remarkable thing, involving computational complexity that is still difficult to fathom, that is to work towards a joint co-ordination of actions with another human being, even when it is very difficult to say what we mean, within a very small number of steps (usually about four) in a very short space of time. Such a capacity involves an ability to make models of the other, read the 'intentions' behind action, make rapid interactional moves in the correct sequence, design actions so that they are perspicuous, and so on.

As Peirce and many more recent writers have been keen to emphasize, deduction and induction are relatively trivial human skills, of no great computational complexity: it is abduction or theory construction which is the outstanding characteristic of human intelligence. Abduction is the leap of faith from data to the theory that explains it, just like the leap of imagination from observed behaviour to others' intentions. While most explicit theories or abductions are wrong, our implicit ones about interactional others are mostly good enough for current purposes (Levinson 1995: 254).

This process of inferential enrichment almost certainly skews our umwelt towards certain interpretations of how the world is. So, for example, we tend to find order where none exists, overdetermine explanations by seeking one all-explaining factor (because interaction requires single-solution thinking), assume that someone is watching us at all times, privilege animistic thinking by presuming that there must be an interactor in the inanimate world, and so on (Tomasello 1999).

In turn, this capacity of inferential enrichment is predicated on two other capacities. One is a very high degree of affective complexity arising out of concern with others' actions and an omnivorous set of senses which encourage 'range'. The affective palette that co-operative living demands means that basic emotions like anger or fear have been progressively extended into all manner of behavioural byways. Indeed, it has even been suggested that rationality and language have grown out of an ability to be so emotional. 'As the emotional brain developed, and we became more emotionally complex and sophisticated, more alternatives and choices arose in our interactions with others. This then required a capacity to think and reflect on our emotions, and this led to the development of the cortex, and in particular, the prefrontal cortex' (Gerhardt 2004: 35) which acts as a kind of control centre from which emotional reactions arising deeper in the brain can be modulated. The other, related capacity is a reliance on communicative movement arising out of the muscular make-up of the body and organs like the hand. As Gehlen (1988: 120) writes, 'much too little attention has been given to the ability of human beings to enjoy a wide range of possibilities for movement unknown among animal species. The combinations of voluntary possible movements available to man are literally inexhaustible, the delicate co-ordinations of movements unlimited'. In a sense, human being is a whirl of movement-space. The development of a range of plastic and adaptable movements is key to human being – to the corporeal schema, to manipulation of tools and the environment, to communication, to expression, to disturbances of perception, and indeed to the whole sense of space (Vesely 2004). Just think of the enormous range of a comparatively simple gestural activity like pointing.

This sense of what the bulk of our thinking is oriented towards also suggests another aspect of human intelligence (Dreyfus 2005). That is conceptuality. Human intelligence is not necessarily linked to the world of tangible things. It has a projective capacity – imagination, theorizing, play, call it what you like – which allows it to point beyond itself to other entities and thereby generate additional concepts and conceive unobservable mental states which, in turn, provide it with high degrees of flexibility in both the physical and social realms. It enables human beings to construct 'explanations for why we (and others) do what we do, and why the world operates in the way it does – an ability not present in other species' (Povinelli 2000: 339). The consequence is that human being is not always constantly occupied with and in things but spends a good deal of its time attempting to understand others in order to understand things:

> to socially learn the conventional use of a tool or a symbol, children must come to understand why, to what outside end, the other person is using the tool or symbol; that is to say, they must come to understand the intentional significance of the tool use or symbolic practice – what it is 'for', what 'we', the users of this tool or symbol, do with it.
>
> (Tomasello 1999: 6)

The animal, in contrast, is to a much greater degree taken by things like food. It has less sense of such things as being-at-hand, as being disclosed. It is less able to suspend and deactivate its relationship with its specific disinhibitors so that it becomes open to possibility. It is more in a relation of enchantment-enchainment to the world (but see Krell 1992).

Finally, we must turn to the aspect of human being that is commonly hailed as distinctively human, namely tool use, and to simultaneously begin to address the place of things. If Heidegger was wrong about this (Nancy 2003), encouraged by his tendency to privilege human existence as the superhero that frees entities from the 'present-at-hand' realm, he was surely right about how we relate to tools. His account is familiar but it is worth reprising.

> Heidegger demonstrates that our primary interaction with beings comes through 'using' them, through simply counting on them in an unthematic way. For the most part, objects are implements taken for granted, a vast environmental backdrop supporting the thin and volatile layer of our explicit activities. All human action finds itself lodged amidst countless items of supporting equipment: the most nuanced debates in a laboratory stand at the mercy of a silent bedrock of floorboards, bolts, ventilators, gravity and atmospheric oxygen. . . .
>
> Heidegger shows that we normally do not deal with entities as aggregates of natural physical mass, but rather as a range of functions or effects that we rely upon. Instead of encountering 'pane of glass' we tend to make use of this item indirectly, in the form of 'well-lit room'. We do not usually contend with sections of cement, but only with their outcome: an easily walkable surface area. As a rule, tools are not present-at-hand but ready-to-hand.
>
> (Harman 2002: 18)

It is unequivocally the case, in other words, that human being is tool-being and that the process of tuning works both ways. As Zizek (2004: 19) puts it 'it is meaningless to imagine a human being as a biological entity without the complex network of his or her tools – such a notion is the same as, say, the goose without her feathers'. Indeed the 'biological' and 'technical' are inexorably linked in ways that are biologically determined. Take the case of the hand. The distinctive anatomical structures of the bones and muscles of the hand allow us to grasp the object world. They have developed in lock step with neural systems in the sensorimotor pathways, and the integrative and coordinative structures of the brain and spinal cord to bring the object world deep inside us. Indeed, it seems likely that the development of manual dexterity and brain size are co-dependent processes in human evolution (Tallis 2003). As importantly, tool-being allows both extension and co-operation. Tools very often require mimetic faculties to learn how to use skilfully, co-operation to use properly, and conversation to continually monitor, as well as to formulate appropriate identities (Hutchby 2001). We can also be sure that tool use is a matter of mutual attunement based on a usability which is attained through a process of historical genesis; 'a technical object lies somewhere between a transient, unstable event and a durable, heavily reproduced structure. Its degree of concretization, to use Simondon's terms, is the technicity of a technology' (Mackenzie 2002: 14). Finally, tool-being can only exist within a network of references and relays. It can therefore have a wide range of styles of thought focused on particular modes of individuation and is continually open to the emergence of new capacities which will emerge in concert with the material being worked (Mackenzie 2002).

This brings us to the last human characteristic, namely human ability to make and remake environments so that they can ask different questions and so provide new kinds of instruction: environments can be more or less articulate. This ability, in turn, allows us to move on to thinking about the world of things in more detail which is the final form of intelligencing that I want to address. For it might be thought that things cannot qualify as sentient beings, even if they are understood as environments 'forever in action, constructing in each moment the sustaining habitat where our awareness is on the move' (Harman 2002: 18). But I want to argue, first, that this is not necessarily the case and, second, that it is, in any case, becoming ever less so. To begin with, things have to be seen as 'wild'(Attfield 2000): 'far from the insipid physical bulks that one imagines, [they] are already aflame with ambiguity, torn by vibrations and insurgencies equalling those found in the most tortured human moods' (Harman 2002: 19). Things enact themselves amidst the system of the world. Most particularly, it is crucial to remember that equipment is not effective just because it is used by people but also 'because it is capable of an effect, of inflicting some kind of blow on reality' (Harman 2002: 20). Then, following on, I think it might be argued that, of late, tools are beginning to take on more and more independent (or, perhaps better, forceful) capacities. Of course, as Heidegger pointed out many times, objects are mutually referential: behind each tool are legions of other tightly interlaced tools. Tools do not function as individual objects, but as distributed networks taking in a range of objects which act as manifold contexts. However, modern tool-being is changing its nature: it has a much greater capacity to influence the comings and goings of bodies than in the past because of the distributed networks in which it is caught up. And for four reasons. First, because we increasingly live in a blizzard of things which possess us as much as we possess them, generated by the fact that capitalism is 'an unreserved surrender to things' (Bataille 1988: 136). Yet this has does not necessarily lessen things' alterity. They can still seem 'wild'. Second, because thought has increasingly been rendered more and more 'thing-like' so that we now seem to live in 'an indeterminate ontology where things seem slightly human and humans seem slightly thing-like' (B. Brown 2003: 13). In particular, the familiar antagonism between abstraction and concreteness does not seem to characterize the present time, as object networks formed from abstract principles increasingly seed concrete events. Third, because things are becoming more complex entities and are therefore beginning to take on, as distributed networks, many of the characteristics of intelligence often thought to be reserved for human beings and animals. Objects are becoming adaptive; within limited bounds some things can self-reproduce, can exhibit emergence, and so on (Dant 2004; Tamen 2001). Fourth, because they provide architectures which force intelligence. Rather as the need to have explicit bodily self-reference in order to get around in the canopy of forests likely forced primate evolution by producing a kinaesthetic self-concept (Povinelli 2001), so an array of things can reciprocally produce a practice of dwelling (Ingold 2002).

Three different means of making worlds (or sets of worlds), then. Of course, these worlds have always intersected. One thinks of the ways in which human intelligencing has been boosted by the prosthetic qualities of animals and things, by, for example, forms of domestication that turned out to have farther-reaching effects on all parties than could ever have been imagined (Whatmore 2002). But I think that it is possible to argue that these worlds are converging at a peculiarly rapid rate at present, thereby producing a more attuned and 'informed' sense of materiality. To begin with, they are converging as a series of systematic knowledges are formed about them which are, in part, replacing or supplementing the tacit knowledges that used to suffice. Many of these knowledges are then migrating into software and other quasi-mechanical means of applying knowledge, thereby turning up in confirmatory ways scattered through and/or constituting new environments. Then, all kinds of conventions cut between these means of world-making. For example, more and more common representational formats are being put in place, particularly around picturing life and various forms of personhood, built around particular senses of narrative (Dumit 2004; Marks 2002). Then again, they are converging as nature and technology adapt and evolve. Thus, just as one instance, many animals are adapting to urban environments, as, for example, in the case of urban foxes that seem to be gradually developing different jaws as a result of scavenging for food from fast-food litter and dustbins rather than hunting live prey (Harris 2004). Meanwhile, technology is becoming more complex, and is taking on more active features; as a result objects are increasingly loaded up with adaptive features which, for example, allow them to communicate with other objects, read interactions, react recursively, and provide various prostheses (e.g. means of producing additional calculation or memory) (Thrift 2004b).

It follows that fragments of each of these intelligencings now crop up in the other's domain on a regular basis, making it possible to think of a more active and mutually implicated materiality in which 'practices of knowing cannot be fully claimed as human practices' (Barad 2003: 829; see also Thrift 2004b). It may not be 'stuff' but we certainly seem to be getting closer to an amorphous state in which human being becomes 'flecks of identity' (Fuller 2005) in wider ecologies of intelligence made up of many things.

Networks of intelligence

But this is only a first step. For each of these intelligencings is in constant interaction with each other. They do not exist singly or apart. This is, of course, a standard mantra of actor-network theory and many other relational approaches. But, as the work of von Uexküll shows, we should not believe that this interaction is taking place in one world. Rather it takes place in a whole series of worlds which are more or less attuned to each other and which have more or less resonance in and with each other (Lorimer 2006). Thus interactions may take place in one dimension (e.g. the character of the fly's visual acuity) or in none. They may produce new affects, or simply run alongside each other. Recently, a number of authors have tried to frame or phrase these attunements. For example, Latour (2000) has argued that the best way to see these interactions is as propositions, in the sense that one entity can be loaded into another by making the second entity attentive to the first. Another way of conceiving this interaction is as part of a more general metaphysics of becoming, that

> can help us to imagine the world before our knowledge of it. On the one hand, the metaphysics serves to put knowledge in its place, as just one part of an evolving cyborg assemblage, rather than as some kind of ethereal simulacrum of the whole thing. On the other hand, though not at all rich or detailed, the metaphysics helps us to imagine the thing itself, the world itself that knowledge is about: entities sporting, coupling, forming temporary unities, and so on.
>
> (Pickering 2003: 107)

What I think this shows is that there is a geographical project based around vital spaces understood as different ways of knowing the world which are, at the same time, ways of living the world. We might, I suppose think of this as a project of comparative ontogenesis in which the task is to investigate how different worlds are composed and interact with each other, rather as the spider and the fly both rely on each other (with the same in-built tensions!). There is a kind of biological metaphor/technological metaphor at work here but it is not the universal phylogenetic tree. Rather, it is the network or fold: 'evolution is basically reticulate' (Woese 2004: 179).

But, having got this far, I then want to try to push a little farther by arguing that the surfaces of biology and technology are being interleaved in ways which question what we mean by intelligence and which, in certain parts of the world, are starting to produce something rather like Robson's carpet of 'stuff' acting as a constantly-on background. Thus, on one side, the world formerly called 'biological' is being loaded up with all kinds of monitors and points of feedback and continuous monitoring and is being treated as a material surface. For example, animals are not just the object of more and more surveillance, ranging from the simple chipping of companion animals through to all kinds of complex ethological surveillance including GPS transmitters attached to smaller and smaller mammals and now birds, continuous video feed into sites which have previously been opaque to detection, and the representation of senses like infra-red that we could not mark before. They are also increasingly thought of, in part no doubt because of this mediated interaction, as the focus of knowledges which are, in certain senses co-operatively generated (Hinchliffe *et al.* 2005). Something similar is happening in the human realm in terms of modern medicine where it is now possible not only to write of 're-ordering life' through new systems of classification and measurement combined with technologies which make the clinical encounter more and more immediate but also to open up more possibilities for co-operation between clinician and patient (Brown and Webster 2004). On the other side, in the world formerly called material, many materials are beginning to have characteristics which used to be reserved for life and biological material is being incorporated into the production of all kinds of things, from plastics to robots (Thrift 2004b). The result is that the realm of 'not-quite-life' is growing apace.

Some writers will want to call 'enough' on this mass miscegenation, seeing a threat to 'nature', 'human nature', and the world of the senses, that might lead to a general 'species suicide' (e.g. McKibben 2003; Habermas 2003). But, I do not believe that an authentic nature/inauthentic technology narrative is a viable one, a point that is only underlined now that crossovers that used to take place in the laboratory are becoming a part of everyday life and are producing new hybrid entities, not as singular bodies but as distributed environments, as autonomic physiologies which have re-organized human being, putting it together again as a skein of bodies, things and spaces. This process of reticulation is becoming so general that it is worth taking some time to consider it. The process consists of six main elements, each of which is inter-related, and which are the twenty-first-century equivalent of the laying down of pipes, cables and roads but with an even more effective grip on human being because they pay more attention to establishing patterns of continually adapting pre-reflective movement which, it might be argued, actually chime rather well with the innate plasticity of human movement.

First, and most obviously, through developments like grid computing, environments are becoming ever more computationally intensive. Elsewhere, I have pointed to the effects of the population of the world with software coupled with general increases in computing power (Thrift and French 2002). In recent work (Thrift 2004a, 2005c), I have been trying to outline what such a 'qualculated' world of continuous and ubiquitous calculation in endless loops will look like, and, in particular, what new capabilities and senses it will bring into being, such as extended reach or the kinds of effects produced by modern mood-altering drugs which depend on computation at every level for their genesis and examination of side-effects. Second, more and more of the world can be seen and heard and tracked through a combination of increasingly ubiquitous screens, sensors, cameras, and the widespread use of the radio spectrum, leading to mobile phones (now including screens), RFIDs and the like, devices which depend on a radioactive world (Thrift 2004a). Third, more and more of the world can be sensed and represented, from the micro to the macro. For example, very large amounts of life can be 'pictured', sometimes in real time and can be made available for self-fashioning. Thus, Dumit (2004) shows how brain scans become part of how people explain themselves: the image becomes lived as part of the person. It constitutes a new sense of what the real is because more and more things will come pre-identified. Fourth, more and more of the world can be named and continuously tracked and this naming will become constitutive, even when it may contain many inaccuracies and distortions. As one example, take the project to produce DNA barcodes which, in theory, will instantly identify every species on the planet on demand, which will, in other words, label every extant form of life. This project has been heavily criticized, not just on grounds of practicality but also for attempting to produce clarity where none exists (B. Holmes 2004). Yet it seems likely that, in time, these barcodes, with all their imperfections, will become a new norm, not so much a gateway on to the natural world as a newly minted world. Fifth, more and more of the world can be remembered (Bowker 2003). The result is that issues like life-logging and digital curation are becoming important topics, as increasingly people record larger and larger amounts of their lives. Sixth, all of these developments take place within a world of constantly shifting spaces which presage a new, pervasive sense of location (Enge 2004). Through the intervention of GPS, GIS, geodemographics, and so on, mobile and constantly adapting spatial and temporal frames have been established which, as I have argued elsewhere, depend (ironically) on an absolute co-ordinate grid (Thrift 2004a). In turn, new kinds of socio-spatial interaction are able to be generated because so many actors can be easily located. For example, the crowds produced by large industrial cities are being supplemented and extended in a number of ways.

To summarize, new kinds of sensing have therefore become possible. Reach and memory are being extended; perceptions which were difficult or impossible to register are becoming routinely available; new kinds of understated intelligence are becoming possible. These developments are probably having most effect in the pre-cognitive domain, leading to the possibility of arguing that what we are seeing is the laying down of a system (or systems) of distributed pre-cognition, a development which I will address in more detail in the next part of the chapter.

Making the world machine readable

To summarize the argument so far, we can begin to see the rise of a new layer of active object environments which constitute an informed materiality in which the activity of the world will be continuously mediated, threaded together and communicated at a very large range of scales and at the same time have added to it a new kind of theoretically charged vitality working in the same way that architecture also does (Vesely 2004). This will be a new kind of building, if you like, a process reality made up of understatements.

This understated building presages a new realism which intends to both extend and/or duplicate the world by anchoring more and more of what was regarded as 'human' in the 'environment' in the form of small cognitive assists but which are drawn on pre-cognitively. These cognitive assists, whose immense range I have laid out above, will aid all manner of root human practices and especially, I suspect, the faculty of interactional intelligence: movement, location, the amount of information available at each moment, what counts as 'near' or 'local', and so on, and stand for essentially theoretical notions of the world – of many kinds – being absorbed back into the warp and weft of everyday practice. Of course, what this process of 'expersonation' might mean in detail is much more difficult to predict. But whatever the actual case this 'stuff' is currently heading out from its Western urban core, like a large carpet, colonizing more and more of the world. The result is that what we count as matter has begun to change: new kinds of mattering are being born (Law 2004). This change is not total. It is currently hesitant and flimsy and parts of it can no doubt be reversed. But it seems to me that the general tendency is towards a world which is being supplemented on a permanent basis.

There are two ways to think about this new state of affairs. One is to argue that it constitutes a gross intrusion which is one further step on the road to a rational-ized dystopia. The other is to argue that it simply adds in another layer of vitality, of 'not-quite-life', which will both punctuate each event with additional informa-tion and will link each event into networks with much larger spatial extent which are underpinned by particular forms of conceptuality. In time, as they coalesce, these developments may bring about a new form of augmented relationality in which technology acts as a constant accompaniment to biology and vice versa.

To understand this spatiality, I want to return to Heidegger. Heidegger, like many authors, tends to contrast a human originary spatiality of the disclosure of being with a homogeneous metrical space of objective and ideal absence intuited by consciousness (Vallega 2003). When originary spatiality is attuned, producing perceptual fulfilment, then all is right with the world. As Todes puts it:

> The percipient's sense of the integrity of his perceptual activity is a sense of achievement, of practical self-composure, of having put-himself-together, inte-grated himself by his skilful practice. This sense is derived from the verification of his anticipations, which allows him to rest assured. It takes the form of an ease or, at best, grace, of poise and movement. He feels, at least momentarily, the absolute master of himself as practical agent. He is fully occupied with his sensible circumstances, but in such a way that he is thereby also fully occupied with a sense of himself as responsive percipient of these circumstances.
>
> (Todes 2001: 128)

What I am arguing in this chapter is that this viewpoint is no longer possible: increasingly human originary spatiality has become not just accompanied but suffused by a metrical space made up out of an army of things which provide new perceptual capacities. In a sense, all are joined together in the domain of bare life in a reworking of the verification of anticipations made possible by an informed materiality.

In other words, we are moving into a new 'a-whereness', one in which what was called 'technology' has moved so decisively into the interstices of the active percipience of everyday life that it is possible to talk about a new layer of intelligence abroad in the world, a layer of intelligence which is beginning to unite living things by virtue of giving them a boosted bare life (Agamben 1998; Thrift 2003b) held more and more in common. Here we have, in other words, a biodigital politics in which 'the body is no longer determined by individual qualities constituting the difference between animal, human and machine' (Parisi 2004: 137).

I want to end this section by addressing the issue of bare life in rather more detail. As originally conceived, bare or simple life was, in effect, intended to describe what might be conceived of as an 'animal' level of consciousness, the simple fact of 'natural' living common to all living beings, that minimal level of consciousness at which life can still be maintained and experienced without cognitive consciousness (and therefore political voice). Now, of course, we know that bare life is in fact full to overflowing. It consists of the vast amounts of computation done by living things in order to simply keep functioning. In human beings, think only of two examples. One is the computation that is necessary to sustain the 'simple' fact of bipedal locomotion. In fact the embodied skills of footwork take up a very large amount of the body's computational attention – and, of course, vary in style substantially from culture to culture (Ingold 2004; Amato 2004; Vogel 2001). Another example is the aforementioned content of interactional intelligence. Much of the computation associated with this intelligence is done in just a few milliseconds and nearly all of it turns up before consciousness, even in human beings. Thus:

> most of what happens in what we call communication or relating happens too quickly, demands too immediate a response, to have an actual correspondence with any of the descriptions that might be made of its 'meaning'. The meaning of the expression or relational act, it is generally assumed, happened earlier as 'intention' or will be recovered later as 'memory'. But of course the 'earlier' and 'later' moments of resolution or synthesis are subject to the same conditions of prospective or retrospective postponement as the original expression or act, as memory and intentionality are themselves but differential 'takes' on the same description.
>
> (Wagner 2001: 8)

So, we now know that what we call 'thinking' in human beings does not occur just in the brain but at a series of sites in the body. We also know that bare life does not just consist of slavish autonomic responses, of blind and unconscious 'vegetative' functions. In both animals and human beings what we see are all kinds of 'unrememberable but unforgettable' (Watt, cited in Gerhardt 2004: 15) cultural subroutines being laid down, most especially in the weeks and months after birth, subroutines that involve imitation, affective response, etc. In other words, bare life is the ground where the biological, technological and cultural collide, and where simultaneously the validity of each of these categories is constantly put under question.

But what is happening now is that bare life is increasingly mediated by things which slip in between its interstices, boosting it here, conditioning it there. The result is that 'humanity . . . has taken upon itself the total management of its own animality' (Agamben 2004: 77). In other words, humanity 'no longer preserves [its] own animality as undisclosable, but rather seeks to take it on and govern it by means of technology' (Agamben 2004: 80).

Notwithstanding the undoubted problems that come from Agamben's reading of technology and indeed biology (see Krell 1992), still it is clear that such a situation could be fraught with real dangers. Most particularly, it makes it difficult to keep events open, since they will have already been forethought: as a result, human beings might become puppets without masters. However, such a negative reading of the more and more explicit engineering of the event also depends upon interpreting technology as a constitutive other, rather than as a part of what it means to be human. If, instead, technology is taken to consist of a series of active mediaries in the Latourian sense, often placed in messy and circuitous conjunctions which only appear as smooth passages because so much of their work has been black-boxed, then maybe it is possible to think in a slightly different fashion. Perhaps, then, in turn, it becomes possible to think of historical parallels with other comprehensive, distributed technological systems.

The most obvious of these parallels, I believe, is with the discovery of writing and the onset of literacy. Writing, and the skills of reading and general literacy that go with it, appears to us now as one coherent system, so near to us that it is hardly ever considered to be a 'technology', but writing only came into being as a comprehensive system through stuttering technological advance and the construction of all manner of slowly evolving institutions of responsive expression and it did not become general in most populations until the nineteenth century – indeed, given figures on global literacy, it is debatable if it is still an entirely comprehensive practice. But writing functioned mainly in the cognitive domain of imagination – as a means of framing time and space, as a set of mental and manual skills, as the means of producing all manner of new cultural modes, from lists to novels, as a new and fertile means of boosting imaginative capacities. Indeed it could and has been argued that it produced much of what we now call cognition. Certainly, it produced a quite different attunement to the world: the onset of this logocentric world has had global effects, producing new kinds of consciousness, new kinds of social and cultural structures, and new kinds of spatiality.

In contrast to writing, the new technologies function mainly in the milliseconds of the precognitive domain of perception (Libet 2004; Donald 2001). Not surprisingly, there is rather less cultural analysis of how this domain functions, but this does not mean there is nothing. For inspiration, we have to reel back to the nineteenth century and the very large amount of work carried out in psychology, and especially German psychology, on involuntary or reflex actions, on habit, as forms of unconscious inference. In particular, this work was picked up by early cultural theorists working on the impact of cinema. The work of Balázs, Kracauer, and others, and of Benjamin on tactility, suggest that technologies of this kind function chiefly as a new surface to the world, adding new ways of touching and being touched, an umwelt in which novel patterns of corporeal habit and inference were laid down simultaneously through the power of new forms of sensation, a new kind of nervous system with its own forms of 'neuropolitics' (Taussig 1993; Connolly 2002; Thrift 2003a).

What I want to suggest here is that we should see the knot of developments that I have outlined as being similar in their effects to the technology of writing (and reading) but mainly taking place in the precognitive domain, in what used to be called the domain of apperception, where attention is brought to focus on an object (Crary 1999). The main effects in this domain of understatement will be on what is regarded as embodiment (for example, on our balance and poise), on the density of the field of perception, on what can be counted as local and near and reachable (as, for example, these technologies make ex-ante spatial links), on the amount of content that is immediately available to feed our imagination and, in general, on our sense of attunement to the world (including what significance we tend to give ourselves).

In turn, there is another way of framing this onset of new silent languages. This new world is one of not-quite-life but so close to the conduct of life that it is not-quite-inert either. In other words, what is required is a new category which is rather like the parasite (Serres 1980) – but in a symbiotic relationship – or perhaps more convincingly the microbe. These 'tiny masters of metabolism and movement' (Margulis and Sagan 2002: 204) form a subvisible world which is a crucial element of the larger worlds of which we are a part. Through the co-optation of strangers in mergers, fusions, incorporations, cohabitations and recombinations, microbes, whether viral, bacterial or eukaryotic, produce ever greater complexity, evolving in ways that extend far beyond the relatively uniform lifestyles and practices of animals and plants. Perhaps the new technologies of understatement are now taking on this role, present in different forms at almost every encounter and, rather like microbes, as likely to make more as less out of them. In turn, such a vision would suggest a new supplementary and teleo-affective spatiality which would provide an underlay to much of what we fondly call 'everyday' life.

Where the people are: by way of conclusions

What I have tried to outline in this chapter is a new fabric of forethought, a new nervous system, coming into being in the world which has at least the capacity to extend environments and make them more articulate (that is, more willing to enter into unexpected connections, provide more expressive opportunities, foster more activity, generate more intermediaries, stand a better chance of being complex, make more entities more active, etc.) or, equally possible, to make them inarticulate by closing all these characteristics down and making the world into a frenzied roundelay of accumulation of not very much at all. The point is that, in these early times, there is a political task to be addressed of producing vital protocols when remarkably few protocols are as yet set in stone and of imagining the new horizons and articulations of momentary enunciation. In other words the new knot of technologies can and should function as means of boosting responsive expression.

I hope that it is clear that I have taken a good deal of inspiration for this chapter from particular forms of process or motion philosophy which stress a recursive metaphysics of association, and in particular the work of Tarde and then Latour, and Whitehead and then Stengers (2002b) and Zubiri (2000, 2003), and Bergson and then Deleuze and Guattari. That work is typified by several key characteristics. First, it earns its living from a relational theory of reality: it refuses to offer an implicit theory of substance existing independently from the relations in which it is involved. Second, it relies on a constructivism of a particular kind, namely a transcendental empiricism (or pan-experimentalism) in which construction never takes place in general but always in relation to a matter of concern and commitment, a lure to our attention which provides an intensification of feeling. Thus, due attention means 'becoming able to add, not subtract, means learning how to get access, not renouncing the possibility of access' (Stengers 2004: 5). Third, it understands reality as a series of complex composites based on an ultimate metaphysical principle of invention; 'the advance from disjunction to conjunction, creating a novel entity other than the entities given in disjunction' (Whitehead 1978: 21). Fourth, it argues that nature cannot be split into, on one side, a causal, objective nature and, on the other, a perceived nature full of so-called secondary properties like odours, sounds, enjoyments and values. And last, it insists that mode of existence and mode of achievement are always related: thus modes of interpretation literally matter.

This brief exposition is necessary because I want to end this chapter by talking about the vexed question of ethics, I will give this topic much less consideration than it deserves but with good reason. I would think it impossible to dispute that all kinds of ethical dilemmas are surfacing or will surface as a result of these developments, and indeed they should – once we find the sites where it makes sense to investigate these dilemmas. After all, in a sense, this new technological world is working directly into our unconscious, acting rather like a substitute for, or, more likely, an extension of, biology. But what I want to address instead is what the domain of ethics should actually be. My argument, briefly put, is that an ontological ethics requires that much more attention should be given to the responsibility of cultivating intelligence and invention, broadly conceived as environments that are made up of informed materials which maximize instruction (Wagner 2001). It is important to state that this kind of ethics which lies somewhere between uprightness in the face of the limits to knowledge and the hope of consolation to be found in an open reading frame (Rabinow 2004) does not preclude a concentration on other ethical moments like justice or equity. Rather, I see it as a supplement. In turn, this means at least the following ethical procedures should be followed by the new ecologies now coming into definition.

In turn, applying these procedures should produce interesting environments that will not only matter but also provide a kind of consolation (Rabinow 2004).

- The world should be added to, not subtracted from. Invention should lead to the actualization of the virtual, rather than the realization of the possible. This is the principle of producing promise.
- The world should continue to be held to be multiple with all the consequences that flow from such a stance, and especially the need for constant ethical brokerage. This is the principle of 'relentless pluralism' (Thompson 2002: 186).
- The world should be kept untidy. It should have negative capability, or as Keats put it 'a man [must be] capable of being in uncertainties, mysteries, doubts without any irritable reaching after fact and reason' (cited in Wagner 2001: 254). This is the principle of messiness.
- The world should be free to display its spectacular and amazing performances through the sacrament of the expressive sign that can pass their energetic demands on. This is the principle of wonder.
- The world should be free to teach us. That means retaining difficulties, uncertainties, inaccuracies since mistakes are a part of the lesson, proof that the problem can still grip us. Indeed, one might argue that there is a pragmatics of error which is crucial in all of this (Wagner 2001). This is the principle of testing life.

None of these principles of an ethics of intelligence should be considered as remarkable. Indeed, it is possible to argue that they should be at the root of any geographical ethics worth its salt but this is a geographical ethics composed for a posthumanist age. For what it is committed to is making more of the world, not allowing it to be reduced, but rather allowing it to be read and writ large.

> For everything that accords with the values of what we call 'civilization', its cities and monumental architecture, its social classes and elaborate lifeways, its incredible technologies, mathematics and self-expression in the control and knowledge of writing and speech, amounts to an overdetermination of the containment of sense by itself.
>
> (Wagner 2001: 30)

8 Spatialities of feeling

> Nobody knows how many rebellions besides political rebellions ferment in the masses of life which people earth.
>
> (Brontë 1993 [1847]: 115)

Introduction

Cities can be seen as roiling maelstroms of affect. Particular affects like anger, fear, happiness and joy are continually on the boil, rising here, subsiding there, and these affects continually manifest themselves in events which can take place either at a grand scale or simply as a part of continuing everyday life.[1] So, on the heroic side, we might point to the mass hysteria occasioned by the death of Princess Diana or the deafening roar from a sports stadium as a crucial point is scored. On the prosaic side we might think of the mundane emotional labour of the workplace, the frustrated shouts and gestures of road rage, the delighted laughter of children as they tour a theme park, or the tears of a suspected felon undergoing police interrogation.[2]

Given the utter ubiquity of affect as a vital element of cities, its shading of almost every urban activity with different hues that we all recognize, you would think that the affective register would form a large part of the study of cities – but you would be wrong.[3] Though affect continually figures in many accounts it is usually off to the side. There are a few honourable exceptions, of course. Walter Benjamin's identification of the emotional immediacy of Nazi rallies comes to mind. So does Richard Sennett's summoning of troubled urban bodies in *Flesh and Stone* (1994). But, generally speaking, to read about affect in cities it is necessary to resort to the pages of novels, and the tracklines of poems.

Why this neglect of the affective register of cities? It is not as if there is no history of the study of affect. There patently is, and over many centuries. For example, philosophers have continually debated the place of affect. Plato's discussion of the role of artists comes to mind as an early instance: for Plato art was dangerous because it gave an outlet for the expression of uncontrolled emotions and feelings. In particular, drama is a threat to Reason because it appeals to Emotion.[4] No doubt, one could track forwards through pivotal figures like Machiavelli, Rousseau, Kant and Hegel, noting various rationalist and romantic reactions, depending upon whether (and which) passions are viewed favourably or with suspicion.[5] Similarly, though at a much later date, scientists have recognized the importance of affect. At least since the publication of Charles Darwin's (1998) *The Expression of the Emotions in Man and Animals* in 1872, and no doubt before that, there has been a continuous history of the systematic scientific study of affect and although it would be foolish to say that we now know all there is to know about the physiology of emotions, equally it would be foolish to say that we know nothing. In turn, literatures like these have been replete with all kinds of more or less explicit political judgements – about which passions are wholesome and which are suspect or even dangerous, about the degree to which passions can or should be allowed untrammelled license, and about how passions can be amplified or repressed.

So why the neglect of affect in the current urban literature, even in the case of issues like identity and belonging which quiver with affective energy? A series of explanations comes to mind. One is a residual cultural Cartesianism (replete with all kinds of gendered connotations): affect is a kind of frivolous or distracting background to the real work of deciding our way through the city. It cannot be a part of our intelligence of that world. Another is concerned with the cultural division of labour. The creative arts already do that stuff and there is no need to follow. A third explanation is that affect mainly figures in perceptual registers like proprioception which are not easily captured in print. No doubt other explanations could be mustered.

Perhaps, at one time, these might have been seen as valid reasons. But they are not any more. I would point to three reasons why neglecting affect is, as much now as in the past, criminal neglect. First, systematic knowledges of the creation and mobilization of affect have become an integral part of the everyday urban landscape: affect has become part of a reflexive loop which allows more and more sophisticated interventions in various registers of urban life. Second, these knowledges are not just being deployed knowingly, they are also being deployed politically (mainly but not only by the rich and powerful) to political ends: what might have been painted as aesthetic is increasingly instrumental. Third, affect has become a part of how cities are understood. As cities are increasingly expected to have 'buzz', to be 'creative', and to generally bring forth powers of invention and intuition, all of which can be forged into economic weapons, so the active engineering of the affective register of cities has been highlighted as the harnessing of the talent of transformation. Cities must exhibit intense expressivity. Each of these three reasons shows that, whereas affect has always, of course, been a constant of urban experience, now affect is more and more likely to be actively engineered with the result that it is becoming something more akin to the networks of pipes and cables that are of such importance in providing the basic mechanics and root textures of urban life (Armstrong 1998), a set of constantly performing relays and junctions that are laying down all manner of new emotional histories and geographies.

In this chapter I want to think about affect in cities and about affective cities, and, above all, about what the political consequences of thinking more explicitly about these topics might be – once it is accepted that the 'political decision is itself produced by a series of inhuman or pre-subjective forces and intensities' (Spinks 2001: 24) which the idea of 'man' has reduced to ciphers. My aims will be three-fold: to discuss the nature of affect, to show some of the ways in which cities and affect interact to produce a politics which cannot be reduced to simply a shifting field of communal self-reflection or the neat conceptual economy of an ideology, and to produce the beginnings of a synoptic commentary. Accordingly, in the first part of the chapter, I will describe some of the different positions that have been taken on what affect actually is. This is clearly not an inconsequential exercise and it has a long and complex history which takes in luminaries as different as Spinoza and Darwin and Freud. But, given the potential size of the agenda, this has meant pulling out four key traditions rather than providing a complete review. This work of definition over, in the second part of the chapter I will then describe some of the diverse ways in which the use and abuse of various affective practices is gradually changing what we regard as the sphere of 'the political'. In particular, I will point to four different but related ways in which the manipulation of affect for political ends is becoming not just widespread but routine in cities through new kinds of practices and knowledges which are also redefining what counts as the sphere of the political. These practices, knowledges and redefinitions are not all by any means nice or cuddly, which is one too common interpretation of what adding affect will add. Indeed, some of them have the potential to be downright scary. But this is part and parcel of why it is so crucial to address affect now: in at least one guise the discovery of new means of practising affect is also the discovery of a whole new means of manipulation by the powerful. In the subsequent part of the chapter, I will focus more explicitly on the way in which these developments are changing what we can think of as both politics and 'the political', using the four traditions that I have previously outlined. I will not be making the silly argument that just about everything that now turns up is political, in some sense or the other, but I will be arguing that the move to affect shows up new political registers and intensities, and allows us to work on them to brew new collectives in ways which at least have the potential to be progressive. Then, in the penulti-mate part of the chapter, I will briefly consider in more detail some of the kinds of progressive political interventions into affect that might legitimately be made, using the ideas stimulated by recent work on virtual art and, most notably, the work of Bill Viola. Finally, I present some too brief conclusions which argue that the current experiments with a 'cosmopolitics' of new kinds of encounter and conviviality must include affect.

In writing this chapter in such a way that it does not simply become a long and rather dry review, I have had to make some draconian decisions. First, in general I have concentrated on current Euro-American societies. This means that I have generally neglected both the rich vein of work (chiefly from anthropology) which has offered up cross-cultural comparisons and the equally rich vein of work which has examined the historical record for evidence of broad shifts in emotional tone and even in what is regarded and named as emotion.[6] Too often, then, in the name of brevity, this chapter will presume an affective common-sense background which does not exist. Sensoriums vary by culture and through history (Geurts 2002).

The chapter therefore risks ethnocentrism in an area which, more than most, has been aware of difference.

Second, I have mainly concentrated on theoretical explorations of affect, although many of these explorations are backed up by solid empirical work. That means, in particular, that I have tended to pass by the very large amount of material in social psychology and cognitive science. This is unfortunate since this work is now going beyond the crude behaviourism of the past but incorporating it would have necessitated not just a supplement but a complete new paper (cf. Davidson *et al.* 2003).

Third, my approach is constrained, if that is the right word, by a specific theoretical background which arises from a particular time in the history of social theory, one in which we are starting to grasp elements of what constitutes 'good theory' in ways that have been apprehended before, but often only very faintly. I will pull out just a few of the principles which are intended to produce new conceptual and ethical resources, mainly because they are so germane to what follows.

1   Distance from biology is no longer seen as a prime marker of social and cultural theory (S.P. Turner 2002). It has become increasingly evident that the biological constitution of being (so-called 'biolayering') has to be taken into account if performative force is ever to be understood, and in particular, the dynamics of birth (and creativity) rather than death (Battersby 1999).

2   Relatedly, naturalism and scientism are no longer seen as terrible sins. A key reason for this is that developments like various forms of systems theory, complexity theory and nonlinear dynamics have made science more friendly to social and cultural theory. Another reason is that, increasingly, the history of social and cultural theory and science share common forebears. For example, since the 1940s systems theory has informed both domains in diverse ways and, consequently, we seem to be entering a period in which post-structuralism is likely to be renewed by its forebear, structuralism.

3   Human language is no longer assumed to offer the only meaningful model of communication.

4   Events have to be seen as genuinely open on at least some dimensions and, notwithstanding the extraordinary power of many social systems, 'revolt, resistance, breakdown, conspiracy, alternative is everywhere' (Latour 2002a: 124). Hence a turn to experiment and the alchemy of the contingent form that such a turn applies (Garfinkel 2002).

5   Time and process are increasingly seen as crucial to explanation (Abbott 2001) because they offer a direct challenge to fixed categories which, in a previous phase of social and cultural theory, still survived though complicated by the idea that one considered their workings in more detail. The multiplication of forms of knowledge and the traffic between them is taken seriously (Rabinow 2003).

6   Space is no longer seen as a nested hierarchy moving from 'global' to 'local'. This absurd scale-dependent notion is replaced by the notion that what counts

is connectivity and that the social is 'only a tiny set of narrow, standardised connections' out of many others (Latour 2002a: 124).

7 In other words, what is at stake is a different model of what thinking is, one that extends reflexivity to all manner of actors, that recognizes reflexivity as not just a property of cognition and which realizes the essentially patchy and material nature of what counts as thought.

What is affect?

The problem that must be faced straightaway is that there is no stable definition of affect. It can mean a lot of different things. These are usually associated with words like emotion and feeling, and a consequent repertoire of terms like hatred, shame, envy, fear, disgust, anger, embarrassment, sorrow, grief, anguish, love, happiness, joy, hope, wonder, . . . Though for various reasons that will become clear, I do not think these words work well as simple translations of the term 'affect'. In particular, I want to get away from the idea that some root kind of emotion (like shame) can act as a key political cipher (Nussbaum 2001).

In the brief and necessarily foreshortened review that follows, I will set aside approaches that tend to work with a notion of individualized emotions (such as are often found in certain forms of empirical sociology and psychology) and stick with approaches that work with a notion of broad tendencies and lines of force: emotion as motion both literally and figurally (Bruno 2002). I will consider four of these approaches in turn but it is important not to assume that I am making any strong judgements as to their efficacy: each of these approaches has a certain force which I want to draw on as well as certain drawbacks. It is also important to note that none of these approaches could be described as based on a notion of human individuals coming together in community. Rather, in line with my earlier work, each of them cleaves to an 'inhuman' or 'transhuman' framework in which individuals are generally understood as effects of the events to which their body parts (broadly understood) respond and in which they participate. Another point that needs to be made is that each of these approaches has connections (some strong, some weak) to the others.[7] Then one last point needs to be made; in each case *affect is understood as a form of thinking*, often indirect and nonreflective true, but thinking all the same. And, similarly, all manner of the spaces which they generate must be thought of in the same way, as means of thinking and as thought in action. Affect is a different kind of intelligence about the world, but it is intelligence nonetheless, and previous attempts to either relegate affect to the irrational or raise it up to the level of the sublime are both equally mistaken.

The first translation of affect that I want to address conceives of affect as a set of embodied practices that produce visible conduct as an outer lining. This translation chiefly arises out of the phenomenological tradition but also includes traces of social interactionism and hermeneutics (cf. Reddy 2001). Its chief concern is to develop descriptions of how emotions occur in everyday life, understood as the richly expressive/aesthetic feeling-cum-behaviour of continual becoming that is chiefly provided by bodily states and processes (and which is understood as constitutive of affect). That has meant getting past two problems that have plagued the sociology of emotions in the past: the problem of decontextualization and the problem of representation. In the first case, the problem is that, more than normally, context seems to be a vital element of the constitution of affect. Very often, the source of emotions seem to come from somewhere outside the body, from the setting itself, but this setting is cancelled out by methods like question-naires and other such instruments. In the second case, the problem is that emotions are largely non-representational: they are 'formal evidence of what, in one's relations with others, speech cannot congeal' (Katz 2000: 323).

> Studies almost always end up analysing how people talk about their emotions. If there is anything distinctive about emotions, it is that, even if they com-monly occur in the course of speaking, they are not talk, not even just forms of expression, they are ways of expressing something going on that talk cannot grasp. Historical and cultural studies similarly elide the challenge of under-standing emotional experience when they analyse texts, symbols, material objects, and ways of life as representations of emotions.
>
> (Katz 2000: 4)

Because there is no time out from expressive being, perception of a situation and response are intertwined and assume a certain kind of 'response-ability' (Katz 2000), an artful use of a vast sensorium of bodily resources which depends heavily on the actions of others (indeed it is through such re-actions that we most often see what we are doing).[8] Most of the time, this response-ability is invisible but when it becomes noticeable it stirs up powerful emotions:

> Blushes, laughs, cryings, and anger emerge on faces and through coverings that usually hide visceral substrata. The doing of emotions is a process of breaking bodily boundaries, of tears spilling out, rage burning up, and as laughter bursts out, the emphatic involvement of guts as a designated source of the involvement.
>
> (Katz 2000: 322)

In other (than) words, emotions form a rich moral array through which and with which the world is thought and which can sense different things even though they cannot always be named.

Between oneself and the world there is a new term, a holistically sensed, new texture in the social moment, and one relates to others in and through that emergent and transforming experience. A kind of metamorphosis occurs in which the self goes into a new container or takes on a temporary flesh for the passage to an altered state of social being. The subjects of our analysis in the first place own the poetic devices (Katz 2000: 343).

The second translation of affect is the most culturally familiar in that its vocabulary is now a part of how Euro-American subjects routinely describe them-selves. It is usually associated with psychoanalytic frames and is based around a notion of drive. Often, it will follow the Freudian understanding that one physio-logical drive – sexuality, libido, desire – is the root source of human motivation and identity. Emotions are primarily vehicles or manifestations of the underlying libidinal drive; variations on the theme of 'desire'. A conception like this, which reduces affect to drive, may be too stark, however. As Sedgwick (2003: 18) puts it, such a move 'permits a diagrammatic sharpness of thought that may, however, be too impoverishing in qualitative terms'.

Sedgwick tries to solve this problem by turning to the work of Silvan Tomkins (Demos 1995; Sedgwick and Frank 1995). Tomkins distinguishes between the drive and the affect system. The drive system is relatively narrowly constrained and instrumental in being concentrated on particular aims (e.g. breathing, eating, drinking, sleeping, excreting), time-limited (e.g. stopping each of these activities will have more or less deleterious consequences after a period of time) and concentrated on particular objects (e.g. getting a breath of air or a litre of water). In contrast, affects[9] like anger, enjoyment, excitement or sadness, shame and distress can range across all kinds of aims (one of which may simply be to stimulate their own arousal – what Tomkins calls their autotelic function), can continually redefine the aim under consideration,[10] can have far greater freedom with respect to time than drives (an affect like anger may last for a few seconds but equally may motivate revenge that spans decades) and can focus on many different kinds of object. 'Affects can be, and are, attached to things, people, ideas, sensations, relations, activities, ambitions, institutions, and any other number of other things, including other affects. Thus one can be excited by anger, disgusted by shame, or surprised by joy' (Sedgwick 1993: 19).

For Tomkins, affect is not subservient to a supposedly primary drive system. In many cases the apparent urgency of the drive system results from its co-assembly with appropriate affects which act as necessary amplifiers. Indeed, affects may be

> either much more causal than any drive could be or much more monopolistic.
> . . . Most of the characteristics which Freud attributed to the Unconscious
> and to the Id are in fact salient aspects of the affect system. . . . Affect enables
> both insatiability and extreme lability, fickleness and finickiness.
>
> (Tomkins, cited in Sedgwick 2003: 21)

Significantly, for Tomkins, it is the face that is the chief site of affect; 'I have now come to regard the skin, in general, and the skin of the face in particular, as of the greatest importance in producing the feel of affect' (Tomkins, cited in Demos 1995: 89).[11] But, for Tomkins, it is important to note that the face was not the expression of something else, it *was* affect in process.

The third translation of affect is naturalistic and hinges on adding capacities through interaction in a world which is constantly becoming. It is usually associated first of all with Spinoza and then subsequently with Deleuze's modern ethological re-interpretation of Spinoza.

Spinoza set out to challenge the model put forward by Descartes of the body as animated by the will of an immaterial mind or soul, a position which reflected

Descartes' allegiance to the idea that the world consisted of two different substances: extension (the physical field of objects positioned in a geometric space which has become familiar to us as a Cartesian space) and thought (the property which distinguishes conscious beings as 'thinking things' from objects).

In contrast, Spinoza was a monist, that is he believed there was only one substance in the universe, 'God or Nature' in all its forms; human beings and all other objects could only be modes of this one unfolding substance. Each mode was spatially extended in its own way and thought in its own way and unfolded in a determinate manner. So, in Spinoza's world everything is part of a thinking and a doing simultaneously: they are aspects of the same thing expressed in two registers.[12] In turn, this must mean that knowing proceeds in parallel with the body's physical encounters, out of interaction. Spinoza is no irrationalist, however. What he is attempting here is to understand thoughtfulness in a new way, extending its activity into nature.

Spinoza's metaphysics was accompanied by an original notion of what we might nowadays call human psychology. For Spinoza, human psychology is manifold, a complex body arising out of interaction which is an alliance of many simple bodies and which therefore exhibits what nowadays would be called emergence – the capacity to demonstrate powers at higher levels of organization which do not exist at others; 'an individual may be characterized by a fixed number of definite properties (extensive and qualitative) and yet possess an indefinite number of capacities to affect and be affected by other individuals' (De Landa 2002: 62). This manifold psychology is continually being modified by the myriad encounters taking place between individual bodies and other finite things. The exact nature of the kinds of modifications that take place will depend upon the relations that are possible between individuals who are also simultaneously elements of complex bodies. Spinoza describes the active outcome of these encounters to affect or be affected by using the term emotion or affect (*affectus*) which is both body and thought.

> By EMOTION (affectus) I understand the modifications of the body by which the power of action of the body is increased or diminished, aided or restrained, and at the same time the idea of these modifications.
>
> (*Ethics* III def. 3)

So affect, defined as the property of the active outcome of an encounter, takes the form of an increase or decrease in the ability of the body and mind alike to act, which can be positive and increase that ability (and thus 'joyful' or euphoric) or negative and diminish that ability (and thus 'sorrowful' or dysphoric). Spinoza therefore detaches 'the emotions' from the realm of responses and situations and attaches them instead to action and encounters as the affections of substance or of its attributes and as *greater or lesser forces of existing*. They therefore become firmly a part of 'nature', of the same order as storms or floods.

> The way of understanding the nature of anything, of whatever kind, must always be the same, viz. through the universal rules and laws of nature. . . .

I have therefore regarded passions like love, hate, anger, envy, pride, pity, and other feelings which agitate the mind . . . as properties which belong to it in the same way as heat, cold, storm, thunder and the like belong to the nature of the atmosphere.

(*Ethics* Pref.: C492)

But affect will present differently to body and mind in each encounter. In the attribute of body, affect structures encounters so that bodies are disposed for action in a particular way. In the attribute of mind, affect structures encounters as a series of modifications arising from the relations between ideas which may be more or less adequate and more or less empowering. In other words, the issue is the composition of an affective relationship. So

euphoria and dysphoria are not the ground of any given emotion any more than musical harmony is the ground of the simultaneous tones which give rise to it. The names of the many emotions we experience are merely the names given to differently assembled euphoric or dysphoric relations, akin to chords.

(Brown and Stenner 2001: 95)

This emphasis on relations is important. Though Spinoza makes repeated references to 'individuals' it is clear from his conception of bodies and minds and affects as manifolds that for him the prior category is what he calls the 'alliance' or 'relationship'. So affects, for example, occur in an encounter between manifold beings, and the outcome of each encounter depends upon what forms of composition these beings are able to enter in to.

Such a way of proceeding from relations and encounters has many echoes in contemporary social science and forms the touchstone of much recent work in human geography. Most especially, it shows up in work which is concerned to find common complexes of relation, such as that informed by contemporary philosophers and most notably Gilles Deleuze. Deleuze (1988b, 1990) added what might be called an ethological spin to Spinoza's assertion that things are never separable from their relations with the world by drawing on the work of writers like von Uexküll on the perceptual worlds of animals and then applying the same kind of thinking to human beings. Thus Deleuze (1988b) considers the simplest of von Uexküll's animals, a tick, whose raison d'être is sucking the blood of passing mammals. It appears to be capable of only three affects: light (climb to the top of a branch), smell (fall on to a mammal that passes beneath the branch) and heat (seek the warmest spot on the mammal). Deleuze then applies the same kind of reasoning to human beings. But there he has to make the considerable reservation that we really have no idea either what affects human bodies or minds might be capable of in a given encounter ahead of time or, indeed, more generally, what worlds human beings might be capable of building, so affects are 'the nonhuman becomings of man' (Deleuze and Guattari 1994: 169). He is therefore led towards a language/practice of different speeds and intensities which can track all the compositions and combinations that human beings might be able to bring in to play.

> If we are Spinozists we will not define a thing by its form, nor by its organs and its functions, nor as a substance or a subject. Borrowing terms from the Middle Ages, or from geography, we will define it by longitude or latitude. A body can be anything; it can be an animal, a body of sounds, a mind or an idea; it can be a linguistic corpus, a social body, a collectivity. We call longitude of a body the set of relations of speed and slowness, of momentum and rest, between particles that compose it from this point of view, that is, between unformed elements. We call latitude the set of affects that occupy a body at each moment, that is, the intensive states of an anonymous force (force for existing, capacity for being affected). In this way we construct the map of the body. The longitudes and latitudes together constitute Nature, the plane of immanence or consistency, which is always variable and is constantly being altered, composed and recomposed by individuals and collectivities.
>
> (Deleuze 1988b: 127–128)

This Spinozan–Deleuzian notion of affect as always emergent is best set out by Massumi when he writes that:

> Affects are virtual synesthetic perspectives anchored in (functionally limited by) the actually existing, particular things that embody them. The autonomy of affect is . . . its openness. Affect is autonomous to the degree to which it escapes confinement in the particular body whose vitality, or potential for interaction, it is. Formed, qualified, situated perceptions and cognitions fulfilling functions of actual connection or blockage are the capture and closure of affect. Emotion is the most intense (most contracted) expression of that capture – and of the fact that something has always and again escaped. Something remains unactualised, inseparable from but unassimilable to any particular, functionally anchored perspective. That is why all emotion is more or less disorienting, and why it is classically described as being outside of oneself, at the very point at which one is most intimately and unshareably in contact with oneself and one's vitality. . . . Actually existing, structured things live in and through that which escapes them. Their autonomy is the autonomy of affect.
>
> The escape of affect cannot but be perceived, alongside the perceptions that are its capture. This side-perception may be punctual, localised in an event. . . . When it is punctual, it is usually described in negative terms, as a form of shock (the sudden interruption of functions of connection). But it is also continuous, like a background perception that accompanies every event, however quotidian. When the continuity of affective escape is put into words, it tends to take on positive connotations. For it is nothing less than the perception of one's own vitality, *one's sense of aliveness, of changeability* (often described as 'freedom'). One's 'sense of aliveness' is a continuous

nonconscious self-perception (unconscious self-reflection or self-referentiality). It is the perception of this self-perception, its naming and making conscious, that allows affect to be effectively analysed – as long as a vocabulary can be found for that which is imperceptible but whose escape from perception cannot but be perceived, as long as one is alive.

(Massumi 2002: 35–36, my emphasis)

I want to foreground one last translation of affect which we might call Darwinian. For Darwin, expressions of emotion were universal and are the product of evolution. Neither our expressions nor our emotions are necessarily unique to human beings. Other animals have some of the same emotions, and some of the expressions produced by animals resemble our own. Expressions, which typically involve the face and the voice, and to a lesser extent body posture and movement, have a number of cross-cultural features. In contrast, gestures, which typically involve hand movement, are not universal: generally, they vary from culture to culture in the same way as language.

Though scientific work on emotions flourished, Darwin's work on emotions was all but ignored for one hundred years or so. However, it has recently enjoyed something of a revival, associated in particular with the work of Ekman (1992, 2003; Ekman and Rosenberg 1997). As Ekman has shown, Darwin's work was important for three reasons. First, it tried to answer the 'why' question: Why are particular expressions associated with particular emotions? Second, it drew on a large range of evidence, not only of a peculiar quantity (Darwin drew on a large amount of international correspondents) but also of a peculiar quality: Darwin's use of engravings and photographs of the face, using a number of sources, has become iconic. Third, there was his claim that there is a strong line of emotional descent running from animals to humans, born out of the evolution of affective expression as a means of preparing the organism for action, a claim arising in part out of a desire to answer critics of evolution.

What Darwin omitted from his study was any communicative aspect of emotion and it is this aspect which has been added in today. Flying in the face of total cultural relativism, neo-Darwinians argue that there are at least five emotions which are common to all cultures: anger, fear, sadness, disgust and enjoyment,[13] and that each of these emotions is manifested in common facial expressions. These common facial expressions are involuntary signs of internal physiological changes and not just a part of the back-and-forth of the communicative repertoire. But this is not to say that emotions operate like instincts, uninfluenced by cultural experience. Communication has its say. 'Social experience influences attitudes about emotions, creates display and feeling rules, develops and tunes the particular occasions which will most rapidly call forth an emotion' (Ekman 1998: 387).[14] In particular, different cultures may not have the same words for emotions or might explain a particular emotion in a radically different way.[15] Further, the specific events that trigger particular emotions can, of course, be quite different between cultures: for example, disgust is triggered by quite different kinds of food according to cultural norms of what is nice and nasty.

Four different notions of affect, then. Each of them depends on a sense of push in the world but the sense of push is subtly different in each case. In the case of embodied knowledge, that push is provided by the expressive armoury of the human body. In the case of affect theory it is provided by biologically differentiated positive and negative affects rather than the drives of Freudian theory. In the world of Spinoza and Deleuze, affect is the capacity of interaction that is akin to a natural force of emergence. In the neo-Darwinian universe, affect is a deep-seated physiological change involuntarily written on the face. How might we think about the politics of affect, given that these different notions would seem to imply different cues and even ontologies? To begin with, we need to think about general changes in the affective tone of Euro-American cultures that are busily redefining the political landscape. That is the function of the next section.

The politics of affect

Of course, affect has always been a key element of politics and the subject of numerous powerful political technologies which have knotted thinking, technique and affect together in various potent combinations. One example is the marshalling of aggression through various forms of military trainings like drill. From the seventeenth century onwards these kinds of trainings have become more and more sophisticated, running in lockstep with 'advances' in military technology. These trainings were used to condition soldiers and other combatants to kill, even though it seems highly unlikely that this would be the normal behaviour of most people on the battlefield. These trainings involved bodily conditionings which allowed fear to be controlled. They allowed anger and other aggressive emotions to be channelled into particular situations. They damped down revenge killings during bursts of rage. And they resulted in particular effects (e.g. increased firing rates and higher kill ratios) which the military had not been achieving heretofore (see Grossman 1996; Bourke 2000; Keegan 1976).

This may appear to many to be an extreme example. But I think it is illustrative of a tendency towards the greater and greater engineering of affect, notwithstanding the many covert emotional histories that are only now beginning to be recovered (cf. Berlant 2000). Similar kinds of thing have been happening in many other arenas of social life, whether on a domestic or other scale, sufficient to suggest that the envelope of what we call the political must increasingly expand to take note of 'the way that political attitudes and statements are partly conditioned by intense autonomic bodily reactions that do not simply reproduce the trace of a political intention and cannot be wholly recuperated within an ideological regime of truth' (Spinks 2001: 23). In this section I want to illustrate how this envelope is expanding in cities by reference to four developments. The first of these developments consists of the general changes in the *form* of such politics which are taking place in the current era, changes which make affect a more and more visible element of the political. In particular, I want to point towards so-called 'agencies of choice' and 'mixed-action repertoires' in line with a general move to make more and more areas of life the subject of a new set of responsibilities called 'choice'. As Norris puts it:

> The expansion of the franchise during the nineteenth and early twentieth centuries generated the rise of traditional channels for political mobilisation and expression in representative government, particularly the growth of extra-parliamentary party organizations, the spread of cheap mass-circulation newspapers, and the establishment of traditional groups in civic society, exemplified by the organized labour movement, civic associations, voluntary groups, and religious organizations. By the 1940s and 1950s, these channels had settled and consolidated and were taken for granted as the major institutions linking citizens and the state within established democracies. Rising levels of human capital and societal modernization mean that, today, a more educated citizenry . . . has moved increasingly from agencies of loyalty to agencies of choice, and from electoral repertoires toward mixed-action repertoires combining electoral activities and protest politics. In postindustrial societies, the younger generations, in particular, have become less willing than their parents and grandparents to channel their political energies through traditional agencies exemplified by parties and churches, and more likely to express themselves through a variety of ad hoc, contextual, and specific activities of choice, increasingly via new social movements, internet activism, and transnational policy networks. Conventional indicators may blind us to the fact that critical citizens may be becoming less loyalist and deferential in orientation toward mass branch parties . . . at the same time that they are becoming more actively engaged via alternative means of expression.
>
> (Norris 2002: 222)

Many of these new forms of choice politics rely on an expansion of what has been conventionally regarded as the urban political sphere. For example, the political nowadays routinely takes in all manner of forms of culture-nature relation (e.g. environmental politics, animal rights politics, pro-choice or anti-life politics, etc.). In turn, this re-definition of what counts as political has allowed more room for explicitly affective appeals which are heavily dependent upon the media, as well as similar appeals which endeavour to reduce these affective impacts (for example, by referring to science, by various means of deconstruction of the 'reality' of an image, and so on) (Boltanski 2002).

This brings me to the second development which is the heavy and continuing *mediatization* of politics. We live in societies which are enveloped in and saturated by the media: most importantly, it is difficult to escape the influence of the *screen* which now stares at us from so many mundane locations – from almost every room in the house to doctor's waiting rooms, from airport lounges to shops and shopping malls, from bars to many workplaces (McCarthy 2001; Knorr Cetina 2001), from the insides of elevators to whole buildings – that it is possible to argue that the screen has taken on a number of the roles formerly ascribed to parent, lover, teacher and blank stooge, as well as adding a whole series of 'postsocial'[16] relations which seem to lie somewhere between early film theory's brute translation of screen-ic force (Balázs 1970; Kracauer 1960) and film theory's later, more nuanced interpretation in which cognitive processes are strained through various conventions and styles (see Thrift 2004). This mediatization has had important effects. As McKenzie (2001) has pointed out its most important effect has been to enshrine the performative principle at the heart of modern Euro-American societies and their political forms. This has occurred in a number of ways. To begin with, the technical form of modern media tends to foreground emotion, both in its concentration on key affective sites like the face or voice and its magnification of the small details of the body that so often signify emotion.[17] Political presentation nowadays often fixes on such small differences and makes them stand for a whole. One line of movement can become a progression of meaning, able to be actualized and implanted locally. Massumi observes this quality in Ronald Reagan:

> That is why Reagan could be so many things to so many people; that is why the majority of the electorate could disagree with him on major issues but still vote for him. Because he was actualised, in their neighbourhood, as a movement and meaning of their selection – or at least selected for them with their acquiescence. He was a man for all inhibitions. It was commonly said that he ruled primarily by projecting an air of *confidence*. That was the emotional tenor of his political manner, dysfunction notwithstanding. Confidence is the emotional translation of affect as capturable life potential; it is a particular emotional expression and becoming – conscious of one's side-perceived vitality. Reagan transmitted vitality, virtuality, tendency, in sickness and interruption.
>
> (Massumi 2002: 41, my emphasis)

Then, political presentation increasingly conforms to media norms of presentation which emphasize the performance of emotion as being an index of credibility. Increasingly, political legitimation arises from this kind of performance (Thompson 2002). And, as a final point, these kinds of presentation chime with the increasingly 'therapeutic' form of selfhood which is becoming common in Euro-American societies (cf. Giddens 1991; Rose 2004). Indeed, Nolan (1998) argues that this therapeutic or 'emotivist' ethos is embedding itself in the structures of the American state to such a degree that it is becoming a key technology of governance, both challenging and to some extent replacing the affective background of older bureaucratic 'machine' technologies, by, for example, recognizing emotional labour, emotion management and emotional learning as key skills (P. Smith 2002);

> Life in the machine has made appeals to the older [traditional] systems of meaning impossible. Instead the individual is encouraged to escape from within and to refer to the language of emotions. The emotivist motif, then, is the 'dictum that truth is grasped through sentiment or feeling, rather than through rational judgement or abstract reasoning'. It encourages a particular ontology that replaces the Cartesian maxim 'I think, therefore I am' with the

emotive 'I feel, therefore I am'. This emotivist understanding of the self shapes the way in which individuals participate and communicate in societal life. In the contemporary context, as Jean Bethke Elshtain observes, 'all points seem to revolve around the individual's subjective feelings – whether of frustration, anxiety, stress, fulfilment. The citizen recedes; the therapeutic self prevails'.

(Nolan 1998: 6)

Thus, a series of heterogeneous knowledges of performance move to the centre stage in modern societies which constitute a new 'disaggregated' mode of discipline, an emergent stratum of power and knowledge. These knowledges construct power in a number of ways – by delivering messages with passion, for example (indeed, it is often the force with which passion is delivered which is more important than the message), by providing a new minute landscape of manipulation (Doane 2002), by adding new possibilities for making signs, and generally by adding new openings out of the event. But, most importantly, they provide a new means of creating 'fractal' subjects challenged to perform across a series of different situations in a way which demands not so much openness as controlled flexibility.[18] As McKenzie puts it:

> The desire produced by performative power and knowledge is not moulded by distinct disciplinary mechanisms. It is not a repressive desire: it is instead 'excessive', intermittently modulated and pushed across the thresholds of various limits by overlapping and sometimes competing systems. Further, diversity is not simply integrated, for integration is itself becoming diversified. Similarly, deviation is not simply normalised, for norms operate and transform themselves through their own transgression and deviation. We can understand this development better when we realise that the mechanisms of performative power are nomadic and flexible more than sedentary and rigid, that its spaces are networked and digital more than enclosed and physical, that its temporalities are polyrhythmic and non-linear and not simply sequential and linear. On the performative stratum, one shuttles quickly between different evaluative grids, switching back and forth between divergent challenges to perform – or else.
>
> (McKenzie 2001: 19)

A third development is closely linked to mediatization and the rise of performance knowledges. It is the growth of new forms of calculation in sensory registers that would not have previously been deemed 'political'. In particular, through the advent of a whole series of technologies, small spaces and times, upon which affect thrives and out of which it is often constituted, have become visible and are able to be enlarged so that they can be knowingly operated upon. Though it would be possible to argue that outposts were already being constructed in this continent of phenomenality back in the seventeenth century with, for example, the growth of interest in conditioning the military body through practices like drill, I would argue that the main phase of colonization dates from the mid-nineteenth century and rests on four developments (Thrift 2000). First, there is the ability to sense the small spaces of the body through a whole array of new scientific instruments which have, in turn, made it possible to think of the body as a set of micro-geographies. Then, there is the related ability to sense small bodily movements. Beginning with the photographic work of Marey, Muybridge, and others and moving into our current age in which the camera can impose its own politics of time and space, we can now think of time as minutely segmented frames, able to be speeded up, slowed down, even frozen for a while. Next, numerous body practices have come into existence which rely on and manage such knowledge of small times and spaces, most especially those connected with the performing arts, including the 'under-performing' of film acting, much modern dance, the insistent cross-hatched tempo of much modern music, and so on. Special performance notations, like Labanotation and other 'choreo-graphics', allow this minute move-ment to be recorded, analysed, and recomposed. Then, finally, a series of discourses concerning the slightest gesture and utterance of the body have been developed, from the elaborate turn-taking of conversational analysis to the intimate spaces of proxemics, from the analysis of gesture to the mapping of 'body language'.

Thus, what was formerly invisible or imperceptible becomes constituted as visible and perceptible through a new structure of attention which is more and more likely to pay more than lip-service to those actions which go on in small spaces and times, actions which involve qualities like anticipation, improvisation and intuition, all those things which by drawing on the second-to-second resourcefulness of the body make for artful conduct. Thus, perception can no longer 'be thought of in terms of immediacy, presence, punctuality' (Crary 1999: 4) as it is both stretched and intensified, widened and condensed.

In turn, this new structure of attention, ironically enough through the appli-cation of greater speed, has allowed us to gain a much greater understanding of what is often nowadays called 'bare life' (Thrift 2003a). An undiscovered country has gradually hoved into view, the country of the 'half-second delay'. This is the period of bodily *anticipation* originally discovered by Wilhelm Wundt in the mid-nineteenth century. Wundt was able to show that consciousness takes time to construct; we are 'late for consciousness' (Damasio 1999: 127). That insight was subsequently formalized in the 1960s by Libet using the new body recording technologies. He was able to show decisively that an action is set in motion before we decide to perform it: the 'average readiness potential' is about 0.8 seconds, although cases as long as 1.5 seconds have been recorded. In other words 'con-sciousness takes a relatively long time to build, and any experience of it being instantaneous must be a backdated illusion' (McCrone 1999: 131). Or, as Gray (2002: 66) puts it more skeletally; 'the brain makes us ready for action, then we have the experience of acting'.[19]

To summarize, what we are able to see is that the space of embodiment is expanded by a fleeting but crucial moment, a constantly moving pre-conscious frontier. This fleeting space of time is highly political. The by-now familiar work of Heidegger, Wittgenstein, Merleau-Ponty, Bourdieu, and Varela shows the ways in which the structure of expectation of the world (the background) is set up by body practices which have complex and often explicitly political genealogies: the smallest gesture or facial expression can have the largest political compass (Ekman 1992, 2003). More recent work has added to this understanding by emphasizing the degree to which these body practices rely on the emotions as a vital element of the body's apprehension of the world; emotions are a vital part of the body's anticipation of the moment. Thus, we can now understand emotions as a kind of corporeal thinking (Le Doux 1997; Damasio 1999, 2003): 'through our emotion, we reach back sensually to grasp the tacit, embodied foundations of ourselves' (Katz 2000: 7).[20]

The result is that we now have a small space of time which is increasingly able to be sensed, the space of time which shapes the moment. Of course, once such a space is opened up it can also be operated on. As Foucault and Agamben make clear, biopolitics is now at the centre of Western modes of power. But what is being ushered in now is a *microbiopolitics,* a new domain carved out of the half-second delay which has become visible and so available to be worked upon through a whole series of new entities and institutions. This domain was already implicitly political, most especially through the mechanics of the various body positions which are a part of its multiple abilities to anticipate. Now it has become explicitly political through practices and techniques which are aimed at it specifically.

A fourth development which involves affect is the careful design of urban space to produce political response. Increasingly, urban spaces and times are being designed to invoke affective response according to practical and theoretical knowledges that have been derived from and coded by a host of sources. It could be claimed that this has always been the case – from monuments to triumphal processions, from theatrical arenas to mass body displays – and I would agree. In the twentieth century, it could be argued that much of the activity of the design of space was powered up again, becoming entangled with the evolution of knowledges of shaping the body (such as the microbiopolitics referred to above), often in a politics of the most frightening sort.[21] But what I would argue is different now is both the sheer weight of the gathering together of formal knowledges of affective response (whether from highly formal theoretical backgrounds like psychoanalysis or practical theoretical backgrounds like performance), the vast number of practical knowledges of affective response that have become available in a semi-formal guise (e.g. design, lighting, event management, logistics, music, performance, etc.), and the enormous diversity of available cues that can be worked with in the shape of the profusion of images and other signs, the wide spectrum of available technologies, and the more general archive of events. The result is that affective response can be designed into spaces, often out of what seems like very little at all. Though affective response can clearly never be guaranteed, the fact is that this is no longer a random process either. It is a form of landscape engineering that is gradually pulling itself into existence, producing new forms of power as it goes.

Changing the political

What might these four developments and others like them mean for the practice of the political (and by implication the definition of the political itself)? In what I hope is a recognizable echo of the papers by Ash Amin and Doreen Massey, I would want to point to a number of shifts, each of which points to new intensities and speeds which have heretofore not so much been neglected as rather been kept firmly in the realm of either the utterly practical or heavily theoretical realms. But now all kinds of corporate and state institutions are trying to formulate bodies of knowledge of these realms which are both systematic and portable, knowledges of complex affective states of becoming, 'regimes of feeling' which are bound to be constitutive of new political practices. It therefore becomes incumbent on those forces which regard these developments as rather worrying – and indeed as likely to produce a new kind of velvet dictatorship – to produce their own analyses and political agendas. As part of the general move towards thinking democracy as a *process* of 'community without unity' (Castronovo and Nelson 2003), I want to try to address this task.

However, how to frame such an agenda? In a general sense, one might argue that the goal is a kind of 'emotional liberty'. But this goal must be tempered by the familiar realization, going back to Plato and before, that the untrammelled expression of emotions is not necessarily a good thing at all. In other words, what is being aimed for is a navigation of feeling which goes beyond the simple romanticism of somehow maximizing individual emotions. That navigation must involve at least three moments. First of all, it needs to be placed within a set of disciplinary exercises if it is to be an effective force, taking in the various forms of agonistic and ethical reflexivity that Foucault grouped under 'care of the self', forms of reflexivity that were intended to produce 'an athlete of the event' (cited in Rabinow 2003: 9). It will therefore *de facto* involve various forms of channelling and 'repression'. Second, it requires a more general expressive exploration of existential territories of the kind that Guattari gives at least a flavour of when he writes:

> there is an ethical choice in favour of the richness of the possible, an ethics and politics of the virtual that decorporealizes and deterritorializes contingency, linear causality and the pressure of circumstances and significations which besiege us. It is a choice for processuality, irreversibility and resingularization. On a small scale, this redeployment can turn itself into the mode of entrapment, of impoverishment, indeed of catastrophe in neurosis. It can take up reactive religious references. It can annihilate itself in alcohol, drugs, television, an endless daily grind. But it can also make use of other procedures that are more collective, more social, more political.
>
> (Guattari 1992: 94)

Third, the more specific means of framing this agenda might be as a politics of hope (Bloch 1986).

Whatever the case, it is quite clear that there are enormous emotional costs and benefits for individuals in being shaped by particular institutions in particular ways but that, equally, it is often difficult to show what is at stake for the individual or groups in submitting to such institutions and embracing certain emotional styles that render them deferential, obedient or humble – or independent, aggressive and arrogant – yet we can all attest to the fact that there are many 'hidden injuries' in the systems we inhabit. Disciplines like psychoanalysis have been very good at searching out the violence done and the costs that have to be borne and laying them bare through indices like physical trauma and tears. But, at the same time, we still lack a politics of emotional liberty[22] or hope which can be both productive and not so attached to Euro-American individualism that it simply reproduces the assumptions of the West in what it strives for: a kind of free to do what one likes, goal-oriented selfishness which actually flies in the face of all the evidence that human individuals (or perhaps better 'dividuals') only exist as faint traces in much larger and more extensive circuits of social relation. As Reddy puts it:

> Can a person who feels that an emotion is a learned response, a product of social construction, be oppressed – in the political sense of the term – by this feeling? The concept of emotions as used in the West is closely associated with the individual's most deeply espoused goals; to feel love for one's spouse or fear of one's opponent, presumably, is to be moved by those things one most authentically wants. It is hard to see how a person can be oppressed by his or her most authentic, most deeply held goals. To make such a claim, that a certain person, group, or community is politically oppressed – without knowing it – would require that one be prepared to assert something about the nature of the individual. Such an assertion, by definition, would have to apply to the individual as universally constituted, outside the parameters of any given 'culture'. Who would have the temerity, today, to make positive claims about this politically charged issue?
>
> (Reddy 2001: 114)

In what follows, I therefore want to point to four of these new intensities and speeds and the attendant navigations of discipline, expressive exploration and hope which are grouping around them, each of which corresponds to one of the forms of affect introduced in the first part of the chapter. In each case, there are some complexities. Foremost amongst these is the fact that these knowledges are not innocent. Each of them represents a striving for new forms of power-knowledge of the kind that John Allen points to in his paper as well as a new kind of political ethic. So, for example, each of the kinds of thinking about affect that I want to foreground have already been drawn on by large capitalist firms, both to understand their environment and to design new products. But they also provide, along with some recent experiments in cosmopolitics, one of the best hopes for changing our engagement with the political by simply acknowledging *that there is more there.*

I will begin by considering the kind of affect associated with embodied practices. The political goal of this strand of work might best be described as *skilful comportment* which allows us to be open to receiving new affectively charged disclosive spaces. This privileging of receptive practices is in contrast to much that currently goes on in Euro-American culture which 'while still structured by receptivity to changing styles of practice, seems to be replacing the substantive good of openness with that of controlled flexibility' (Spinosa *et al.* 1997: 180). Thus, the political project in all cases is to make receptivity in to the 'top ontological good' (Spinosa *et al.* 1997) but, of course, no clear principle of receptivity can be adduced. Rather, what is being stated is something like a political ethic of the kind laid out by writers like Varela. Here, I want to point to Varela's emphasis on the potential for understanding new forms of affect born out of the task of producing new practices which are not reliant on an implicit or explicit promise to satisfy some request. For Varela, it is possible *to learn to be open* through a combination of institutional transformation and body trainings which utilize the half-second delay to act into a situation with good judgement.[23] Such a politics might be one of attempting to redefine education so that it emphasizes good judgement (cf. Claxton 2000) or, at a more mundane level, designing new 'affective' computer interfaces which can wrap themselves around their subjects' concerns in ways which do not, however, act just as a confirmation of the world but also provide challenges.

The second kind of affect is associated with psychoanalytic models of affect of the kind produced by Tomkins and is an attempt to move outside 'the relentlessly self-propagating, adaptive structure of the repressive hypothesis' (Sedgwick 2003: 12). In one sense, this is clearly an attempt to continue the Foucauldian project. In another sense it is an attempt to move beyond it by valorizing what Sedgwick (2003) calls the 'middle ranges of agency'.

> [Foucault's] analysis of the pseudodichotomy between repression and liberation has led, in many cases, to its conceptual reimposition in the even more abstractly reified form of the hegemonic and subversive. The seeming ethical urgency of such terms masks their gradual evacuation of substance, as a kind of Gramscian-Foucauldian contagion turns 'hegemonic' into another name for the status quo (i.e. everything that is) and defines 'subversive' in, increasingly, a purely negative relation to that (an extreme of the same 'negative relation' that had, in Foucault's argument, defined the repressive hypothesis in the first place). . . . Another problem with reifying the status quo is what it does to the middle ranges of agency. One's relation to what is risked becoming reactive and bifurcated, that of a consumer: one's choices narrow to accepting or refusing (buying, not buying) this or that manifestation of it, dramatizing only the extremes of compulsion or voluntarity. Yet it is only the middle ranges of agency that offer space for effectual creativity or change.
>
> (Sedgwick 2003: 12–13)

In particular, it is here that it is possible to work on negative affects (e.g. paranoia) by taking up reparative positions that undertake a different range of affects, ambitions and risks and thereby allow the release of positive energies which can then be further worked upon. Seek pleasure rather than just forestall pain. Again, what we find here is an ethical principle.

Such projects of *reparative knowing* are, of course, becoming commonplace as means of producing affective orientations to knowledge which add another dimension to what knowing is. I am thinking here of many studies in the spheres of postcolonial struggles or struggles over sexual or ethnic identity in which a coalition of activists has been gradually able to change the grain and content of perceptual systems by working on associating affective response in both thought and extension.

The third kind of affect is that in the tradition offered by Spinoza and Deleuze. Here I want to point to two possibilities. One is a very general one. That is a model of *tending*. Here the simple political imperative is to widen the potential number of interactions a living thing can enter into, to widen the margin of 'play', and, like all living things, but to a greater degree, increasing the number of transforms of the effects of one sensory mode into another. Massumi frames this kind of 'intercessor' approach in relation to the future mission of cultural studies.

> If radical cultural studies semi-artistically refuses to set itself up as a model of any kind, yet lacks powers of contagion, how can it be effective? What mode of validity can it achieve for itself? Consider that the expanded empirical field is full of mutually modulating, battling, negotiating process lines liberally encouraged to develop and sharply express self-interest across their collectively remaindered, ongoing transformations. The anomaly of an affectively engaged yet largely disinterested process line could be a powerful presence if it were capable of conveying its (masochistic?) removal of self-interest. The reciprocal re-adjustments always under way in the empirical field make the pursuit of politics an ecological undertaking, whether it thinks of itself that way or not. . . . This is a political ecology. The 'object' of political ecology is the coming-together or belonging-together of processually unique and divergent forms of life. Its object is 'symbiosis' along the full length of the nature-culture continuum. The self-disinterest of cultural studies places it in a privileged position to side with symbiosis as such. What cultural studies could become, if it finds a way of expressing its own processual potential, is a political ecology affectively engaging in symbiosis-tending.
>
> (Massumi 1997b: 220)

This approach will appear a little high and mighty to some. So let us turn in a slightly different direction to end this catalogue of new political directions.

Here I want to concentrate on the idea of a politics aimed at some of the registers of thought that have been heretofore neglected by critical thinkers even though, as already pointed out above, those in power have turned to these registers as a fertile new field of persuasion and manipulation. The motto of this politics might be Nietzsche's phrase 'Between two thoughts all kinds of affects play their game; but their motions are too fast, therefore we fail to recognise them' (1968: 263). But today 'the dense series of counterloops among cinema, TV, philosophy, neurophysiology and everyday life' mean that we do recognize the realm between thinking and affects and are beginning to outline a '*neuropolitics*' (Connolly 2002) that might work with them. It is a politics that recognizes that political concepts and beliefs can never be reduced to 'disembodied tokens of argumentation. Culture has multiple layers, with each layer marked by distinctive speeds, capacities and levels of linguistic complexity' (Connolly 2002: 45). Take difference and identity as one example of this geology of thinking. The political literature in this area has tended to foreground signification at the expense of affect and has therefore enacted culture as a flat world of concepts and beliefs which can be changed simply by engraining other new concepts and beliefs. It might be possible to point to (and domesticate) the vagaries of thinking in everyday life via a concept like habitus but that is about it. But difference and identity isn't like that. It operates on several registers, each with their own organizations and complexities:

> on one register it is a defined minority that deviates from the majority practice. On a second, it is a minority that varies from other constituencies in a setting where there is no definitive majority. On a third, it is that in an identity (subjective or intersubjective) that is obscured, suppressed, or remaindered by its own dominant tendencies – as in the way devout Christians may be inhabited by fugitive forgetfulness and doubts not brought up for review in daily conversations or in church, or in the way that militant atheists may tacitly project life forward after death when not concentrating on the belief that consciousness stops with the death of the body. The third register of difference fades into a fourth, in which surpluses, traces, noises, and charges in and around the beliefs of embodied agents express proto-thoughts and judgements too crude to be conceptualised in a refined way but still intensive and effective enough to make a difference to the selective way judgements are formed, porous arguments are received, and alternatives are weighted. And in a layered, textured culture, cultural argument is always porous. Some of the elements in such a fugitive fund might be indicated, but not of course represented, by those noises, stutters, gestures, looks, accents, exclamations, gurgles, bursts of laughter, gestures and rhythmic or irrhythmic movements that inhabit, punctuate, inflect and help to move the world of concepts and beliefs.
>
> (Connolly 2002: 43–44)

So we require a microbiopolitics of the subliminal, much of which operates in the half-second delay between action and cognition, a microbiopolitics which understands the kind of biological-cum-cultural gymnastics that takes place in this realm which is increasingly susceptible to new and sometimes threatening knowledges and technologies that operate upon it in ways that produce effective outcomes, even when the exact reasons may be opaque, a micropolitics which understands the insufficiency of argument to political life without, however, denying its pertinence. That micropolitics might be thought to be composed of three main and closely related components. One is quasi-Foucauldian and consists of attention to the arts of the self of the kind already signalled. The second is an 'ethic of cultivation', an ethico-political perspective which attempts to instil generosity towards the world by utilizing some of the infrasensible knowledges that we have already encountered on a whole series of registers (Connolly 2002). The third involves paying much greater attention to how new forms of space and time are being constituted. In an era in which several new forms of time and space have been born (e.g. cinematic time and the movement image, standardized space and the ability to track and trace) this latter component seems particularly pressing.

The fourth kind of affect is that associated with a neo-Darwinian approach. That approach tends to focus on the face and faciality as an index of emotion and it is this aspect that I want to take up in the next section by concentrating on a particular case study. After all, for most of us, 'the living face is the most important and mysterious surface we deal with. It is the center of our flesh. We eat, drink, breathe and talk with it, and it houses four of the five classic senses' (McNeill 1998: 4). So let's face it, most especially through the medium of the screen which has now become such a dominant means of connecting Western cultures.

I do not know what it is I am like[24]

The discussion so far will be trying for some because of its lack of concreteness. So, in this final section I want to bring some of the elements of my argument together in a concrete example which takes elements from the four approaches to affect that I have identified (and especially the neo-Darwinian obsession with the face) and extends them into politics conceived as an art of showing up showing up differently. I want to set out at least some elements of the last kind of politics I want to further by venturing into the realm of video art (taking in any screened art) (Rush 1999; Ascott 2003). I have chosen this field for four reasons. First, the film and video screen have become a powerful means of conveying affect in our culture, drawing on a set of historically formed stock repertoires for manipulating space and time which have existed now for nearly a century (Doane 2002). Second, because video art has slowly come of age as the available technologies have become more adaptable to expression[25] and has gradually been able to forge a common vocabulary of spacing and timing differently which can travel across a number of screened media and which is now also becoming interactive (film, video, web, virtual reality, etc.). The blurred and crudely lit video art of the past, often not much more than a means of recording performance art, has been replaced by degrees of colour, texture and motion that make genuine and concerted demands on attention (Campbell 2003). Third, because new developments like the web give video artists large and culturally primed audiences which were not available when works had to be sited in the aspic of galleries and which spread out beyond self-defined cultural elites. Fourth, because this work has engaged explicitly with affect. A good example is Roy Ascott's notion of telematic love, built on Charles Fourier's theory of 'passionate attraction' (see Amin and Thrift 2002), which was described by him as 'the drive given us by nature prior to any reflection . . . toward the co-ordination of the passions . . . and consequently toward universal unity' (Fourier, cited in Shanken 2003: 75). On this base, Ascott builds a kind of telematic cosmopolitics, in which telematics forms the beginnings of a global networked consciousness[26] based on continuous exchange which is both cognitive and affective. Ascott has built a set of artworks on this premise which act as a machine for imagining life as it could be.

However, it is not just for these reasons that I want to turn to video art. It is also because it can show something about the energetics of movement and emotion and how that relationship is formed and made malleable in cities in which, as I pointed out above, screens, patches of moving light populated chiefly by faces, have increasingly become a ubiquitous and normal means of expression, populating more and more urban spaces and producing a postsocial world in which *faces loom larger than life* (Balázs 1970).[27] To help me in this endeavour, I want to call on the work of Bill Viola (1995, 2003). Why Viola?[28] I want to point to three reasons. First, and very importantly for me, because he gets real audience response: his works have grip. The mix of unnatural naturalism and magical realism he projects in his works stirs spectators and sometimes stirs them mightily. His exhibitions are not only popular but they also regularly produce extreme emotional responses in their audiences which sometimes seem to cross over into the therapeutic and even redemptive (cf. Gibbons 2003).

Second, because he is intent on engaging affect but through a series of depictions which knowingly engage the unconscious history of affect, pulling on heartstrings developed over many centuries. In other words, in what is often only a few seconds, Viola is producing an archaeology of the contemporary past which is both trans-cendent and therapeutic and perhaps, in certain senses, redemptive (Buchli and Lucas 2001). At a minimum, this archaeology recalls the following histories and cartographies of the contemporary past:

- The history of the representation of the agonies of Christ and other Christian imagery from the Middle Ages and Renaissance. This is a tradition of depiction which harks back to the ancient Greek term pathos (which simply signified 'anything that befalls one') and the way that this term became mixed up with the Christian notion of passion which named the suffering and crucifixion of Jesus and was heavily loaded up with emotion (Meyer 2003).
- The history of exact scientific representation of the expressive face from the early days of physiognomy (as in Le Brun's seventeenth-century depiction of faces transported by extreme emotion) through the writings of nineteenth-century anatomists and physicians on facial musculature and expression to Rejlander's carefully staged photographic contributions to Darwin's work and on to the current interest in the face to be found in the so-called affective sciences.
- The hop, skip and jump delay of scientific experiment on human perception, as found in, for example, nineteenth-century German psychophysics. This genealogy may be best tracked through the history of the invention and operationalization of the feedback loops of cybernetics and so on into the

elementary forms of capitalist life to be found in the minimal presences of the brand and other such sigils.

- The sensate assault on vision which begins with the technological reproduction of reality in the linked images of silent film flitting by and which allows a certain kind of intense faciality of the kind found especially in the close-up observations of silent film (R.O. Moore 2000), the 'raw vision' so beloved of Benjamin and Epstein which presses too close and hits us between the eyes in its jerky nearness (Crary 1999); 'film moves, and fundamentally "moves" us, with its ability to render affects and, in turn, to affect' (Bruno 2002: 7). Again, there are direct links to physiognomy in the use by directors of actresses and actors whose facial deftness allows them to display a map of emotions, and involves the spectator in an intricate process of watching and searching for clues (Taussig 1999; Bruno 2002).
- The clichés of modern press reporting and photography which provide a kind of habitual visual taxonomy through which we face/feel the world which is thing-like in its material presence.
- The oligoptic gaze of the dry schemata of modern facial recognition systems that are increasingly being used in a plethora of systems of surveillance and whose genealogy again reaches back to physiognomy (Elkins 1999).
- The recent struggles of performance and various kinds of performance art to capture the kernel of the videoed face, building on the legacy of movements like behaviorist art, various cybernetic models, kinetic art and interactivity generally (Ascott 2003).

Viola enacts this multiple historical/cartographic legacy by, for example, using close-up and slow motion[29] on state-of-the-art LCD flat screens which recall the multiple screens of medieval polyptychs. The depictions stretch out time in such a way that they allow nuances of feeling to be observed that would barely be noticed in the to and fro of everyday life. They are carefully staged and scripted, sometimes involving a huge cast of actors, as well as stunt people, hundreds of extras, and a panoply of scene designers, plus set builders, a director of photography, wardrobe, make-up, lights, and so on, all for takes which may be less than one minute in length, given the limited capacity of a film magazine at high speed (Wolff 2002). The intent is clearly to let facial expression or other body movements (and, most obviously, the hand), patterns of light and different spatial formations interact in telling ways, providing 'turbulent surfaces' in which emotional and physical shape coincide in arcs of intensity. At the same time, the depictions knowingly point to their own operations, pulling in paratextual elements (like frames and times) as integral parts of the performance.

Third, Viola's works point to aspects of cities which are too often neglected. In particular, he has been concerned to highlight the face as a primary composer of affect and maker of presence (Taussig 1999). Viola sees the face as a colour wheel of emotions and constantly places emotions together as sequences which illustrate this shifting spectrum of affect. But it is not just the face, it has to be said. Viola also considers the hand as an index of affect (Tallis 2003). He also uses the whole body to index more general affective practices of coping, of which the most notable is probably crying (cf. Thrift 2004). So, the city as a sea of faces, a forest of hands, an ocean of lamentation: these are the building blocks of modern urbanism just as much as brick and stone. In other words, Viola provides an affective history of the city, understood as a chronicle of faces and hands and tears. This is an intimate geography through which and as which affect makes its way, a set of histories of the way in which affect takes hold told by foregrounding a set of affective practices which are too often neglected: seeing visions, praying, crying, each of which has their own cultural history. But Viola is also quite aware that these ecstatic practices are usually part of a daily round which can itself become his focus of attention; a chain of ordinary tasks themselves become a spiritual practice, a set of margins constantly edging forward, recomposing as they go.

But what, then, is the political import of Viola's 'slowly turning narratives'? I think it is threefold, with each succeeding element more important than the one before. One element is showing the complex process of mimesis by which we learn to generate affect. Viola is able, by slowing things down, to show how each element of the body (and most especially the face) takes its part in a show of emotion which has its own contested cultural history. He presents us with a kind of affective historical geography of expressive elements of the body like the face, maps of the way our bodies are socialized through mimesis[30] and other processes from birth onwards which have been created over many centuries, quite literally producing a release of meanings from the past. The mapping of the spatial play of affect may not be particularly original[31] but Viola does it beautifully, using all the aesthetic cues that have come down to us as cultural signifiers of intensity which we learn from infancy on. In turn, the audiences react to their own processes of emotional learning, playing these corporeal 'memories' back in their body and very often amplifying them through the step-by-step of Viola's depictions in ways which may legitimately be described as therapeutic.

Then, second, Viola embeds affect in space and time. His sets, whether they are an iconic human face, a country walk or a house in flood, are carefully cued spatial and temporal transformations which resist the reading-writing-text paradigm but are still comprehensible to a critically alert audience as various forms of (e)motion. Their visual 'vocabulary' cracks open familiar horizons of space and time and shows the way that wheres can also be elsewheres, and how these new alignments might offer new affective resonances and resources. By operating on space and time (stretching, transforming, miniaturizing, etc.) they become a kind of threshing floor for the emotions from which new instinctual traffic may come. Kracauer once argued that film was a redemptive art of estrangement that could put us back in touch with reality (Carter 2002).[32] Too grand a statement, no doubt. But, in Viola's case, it seems to bear some relevance to his ambitions (cf. Viola 2003).

Third, Viola is able to show something about the elementary affective forms of the modern world as they are produced in screens and then transmitted into urban bodies and other byways as a kind of visceral shorthand existing only in very small subliminal spaces and times. Marcus puts it well when he writes that 'When a movie has become part of the folklore of a nation, the borders between the movie and the nation cease to exist. The movie becomes a fable; then it becomes a metaphor. Then it becomes a catchphrase, a joke, a shortcut' (2002: 104). Viola shows us all the affective catchphrases, jokes and shortcuts that typify Western cultures but, through slow motion and close-up, restores them to their original step-by-step nature so that we can see them at work. They may be difficult to describe in words since they are non-representational but we can still detect them through Viola's laying out of the minute and diagrammatic clues we usually work on in everyday life as something more akin to large signposts.

Of course, what Viola points to is not regular politics but, unless the matter of how we are made to be/be connected is to be regarded as somehow out of court, what he is focusing on is surely an intensely political process, one which matters to people. Without this kind of affective politics, what is left of politics will too often be the kind of macho programme-making that emaciates what it is to be human – because it is so sure it already knows what that is or will be.

Conclusions

So let me briefly conclude. There is more to the world than is routinely acknowledged in too many writings on politics and this excess is not just incidental. It points in the direction of fugitive work in the social sciences and humanities which can read the little, the messy and the jerry-rigged as a part of politics and not just incidental to it. It points as well in the direction of work that wants to give up the ancient settlement between knowledge and passions (and nature and culture, and people and things, and truth and force) in favour of considering what ties things together as an explicit politics (Stengers 1997). I think we live in exciting times because these two 'traditions' have become mixed up, most especially in experiments in thinking about the politics of encountering the spaces of cities which we are only just at the start of laying out and working with.

In particular, I would want to end with the work currently being undertaken as a result of alliances between social sciences and artists. The marriage of science and the arts is often called 'engineering' and this seems to be the right term for the kind of theoretical-practical knowledges that are now being derived, ad hoc[33] knowledges of the ad hoc which can simultaneously change our engagements with the world. In struggling to represent some of the issues dealt with in this chapter the foundations of a new kind of cultural engineering is gradually being constructed upon which and with which new forms of political practice which value democracy as functional disunity will be able to be built. I have heard a number of commentators argue that these kinds of engineering experiments are essentially trivial and that we need to get back to the 'real' stuff. I am not persuaded. I am not persuaded at all. It seems to me that *no choice has to be made*. We need to pursue many of the older forms of politics and the political as vigorously as before but we also need the 'research and development' that will allow us to expand the envelope of the political and so both restore the spaces of moral and political reflection that 'man' has collapsed and bring new forms of politics into being. If we don't do it, others most surely will.

9 But malice aforethought

You may talk of the tyranny of Nero and Tiberius; but the real tyranny is the tyranny of your next-door neighbour.

(Bagehot, cited in Lane 2004: 15)

Perhaps he doesn't wait even for the end of the conversation, but gets up at the point where the matter has become clear to him, flies through the town with his usual haste, and, before I have hung up the receiver, is already at his goal working against me.

(Kafka 1988: 425)

He who says neighbours says enemies.

(France 2002 [1909]: 9)

Introduction

The idea of the city as doomed is one of the common tropes of urban representation, as Mike Davis (2002) has illustrated at length in one of his latest books.[1] For Davis, the Western city is rapidly coming unglued. It is a runaway train fuelled by equal parts hubris and fear. It is Roadrunner suspended over the abyss. In tapping in to this anxious tradition of writing on cities, Davis is hardly alone. For example he cites approvingly that rather idiosyncratic Marxist Ernst Bloch, in equally apocalyptic mode, arguing much earlier that, in contrast to the adaptive and improvisatory pre-capitalist city, the capitalist city is in a continual state of radical insecurity and dread. Transfixed by the idea of a totally safe and calculable environment, the capitalist city is fixed and unbending in the face of unexpected events: 'it has rooted itself in midair'. And so it is heading for a fall; 'where technology has achieved an apparent victory over the limits of nature . . . the coefficient of known and, more significantly, unknown danger has increased proportionately' (Bloch 1998 [1929]: 307, 309).

Well maybe. I thought that I would begin this chapter by arguing against these increasingly common nightmare scenarios which seem to be so prevalent that they are now producing all kinds of echoes – such as the growing historical literature on metropolitan catastrophes.[2] I believe that on many dimensions the contemporary Western city is more robust than it has ever been and I will want to explain why (cf. Massard et al. 2002). But I am also sure that the inhabitants of Western cities often think the opposite and I will try to explain that why too: my thesis will be that it is not only the images of war and disaster flooding in from the media that have generated a pervasive fear of catastrophe but also a more deep-seated sense of misanthropy which urban commentators have been loath to acknowledge, a sense of misanthropy too often treated as though it were a dirty secret.

This is not, I hasten to add, a Panglossian account. I do not think that all is well in the urban world or that all will be well – of course, cities are and will no doubt continue to be vulnerable to all kinds of catastrophic events, from terrorist attacks to earthquakes to influenza epidemics. Rather, I want to provide a qualified account which by excavating the everyday life and varying time signatures of cities might lead the discussion of the future politics of cities in slightly different directions.

To this end, I will begin the chapter by noting that cities often bounce back from catastrophe remarkably quickly. I will argue that there are good reasons why that is: most particularly, the fact that Western cities are continuously modulated by repair and maintenance in ways that are so familiar that we tend to overlook them but which give these cities a good deal more resilience than Bloch, Davis, and many others before and since have been willing to give them credit for.

Then, in the second part of the chapter, I want to take a more philosophical turn and start to address why urban inhabitants might have a sense of foreboding about cities. I am not sure that the evidence would suggest that cities are any more on a knife edge than they have ever been but a Cassandra tendency seems to infect many of the recent writings on cities. Why might this be? I want to suggest that this requires an analysis of the prevailing urban mood. In other words, I want to turn to a consideration of affect arising out of a series of papers I have published recently[3] which have attempted to engage with various technologies of affect. In particular, I will consider the sheer incidence of misanthropy in cities and how it has been framed since industrialization. My argument is that it is only by facing this misanthropy square on that we can start to understand kindness and compassion. I will want to argue that a certain amount of dislike of one's fellow citizens is, given the social-cum-biological-cum-technological make-up of human beings, inescapable: the ubiquity of aggression is an inevitable by-product of living in cities.[4] But I also want to argue that part of the impetus for the increasing interest in the misanthropic side of cities that may not celebrate but certainly does not shy away from the darker side of human nature lies in the fact that modern urban spaces are increasingly seen as themselves implicated in human imperfectibility in that rather more of their substance than was formerly acknowledged takes its cue from models of organization that are founded on the systematic delivery of violence, which are so engrained that we hardly notice their dictates, yet alone understand their origins. Certain kinds of violence have become engrained in our 'natures' by these models of organization and our environment now simply confirms these truths.

Then, in the final part of the chapter, I want to argue that there is a nascent politics of foreboding centred around the idea of a politics of hope which involves engaging with the sentiment of compassion but is not thereby sentimental.

In other words, in this chapter I want to walk the line, veering between hope and then pessimism, and then hope again. To begin with I want to argue straightforwardly that, even though 'the myth of terrible urban vulnerability endures' (Konvitz 1990: 62) cities are much more robust entities than they are usually given credit for, continually being re-placed by activities of maintenance and repair.

But then I want to move on to argue, perversely some will say, for a more pessimistic view of the moral life of cities than is often put forward nowadays for I do not believe that advances in material civilization necessarily lead to moral progress. This is hardly a novel position. After all, it was forcefully put forward by Rousseau in his *First Discourse*. But, even now, it is still an uncomfortable one, sometimes associated with fascism or various forms of mysticism, and most clearly articulated by an almost forgotten set of social theorists like Gobineau, Le Bon, Sorel and Schmitt whose politics were not always attractive, to put it but mildly (Llobera 2003). However, of late, it is possible to argue that there has been a largely unacknowledged revival of this kind of thinking as a result of a number of developments, of which I will highlight just three. First, there has been a greater and greater interest shown in the biological constitution of human social orders. Whilst, arguably, a strain of eugenic thinking persists in modern societies (cf. Duster 1990), still it has become possible to talk about biology without being immediately accused of determinism and, in turn, to address issues like violence and aggression and hatred as though they might have biological determinants without immediate censure. Second, there has been a renewed interest, in the guise of work on so-called agonistic politics, in forms of politics which are willing to tolerate a depiction of societies as not premised on the maintenance of shared orders but as, in large part, being the result of the carving out of very different worlds, worlds which cannot be expected to reach agreement and which may obdurately disagree because they do not even share shared premises about the world. Such work argues that politics is about disagreement as much as it is about consensus (cf. Rancière 1999; Mouffe 2002).[5] Third, there has been a general falling away of belief in the efficacy of large-scale projects of social change and their corresponding goals of forging a bourgeois or socialist heavenly kingdom, not just because they so often seem to crush difference, but also because they so often seem to unleash mythopoetic forces that their own proponents do not seem to understand.[6]

Then, in conclusion, against this rather sombre background, I want to return to the later work of Ernst Bloch and argue for a politics of affective 'repair and maintenance' based around hope. This should not be interpreted as a call for blind optimism. Rather, it is an argument for a politics of disagreement which can still find a place for a sort of practical utopianism which cleaves to the idea that the 'the essence of the world is cheerful spirit and the urge to creative shaping' (Bloch 1986 [1959]: 16). Cities may have, as I will argue, a large reservoir of enmity but they also have a surplus of hope, an unconscious hunger for the future as well as the past.

In what ways vulnerable? The hum of maintenance and repair

In both old and more recent work, I have been trying to see the city as an object which has temporal extension into the future, rather than as a snapshot. It consists of a myriad of partially connected processes going forward at different rates and speeds (Amin and Thrift 2002) and across many 'scales' simultaneously.[7] This vision has particular relevance in arguing about urban vulnerability. For it is often argued that cities are vulnerable and cannot survive the trauma of war and other dramatic events of destruction easily. This is an extreme judgement. To begin with, it tends to rely on thinking of cities as caught in the temporal aspic of the present, as if urban trauma only consisted of the act of destruction itself and its immediate aftermath. But there is another tradition of thinking about cities which thinks of them as existing over the longer term, for example by using devices like building cycles with their various amplitudes, and would judge urban trauma using this longer-term perspective. This kind of work has fallen out of favour (see Parkes and Thrift 1980 for a review) but it has the useful by-product of conceptualizing cities as having all kinds of periods of temporal return, many of which may extend over decades.[8] Then, there is a simple empirical point. Cities generally tend to recover quite quickly from even the most damaging catastrophes. For example, back in the 1980s when I considered the history of large Vietnamese cities in the 1960s and 1970s (Thrift and Forbes 1986) and British cities in the Second World War (Thrift 1996), I was struck by the fact that their populations could survive repeated attacks quite well. Some decanting of population took place but many people soon returned. This resilience existed for all kinds of reasons, of course, not all of them good. For example, many people, and especially working-class people, had nowhere else to go. But there was one factor which was apparent at the time but whose wider significance I have only lately seen. Cities are based in large part on activities of repair and maintenance, the systematic re-placement of place, and this ability is still there in times of trouble to be adapted to the new circumstances. These activities provided a kind of glue, which hastened cities' recovery times, most especially because all kinds of processes are being intervened in, some of which are pretty easy to deal with quickly (e.g. broken power lines), others of which take far longer to mend (e.g. broken hearts). Cities, in other words, took hard knocks but with the aid of all these activities they could get up, dust themselves off, and start all over again. This is a point I want to develop in more detail.

Repair and maintenance covers a whole host of activities and it has become, if anything, more prevalent since I was working on the impact of war on cities. To begin with, Western cities nowadays are populated by large national and international companies[9] which specialize in activities as different as various kinds of cleaning, all forms of building maintenance, the constant fight to keep the urban fabric – from pavements and roads to lighting and power – going, emergency call-out to all manner of situations, the repair of all manner of electrical goods, roadside and collision repair of cars, and so on. These mundane activities, the quartermasters of urban culture as Loos (1982 [1898]) might have put it, may have been neglected by most urban commentators but it is possible to argue that they are vital, not least because of the large and systematized knowledge bases that underpin them which are currently seeing an unparalleled expansion. That expansion is taking place in three domains: new materials and techniques that are extending the service life of all the infrastructure that surrounds us; new means of presenting and commodifying this knowledge (for example, there are now substantial degree programmes in topics like logistics and facilities, maintenance and repair); and the fact that what counts as repair and maintenance is constantly extending into new fields (for example, into the biological domain through activities as diverse as bioremediation (effectively, environmental repair) and the repair of DNA). To give some sense of the current spread of activities, consider only the vaguest of snapshots provided by Table 9.1.[10] Then, much of the general population is also constantly involved in maintenance and repair. The growth of activities like do-it-yourself (DIY) indexes the way in which home maintenance and repair (including the maintenance of gardens, cars, and the like) has itself produced a set of thriving commodity markets, made up of all kinds of electrical and other goods.[11] And, finally, these activities often involve a high degree of improvisation, even in their most systematized form. They involve solutions to very diverse situations which still resist standardization, and so may often retain a good deal of often un- or under-appreciated skill and all kinds of 'underground knowledges'.[12]

What is interesting is that we have little idea if the increasing reach and complexity of activities like these have made cities more or less vulnerable to catastrophe. Some 'risk society' commentators might argue that their contribution is piffling when compared with the new generation of global risks that are now emerging. But, equally, it would be possible to argue that cities are constantly adding new circuits of adaptability: the city is a knot of maintenance and repair activities which cannot easily be unravelled and which allow it to pick itself up and start again, so to speak, relatively easily. All we can say at the moment is that modern urban dwellers are surrounded by the hum of continuous repair and maintenance and that, furthermore, some of the quintessential everyday urban experiences are generated by them, from the noise of pneumatic drills boring into roads to the knock or ring of a repairman come to mend a broken-down this or that.[13] The point becomes even more germane if the emergency services are added in, with their knowledges of clearing up small but sustained disasters like accidents, fires, and the like, all the way from the actual incident itself to the smooth running of the aftermath, which may involve all kinds of allied actors from builders to insurance assessors.[14] Again, the sight and sound of these services is a quintessential everyday urban experience.

Recently, this general hum of activity has been powered up by information technology. True, the speed, interconnectedness and complexity of information and communications technology has produced new vulnerabilities. For example, on one estimate, an average large firm's computer networks are down for an unplanned 175 hours per year and as much as '70–80% of [corporate] IT spending goes on fixing things rather than buying new systems' (Kluth 2004: 4). But, generally speaking, information and communications technology has probably made cities more robust by adding more degrees of redundancy and new forms of knowledge. Simple things like risk analysis and other institutionalized forms of diligence, booking systems, etc. have made the business of maintenance and repair easier to carry out and, indeed, are beginning to automate at least some of this activity (as in, for example, the instance of machines that send messages that they are breaking down). More to the point, in situations of breakdown, whether epic or mundane, the humble mobile phone has extended the city's interactivity and adaptability in all kinds of ways and may well have been the most significant device to add to a city's overall resilience by adding an extra thread to the urban knot. In addition, all kinds of knowledges of maintenance and repair which are heavily dependent upon information and communications technologies are coming to the fore, all the way from logistics to disaster planning itself (which, in certain senses, is a branch of logistics).

I want to argue that this activity constitutes an urban technological unconscious which helps to keep cities as predictable objects in which things turn up as they are meant to, regularly and predictably (Thrift 2004a). Modern Western cities are in many ways mass engineerings of time and space and this engineering increasingly involves working with very small spaces (of the order of millimetres) and times (of the order of milliseconds). At this scale, this means working on the structure of anticipation, producing a comforting sense of regularity and a corresponding (and probably amplified historically) sense of annoyance when things do not play out exactly as it is intended that they should. In a sense, speed has produced a new landscape of anticipation. Some commentators see this landscape as a threat, likely to institute a new 'dromocracy'. I am more ambivalent. It seems to me that it offers possibilities too, and not least in providing rapid reaction to problems large and small. Indeed, as information technology systems come in which are based on continuous updating of information, some degree of capacity to track and trace and the ability to forecast forward in a very limited way (for example, through profiling systems), so it seems to me that cities will add another landscape to their repertoire, one which works a few seconds or minutes or, in extreme cases, hours ahead of the present and which will add markedly to their resilience. Of course, there is a new repertoire of risk associated with this landscape of foresight but whether it is that much larger than many other developments remains to be seen. Computer systems are vulnerable to attack just like any other system but it is also important to remember the continuous amount of repair and maintenance which goes into these systems anyway, and reactions to attacks by worms or viruses are rapidly being incorporated into this burgeoning structure.

Of course, there is a partial exception to this story of relative resilience: cities in the South. It could be argued that some of these cities are in a recurring state of emergency (Schneider and Susser 2003). They have not benefited from many of the recent developments in information technology and may even have had much risk transferred to them by the vagaries of uneven development but, whatever the cause, such cities, have much less in the way of repair and maintenance infrastructure to begin with.[15] Writers like Koolhaas (2007) have celebrated the informality of these cities and argued that they present a new model of flexibility:

Table 9.1 A sample of facilities, maintenance and repair jobs

Aircraft Electrician jobs	Level I Electrician jobs	Level III General Maintenance Worker jobs
Aircraft Maintenance Supervisor jobs	Level I Facilities Maintenance Manager jobs	Level III HVAC Mechanic jobs
Airframe and Engine Mechanic jobs	Level I General Maintenance Worker jobs	Level III Operations Research Analyst jobs
Assembly Supervisor jobs	Level I HVAC Mechanic jobs	Level III Painter jobs
Concrete and Terrazzo Finisher jobs	Level I Operations Research Analyst jobs	Level III Plumber jobs
Construction and Building Inspector jobs	Level I Painter jobs	Level III Rep., Electro/Mechanical Equipment Field Service jobs
Copy Machine Field Service Representative jobs	Level I Plumber jobs	Level III Rep., Electronic Equipment Field Service jobs
Dairy Processing Equipment Repairer jobs	Level I Rep., Electro/Mechanical Equipment Field Service jobs	Level III Rep., Telecommunications Equipment Field Service jobs
Electric Home Appliance and Power Tool Repairer jobs	Level I Rep., Electronic Equipment Field Service jobs	Level III Spares Coordinator jobs
Electric Meter Installer and Repairer jobs	Level I Rep., Telecommunications Equipment Field Service jobs	Level IV Operations Research Analyst jobs
Electric Motor Assembler jobs	Level I Spares Coordinator jobs	Level IV Spares Coordinator jobs
Electrical Powerline Installer/Repairer jobs	Level II Aircraft Maintenance Manager jobs	Level V Operations Research Analyst jobs
Electrical Utility Trouble Shooter jobs	Level II Aircraft Painter jobs	Level V Spares Coordinator jobs
Elevator Installer/Repairer jobs	Level II Carpenter jobs	Maintenance Supervisor jobs
Estimating Manager jobs	Level II Electric/Electronics Technician jobs	Operations Research Analysis Manager jobs
Facilities Maintenance Supervisor jobs	Level II Electrician jobs	Operations Research Analysis Supervisor jobs
Facilities Manager jobs	Level II Facilities Maintenance Manager jobs	Parking Lot Attendant jobs
General Labourer jobs	Level II General Maintenance Worker jobs	Security Guard jobs
Groundskeeper jobs	Level II HVAC Mechanic jobs	Senior Airframe and Engine Mechanic jobs
Head of Housekeeping jobs	Level II Operations Research Analyst jobs	Senior General Labourer jobs
Housekeeper jobs	Level II Painter jobs	Senior Groundskeeper jobs
Housekeeping Supervisor jobs	Level II Plumber jobs	Senior Janitor jobs

Interior Aircraft Assembly Manager jobs

Interior Aircraft Assembly Supervisor jobs

Janitor jobs

Jig and Fixture Builder jobs
Lawn Service Manager jobs
Level I Aircraft Maintenance Manager jobs
Level I Aircraft Painter jobs
Level I Carpenter jobs
Level I Electric/Electronics Technician jobs

Level II Rep., Electro/Mechanical Equipment Field Service jobs
Level II Rep., Electronic Equipment Field Service jobs
Level II Rep., Telecommunications Equipment Field Service jobs
Level II Spares Coordinator jobs
Level III Aircraft Painter jobs
Level III Carpenter jobs
Level III Electric/Electronics Technician jobs
Level III Electrician jobs

Senior Security Guard jobs

Senior Structural Assembler jobs

Spares Coordination Manager jobs

Spares Coordination Supervisor jobs
Structural Assembler jobs
Vehicle Washer/Equipment Cleaner jobs

Source: www.salary.com

I doubt it! It seems more likely to me that these cities, through general lack of resources, are likely to have less maintenance and repair infrastructure and that they are forced to make up this deficit through even more acts of inspired improvisation and the widespread use of informal networks of help like family and friends. Of course, in extremis, as in forced acts of 'de-modernization' such as are found in Palestine, repair and maintenance infrastructures may start to break down completely (indeed, it could be argued that one of the tactics of 'urbicide', to use Steve Graham's (2003) felicitous phrase, is to mount an assault on precisely these structures).

What cities of the South do illustrate is the importance of another kind of repair and maintenance to which I will return later in the chapter. That is what we might call the social repair occasioned by social networks of various kinds, kin and friendship networks which may offer a range of support. This is more, so far as I am concerned, than just so-called 'social capital'. It is practical political expression.

Dark feelings

So why, if the evidence for the increased vulnerability of cities is certainly ambiguous, and even at times downright tenuous, especially when compared with an everyday event like, say, global traffic carnage (now standing at well over a million killed per year around the world) does a certain sense of defencelessness and foreboding persist in the populations of many Western cities? Why is fear of and for the future seemingly so widespread, to the point where the level of anxiety has touched off what Mike Davis (2002) calls a whole urban 'fear economy' of surveillance and security? Why do so many seem to feel that their definition of the real is under threat, such that, for example, the normative relays between personal and collective ethics have become frayed and worn? To begin to understand this dynamic of unease, we need to stray onto the territory of affect and begin to think of cities as emotional knots.

I have been involved in investigations of urban affect or mood for a number of years now but can say that touching this sphere remains an elusive task, not least because so many definitions of affect circulate, each with their own problematizations. For example, affect can be understood as a simple or complex biological drive, a pragmatic effect of the pre-cognitive or cognitive interactions of bodies, a set of capacities for affecting or being affected by, the communicative power of faciality, and so on (Thrift 2004b). In other words, affect is as much a nexus of a set of concerns – with what bodies can do, with the power of emotions, with the crossover between 'biology' and 'culture' – as it is a finished analytic.

But even given this diversity of focus, we can point to obvious causes of a sense of defencelessness and foreboding, none of which I would want to gainsay. There is the evident peril of the current geopolitical conjuncture with all its pitfalls. More importantly, probably, there is the emotional aftermath of 9/11 and similar terrorist attacks. Images of these events have probably come to stand for something greater in many Western city dwellers' minds, not just the threat to life and limb but also the disruption of the pace and rhythm of everyday life, the sheer turn-up again-ness of each urban moment and the quantum of hope that goes with it. Further, these images have been amplified by the media which has a constitutive interest in presenting them as inherently magnified. Why? Because, fear sells. There is a market in anxiety.[16] As Altheide (2002) shows in his seminal book on the subject, the overwhelming message of news reports is fear. Further, safety is increasingly promoted through association with fear. In other words:

> Fear has shifted from concerns with the physical world and the spiritual realm of salvation during the last four hundred years to the social realm of everyday life. It is other people but not just immigrants – the historical other that have troubled previous immigrants-now-solid-citizens; it is the 'other', that category of trouble that can unseat solid expectations and hopes for a future that can never be realized in what is perceived to be a constantly changing and out-of-control world. Fear rests on the borders between expectations and realizations, between hope and reality.
>
> (Altheide 2002: 26)

But I want to go farther into this sense of the future by considering the typical make-up of the 'unconscious' of the modern Western urban dweller. I shall argue that the current urban trauma is the particular expression of a more general set of affective potentials. But I shall not, on the whole, resort to Freudian explanations of this affective undertow. Rather, I will argue that the contemporary Western urban unconscious consists of sedimented cultural-cum-biological-cum tech-nological (the clumsiness of these terms themselves suggesting that they are unsatisfactory representations) shortcuts which produce particular kinds of interactional intelligence, stances towards how the world is negotiated. Human interactional intelligence is, so far as we know, predicated upon five qualities. First, it assumes sociality. As Levinson (1995) points out, human is biologically and socially predicated upon co-ordination of action with others: 'it is cooperative, mutual intersubjectivity that is the computational task that we seem especially adapted to' (Levinson 1995: 253). So, for example, selfishness seems to be a second-ary characteristic; 'people care both about other people, and about how social transactions occur – not just the outcomes' (Heinrich *et al.* 2004: 1). Second, and consequentially, human interaction recognizes and privileges the special kind of intention with which a communicative act is produced. Third, human assumes the presence of tools which will be actively used and which are assumed to be active. (Indeed it is arguable that certain human bodily characteristics like the hand and associated parts of the brain have co-evolved with tool use). Fourth, human interaction utilizes a massively extended affective palette which is learnt from birth (Gerhardt 2004). Fifth, human because of these characteristics tends to animistic thinking, which humanizes the environment and assumes that the environment interacts with it on similar terms, rather than as a series of partially disconnected and perceptually very different umwelts.

This interactional intelligence is perpetually criss-crossed by affect which acts both as a way of initiating action, a reading of the sense of aliveness of the situation and an intercorporeal transfer of that expectancy. Affect, in other words, acts as the corporeal sense of the communicative act. In the literature, some prominence has tended to be given to euphoric affects like happiness, hope, and joy. But, there are a range of dysphoric affects that also repay attention which have also been studied, like greed, cruelty and shame. I want to argue that interactional intelligence has therefore both a positive bias to sociality but also, in part precisely because of this, some misanthropic aspects.

One thing which is often neglected about affect is that it involves temporal extension. Perhaps because Freudian concepts of repression have circulated so widely, it is often thought that affect is solely concerned with projections of the past. But, there is every reason to believe that affect is as concerned with projection or thrownness into the future, as a means of initiating action, as the power of intuition (Myers 2002), as a hunger for the future (as found in, for example, daydreams), as a set of fantasies (for example, concerned with romantic love, which I will address again below), and as a general sense of physical motility (Balint 1959).

The rather longwinded preface to this section allows me to argue something about the nature of interactional intelligence which has often been neglected, namely that although it has a social bias, there is another side to that bias. That is that achieving sociality does not mean that everything has to be rosy: sociality is *not* the same as liking. In particular, it seems likely that from an early age interactional intelligence, at least in Western cultures, is also premised on exclusion and even aggression. Children tend to learn sociality and sharing, at least in part, through intimidation, victimization, domination and sanction. In other words, the kind of empathy required by interactional intelligence does not preclude a good deal of general misanthropy. Though it hardly needs saying, sociality does not have to be the same thing as liking others. It includes all kinds of acts of kindness and compassion, certainly, but equally there are all the signs of active dislike being actively pursued, not just or even primarily as outbreaks of violence (for example, road rage or Saturday night fights) but more particularly as malign gossip, endless complaint, the full spectrum of jealousy, petty snobbery, personal deprecation, pointless authoritarianism, various forms of *Schadenfreude*, and all the other ritual pleasures of everyday life.[17]

None of this is to say that it is necessary to condone virulent forms of racism or nationalism or other forms of mass identification which often involve systematic exclusion and violence. It is to say, however, that we need to think more carefully about whether we really have it in us to just be unalloyedly nice to others at all times in every single place: most situations can and do bring forth both nice and nasty. Perhaps, in other words, we are unable to resist at least some of the forms of resentment and even cruelty that arise from the small battles of everyday life: recent work in the social psychology of childhood development, for example, shows how children gradually come to understand sharing and turn-taking but can also be 'happy victimizers' (Killen and Hart 1995). However, at some point, most (but by no means all) children link the two: the pain and loss of the victim begin to modify and reduce the victimizer's happiness. In other words, they begin to construct a practical *morality*.

Morality is not, of course, a purely cognitive process. It has strong affective components. It is quite clear that all kinds of situations are freighted with affective inputs and consequences that are central to their moral outcomes which come from affective histories that arise from complex histories of being victims and of victimization that produce a sense of fairness and concern that will build into a consensus in some situations and not in others. How is it possible to apply insights like this to the affective fabric of cities? That is what I will now begin to attempt to elucidate.

The misanthropic city

Cities bring people and things together in manifold combinations. Indeed, that is probably the most basic definition of a city that is possible. But it is not the case that these combinations sit comfortably with one another. Indeed, they often sit very uncomfortably together. Many key urban experiences are the result of juxtapositions which are, in some sense, dysfunctional, which jar and scrape and rend. What do surveys show contemporary urban dwellers are most concerned by in cities? Why crime, noisy neighbours, a whole raft of intrusions by unwelcome others. There is, in other words, a misanthropic thread that runs through the modern city, a distrust and avoidance of precisely the others that many writers feel we ought to be welcoming in a world increasingly premised on the mixing which the city first brought into existence.

This is often framed in liberal accounts as a problem of alienation: the city produces solipsistic experiences which, in some sense, cut people off from each other and, presumably, from the natural condition of inter-relation they feel in smaller, rural communities.[18] But, as is now clear, I would want to argue for a different course, one in which misanthropy is a natural condition of cities, one which cannot be avoided and will not go away and which may even have been amplified by the modern mass media with their capacity to extend the reach of what counts. I want to argue that cities are full of impulses which are hostile and murderous and which cross the minds and bodies of even the most pacific and well-balanced citizenry. Perhaps, indeed, we need to face up to the fact that this underside of everyday hatred and enmity and malice and vengeance may be one of humanity's greatest pleasures, sieved through issues as diverse as identity (as in who belongs and who doesn't), sexuality (as in unfettered masculinity) and even the simple turn-taking of conversation (as in rude interruptions and the like). In other words, humanity may be inching towards perfectibility but, if that is indeed so, it is an even slower progress than we might have thought, worked through daily lacerations and mutilations of social relations. In turn, perhaps we cannot simply explain away this malign background but must learn to tolerate it, at a certain level at least, as a moral ambiguity which is part and parcel of how cities are experienced, an ambiguity which cannot be regulated out of existence.

However, I do not want to be misunderstood. This is not to express some cathartic horror of urban humanity in a long tradition which stretches back to at least Victorian times and no doubt before. It is rather an attempt to write back into social science accounts of the city a thread of understanding which has for too long been left to wither, a tradition which briefly flowered in the works of philosophers like Schopenhauer and Stirner,[19] philosophical novelists like Dostoyevsky, and social scientists and political theorists like Le Bon, Sorel, Schmitt and others, but which has generally been left to novelists and poets to enquire in to. This is surprising, not least because it could be argued that the foundation of social science itself rests on the response to various religious crises which prompted the production of increasingly secular and societal remedies for what had once been considered theological and metaphysical concerns: as Comte explained, theology's 'treatment of moral problems [is] exceedingly imperfect, given its inability . . . to deal with practical life' (cited in Lane 2004: 5). Hence, his 'system of positive polity'.

What seems certain is that the actual expression of the misanthropy has been more or less excusable as an urban condition through the course of history. Thus, in eighteenth- and early nineteenth-century England, misanthropy was understood as a problematic state but certainly not a state that was mad, iniquitous or perverse. For example, Hazlitt could argue that 'there is a secret affinity, a hankering after evil in the human mind [and] it takes a perverse, but a fortunate delight in mischief, since it is a never-failing source of satisfaction' (cited in Lane 2004: 9). But by the middle of the nineteenth century, such sentiments were fast becoming out of fashion in the face of a more pious stance to life which valued a controlled and benevolent heroism of the everyday and which increasingly regarded people-hating as a psychological affliction (often, indeed, caused by unrequited love) which must needs be combated by social programmes and self-restraint, although in mid- and even late-Victorian literature a series of radical or maudlin haters still continue to crop up as characters and attitudes, as instanced by authors like Dickens, Brontë, Eliot, Browning, Hardy and Conrad. The turn against misanthropy may have been hastened as well by other cultural shifts and, not least, the discovery of evolution and of animal passions that might seem all too natural if not shackled by reason (Gay 2002).

In general, one might argue that this Victorian attitude to intolerance or even hatred of others as failed civility still inhabits Euro-American cities, leaving a large amount of *surplus enmity* as hard to express and likely to be interpreted as a sign of a subject not fully in control of their behaviour. Western cities are, indeed, chock full of institutions and mechanisms that are intended to channel and domesticate anger towards and hatred of others, all the way from institutions of socialization like schools through to all the paraphernalia of emotional control or appropriate expression that occur subsequently. But Western cities are also full of outbursts of violence and rancour, all the way from seemingly all but random outbursts of road rage through the drunken mayhem typical of, say, British cities on a Saturday night, which suggest that a certain amount of hatred and rancour can still be generated in and by cities surprisingly easily. I would argue that the sense of defencelessness that is now being felt in large part is being channelled by and from this underside: it actually consists of the victimizations of childhood and the run of daily life more generally feeding back into the city's fabric as an undertow of spite. It is ourselves turning back on ourselves. It is the thin veneer of altruism at its thinnest.

But I want to go farther than this and suggest that this sense also arises from the fact that modern cities are criss-crossed by systems that channel and control anger and hatred in ways which are likely to produce random outbursts and occasional mayhem on a fairly regular basis amongst the citizenry which go beyond acts which are necessarily labelled as 'criminal'. I want to argue, in other words, that the potential for different combinations that are brought into existence by cities has, as an inevitable correlate, a dark side that we have too soon wanted to label as pathological. There are a number of sides to this problem. First, some of this dark side can be ascribed to biological pressures that we can only probably abate. Frankly, we cannot tell because we do not know what kind of animal we are and the range of territorial and other adaptations we can comfortably make. For example, it is by no means clear what the range of intuitive spatial behaviours of human beings can be (Levinson 2003). Second, many social structures them-selves may generate enmity as they try to damp it down, a point close to Freud's (2002 [1930]) argument in *Civilization and Its Discontents* that civilization is a key cause of antagonism: 'society, in trying to protect us from what we want (ultimately, an end to internal tension), instills in subjectivity a profound malaise, while providing "an occasion for enmity"' (Lane 2004: 28).[20] Third, the issue becomes even more complex because some of our dark side comes from formally structured cultural behaviours which tap into these pressures and constraints and work with them to deliver anger and hatred in a structured and predictable way.[21] Engrained within cities are all kinds of imperatives towards enmity and rage which arise out of social institutions of feeling which are only just beginning to be understood.[22]

Let me take a particularly relevant example. That is the echoing presence of armed force and, in particular, militaristic organization. I think it could be argued that military organization has had rather more influence on cities than is conven-tionally allowed in most accounts. This is not just about the matter of the presence of armed forces, trained in ways of structuring violence that can have lasting impacts, though this presence can be extensive (see Woodward 2004). It is not just about a series of military innovations which have made their way into the everyday life of cities, such as logistics.[23] It is not even just about the construction of militarized bodies through the proliferation of disciplined routines which have at least some military forebears, like boxing and martial arts, bodybuilding, and even some of the forms of warrior charisma beloved of business (see Armitage 2003). And it is not, finally, just about the apparent ambition of so many forms of modern entertainment to recreate the heat of the battlefield by battering the senses into a non-representational sublimity (Ferguson 2004).

I want to suggest that military imperatives are much wider even than this and have led to the deployment of anger and hatred and resentment in cities on an even more systematic basis. In particular, I want to point to the way in which domesticity has been organized on military lines through the institution of the suburb and other normalizing spaces to enforce a particular notion of domestic normalcy which at the same time very often leads to everyday violence. Here I want to draw on the provocative work of writers like Lauren Berlant and Laura Kipnis to argue, provocatively I hope, that militarized imperatives are a part of the structure the domestic system (and especially its spatial correlates) and produce and channel a surplus enmity which cannot easily be satisfied but tends to reveal itself in petty acts of cruelty, as well as actual violence.

Thus, the figures demonstrate that domesticity is associated not just with love and care but also with violence so widespread that it is difficult not to believe that it has a systematic nature based on 'happy victimization'. For example, in the UK one in four women will be a victim of domestic violence in their lifetime and domestic violence accounts for more than a quarter of all violent crime (including over 150 murders each year). In the EU, one woman in five has been at least once in her life the victim of violence by her male partner and, as in the UK, a quarter of all violent crimes involves a man assaulting his wife or partner. And this is before we arrive at the figures for child abuse.

This system cannot be easily undone because, ironically, of the surplus of hope that also structures the system of domesticity in Euro-American societies in the shape of the notion and practices of romantic love. There is no doubt that romantic love has its positive tropisms. It clearly represents a kind of last and best hope in many people's lives, providing an emotional world to which they can escape or which they can use as a goal to escape to, an imagined future outside of the humdrum world. 'Romance is, quite obviously, a socially sanctioned zone for wishing and desiring, and a repository for excess' (Kipnis 2003: 43). Thus, as Kipnis points out, adultery is very often a kind of affective escape attempt founded on the notion of an irresistible romantic love:[24]

> Among adultery's risks is the plunge into a certain structure of feeling: the destabilizing prospect of deeply wanting something beyond what all conventional institutions of personal life mean for you to want. Yes, all these feelings may take place in the murk of an extended present tense, but nevertheless, adultery, like cultural revolution, always risks shaking up habitual character structures. It creates intense new object relations at the same time that it unravels married subjects from the welter of ideological, social, and juridical commandments that handcuff inner life to the interests of orderly reproduction. It can invent 'another attitude of the subject with respect to himself or herself'. In adultery, the most conventional people in the world suddenly experience emotional free fall: unbounded intimacy outside contracts, law, and property relations. Among adultery's risks would be living, even briefly, as if you had the conviction that discontent wasn't a natural condition, that as-yet-unknown forms of gratification and fulfilment were possible, that the world might transform itself – even momentarily – to allow space for new forms to come into being. Propelled into relations of non-identity with dominant social forms, you're suddenly out of alignment with the reality principle and the social administration of desire. A 'stray'.
>
> (Kipnis 2003: 41–42)

But it is not difficult to argue that romantic love is also oppressive because it blots out so much of the affective else which may be less intense but socially more important, making everything else appear an insufficiency. Yet, in a striking parallel with misanthropy, anyone who declares themselves incapable of romantic love would be regarded by the majority of people as abnormal: 'all of us [are] allied in fearsome agreement that a mind somehow unsusceptible to love's new conditions is one requiring professional ministrations' (Kipnis 2003: 26).[25] Thus, as Kipnis puts it:

> It's a new form of mass conscription: meaning it's out of the question to be summoned by love, issued your marching orders, and then decline to pledge body and being to the cause. There's no way of being against love precisely because we moderns are constituted as beings yearning to be filled, craving connections, needing to adore and be adored, because love is vital plasma and everything else in the world just tap water. We prostrate ourselves at love's portals, anxious for entry, like social strivers waiting at the ropeline outside some exclusive club hoping to gain admission to its plushy chambers, thereby confirming our essential worth and making us interesting to ourselves.
>
> (Kipnis 2003: 3)

Yet, at the same time, it would be difficult to deny that romantic love can also contain large amounts of care, compassion and intimacy and it is to values of attachment like these that I now want to turn, values which exist somewhere between the poles of romantic love and misanthropy but which aren't quite so demanding, perhaps, so difficult to live up (or down) to.

The politics of urban trauma: from love to kindness

The notion of cities as potential nests of kindness has been at the root of the notion of social science since its inception. For example, Comte's *System of Positive Polity, . . . Instituting the Religion of Humanity* argued that 'in human nature, and therefore in the Positive system, Affection is the preponderating element' (1877). Comte wanted to transform self-love into social love by promoting what he called, coining a new word, 'altruism'.[26] From there, it was but a short step to the notions of 'community' which have so entranced writers on cities who have been trying to increase the sum total of altruism in cities, from Park through Jacobs to Sennett.

I am perhaps less starry-eyed about the practice of altruism than these authors (though none of them could be counted as romantics). I have already rehearsed some of my reasons: for example, the prevalence of misanthropy and romantic love and the fact that we live in heavily militarized societies which are based in part around understanding cities as if they were armed camps – the model of armed force and the armed camp can be argued to be one of the organizing principles of the modern city, rather than being a new alternative (Agamben 2001). But there are others too. For example, most subjects most of the time are clearly the receptacles of all kinds of contradictory desires; 'contradictory desires mark the intimacy of daily life: people want to be both overwhelmed and omnipotent, caring and aggressive, known and incognito' (Berlant 2004b: 5). Then again, most subjects are more often than not ambivalent about the dilemmas that they face and often prefer that things should remain that way: they don't necessarily want them to become 'issues' that they have to explicitly address. As Berlant puts it with regard to intimacy:

> When friends and lovers want to talk about 'the relationship'; when citizens feel that the nation's consented-to qualities are shifting away; when news-readers or hosts of television shows bow out of their agreement to recast the world in comforting ways; when people of apparently different races and classes find themselves in slow, crowded elevators; or when students and analysands feel suddenly mistrustful of the contexts into which they have entered in order to change, but not traumatically, intimacy reveals itself as to be a relation associated with tacit fantasies, tacit rules and tacit obligations to remain unproblematic.
>
> (Berlant 2004b: 6–7)

But I also believe that a politics of disagreement of the kind formulated by writers like Rancière (1999) can take the practice of altruism under its wing and forge a critical politics of feeling which is inherently optimistic (Berlant 2004b) but also realistic; that is, it does not demand too much – which is not, of course, the same as saying that it demands nothing at all! Thus, in what follows, I will want to argue that it is possible to think about a practical politics of the maintenance and repair of the city's structure of kindness. In turn, such a politics can begin to understand rather better what makes cities tick.

So far, we have mainly considered the temporal politics of foreboding, the sense that round the corner lies something rotten, something to be fearful of. But there is another kind of temporal politics that is also possible, a politics that amplifies the sense that around every corner is an opportunity – to open up and take hold of the future, to endow it with values like care and compassion, to value expectancy. I want to begin to open up this problem by returning to the work of Ernst Bloch.[27] For Bloch is probably best known not for his apocalyptic comments on cities but for his much later work on the politics of hope.[28] Bloch was concerned with a temporal sense that he called the method of 'hope' whose 'goal' was the amplification of moments of hope: 'any attempt to objectify these moments and turn them into outcomes of some process, as philosophy and history tend to do, are destined to fail to capture the temporality of these moments' (Miyazaki 2004: 23). Thus, for Bloch, 'hope' signed a kind of thirst or hunger for the future, a venturing beyond, a forward dreaming which mixes informed discontent with an ineluctable forward tendency; 'a heap of changing and mostly badly-ordered wishes' (Bloch 1986 [1959]: 50). What Bloch wanted to foreground was a politics of anticipation, a feeling of striving towards the future, an eager looking-forward and reaching forth, a source of fresh strength, a production of the New, a dawning. And, for Bloch, this fresh strength could be mapped: it would be found particularly amongst youth, in times on the point of changing, in moments of creative expression, and so on.

Using this framework amongst others, I want to turn to the embryonic politics of this chapter by considering some of the ways in which an *active*, so-called 'prosocial' everyday form of kindness might be installed in cities as a value which goes beyond 'simple' civility. This would not consist simply of the installation of good manners, as in certain middle-class mores, or of the inculcation of a kindness militant, as in certain religions, or the installation of a forced state project, as in the proposals to build up 'social capital' being proposed by many governments around the world currently. Rather, it would be a way of producing generosity in the body from the start by emphasizing what Bloch calls 'productivity', the construction of a new horizon out of the subconscious, the conscious and the not-yet-conscious. Writing from another context, Diprose (2002) has called the ethical correlate of this kind of transhuman approach, which privileges emergence and becoming,[29] 'corporeal generosity' but I think that this phrase runs the risk of falling back into the domestic model of kindness that I am concerned to escape, a model that too often ignores the fact that force and violence permeate political life and, to an extent at least, define politics as a domain and that mean, to use a classically Weberian insight, that nicely honed ethical actions do not necessarily lead to morally desirable consequences (Warner 2002). This is not, then, intended to be some starry-eyed account. I am quite clear that such a stance would not only be utopian in the worst sense but may also be trying to act against the basic features of interactional intelligence.

Of course, it would be possible to argue that certain kinds of generosity are being installed in cities continually in the many daily acts of everyday life. For example, a mother instructs her child not to pull another child's hair. Or someone helps a frail person to cross the road. But I want to go a little farther than this in that it seems to me that a kind city has to work on a number of dimensions, not all of which are conventionally 'human'.[30] Kindness has to be extended to other kinds of urban denizen, including animals. More to the point this kindness has to be built into the spaces of cities. Thus cities have to be designed as if things mattered, as if they could be kind too. Cities would then become copying machines in which a positive affective swirl confirmed its own presence.

So what kinds of relationships should be possible in cities, given that there is rather more misanthropy than commentators are willing to own up to, and equally rather too much romantic love?[31] I have tried to argue that too little has been made of kindness and compassion as a means of structuring cities in the race for a higher plane which just isn't there. In turn this suggests a twofold political task. On one side, we obviously need to continue to pursue a conventional macropolitics of urban care which draws on the deep wells of caring and compassion that currently typify many cities, the result of the often unsung work put in by the employees of various welfare systems, all manner of voluntary workers, and the strivings of an army of 'carers'. On the other side, we need an affirmative micro-politics of productivity which attempts to inject more kindness and compassion into everyday interaction, the arena on which I will concentrate (see Thrift 2004b).

In other words, I want to think of kindness as a social and aesthetic technology of *belonging to a situation*, rather than as an organic emotion.

To illustrate the point, I want to return initially to the military. For what is clear is that the military demonstrates the way in which kindness and compassion can be systematically generated and amplified by war – but, generally speaking, in small combat groups only. In these groups, which usually consist of six to ten 'buddies', people routinely look out for each other, even die for each other, bound together by learned mechanical behaviour and tight social bonds which can, at least to an extent, banish fear (Holmes 2003; Ferguson 2004). Indeed it has been argued, ironically, that these tight-knit groups are the bedrock of the deployment of successful armed force; their intense sociality acts as a structured means of producing death. Many other social orders have this same intensity but that intensity sometimes seems to summon up too much love/hate. Which is why, perhaps, lighter touch forms of sociality are now receiving so much attention, what one might call, following Latour (2004b), 'gatherings'. These systems of more intensive encounters are not attempts to build utopian realities so much as they are attempts to 'produce ways of living and models of action within the existing real', thereby 'learning to inhabit the world in a better way' (Bourriaud 2002: 13). They can, in other words, be counted as attempts to privilege a little more expectation of *involvement* which do not, however, try to go over the affective top, to continue the military metaphor: these are attempts to construct affective shortcuts which can add a little more intensity. Equally these are attempts to foster an expectation of civility which does not try to set its hopes too high. Instead of performing opposites like stranger-intimate (Warner 2002) by building categories of inclusion and exclusion that are too categorical, and that immediately begin to make rights-based claims on the state, the 'goal' is to construct counterpublics that are based on a certain conviviality arising out of a mutable, itinerant culture. As Gilroy (2004: xi) puts it, 'the radical openness that brings conviviality alive makes a nonsense of closed, fixed and reified identity and turns attention towards the always unpredictable mechanisms of identification'.

But how to construct this lighter-touch urban politics of assembling intimacy, kindness and compassion, understood as a range of social and aesthetic technologies of belonging? This practice of 'relational aesthetics' (Bourriaud 2002) is both a difficult one to uncover and a difficult one to demonstrate.[32] For a start, it can easily be confused with other agendas, for example in attempts around the world to build 'social capital' or simply to enforce civility, as in the United Kingdom's current war on anti-social behaviour.[33] Then, compared with other forms of politics, it can appear to be such a faint proposition that it may seem to be hardly worth pursuing (Bennett 2001). And finally, it operates in a domain of hope and expectation which is hard to see and whose results may be hard to discern until long after the event. It operates in the background – which is, of course, the point. Such a politics, in other words, is bound to provoke cynical reactions of various kinds. It's too prim and proper. It's now you see it, now you don't stuff. It's weak and feeble: what do you say to racist thugs or vigilante groups? But just because cynical reactions can be predicted is no reason not to begin the task.

So, as an envoi, I want to highlight four of the sites – sites which can be built upon – at which these kinds of gatherings can be found currently, gatherings which are mobile, often times ambiguous, and which encompass a multivalent host of forms. In each case, as I have argued elsewhere, the gathering operates as much in the precognitive realm as the cognitive, based around forms of expression which are not conventionally regarded as political but which may well conjure up all kinds of sometimes ill-formed hopes and wishes which can act to propel the future by intensifying the present. This proto-political domain of added strength afore-thought, of a politics of readiness, of what Lefebvre called *the politics of small achievements*, is now hoving into view as a much more explicit site of political effort than in the past, one which has much more time for affect since it is in this domain that so much affect is generated (see, for example, Connolly 2002; Thrift 2004b).

The first site concerns *the domain of politics itself*. In the past, politics has often been considered to be a case of building local coalitions which are able to assembled into ever larger movements which in time will become political forces in their own right. But I am struck by how many recent forms of politics do not necessarily have this goal in mind. They are determinedly local and have no neces-sary expectation of wider involvements. An example might be the growing number of urban environmental struggles based on fauna and flora that has usually been considered as mundane and/or disposable but for which people may have con-siderable affective bonds, or on leisure activities like gardening which require considerable expressive capacities but, until recently, have been seen as without the right kind of cultural authenticity. Another example might be the choice of minor key targets for political action which are unexpected but have grip, such as garbage (Chakrabarty 2002) or even paving stones (Massey 1991). These are forms of politics that can work round emotional impasses, that can boost expressive capacities and that can generate trust and familiarity for their own sakes. This is not to say that they do not relate to wider concerns – they do – but their main concern is, to repeat Bourriaud's little/big phrase, 'learning to inhabit'.

The second site is the city's light-touch, partially engaged, partially disengaged *modes of social interaction*. Long derided as the fount of blasé attitudes or cynicism or various other forms of alienation,[34] it might just be that they can be perceived as something quite different if they are understood as spaces of affective display and style in the manner recently argued by Charles Taylor (2004), as a kind of continuously mobile sphere of public opinion expressed as much through mood as through any definite cognitive process.

> Spaces of this kind become more and more important in modern urban society where large numbers of people rub shoulders, unknown to each other, with-out dealings with each other, and yet affecting each other. As against the everyday rush to work in the Metro, where others can sink to the status of obstacles in my way, city life has developed other ways of being, as we each take our Sunday walk in the park or as we mingle at the summer street festival or in the stadiums before the playoff game. Here each individual or small group acts on their own, but with the awareness that their display says

something to others, will be responded to by them, will help build a common mood or tone that will color everyone's actions.

(Taylor 2004: 168)

Taylor shows that these light-touch gatherings[35] are different from their nineteenth-century forebears in a number of ways. Most particularly, through the power of the modern media, they often rely on audiences dispersed beyond the space of the immediate event. But what seems clear is that these gatherings can constitute a binding affective force which, though 'not enframed by any deeply entrenched if common understanding of structure and counterstructure' can still be 'immensely riveting, but frequently also wild, up for grabs, capable of being taken over by a host of different moral vectors' (Taylor 2004: 170).

A third site is the institution of *friendship*. It seems to me that in the end it is the kind of lighter touch social relationship signalled by the notion of 'friend' that probably has most to offer cities in making them resilient. Of course, the notion of 'friend' has changed historically over time (Bray 2004; Pahl 2000; Traub 2002; Vicinus 2004) from the remarkably intense relationships signalled by the term in the sixteenth and seventeenth centuries but I think that it is possible to suggest that the looser ties of friendship and conviviality, and the kind of stance implied by the term now, have had the most to offer in keeping cities resilient and caring. For, in the end, cities have survived trauma because they are concentrations of knowledges of routine as found in activities like repair and maintenance, and also of the kind of energy and resourcefulness which has a large part of Bloch's quality of hope engrained within it, mediated by mundane but crucial social ties like friendship.

Friendship has three main things to recommend it. First, it is still widespread. For all the stories of the demise of sociality in alienated Western cities, the evidence suggests that friendship is still thriving, though inevitably mediated by all kinds of factors such as stage in life course (Pahl 2000). Then, the practice of friendship offers a model for intimacy and compassion which is achievable and which offers an automatic reaction to distress: a friend acts to help. It offers, in other words, a model of the future in which bad, even terrible, things may still happen but one in which 'my friends will still be there for me'. At its best, the help of friends is often given automatically as a subconscious attachment to a situation. Finally, it can be shown that these kinds of networks do work when catastrophe beckons. For example, in a recent brilliant book, Eric Klinenberg (2003) has looked at the way in which the populations of two relatively alike areas of Chicago reacted to the catastrophe of the week-long 1995 heatwave in which over 700 died. In one area, the death toll was low, in another it was high. The difference could be explained by a number of factors including poor or unresponsive public services but also, pivotally, by the actions of friendship networks. In one area, these were active and acted as both glue and as a means of social maintenance and repair. In the other area, no such networks existed and the area proved correspondingly brittle.

Again, it is important not to be starry-eyed. Friendship can involve all kinds of negative emotions and tensions. It may involve quite high degrees of competition.

It does not necessarily do anything to lessen social divides.[36] But friendship can also form a kind of moral community, whose power should not be underestimated in its reaching across.

Then, as a final site, I want to point to the outpouring of various kinds of *practical affective politics*. I have reviewed these elsewhere (see Thrift 2004b), so I will only briefly reprise them here. What is important to note is the increasing range of performative methods that are now going to make up the practices of politics, many of which involve the explicit mobilization of affect. These methods are often precisely involved in the stimulus of kindness and compassion and range from various kinds of work on the body (including manifold trainings, new means of showing awareness, various forms of pedagogic and co-operative psychology, and so on) to attempts to use urban space in ways that will produce new understandings of the moment (as in various kinds of performance art, psychogeography, and other forms of spatial play). In every case, the intention is to engineer intention and increase capability by constructing automatic reactions to situations which can carry a little more potential, a little more 'lean-in', a little more commitment.

To summarize, in this chapter I have wanted to see cities as oceans of hurt resulting from the undertow of the small battles of everyday life but also as reservoirs of hope resulting from a generalized desire for a better future. My intention has been to consider the darker sides of cities by concentrating on the subject of misanthropy but equally to balance this picture up by injecting a wash of kindness. My intention has therefore been to approach, or more accurately sidle up to, the subject of moral progress but to discuss this issue in a much less grand way than is normally found in the literature.

In alighting on the difficulties of making moral progress I am not, of course, giving up all hope of such progress. Rather I have wanted to approach the subject by considering qualities like kindness and compassion which are far from the unstinting love for others that is often envisaged as the ultimate measure of such progress. Put very simply, I want to conceive of kindness and compassion as elements of urban life we would want to nurture and encourage, against a background that often seems to militate against them. I want, in other words, to argue that in an agonistic city, where agreement is thin on the ground, a little more kindness may be what we should hope for and what we can get, whereas love is a bridge too far.[37]

As a parting thought, over the years, cities have been routinely lauded or deplored for the feelings they induce. Some cities have come to be regarded as generous or friendly. Others are regarded as hard-edged and hyper-competitive. Wouldn't it be interesting if, in the future, city spaces were increasingly pulled out of the mass on criteria such as some of the ones I have just mentioned? These spaces would become known in new sensory registers, through haptic maps of affective localities (Bruno 2002), and not least as geographies of kindness and compassion, geographies that might then leak out into the wider world.

10 Turbulent passions

Towards an understanding of the affective spaces of political performance

Why did the chicken cross the road?

Because its dopaminergic neurons fired synchronously across the synapses of its caudate nucleus, triggering motor contractions propelling the organism forward, while emitting 'cluck' distress signals, to a goal predetermined by its hippocampal mappings.

(Standard e-mail neuroscience joke)

The cultural process, as the supra-natural growth of the energies of things, is the manifestation or embodiment of the identical growth of our energies. The border-line at which the development of specific life-content passes from its natural form into its cultural form is indistinct and is subject to controversy.

(Simmel 1990 [1900]: 448)

Someone possesses my soul and governs it. Someone directs all my actions, all my movements, all my thoughts. I myself am nothing but a terrified, enslaved spectator of the things I am accomplishing.

(Guy de Maupassant, cited in Peters 1999: 104)

If human beings suddenly ceased imitating, all forms of culture would vanish.

(Girard 1987: 7)

Testing my faculties I found a stealth
Of passive illness lurking in my health

(Gunn 1965: 392)

Introduction

This final chapter provides an investigation of the affective realm of political feeling, understood as the history of the development of a series of affective technologies, and follows on from Chapters 7 and 8). In particular, I want to understand what might be best called 'motivational propensity' or 'disposition', the means by which masses of people and things become primed to act. This requires, most particularly, an understanding of affect, since such a propensity must include at its heart moods that we (howsoever defined) cultivate.[1]

Affect has, of course, become a term which is sprinkled through many recent writings, often adding nothing much more than a mere cultural frisson or, even worse, a highly questionable means of choosing choice which omits, ignores or diminishes many of the negative and obvious links to the exercise of power (Hemmings 2005).[2] But that does not mean that affect can therefore be written off as just a passing intellectual fad for it addresses real issues about fundamental understandings of what constitutes the 'social', and, indeed, whether the 'social' is an adequate descriptor of the work of the world.

Broadly speaking, *affect* is an attempt to avoid an easy psychologism. Put most simply, as in, for example, a Spinozan interpretation, it refers to complex, self-referential states of being, rather than to their cultural interpretation as emotions or to their identification as instinctual drives, although, to muddy the waters, it is clear that affect is not easily separated off from either emotion or drive and that a good part of the current rampant confusion in the literature derives from the difficulty of making such easy dividing lines. Thus, we might say, in line with Griffiths (1997), that *emotions* are everyday understandings of affects (such as the Western folk model that understands emotions as introspective sensations), constructed by cultures over many centuries and with their own distinctive vocabulary and means of relating to others. In a sense, they are a kind of folkbiology, a set of continually emerging beliefs about efficacy. The central Western concept of emotion is unlikely to be of more use than this because it assumes that one process category underlies all human behaviours, and can somehow explain them. But there is no evidence to suggest that this is the case.

> There is no one process that underlies enough [human] behaviour to be identified with emotion. Emotion is like the category of 'superlunary' objects in ancient astronomy. There is a well-designed category of 'everything outside the moon' but it turns out that superlunary objects do not have something specially in common that distinguishes them from other arbitrary collections of objects.
>
> (Griffiths 1997: 79)

Drives, in contrast, arise out of basic biological functions, such as hunger, sex, aggression, fear and self-preservation. They are often viewed as the source of many affects but, unlike drives, affects can be transferred to a wide variety of objects in order to be satisfied.

What seems certain is that any consideration of affect has to involve merging two collections of analytical objects that have been conventionally kept apart, namely 'the social' and 'the biological' (S.J. Williams 2001). As Brennan puts it:

> This is not especially surprising, as any enquiry into how one feels the others' affects, or the 'atmosphere', has to take account of physiology as well as the social, psychological factors that generated the atmosphere in the first place. The transmission of affect, whether it is grief, anxiety, or anger, is social or psychological in origin. But the transmission is also responsible for bodily

changes, as in a whiff of the room's atmosphere, some longer lasting. In other words, the transmission of affect, if only for an instant, alters the biochemistry of the subject. The 'atmosphere' or the environment literally gets into the individual. Physically or biologically, something is present that was not there before, but it did not originate sui generis: it was not generated solely or sometimes even in part by the individual organism or its genes.

(Brennan 2004: 1)

Notice here how Brennan does not assume that the transmission of affect is from individual to individual, contained within one skin and being moved to another. Rather, that transmission is a property of particular spaces soaked with one or a combination of affects to the point where space and affect are often coincident.

Thus, as I hope is clear, I will be following a broadly posthumanist agenda. I am not, on the whole, interested in individuals but rather in how particular hybrid compositions attain and keep coherence, become bodies of influence, so to speak. Thus, my interest is in trying to answer questions like 'What would the study of affect look like if it did not focus on the subject and subjectivity?' 'How do political formations generate affect?' and 'To what extent is affect a political form in itself?' However, as I have made clear in Chapter 6, I would not want to take this agenda to its limits. I believe that singular bodies can make an inventive difference which is sometimes of a different order from other hybrids. In certain situations, these bodies can stand out of the crowd as monad-like nodes of performativity constructed by the mass before falling back into the mass,[3] as certain individuals seem capable of achieving for longer or shorter periods (see Elliott and Lemert 2006). But, equally, all kinds of other bodies are possible. There are, in other words, no stable ways to be a human being because '"human" is not the name of a substance, in the Aristotelian sense of the term, but the name of a relation, of a certain position in relation to other possible positions' (Viveiros de Castro 2005: 155).

And why the emphasis on affect? Because there is a political diagnosis to be made. Most obviously, this is a time of great political passions on both right *and* left (Nelson 2006). But more importantly, it seems to me that we are living in a time of greater and greater authoritarianism. But this is an authoritarian capitalism which relies on sentiment, media, and lack of attention and/or engagement to most political issues to hold sway, a capitalist socialism or, at least, a neo-authoritarian new deal whose main interest is in accelerating innovation. At this moment in time, or so it seems to me, the left has very little purchase on how to combat this post-liberal form which privileges media (news) time and election time over historical time (Runciman 2006), not least because it has so little purchase on how this form is able to use alternative modes of affective intelligence to produce compelling political impressions. Too often it falls back on the orthodox politics of resentment of left radicalism which has become an increasingly sterile political repertoire whose appeals to unity simply repeat the old terms of succession within a foreclosed 'radical' community intent on the pleasures of victimization (Amin and Thrift 2005a). The only alternative to left moralism often seems to be a mystique of protest which can call forth 'a community of angry saints in which the fire of pure opposition burns', as Sloterdijk (in Funcke 2005: 5) aptly puts it, which then provides, simply through its existence, an apparent revolutionary justification. Interestingly, a good part of this community finds its practices confirmed through a kind of affective charge. However, this alternative seems close to the prevailing regime too in that it relies on an appeal which is too often simply an appeal to affective force as if that somehow validated the political analysis. In other words, we need to find other keys to organizing and enduring which can combat the motivational propensities now being diffused. So, I am searching for another way of going on, a different kind of politicalness which has its roots in new intellectual-practical formations which have cried 'enough' to the usual knee-jerk left analyses and are attempting to re-materialize democracy. Such formations do not rely either on a politics of resentment or on the kind of 'spiritualism' that too often emerges in its stead, and in their search for a political reanimation they take biology seriously as a key to thinking about the political as a part of a more general search for political forms that are adequate to current modes of being: forms of multi-naturalism rather than multiculturalism, if you like (Viveiros de Castro 2005). This search must be both an experimental and a vigilant activity. After all 'a subversive political theory must reveal an empty place that can be filled by practical action. Any political theory worthy of the name must await the unexpected' (Virno 2006: 42).

This chapter is therefore in five main parts. In the first part, I simply outline the main ways in which affect has been defined before going on to address the kinds of thinking about biology that are currently to be found in the social sciences, broadly defined. These means of thinking about biology provide a platform for the next part of the chapter which is concerned with understanding affective contagion: how it is that affect spreads and multiplies, most especially through imitation. The subsequent part of the chapter then looks at how affect has become increasingly engineered by concentrating on the corporate sector and especially the ways in which knowledge of the commodity increasingly includes affective technologies which are important inventions in their own right. This section acts as a prolegomenon to the next which deals with the political engineering of affect by concentrating on those same practices as they are found within the corporate sector. The chapter ends with a short discussion of the counter-politics of affect.

Scenes of effusion

Broadly speaking, there are five schools of thought about affect that populate modern social thought (Thrift 2004b). The first and most visible of these is the 'affect program' theory, derived from a Darwinian interpretation of emotions (Darwin 1998 [1872]; Ekman 1972; Griffiths 1997) which concentrates on short-term bodily responses which it is clamed are pan-cultural (that is, present in most human populations).[4]

> In its modern form, the affect program theory deals with a range of emotions corresponding very roughly to the occurrent instances of the English terms

surprise, fear, anger, disgust, contempt, sadness, and joy. The affect programs are short-term stereotypical responses involving facial expression, autonomic nervous system arousal, and other elements. The same pattern of response occurs in all cultures and homologues are found in related species. These patterns are triggered by a cognitive system which is 'modular' in the sense that it does not freely exchange information with other cognitive processes. This system learns when to produce emotions by associating stimuli with broad, functional categories such as danger or loss. . . . It is not possible to do justice to Ekman's views using the common opposition between 'naturalistic' and 'social constructionist' views of emotion. . . . The 'naturalist' is normally claimed as someone who believes that all or some emotional responses are the same in all cultures. But at the very least a distinction must be drawn between the input and output sides of emotional responses. Ekman claims that the output side of affect programs is stereotyped and pancultural, but he makes no such claim about the eliciting conditions of affect programs.

(Griffiths 1997: 79)

In other words, the affect programme approach makes a case for the view that certain so-called lower order affects at least have some degree of cultural generality but are not therefore necessarily innate. It makes no such claim for so-called higher cognitive affects such as love, jealousy, guilt and envy.

The second school of thought is that of William James and Carl Lange, often referred to as the James–Lange theory. This famous theory essentially argues that bodily responses give rise to affective states and is popularly rendered by statements such as 'crying makes us sad'. The primacy that James gave to bodily changes, following in part from Descartes' belief that emotions are passive perceptions of bodily motions, has become a crucial element of modern experimental psychology, in that it makes affect a matter of visual and auditory observation and so focuses attention on physiological change. The theory is undergoing something of a revival through the work of Antonio Damasio as the notion that emotion-feeling is the perception in the neocortex of bodily response to stimuli, mediated through lower brain centres. At the same time, the James–Lange theory is recognized to have serious defects and not least its overly simple model of causality.

The third school of thought is that of Sylvan Tomkins, whose main concern was to differentiate affects from drives. Unlike drives, affects can be transferred to a range of objects so as to be satisfied: they are therefore adaptable in a way that drives are not.

So, affect can enable the satisfaction of a drive (excitement might prepare the body for the satisfaction of hunger) or interrupt it (so that disgust might interrupt that satisfaction if you were served a rotten egg to eat). . . . Tomkins was the first to suggest that they have a singularity that creates its own circuitry. Thus affect may be autotelic (love being its own reward) or insatiable (where jealousy or desire for revenge may last minutes or a lifetime).

In terms of our relations with others, Tomkins asked us to think of the contagious nature of a yawn, smile or blush. It is transferred to others and doubles back, increasing its original intensity. Affect can thus be said to place the individual in a circuit of feeling and response, rather than opposition to others. Further, Tomkins argues that we all develop complex affect theories as a way of negotiating the social world as unique individuals.

(Hemmings 2005: 551–552)

The fourth school of thought is that of Gilles Deleuze. For Deleuze, affect stands for the unruly body's ability to go its own way which cannot be reduced to just social organization. For Deleuze, therefore, the focus is on bodily displacement, the movement between bodily states, the map of intensities. As Hemmings again succinctly puts it:

Deleuze proposes affect as distinct from emotion, as bodily meaning that pierces social interpretation, confounding its logic, and scrambling its expectations. In contrast to Tomkins, who breaks down affect into a topography of myriad, distinct parts, Deleuze understands affect as describing the passage from one state to another, as an intensity characterized by an increase or decrease in power.

(Hemmings 2005: 552)

The final school of thought is psychosocial. It can be traced from Aristotle through Hobbes to Leibniz and shares an emphasis on corporeal dynamics based on the Aristotelian rather than the Cartesian model. It describes what might be called a political economy of affect in that affects are not seen as having equal purchase in all bodies. In opposition to the idea that the passions are something that are housed in a body and shared by all human beings equally, affect consists of the contours of a dynamic social *field* 'manifest in what's imagined and forgotten, what's praised and blamed, what's sanctioned and silenced' (Gross 2006: 15). They are constituted *between* politically and historically situated agents. In turn, this suggests that it makes a difference 'not only what sort of passions are distributed to whom, but also how they are hoarded and monopolized and how their systematic denial helps produce political subjects of a certain kind' (Gross 2006: 49).

Significantly, each of these five schools of thought involves a substantial biological component. In each case, the body is given its own powers that are outwith social organization, *sensu strictu*, although obviously, in practice, it is very hard to tell the difference. For example, take the case of bipedal motion: Ingold (2004) has shown that gait is culturally striated in all sorts of ways.

Whatever the case, it is clear that affect signals a number of challenges to social theory as currently constituted[5] but, most especially, as I have already pointed out, a challenge to any easy dividing line between the 'social' and the 'biological' and to the apparent roles of each. This particular chapter is therefore stimulated by two main currents of work, both of which either set out from the biological or at least take the biological seriously as important elements of affect which cannot be either wished away, shoved into a box marked 'naturalism', or made secondary to the social. These associative currents of work subscribe to the view that the biological is not something different in kind from the social but is an integral part of the business of building collectives. But they also index the rise of 'biosocieties' which include all manner of industries based on the manipulation of heritability and explicit biological engineering of various kinds (e.g. bionanotechnology), the direct manipulation of body parts via procedures like transplantation, and now xenotransplantation, the number of public currents of concern that refer to biological issues, from the treatment of farm or laboratory animals through concerns about genetically modified organisms through to all the different means of cohabitation that have now become apparent, and the consequent proliferation of social imaginaries that now refer to the biological as constitutive. In other words, this work tries to lay out reasons for the urgency and heat of affect and how it effects what we have too easily named as the social.

The first current of work is concerned with a direct revaluation of the biological, a revaluation which has been going on for some time now. Led by an evolutionary momentum which derives from three chief sources – the debate around culture and evolution, the debate around animals, and the rediscovery of the process philosophy of Whitehead – this work has been going back to first principles, and especially the intersection between evolution and culture, in order to discover what it means to be human if human is understood as process of situated flow within which human bodies are just one of the sets of actors. It is no longer possible to avoid this fulcrum of activity, with all its undoubted historical baggage, since it both speaks to a time in which biopower has become biopolitics (Lazzarato 2002a) and because the questions now being raised by biology press on that knot of interests formerly known as the social.

Thus, the first debate attempts to understand culture as a part of the biosphere, as both caught up in evolution and as a vital part of evolution, giving 'cultural evolution its due weight without divorcing culture from biology' (Richerson and Boyd 2005: 17). Such a renovation of Darwin's 'inherited habits' has become much easier to countenance as it has been realized just how quickly biological adaptation can take place in humans, as in other animals, not only through so-called gene-culture co-evolution[6] but also through epigenetic traits. In other words, not only human behaviour but also anatomy,[7] broadly understood, is labile with the consequence that the 'superorganic firewall' (Richerson and Boyd 2005: 17) between the social and the biological has been breached, thus bringing both categories into question, as well as underlining how the same environment can be used in radically different ways. In turn, the sheer complexity of cultural variation has become ever more apparent as a force in evolution. There is much more to heredity than genes (Jablonka and Lamb 2005). Three examples, all but one drawn from Levinson (2005), will suffice. One is that cultural knowledge about the environment makes it possible to build a larger population as, for example, when cultures accumulate a myriad of successful and adaptive experiments with different kinds of foods. So, for example, the appearance and diffusion of cooking is now interpreted by many as a major evolutionary leap; cooking provides a short cut to extra energy and can be thought of as a new element of human physiology, leading to, for example, an increase in body mass, a consequent sharp decrease in sexual dimorphism, a reduction in the size of tooth and jaw complex and gut size, and a significant rise in brain volume.[8] Another is the formation of groups able to function as an effective 'giant superorganism' which is both a culture-bearing entity and a technical ensemble and which is able, through the specific cognitive abilities gained, to overcome disasters like cyclones and therefore produce population selection. One more example is microadaptation to genetic impairment, as in the overcoming of hereditary deafness through the use of sign language, an adaptation that proves to be common around the globe. It is true that the parallels drawn between genetic and cultural evolution can, sometimes, in the hands of neo-Darwinians, seem forced but they also underline the presence of the demanding human capacity for cooperation and detection of cheating (the two being related). This capacity, based on the ability to 'read' others' intentions by constructing 'theories' about them, has been a (perhaps the) crucial evolutionary step, essential to enhanced adaptation (Levinson 1995).

The second debate has been concerned with the nature of animals, addressing the question, 'What do the relatives know?' (Csányi 2005). There is now a very large corpus of work addressing animal behaviour, sufficiently large to draw a series of conclusions about affect in other species. This work has shown that animals have rich affective lives, though it is clear that they rarely display emotions in quite such a transparent way as human beings, whose complicated social life demands that its members are 'on the same wavelength'. For example, animals show the central role of some affects, at least across mammalian species. In particular, anger, fear and anxiety seem to be common to all mammals, as does a degree of emotional identification. But animals show other aspects of affects too. I will point to just four of these. To begin with, recent research has shown just how important systematic hormonal change is to animal behaviour. A good example is the production of new and unexpected kinds of affective palettes as various kinds of genetic manipulation are achieved through selective breeding which unexpectedly alter animals' affective constitution, producing all kinds of unexpected and unwanted emotional behaviour (Grandin and Johnson 2005). So-called pure breed domestic animals are, not surprisingly, particularly susceptible because affective side-effects are ignored in the race for other kinds of perfection. (Such side-effects are then made worse by the lack of socialization that these kinds of animals may suffer, as owners attempt to keep them apart from the mass). Then it has shown the sheer variety of animal affects, even within apparently homogeneous species. For example, consider the enormous differences between the affective make-up of chimpanzees and bonobos (de Waal 2005). The bonobo has a vastly different temperament from the chimpanzee. Chimpanzees are aggressive, territorial and hierarchical whereas bonobos are gentle and empathic, not least because they use sexuality as an utterly prosaic means of pleasure and social bonding as much as a means of reproduction. For bonobos, sexuality is a means of – often frantic – social contact that serves to calm tempers and pave the way for sharing. Then, animals can teach us about the diverse range of registers of communication bodies have. For example, take the case of ectohormones[9] or pheromones. Pheromones are so-called semiochemicals, small molecules emitted by a creature through the skin or by specialized glands or secretory organs which have some effect on creatures of the same species,[10] usually a definite behaviour or a developmental process. They are normally detected by smell (Thrift 2003a), although they can also be detected through touch (Wyatt 2003). Thus, very often no direct contact is needed for their transmission: pheromones are in the air. Though often associated only with sexuality and reproduction, pheromones have a wider compass, often acting as means of unconscious communication. Pheromones are a powerful means of transmitting affect through smell and taste, along with sight (understood as grip), sound and rhythm, with its insistent beats. 'Across the animal kingdom, more interactions are mediated by pheromones than by any other kind of signal' (Wyatt 2003: 4), not least because the metabolic costs of this kind of signalling are so low. The importance of pheromones for human behaviour is only just becoming clear, not least because humans cannot smell most of the chemicals important to other animals so that this branch of biological research has languished. That is now changing. It is recognized that chemical cues are crucial in the recognition of kin and familiar people, seem to be important for human sexuality and are vital in producing synchrony of some human functions (e.g. menstruation) (Wyatt 2003). Equally, it is now recognized that different cultures have different olfactory palettes. Most importantly for the purpose of this chapter, chemical cues function as mood changers, affective switches that can tone and tune situations. Animals provide one more piece of relevant information about affect. That is that it is crucial to time and decision-making (Grandin and Johnson 2005). Like people, animals use affects to predict the future and make decisions about what to do next; affects provide information about the future and what to do about it. Without affects, cognitive systems collapse: nothing is affectively neutral because emotions provide vital information about every bit of information. They are a key element of all decisions (T.D. Wilson 2002).

The third debate has revolved around the rediscovery of the work of A.N. Whitehead, and most especially his work on the metaphysics of a non-bifurcated nature, that is a nature which is no longer considered to have primary and secondary qualities (such as the kind of causal laws supposedly discovered by science and an apparent nature, nature as we perceive it), and on the characteristics of what might be thought of as a creative organism, able to remain in existence – to endure, to achieve togetherness, to become obstinate[11] – and able to affect its environment and be affected by it, that is, at least in part, to be able to shape its environment, often, paradoxically, by becoming impatient against the very habits that allow the organism to endure. Thus, biology means being able to innovate, to produce original answers to changing conditions.

In his striving to construct a process-based view of the world without human subjectivity, Whitehead produced a metaphysics which attempted to invent new modes of abstraction founded on the idea that 'everything that may be told to exist will be concerned' (Stengers 2005: 10), through adventures of thought that make the possibility of relevant novelty matter, that rely on the irreducibility of possibility, 'transforming potentiality into its own actuality, as it decides for itself how it will fulfil its own process of becoming itself' (Stengers 2005: 12). Such a viewpoint has led to a flowering of all manner of approaches (from Deleuzian pragmatics through actor-network theory to many different kinds of performance) which might be termed naturalistic, both in their attention to a vivid, irridescent world in which there is no deciding subject because the decision is producing the subject and in their emphasis on adaptation which is no longer conceived as continuity through modification but as adventure, irrational hopes, foolish enterprises.

The second current of work approaches the biological in a less direct fashion. It has tried to take up the idea that it is possible to derive a thinking that is not conditioned or compressed by time but is of what might be called an ethological nature, recognizing the prime importance of territory since an object like affect is no longer regarded as in some sense 'internal' but is regarded rather as a moving map of passions making their way hither and thither. In terms of current thought, such a processual move towards a *spatial thinking* (cf. Buchanan and Lambert 2005) has most often been associated with the work of Gilles Deleuze.

> He asks whether it is possible not only to criticize Kant in order to offer a theory of thought fractured by time in a non-Kantian way, but also to think a radically different thought that would be neither temporal, historical, reflexive, nor active, and instead geographical, inorganic, passive and vegetal.
>
> (Arsic 2003: 126)

But I want to turn to three other developments in spatial thinking instead. Though each one of them has a relation to Deleuze, they can also be used to go beyond his work and to think about the nature of shared animated space more deeply. The first is the work of Gabriel Tarde. Tarde was a formative influence on Deleuze's thought on difference and repetition but he offers much more than that of an extended footnote. The second is the work of the Italian *operaismo* Marxists, Paolo Virno and Maurizio Lazzarato. Both Virno and Lazzarato have become increasingly influenced by both Deleuze and Tarde but they provide a diagnostic reading of capitalism that is only faintly present in Deleuze. Finally, there is the work of Peter Sloterdijk, and especially his 'Spheres' trilogy (Sloterdijk 1998, 1999, 2004). Sloterdijk shares an interest in Deleuze but in his *Sphären* trilogy arguably he demonstrates a much more acute sense of space.

Why would authors like Virno and Lazzarato and indeed lately Sloterdijk become interested in Tarde, whose work has been resurrected by the presence of a French reissue of nearly the whole of his corpus under the editorship of Eric Alliez, and by publication in German and Danish too?[12] There are five main reasons, I think. First, his work seems to prefigure a modern landscape in its commitment to an epidemiological model in which imitation and invention are a key form of the 'universal repetition' that Tarde conceived as at the base of all action (Rogers 2003; Beirne 1987). The entities that Tarde is dealing with are not people, but innovations, understood as quanta of change with a life of their own.[13]

> This is why any social production having some marked characteristics, be it an industrial good, a verse, a formula, a political idea which has appeared somewhere in the corner of the brain, dreams like Alexander of conquering the world, tries to multiply itself by thousands and millions of copies in every place where there exists human beings and will never stop except if it is kept in check by some rival production as ambitious as itself.
>
> (Tarde, cited in Latour 2005: 15)

Second, and notoriously, Tarde questioned the idea of society. Insofar as he was willing to countenance the use of the word at all, it was to refer to the complete range of entities that exist in association.

> Tarde's sociology is not a science of the social according to the categories of sociology. It is an understanding of 'associations', of co-operation, with no distinction made between Nature and Society. It is the sociology of atoms, of cells, and of man. Tarde takes Durkheim's premise that the social is a fact and must be analysed as such and turns it on its head. 'All phenomena is social phenomena, all things a society'.
>
> (Lazzarato 2005a: 17)

Necessarily, Tarde therefore places biological entities on an equal footing with 'social' ones, mixed together in many hybrid forms. Third, Tarde's work is exactly concerned with passions, passions transmitted, most particularly, through a semiconscious process of mimesis (Leys 1993); feeling becomes a propensity to engage in conduct considered 'automatic' and 'involuntary'. In other words, Tarde was a part of a long tradition of work on imitation-suggestion, which would subsequently take in Freud, Prince, and Ferenczi, amongst others, as the very ground and origin of psychic experience (Leys 2000). For example, in *Psychologie Économique* Tarde produces a model of the economy in which bodies of passion multiply as so many animations.[14] Fourth, Tarde's is a material world, but one in which there are passionate relationships with things and these passionate relationships form a matrix of property, of things chosen to be interpreted as affecting and centrally involved in person-making (Tamen 2001). Fifth, for all these reasons, for Tarde space is key. But this is a particular kind of space, one which continually questions itself by generating new forms of inter-relation. It is a space which is as likely to value the indirect as it is the direct: it bears therefore some relation to models of action-at-a-distance like those found in theology, spiritualism, mesmerism, hypnosis, telepathy, immunology, epidemiology, and so on.[15]

In other words, Tarde provides a gathering point for those who believe that the term 'society' and the models of socio-cultural inscription which are its main theoretical legacy are completely exhausted and who want to work instead with a form of associationism which is regarded as the only way of following the multiplication of collectives, and forming 'landing strips' (Latour 2005) for new ones.[16] Most particularly, Tarde's work suggests the possibility of resurrecting an epidemiological model which is based on processes of imitative contagion, not least because the spread of feelings (through gesticulation, bodily movements, motor co-ordinations and repetitions, as well as all the technologies of the body that now exist) is such fertile ground for thinking about mental contagion. Such epidemiological models of mimetic 'vibrations' held sway in good parts of the social sciences at the turn of the nineteenth century as means of explaining phenomena as different as crowd behaviour (as in the work of Le Bon, Trotter or McDougall, and subsequently luminaries like Freud and Bion) and the diffusion of different kinds of cultural object (as in the work of anthropologists like Tylor) but they went in to steep decline as means of explanation for a variety of reasons, not least their association with right-wing diagnoses of disorder as pathological and irrational based on ideas such as that crowds were likely to regress to lower levels of mental functioning, and/or were highly suggestible, in both cases leading to loss of personality. However, they have periodically continued to grip the imagination. One thinks, for example, of work in history on affect which has resorted to these models, as in the case of the history of fear (Lefebvre 1973) or various kinds of sentimentality (Vincent-Buffault 1991) or even crowd behaviour like riots (Hobsbawm and Rudé 1985). And, as Leys (2000) argues, they were implicit in many later theories, for example many current theories concerning the power of trauma often deploy an implicit mimetic mechanism. Of late, epidemiological models have begun to make something of a comeback. That comeback is based on the ability of these models to express expression and to frame sympathetic induction. Such models provide a much better sense of how particular kinds of affective phenomena do their work. A good example is provided by the seminal work of Brennan (2004) who tracks affect as so many 'atmospheres'.

It is probably against this background that the recently rehabilitated work of Tarde makes the most sense. Indeed it might be more accurate to say that Tarde has become more relevant, has even found his time (Thrift 2006b). In particular, Tarde provides access to a time when unconscious influence was thought to be of the greatest importance, the key to understanding motivation and disposition:

> Men are ever touching unconsciously the springs of motion in each other; one man, without thought or intention or even consciousness of the fact, is ever leading some others after him. . . . There are two sorts of influence belonging to Man: that which is active and voluntary, and that which is unconscious; that which we exert purposely, or in the endeavour to sway another, as by teaching, argument, by persuasion, by threats, by offers and promises, and that which flows out from us, unawares to ourselves.
>
> (Bushnell, cited in Wegner 2002: 315)

In turn, Tarde provided a series of psychosocial models of that which flows out from (or perhaps more accurately, through) us unawares, namely models of *imitation* and *invention*. These models serve the present moment well, emphasizing as they do non-conscious perception, dissociation, suggestion and suggestibility, and social influence as forming a part of a stream of thought, rather than a threat to the boundaries of an individual. Though Tarde was of his time, he was also an original in his emphasis on understanding imitation as a process of snowballing mimetic desire, as reverberating circles of influence, rather than as simple mechanical copying, and on his insistence that imitation formed a basic process of social life that was governed by laws of regularity which could be attributed to the action of invention. For invention itself was also considered as a social process by Tarde, one which determined which ideas spread – and which did not.

Interestingly, Tarde provides another kind of link to the past in the present in that, along with Bergson, James and others, he was involved with the Institute of Psychical Research in Paris, established in 1900 (Blackman 2001), which investigated all manner of psychic phenomena as semiconscious capacities to be affected, including mesmerism, hypnosis, trance, telepathy, mediumship, and so on. This is hardly a surprise: the history of early psychology was bound up with the new 'continent of the unconscious and the peninsulas of neurosis and hypnosis' (Peters 1999: 91) as expressed through phenomena like these. For Tarde, imitation was akin to these kinds of phenomena in that it involved dissociation within which suggestion could thrive.

> Tarde made dramatic use of the findings of the new science of hypnotism, especially in the work of Hypollite Bernheim, to support his theory by classing imitation, defined as 'the action at a distance of one mind on another' or the 'quasi-photographic reproduction of a cerebral image upon the sensitive plate of another brain', with somnambulism and hypnotic suggestion. As he declared in a characteristically stylish formulation, 'I shall not seem fanciful in thinking of the social man as a veritable somnambulist. . . . Society is imitation and imitation is a kind of somnabulism'. And: 'The social state, like the hypnotic state, is only a form of dream, a dream of command and a dream of action. To have only ideas that have been suggested and to believe them spontaneous: such is the illusion of the somnambulist and also of the social man'.
>
> (Leys 1993: 279)

That formulation is interesting on three grounds, First, it links directly to semiconscious automatisms about which I will have more to say later. 'Both the somnambulist and the social man are possessed by the illusion that their ideas, all of which have been suggested to them, are spontaneous' (Tarde 1962: 77). Second, it also suggests an impulse to explain phenomena like the spread of ideas as flow phenomena when they have so often been argued to be simply a function of institutions, not least because the self itself arises from an unconscious imitation of others (Potolsky 2006). Third, it can be argued that it foreshadows the way that phenomena like hypnotism have provided a fund of images for the redemptive and diabolical features of mass communication – from the telegraph on – which lives on in numerous, often unacknowledged forms. For example:

mesmerism's afterlife helped shape the understanding of mass media in the twentieth century as agents of mass persuasion that somehow, via their repetition, ubiquity, or subliminally iniquitous techniques, bypassed the vigilant conscience of citizens and directly accessed the archaic phobias (or ignorance and sloth) of the beast within.

(Peters 1999: 94)

The second school of thought is Italian workerist (*operaismo*) Marxism. Such a variant of Marxism is often associated with the name of Antonio Negri and his gradual journey from a Marxism that was still faithful to the *Grundrisse* (and most especially to that small part of the *Grundrisse* which expounded the idea of general intellect) to a Marxism that seems to be more faithful to Spinoza (cf. Negri 1988; Wright 2002). However, arguably more interesting developments have occurred in the work of Paolo Virno and Maurizio Lazzarato who both started from some of the same ideas as Negri but have diverged subsequently, increasingly taking on neo-vitalist ideas as they track from capital-labour to capital-life in which capital takes on all the powers of the transindividual general intellect – 'knowledge, the subjective spirit of invention, invention-power' (Virno 2005: 21) – by tapping in to the full range of powers of the human body rather than just labour; 'abstract expenditure of psychophysic energy' (Virno 2005: 21) and making it into a pre-individual thing that can be operated on.[17] 'In a way, labour is today truly productive (of surplus value and profit) only if it coincides with the human abilities that previously explicated themselves in non-labour' (Virno 2006: 38). So 'labour power has become invention-power' (Virno 2006: 37). In other words, the whole of human praxis, all of the generically human gifts, come to be included in the productive process, all those aspects of forms of life that exist outside its stringent rationality and that allow this expanded praxis to both produce, hasten and adapt to a nonlinear productive fluctuation. 'Contemporary capitalist production mobilizes to its advantage all the attitudes characterizing our species, putting to work *life* as such' (Virno 2005: 35, author's emphasis).

In particular, Lazzarato (2002a, 2005a, 2006b) has taken up the gauntlet of Tarde's work on the power of invention, concentrating on the modes of production of communication and knowledge that lead beyond economy, as well as Foucault's work on biopower as a new political economy of forces that act and react against each other, in order to forge a new synthesis. This synthesis constitutes a description of the new modes of extracting a surplus of power from living beings, modes of extraction which harness 'freedom' to the production and government of new forms of life that are based on relationships of differentiation, creation, and innovation. This Tardean-Foucauldian synthesis which uses the presence of others as a transindividual resource underlines the existence of strategic relations that can escape (or at least minimize) domination by being based on sympathy and not just on asymmetry (and therefore domination-resistance):

A prominent sociologist recently defined social relations, in a way that is so narrow and far removed from the truth, by claiming that the principal characteristic of social acts is that they are imposed from the outside, by obligation. To make this claim is to recognise as social relations only those between the master and the slave, between the professor and the student or between parents and children, without any regard for the fact that free relations between equals exist. One has to have one's eyes shut not to see that, even in the schools, the education that the schools acquire on their own, by imitating each other, by breathing in, so to speak, their examples, or even those of their professors, the education that they internalize, has more importance than the one they receive or are forced to hear.

(Tarde 1999: 62)

The third school of thought arises from the work of Peter Sloterdijk on the genesis of manufactured environments (Thrift 2005a). In his *Sphären* trilogy, Sloterdijk takes Heidegger on dwelling as a point of reference[18] but then spatializes his thinking by posing the question of being as the question of being-together: 'one is never alone only with oneself, but also with other people, with things and circumstances; thus beyond oneself and in an environment' (Sloterdijk 2005d).[19] 'Being-a-pair' or a couple precedes all encounters.[20] In other words, Sphären is concerned with the dynamic of spaces of co-existence, spaces which are commonly overlooked, for the simple reason that 'human existence . . . is anchored in an insurmountable spatiality' (Sloterdijk 2005d: 229).

Continuing on with this spatial problematic, like Tarde, Sloterdijk is concerned with how distances intercalate. Sloterdijk identifies three waves of globalization, each with its corollary of new forms of 'artificial' construct. The first wave is the metaphysical globalization of Greek cosmology, the second wave is the nautical globalization of the fifteenth century on, and the third wave is now upon us. Whereas the first wave created an esoteric geometricism and the second wave created an exoteric cosmopolitanism, the third wave of rapid communication is producing, through the work of 'joining the nervous systems of inhabitants in a coherent space' (Sloterdijk 2005d: 226), a global provincialism of 'connected isolations', of microclimates in which 'communicative relations are replaced by the inter-autistic and mimetic relations, a world that is constructed 'polyspherically and interidiotically' (Funcke 2005: 2). Thus:

At the centre of the third volume is an immunological theory of architec-ture, because I maintain that houses are built immune systems. I thus provide on the one hand an interpretation of modern habitat, and on the other a new view of the mass container. But when I highlight the apartment and the sports stadium as the most important architectural innovations of the modern, it isn't out of art- or cultural-historical interest. Instead my aim is to give a new account of the history of atmospheres, and in my view, the apartment and the sports stadium are important primarily as atmospheric installations. They play a central role in the development of abundance, which defines the open secret of the modern.

(Funcke 2005: 3)

Sloterdijk suggests, on the basis of this analysis, that what is needed is an 'air-conditioning project' that can sweep through the gentle, all-absorbing hum of the totally managed and domesticated spatial environments of current social entities, entities which are entangled in a paradox of heightened isolation and heightened connection (Latour 2006). The challenge is how to achieve the *ventilation* of the atmospheres of modern life (Sloterdijk 2006). Is it possible to change the socio-spatial terms of trade by providing new environments in which novel doctrines of living can thrive, environments which will provide the breathing space with which democracy can be re-invented, just as the original Athenian democracy was critically dependent upon the city and 'the pre-logical or pre-discursive premises of the art of urban co-existence' that were able to be constructed from it, premises that were the result of 'the skilful application of anti-misanthropic procedures' (Sloterdijk 2005c: 947) that included, most especially, explicit affective engineering. Significantly, for Sloterdijk, one of the ways of constructing such new 'aired' environments (Latour 2006) may be by reviving metaphors of contagion and infection which once circulated as ways of understanding relationships of togetherness and intermingling, metaphors which can also function as means of capturing attentiveness (Ten Bos and Kaulingfreks 2002).

In what follows, I want to combine these different but related bodies of work by focusing on the vexed topic of affect, understood especially as a function of the workings of capitalism. In particular, I want to consider how disposition itself is being changed by more and more explicit engineering of affect. Then, in turn, I want to look at how the lessons learnt are being transferred to the political sphere.

Understanding affective contagion

What is particularly hard to cope with in writing about affect is not so much its insubstantial nature as finding a model that can encompass its powers. As I have pointed out, that model must be, in part, biological, which adds to the challenge. What seems clear now is that such a task must mean attempting to understand affective contagion, for affect spreads, sometimes like wildfire. This was a central concern of turn-of-the-nineteenth-century social science in the form of the study of imitation and suggestibility. Imitation and suggestibility took shape as particular kinds of object through a hypnotic paradigm which worked themselves out through an interest in particular forms of psychopathology (such as hallucinations and delusions), and an interest in spiritualist forms of communication. Imitation and suggestibility were sites for exploring all manner of issues, such as consciousness, memory, personality, and communication. In particular they signified a 'taking over' of the subject that defied normal economies of subject-object relations. However, subsequently, a move to psychoanalytic models of desire, or to more discursive approaches to subjectivity, ruled imitation and suggestibility out of court and they fell into disrepair as a way of approaching social structuring.

But, of late, imitation and suggestibility have been making a return. Within cultural theory, viral models of contagion have been posited as explaining the workings of a range of phenomena, including ideology, governance, self-cultivation, and even resistance but often in highly speculative ways that posit a kind of performative energetics but without usually specifying what the source or content or form of that energy might consist of. But there is no need for this (often convenient) opacity, as I hope to show in this section through a more detailed examination of the grip of affect.

Let me begin by summarizing what we have gleaned about affect so far. To begin with, that means understanding affect as in large part a biological phenomenon, involving embodiment[21] in its many incarnations, but a phenomenon that is not easily captured via specular-theatrical theories of representation (Brennan 2004). It brings together a mix of a hormonal flux, body language, shared rhythms, and other forms of entrainment (Parkes and Thrift 1980) to produce an encounter between the body (understood in a broad sense) and the particular event. Then, affect is generally semiconscious, something not that far from William Harvey's 'certain sense or form of touch', sensation that is registered but not necessarily considered in that thin band of consciousness we now call cognition (Blakemore 2005).[22] Further on again, affect is understood as a set of flows moving through the bodies of human and other beings, not least because bodies are not primarily centred repositories of knowledge – originators – but rather receivers and transmitters, ceaselessly moving messages of various kinds on; the human being is primarily 'a receiver and interpreter of feelings, affects, attentive energy' (Brennan 2004: 87).

In turn, this depiction points to one more important aspect of affect, namely space, understood as a series of conditioning environments that both prime and 'cook' affect. Such environments depend upon pre-discursive ways of proceeding which both produce and allow changes in bodily state to occur (Thrift 2006b). Changes in bodily state require understanding that essentially autonomic hormonal and muscular reactions are continually transferring between people (and things) in ways that are often difficult to track. At the same time, they challenge the idea that the body is a fixed component of humanity. It might be more accurate to liken humans to schools of fish briefly stabilized by particular spaces, temporary solidifications which pulse with particular affects, most especially as devices like books, screens and the internet act as new kinds of neural pathway, transmitting faces and stances as well as discourse,[23] and providing myriad opportunities to forge new reflexes. Thus, concentrating on affect requires a cartographic imagination in order to map out the movement between corporeal states of being which is simultaneously a change in connectivity. Only a very limited range of spatial models currently exist which can understand flows of imitation/suggestion, mainly familiar cartographic motifs from diffusion studies, certain very general metaphors that have arisen from the recent emphasis in social theory on mobility, a range of models of the staging of space that can be found in performance studies (which are usually excellent at showing how affect is conducted in intimate situations but often tail off when it comes to mediated contexts), a set of artistic experiments with sites of affective imitation that have often used the possibilities of modern electronic media, and various kinds of conversation maps (Abrams and Hall 2006).

However, it is also clear that certain technological advances, and especially those to do with mobile telephony and the web, are making it easier to visualize flows of imitation, not least because they are themselves prime conductors.

Now we can also add in what we currently know about imitation and suggestibility. For, imitation has become a paramount concern of the contemporary cognitive sciences, and this work is worth exploring in a little more detail, since it contains many insights. In particular, imitation is now understood as a higher level cognitive function,[24] mirroring both the means and ends of action, and highly dependent upon the empathy generated in an intersubjective information space that supports automatic identifications. For example, hearing an expression of anger increases the activation of muscles used to express anger in others. There is, in fact, only a delicate separation between one's own mental life and that of another, so that affective contagion is the norm, not an outlier. What differs between different cultures is rather what is regarded as the result of agency. Thus, for Western cultures it can be a painful realization to understand how little of our thinking and emotions can in any way be ascribed as 'ours'; it is often very hard for Westerners to accept that broad imitative tendencies apply to themselves – both because they are unconscious and automatic, so that people are not aware of them, and because the preponderance of apparently 'external' influences threatens the prevailing model of an agent as being in conscious control of themselves.

At the same time, it is important to stress that imitation is more than mere emulation. Imitation is different from simple emulation in that it depends upon an enhanced capacity for anticipation, so-called mind-reading (Thrift 2006b).[25] In particular, much of human beings' capacity for mind-reading (whether this be characterized as inference or simulation) develops over years of interaction between infants and their environments, and involves processing the other as 'like me', and the consequent construction of high-level hypotheses like deception. That is, it involves a form of grasping which is innately physical and non-representational since our privileged access is to the world, not to our own minds.

Whatever the exact case might be, most imitation is clearly rapid, automatic and unconscious and involves emotional contagion, in particular (down to and including such phenomena as moral responsiveness). In particular, people seem to be fundamentally motivated to bring their feelings into correspondence with others: people love to entrain. What seems clear, then, is that human beings have a default capacity to imitate, automatically and unconsciously, in ways that their deliberate pursuit of goals can override but not explain. In other words, most of the time they do not even know they are imitating. Yet, at the same time, this is not just motivational inertness. It involves, for example, mechanisms of inhibition, many of which are cultural.[26]

In turn, imitation leads to other affective states such as empathy, not only because the self-other divide can be seen to be remarkably porous but because across it constantly flow all kinds of emotional signals. But this is a kinetic empathy, of the kind often pointed to in dance, a kinaesthetic awareness/imitation which is both the means by which the body experiences itself kinaesthetically and also the means by which it apprehends other bodies (Foster 2005).

More generally, human imitative skills may be regarded as part of a widespread human capacity for mimesis.

> Mimetic capacities evolved as primarily motoric adaptation in hominids about two million years ago and remain just out of reach for most primates. Mimesis involved not just imitation but also the rehearsal and refinement of skills, the public motoric display of perceived or remembered episodes, social coordination and ritual, non-linguistic gesture and pantomime, and reciprocal emotional display or mirroring.
>
> (Hurley and Chater 2005: 42)

However, in contrast to many interpretations, for example those of Benjamin or Horkheimer and Adorno, I do not accept that the mimetic capacity has to be interpreted as somehow a primordial cognitive faculty which modernity has caused to decay. Many authors still want to argue that the main outpouring of mimesis now is in the play of children and is given up as the adult world approaches,[27] or they consign mimesis to supposedly archaic categories like magic. In contrast, I would argue that mimesis is in fact a perennial human imitative capacity, closer to a biological drive, and that it is an additive capacity for desire created out of a third term which René Girard calls the model or mediator. It is therefore neither autonomous nor innate.[28] There is no exact copy so that our desires can never properly be ours (Fleming 2004). Rather, our desires are second hand and socially oriented; we always desire what others desire, in imitation of them, and not under our own impetus. Take the case of modern advertising:

> advertisers rely on external mediation when they pay celebrities to use a product, and make use of internal mediation when they depict common people using common products. In the first case, they want our admiration for the celebrity to spark a desire for the product, and in the second case, they want us to 'catch' the nearby desire of someone like ourselves.
>
> (Potolsky 2006: 147)

But, at this point, it is important to make three points about this imitative notion of affective corporeality which are important for the arguments in this chapter. To begin with, it is important to note that, though much of the flow of affect can be described as a form of thinking, understood as part of a ceaseless flow of mind-readings, it is not necessarily instrumental or knowledgeable, that is oriented towards determinate goals like comprehension, purpose or intention. Rather, it is oriented to the achievement itself. This point is well illustrated by the fact that a large part of corporeal life is simply oriented towards concern over the body's extreme vulnerability. And not surprisingly: bodies make mistakes, trip or fall, get toothache or migraine, can see only partially or not at all, get chronic diseases like arthritis – or simply drop dead. One of the remarkable facts about the recent interest in the social sciences in embodiment, practice and performance, and the body-in-action generally, is the lack of thought that has been given to the fact of this vulnerability and how it wraps back into mind-reading. The primary role in the theorization of embodiment across a number of theoretical perspectives is still played by intentional or auto-affective action. Vulnerability remains not only unthought-of but potentially un-thinkable within much current work on the body within Anglo-American social science. But much corporeal experience is based on bodily states that underline corporeal vulnerability, such as fatigue and exhaustion or pain and suffering or exposure to extreme cold or heat or lack of sleep (Wilkinson 2005). In other words, corporeal life is inherently susceptible, receptive, exposed; open beyond its capacities to comprehend and absorb. One should not overdo this condition of vulnerability, of course (for example, for some, fatigue, weariness and general inaction can involve considerable psychic investments from hypervigilance to a certain kind of somatic self-regard and have themselves been the subject of affective firestorms (cf. Nunn 2005), but neither should one underplay it.

Then, it is also crucial to underline the role of things. Of late, the prosthetic impulse provided by the role of things has become a key theme in social sciences (Smith and Morra 2006) but, because of the social sciences' roots in interpretation, the emphasis still tends to fall on objects' meaning, on objects as cultural inscriptions. However objects do far more than represent. In terms of the argument of this chapter it is crucial to underline their other roles; 'the prosthesis is not a mere extension of the human body; it is the constitution of this body qua "human"' (Stiegler 1998: 152–153). In particular, objects form shields to human vulnerability by extending the body's circumference. They provide mental and physical resources to allow the body to be in the world, they add to what and how the body can experience, and they have their own agency, an ability to move bodies in particular ways. Thus clothes are not just ornamentation and display, they protect from the weather, provide resources for all kinds of specialist situations, and they produce particular corporeal stances. Similarly, houses provide a safe environment which wraps the comforting aura of familiarity around bodies. Thus, things redefine what counts as vulnerable. One of the key moments of affect is therefore an ability to produce affectively controllable worlds. That is difficult to do and often things substitute for bodies in such cases. Thus the popularity of robots in Japan seems, at least in part, to be a function of the complexity and correspondingly rich affective load of social life in Japan where there is no singular, internalized mental system of the kind regarded as normal in the West but rather a series of relays each of which must be performed correctly: robots are predictable partners in such interaction and therefore act as less stressful affective presences (*The Economist* 2005a).

Last of all, I want to stress – once again – the involuntary and precognitive nature of much of what is being described here. So, for example, feelings of vulnerability may not necessarily be expressly articulated though they may well be expressed in other ways, for example through bodily stances.[29] Thus we arrive again at the subject of *automatism*. Generally speaking, affect is a semiconscious phenomenon, consisting of a series of automatisms, many of them inscribed in childhood, which dictate bodily movement, which arise from suggestion, and which are not easily available to reflection (Wegner 2002; T.D. Wilson 2002). These automatisms may often feel like wilful action but they are not and they have powerful political consequences, not least because they form a kind of psychic immune system which means that certain issues can be avoided or perversely interpreted as a matter of course (T.D. Wilson 2002; Milton and Zizek 2005). Equally, suppositions of causality may become firmly entrenched. For example, it is relatively easy to promote in populations feelings of responsibility over events for which they could not possibly have had any responsibility at all. Affect is, in other words, a series of highways of imitation-suggestion. As Wegner (2002: 314) puts it, we live in a 'suggested society' in which 'the causal influences people have on themselves and each other, as they are understood, capture only a small part of the actual causal flux of social relations'. In other words, societies are thought of, quite literally, as *en-tranced*, as only half-awake.[30]

I will attempt to come to terms with the terms that affective contagion lays upon the world through an attempt to show how affect can be engineered to produce a politics which is able to act as a dark force which is part and parcel of the new liberal settlement. My argument will be as follows. Against a background of a general, if differential, loss of belief in formal modes of efficacy, and especially political engagement, Western cultures are becoming increasingly prone to brief moments of engagement tied to the affective texture of particular events shaped by a series of political inventions made in the last 40 years or so. Most of the time Western democratic cultures tend to be disengaged but they can be 'switched on' by particular issues with high affective resonance. Thus a growth in disengagement and detachment (Ross 2006) is paralleled by moments of high engagement and attachment. Part of the reason for this change in the affective time structure is, I hypothesize, the growth of anxious, obsessive and compulsive, behaviours, with interesting consequences of various kinds for politics and the political. Even though notoriously difficult to define and ask questions about, all the available surveys show that these behaviours are growing apace, filling up more and more of the Western psychic space (cf. Salecl 2004 and, most recently, Huddy *et al.* 2005).[31]

What might I mean by the performatives of 'anxiety', 'obsession', and 'compulsion'? Anxiety, defined by the dictionary as 'a state of apprehension, uncertainty and fear resulting from the anticipation of a realistic or fantasized threatening event or situation', can be understood as the affective reaction to an expected danger, sometimes muddied by the concern that the reaction will not be reciprocated. The dictionary defines obsession variously as a 'compulsive preoccupation with a fixed idea or an unwanted feeling or emotion, often accompanied by symptoms of anxiety', or 'an irrational motive for performing trivial or repetitive actions against your will', or 'an unhealthy and compulsive preoccupation with something or someone', thus signalling that obsession is close in nature to the other affect in which I am interested, namely compulsion; 'an irresistible impulse to act, regardless of the rationality of the motivation'. In other words, the nub of anxiety, obsession, and compulsion is a certain lack of free will: people have little or no agency over their bodies or environments but are under the control of an affective force. That is, they are powered by automatisms: the body is the medium for the transmission of force but without any conscious volition. Unconscious 'thoughts' cause the bulk of actions. Described in this way, the study of such auto-feelings has a long history which goes back until at least the eighteenth century. But what I think is different now is that these feelings are increasingly available to be worked on and cultivated through a kind of performance management, as I will show below in the case of business and politics (Ross 2006).[32]

Now it is, of course, perfectly possible to ramp up affects like anxiety, obsession, and compulsion in dangerous ways. They can be related, for example through psychoanalytic analyses, to the death instinct and the fear of annihilation, to various splits in the subject involving the externalization of what are internal situations (the projection of the self), and so on, producing in turn a general diagnosis of Western civilization as most especially based on 'firework' affects like fear (Robin 2004) or anger, and on their overt results such as the kinds of inflamed imaginaries that produce conspiracy theories, millenarianism, and the like. Equally, it is possible to start linking these affects to all kinds of other affects – like melancholy or guilt or shame – in the process producing a never-ending compendium of misery which has the same cumulative effect of producing a glacier of all too capable incapability. And finally, it is possible to paint these affects as purely negative when they can have positive aspects. Take the case of anxiety and political judgement. Marcus, Neuman and Mackuen (2000) show how anxiety can be a means of sensing political dangers, informing people who rely on routine responses that these routines need re-assessment. In other words, it can act as an automatism that, in making people feel uncomfortable, spurs them to re-assess a situation. No wonder that in political terms, anxiety is often portrayed positively as a condition of the vigilance that so many years ago Thomas Paine argued was the burden of a free people (Brader 2006).

So, bearing these caveats in mind, I want to link these three affects more closely in to everyday life. In doing so, I am certainly not trying to deny that the stronger 'firework' affects like anger and fear do not have their say in the interstices of the everyday – consider only the play of domestic violence or the massive incidence of self-harm as a counter to that kind of argument, yet alone other violent incidents of various kinds (see Chapter 9).[33] Rather, I want to signal anxiety, obsession, and compulsion as outcomes of a different condition, one that is shackled to the subject's often unconscious sense of corporeal vulnerability in time which is in part the atmosphere of a particular habitat and thus cannot be undone by simple behavioural changes. In other words, I want to see these affects as a part of 'the very condition through which people relate to the world' (Salecl 2004: 15), affirmed by their own presence and not bracketed by meaning (Gumbrecht 2004).

But how do people relate to the world? Of late, it has become almost a standard account that human life is based on a creative corporeality which displays an almost continuous intentionality; a constant release of energy, if you like. Writers as different in theoretical background as hard-line phenomenologists, for whom consciousness is the measure of the world, and hard-line poststructuralists, who abjure any mention of the subject, are united by their emphasis on the 'bliss of action' (Deleuze 1988a: 28). But this is to overlook a feature of embodiment which is crucial: effort. It takes effort for the body to be in the world, to produce an expenditure of energy, to conserve some kind of equilibrium. But, too often, it is simply assumed that bodies are bodies-in-action, able to exhibit a kind of continuous intentionality, able to be constantly enrolled into activity. Every occasion seems to be willed, cultivated or at least honed. But the experience of embodiment is not necessarily like that at all. It also includes vulnerability, passivity, suffering, fatigue, indolence, even simple hunger (Wilkinson 2005). It includes episodes of insomnia, weariness and plain exhaustion, a sense of insignificance and even sheer indifference to the world. It includes tripping over, falling,[34] missing a catch or a target, walking into an obstacle. In other words, bodies can and do become overwhelmed. The unchosen and unforeseen exceed the ability of the body to contain or absorb (Harrison 2007). There is a sense of being unworthy of events, and a general reluctance to take up the challenges of being. And this is not an abnormal condition: it is a part of being as flesh. This *corporeal vulnerability* is a crucial experience in people's lives.

Rather than focusing on the more overt epidemics of fear or anger (cf. Thrift 2005b, 2006b), it seems crucial to me to concentrate on an underlay of *reluctance to engage*, arising partly out of this corporeal vulnerability. For it seems to me that this reluctance also has a wider political significance since it is these points of unconscious volition (or non-volition, perhaps) which are often so crucial in influencing the course of politics by inducing an active passivity (Eliasoph 1998).

Such tendencies have been only strengthened by the growth of the media which makes it much easier to work on bare life, and most especially the ability to arrest time and examine and work with it (Thrift 2001; Mulvey 2005). Delay in time allows detail which has, so to speak, lain dormant to be noticed and worked with. Thus, more and more action becomes deferred, often for very small periods of time, and during this period of deferral it can be pre-treated in various ways, thus allowing the automatisms I have discussed above to become routinely embedded in action. At the same time, the advent of mass media has almost certainly increased levels of anxiety by speeding up the reception of events so that giving any considered political voice to them becomes particularly difficult. Indeed, increasingly, notwithstanding a general increase in news outlets (Bennett and Entman 2001),[35] this political voice tends to be restricted to certain widely circulated clichés of presentation which foreground affect as a means of gaining a speedy impact, an effect that is exacerbated by the heightened levels of competition to find presentations with grip. For example, mass media images of risk nearly always focus on suffering; 'More often than not, "risk" is communicated for public attention in graphic portrayals of bodies in pain and harrowing images of people in mourning and distress' (Wilkinson 2005: vii). In particular, an affective platform like melodrama, which involves the generation of high levels of anxiety, has become, through the media, an accepted affective automatism (Huddy *et al.* 2005; Thrift 2006a). Furthermore, the proliferation of mass media tends to both multiply and keep this kind of affective platform in the public mind in a way which promotes anxiety and can sometimes even be likened to obsession or compulsion.

In other words, what I am trying to point to is the rise of more and more affective techniques, premised on making appeals to the heart, passion, emotional imagination, to and through a realm of affect that is co-present with the psychic and the emotional rather than the intellect and reasoning. To put it another way, I want to recall Tarde by paralleling imitation with invention. Moscovici (1985) is writing about another less mediated time but his work seems particularly relevant to the new mediated age of the imitative crowd we now inhabit, an age which might well be caricatured as mass mesmerism gone bad (Barrows 1981; Peters 1999; J. Miller 1983). For Moscovici argues that affective appeals try to create an 'illusion of love' via a range of techniques – affective, corporeal, and psychological – aimed at maximizing processes of suggestion and imitation, including the use of symbols, images, flags, music, affirmations, phrases, speeches, and slogans, all jammed, as I see it, into the half-second delay between action and cognition. These are delivered through the hypnotizing use of repetition rather than didactic command and instruction. Thus, the population is touched in ways which might be non-conscious and may well instil the feeling that they are the originator of that thought, belief, or action, rather than simply and mechanically reproducing the beliefs of a charismatic other. The principle is to extend and reinforce 'mental touch'. In other words, waves of affect are transmitted and received, transmitted and received, constantly challenging the Lockean citadel of the consenting self (Barrows 1981) as they cook up an affective storm.

To begin to understand this process of continuous biocultural contagion, I will begin by taking the corporate circuit as an exemplar, rather than the more obvious cultural sources, like the arts. Why? First, at least arguably, large corporations now rival states as generators of political power. Not only are they at the heart of the economic system but they are also endowed with considerable political power, both directly through the influence they can exert on the political process and indirectly through the practices of government that they are able to disseminate. Then, second, because they are a fertile ground of invention for techniques of imitation-suggestion, affective, semiconscious imitation-suggestion. From the early days of marketing through to the latter days of brand formation, they are skilled in the art-cum-science of influencing disposition through various methods of entrancement. In this sense, they constitute a 'système sorcier' (Pignarre and Stengers 2005), able to deliver effective affective charges, if not with impunity then certainly with a (lack of) will.

The affective corporation

The modern corporation has become an increasingly political entity. Of course, since their inception, corporations have wielded political influence. Think only of the East India Company or, later, the ways in which various plutocrats wielded power in the USA. By the turn of the century, the political power of the corporation – and how to control it – had become a favourite theme. But this power has become much greater of late. For example, currently, 51 of the largest 100 economies in the world are corporations and the 100 largest corporations control about 20 per cent of global foreign assets (Ginsborg 2005). Yet, taken singly, these corporations are remarkably vulnerable entities, seething with uncertainties.

It is therefore surprising that a considerable part of the academic literature on business seems to want to set affect to one side as having no official place in business, perhaps as a result of an untoward emphasis on calculation. Yet all relevant research shows that corporations are a series of affective soups. It is a truism that all corporations are emotional entities and since the death of the robotic 'organization man' in the 1960s that truism has slowly become accepted. These are organizations where emotional attachments are formed out of the play of anger, elation, envy, disappointment, shame, suffering, even violence of various kinds, as numerous films (*Citizen Kane, Wall Street*) and novels (*Bonfire of the Vanities*) have set out to show. These are organizations where thriving traditions of emotional engineering have grown up, most especially in human resources and marketing but now extending over into commodity design and engineering. And these are organizations which are now starting to receive due academic attention as emotional formations, for example in the study of international finance (Pixley 2004), internet commerce (Kuwabara 2004), and innovation.

For quite some time, emotions were thought of as important to the conduct of business but as essentially epiphenomenal. For example, they might be thought of as ties that were formed only because the correct organizational structure could not be found (Jaques 1995). If not dysfunctional, they were usually regarded, therefore, as informal elements of organization. But the change in the modern corporation to flatter management structures, coupled with a determined push by numerous elements of the cultural circuit of capital to highlight the emotional elements of corporate life since at least the 1960s has changed all that. Emotion is now something of a corporate watchword and in innumerable workshops and seminars all kinds of workers, from the highest manager to the lowliest worker, are being taught at least some bowdlerized principles of emotional intelligence. This is no coincidence. There are at least five reasons why emotion has become accepted as an explicit element of all corporate life. One is the rise of the aforementioned flatter management structures. The fluidity and subsequent lack of clarity of relations of accountability and authority and the substitution of networks of influence and persuasion for formal lines of authority in these management structures, coupled with the subsequent need to generate trust, have all highlighted the importance of affective ties and skills as key elements in the corporation, as well as in all manner of corporate interactions – from interacting with the customer to interacting with other corporations. Second, as corporations expand into new areas of business, often buying up whole new areas of expertise which have their own cultures, corporations can often become affective swamps. Indeed, many mergers and takeovers have failed precisely because corporations have been unable to attune their cultures, and not least their emotional cultures. Third, the pressure for higher rates of innovation in many corporations has promoted high interaction cultures which often have very high emotional strains attached to them (Thrift 2006a). Fourth, it seems possible that the context within which organizations find themselves is more dynamic. Certainly, it is often *felt* to be so, a fact not entirely uncoincident with the constant barrage of publications and surveys that insist that this is the case. Fifth, and finally, corporations have much more diverse workforces than formerly. The need to negotiate gender, ethnic and other divides has produced a different corporate ambience, one that speaks to values like creativity and discovery and mobilizes affects like hope but one which again takes an emotional toll.

Thus, corporations have become emotional soups, full of (quite understandable) hopes and anxieties: Jacques' (1995) so-called 'paranoiagenic zoo', in which anxiety levels are constantly high. At the extreme, the cult of 'leadership' currently found in many organizations, which elevates the charismatic authority of CEOs and others, in part by investing them with celebrity status, can be seen as a need to affectively embody the enterprise in the absence of traditional boundaries.

But, more to the point, as they have recognized the power of the affective forces that push them hither and thither and as affect has made its way up corporate agendas as an element that is not incidental but can be worked on, so corporations have also been able to generate new performative knowledges which depend upon the staging of affect, most of which revolve around *generating engagement* through the manipulation of mood. Of these, the most important has been making the maximum affective impact with the commodity by producing what might be called customized individualization, a collective individuation that draws on the whole intellect of the consumer in order to induce emotional identification with the commodity. This process of generating the same wavelength – which is only strengthened by the Christian–Romantic ideal of personal relations which allows commodities not just to figure as a part of commitments to a relationship but to become commitments in their own right (Gray 2002) – has occurred in at least five ways. When taken together, these five developments have produced a new 'flock and flow' consumer technology which is redefining wanting as insertion into a steady, continuous stream of low-level imitative excitements, fuelled by all manner of anxieties and enthusiasms.

First, there has been a massive increase in the mediation of society, producing a fertile ground for the imitative transmission of affect. Just one example of this kind of suggestibility will suffice, precisely because it is so powerful. Celebrity has become a particular means of relating to the world, a form of obsessive contact and identification with familiar strangers who, through a variety of media, can be inserted into the fabric of everyday lives, becoming a culturally pervasive aspect of the affective background, quite literally a means of catching breath (G. Turner 2004).

Second, commodities are increasingly elements in the generation of passions, both through the invocation of 'sensory design' (Malnar and Vodvarka 2004) which increases the commodity's sensory range by producing commodities that function as phenomenological fishing nets and through the affective extension of the commodity as a result of devices like the brand and celebrity (Thrift 2006a). This process of adding affective value is often described in psycho-sexual terms. For example, most recently, Steinberg (2005) has described commodities as having a 'quasi-erotic' aura because they are sold with promises of ease, fun, sexual attraction, and the like. Yet, it is difficult to reconcile such accounts with close ethnographies of consumers which show that consumers very often see through such appeals, as they do through technologies like brands which are often mooted as the affective extensions of commodities (Lury 2004). Hence the need to fix on the automatism: a substrate of the will which is not conscious. One way to describe this would be through psychoanalysis but I think it is much simpler just to concentrate on the play of affects like anxiety, transmitted in a semiconscious way through imitation, and the way that these affects can be boosted. For example, feminist theorists have shown the way in which corporations are able to produce or exaggerate anxieties about body image but they have very often taken this to be a conscious cognitive choice, based on representations. However, it might be more interesting to think about these anxieties as being transmitted and received by a moving mind that has been caught up in the business of what Blum (2005) calls 'as-if beauty', the generation of paradigms for others to emulate (based, for example, on celebrity) and, correspondingly, the assumption of the characteristics and behaviours of those persons you want to be, which are often fixed in episodes of childhood imitation before identification becomes permanent. Most recently, business has become involved in the design of commodities that reach out to consumers by actually simulating them and this activity is totally bound up with affect since it involves the imitation of imitation, so to speak. Thus, recent work in robotics has exactly tried to capture affect. But it has also faced extreme difficulties of characterization and specification of generally vague principles (Fellous and Arbib 2005).

Third, whom commodities of particular kinds can be sold to has become an increasingly precise business based on the rise of customized customer intelligence (including data enrichment, profiling, and data mining); 'customer intelligence describes the knowledge that an organization has concerning the likely future intentions of its customers or prospective customers' (Kelly 2006: 1). The consequent rise of geodemographics has produced a series of detailed maps of what might be called susceptibility to particular affective cues amongst an increasingly fragmented set of consumers which call for mass customization. Thus, most interestingly, geodemographic descriptions often now include extensive affective information (e.g. on levels of fear and worry and a corresponding requirement for safety) (M.J. Weiss 2000).

Fourth, using the internet in particular, corporations have devised new ways of maintaining constant contact with and cultivating consumers. The result is that it is now much easier to make consumption into a relationship which gathers, manages and plays on and with consumer loyalties, engagements, and even obsessions. Consumers are enabled to become 'fanatics without convictions' much more easily. Thus, interestingly, a search of books on obsession is as likely to produce books on fell running and other extreme sports, chocolate, lawns, football, and various kinds of music, religion and automobiles as on conventionally psychosexual topics.

Fifth, as a result of all these processes, commodities are increasingly seen as unfolding in time. Not only may commodities have a temporal profile, for example through being continuously updated, but they are tied closely to events. It is no surprise then that, at this point in time, event-oriented marketing has become so important. Increasingly, the idea is to tie commodities into the affective landscape of consumers by tracking their lives through a parallel information landscape. This landscape has speeded up the ways in which commodities can be inserted into the lives of consumers, thereby producing more consumption opportunities in a continual semiconscious onflow. Thus, time itself is shaped so that it becomes more and more like an analogue of the kind of political time that Machiavelli wanted to construct, a time that is 'importantly psychological in its effect, capable of producing different responses – panic, fear, boldness, lassitude – according to the seeming imminence or remoteness of a danger or possibility' (W. Brown 2005: 8).

To summarize, corporations are in the business of making hormonal splashes through increasingly close contact with consumers, contact predicated on the development of new forms of the media which allow individual-level relationships to be constructed, as opposed to the kinds of relationship dictated by the mass audiences of old (Bennett and Entman 2001). Corporations are not only delineating the affective field and starting up new affective cascades but also adding in to the field by producing new combinations, new sensings if you like, that add in new affective shadings. The result is that they have found powerful new means of not only confabulating intentions (that is, revising what actors thought they intended to do after the action, especially the inference of desires) but of working on intention itself, before it necessarily comes to fruition. The coalface is, in other words, the invention of inventions that can shape subconscious intentions.

The political arena

> Bush is the product. Rove is the marketer. One cannot succeed without the other.
>
> (Moore and Slater 2003: 11)

In this penultimate section, I want to argue that these corporate impulses are now spilling over into political life.[36] Now, it can hardly be said that affect has never played a visible part in political life. Politicians routinely ask the 'How do they feel?' question, recognizing just how important that question is, and are continually being accused of preying on the people's hopes and fears,[37] the two emotions that they are most likely to appeal to (Brader 2006). In the Greek polis, it is at least arguable that the most important innovation was the production of a space that could dampen emotions sufficiently to produce a time structure of waiting one's turn to speak (Sloterdijk 2005b). In any case, even before Aristotle declared that we are all political animals, underlined the importance of emotions for good moral judgement, and drew attention in the *Rhetoric* to emotion as a key component of political oratory, the arts of rhetoric had been a staple of political life (Koziak 2000; Chilton 2003). These arts are, in part, precisely about swaying constituencies[38] through the use of affective cues and appeals which are often founded in spatial arrangement; think only of a book like Thomas Wilson's (1993 [1553]) *The Art of Rhetoric* and the careful attention it pays to staging as an affective key. Certainly, as Koziak (2000) has pointed out, few canonical political philosophers and even fewer contemporary political theorists have tackled the role of affect in politics, even as they have spent a good deal of time challenging the supposed certainties of liberal political theory. But that is not to say that there is nowhere to turn. Think only of Paul Lazarsfeld's seminal study of political communication and voter decision-making during the 1940 US presidential election, Richard Hofstadter's classic (1964) essay 'The paranoid style in American politics', expounding on the power of 'angry minds', George E. Marcus's (2002) work on affective intelligence and political judgement, Lauren Berlant's remarkable series of works on affective democracy and compassion, or the growing feminist literature on politics, for example. But I think that it is fair to say that much of this interest has not been systematic and has been bedevilled by the view that politics ought to be about conscious, rational discourse with the result that affect is regarded as at best an add-on and as at worst a dangerous distraction (see Thrift 2006a).

Yet politics is susceptible to and is based on many of the same subconscious processes of imitation as consumerism. Take just the realm of political advertising. Think only of the classic hopeful 1984 Ronald Reagan 'Morning in America' ad campaign or the scary 1964 Johnson 'Daisy' ads: each of these campaigns, repeated many times since in different variants, testifies to the influence of affect on politics and the importance of imitation as a constituent element of affective contagion (Brader 2006). And this is no surprise. As Popkin (1991) pointed out in the classic *The Reasoning Voter* a good part of politics in a mediated environment is based on intangibles that briefly fix attention – which he calls 'low-information signalling' – chiefly affective short-cuts that convey just enough of the character of candidates to voters and which are open to all kinds of manipulation, particularly via the use of nonverbal cues like music and imagery. Such fleeting impressions, in which 'our brains often identify cues and respond to them without our awareness' (Brader 2006: 14), often count for more than cogent policies and often pass as voters' political reasoning.[39] In turn, this puts much more emphasis on the individual politician who acts as a kind of affective bellwether. Indeed recent work in political psychology suggests that voters can often make inferences of competence based solely on the facial appearance of candidates, and do so remarkably rapidly – within milliseconds (Todorov *et al.* 2005; Todorov and Willis 2006).

In particular there has been a wide-ranging set of changes in political technology (Table 10.1), many of which take their cue from corporate practices of generating engagement. These technologies supposedly make the conduct of electoral and other forms of politics more effective but too often they confuse the consumption of democracy with the practice of democracy (Orlie 2002; Klein 2006).

Perhaps the most obvious sign of this crossover is the new political alignment between consumerism and politics, as 'we watch Sharon Stone, Angelina Jolie and Bono petitioning the corporate hierarchy at Davos for more concessions to social and environmental concerns' (Nelson 2006: 11). But the crossover goes far

Table 10.1 Progressive technological change in detecting biosocial political tendencies

1930s	national polls (Gallup, Harris, Quayle)
1940s	audience research
1969	first intensive polling firm
Mid-1970s	telephone polling and focus groups and direct mail fundraising
1976	on permanent campaign
1992	dial groups
1980s	daily tracking polls
1990s	one-on-one sessions in shopping mall offices
2003	use of Web in Howard Dean campaign to organise monthly meetups (Create own crowds). Decentralized campaign using websites. Use of email and blogs instead of focus groups and such to gauge opinion. House meetings.

beyond these kinds of show-business. In effect, it is based on the five processes of comprehensive commodification that I outlined in the previous section.

Thus, to begin with, there has been a mass mediation of politics. It is something of a cliché to note the influence of the media on politics – even in the nineteenth century this was a favourite topic for jeremiads – but this has now become pervasive, based especially in; the interaction between techniques like opinion polling and media presentation (Brace and Hinckley 1992), the result of an increasing familiarity with television technique, growing professionalization of the presentation of politics (as symbolized by growing numbers of consultants[40] and the fame of formative guru-cum-inventors like Lee Atwater, Dick Morris, and Karl Rove), the burgeoning of available media outlets and the subsequent net expansion of political programming, and increased media access. When a New Labour spin doctor declares that 'what they can't seem to grasp is that communications is not an after thought to our policy. It's central to the whole mission of New Labour' (cited in Franklin 2004: 5), this is no longer a partisan point – it is typical of the modern mediated Western democracy.

Second, political actors are increasingly treated as commodities to be sold, in part, perhaps, because so many citizens lack the attention span or inclination to follow political issues and tend to invest their trust in the low-information signals emanating from iconic figures instead. Such marketing involves more and more use of the small signs of affective technique structured as various kinds of performance of style: a politician's ability to perform in public becomes a crucial asset but it is very often a performance in which unexpected emotions are bleached from the process because of the dangers of 'expressive failure'. Spontaneity has to be carefully structured. So, for example, the practices of celebrity are becoming more and more common in the political arena. Think only of the way in which that languorous extremist Ronald Reagan's face has become an abiding source of contemplation by political commentators because of the affective power of its ability to convey comfort and avuncular authenticity and warmth and even serenity

(Massumi 2002), or the careful prepping of Bill Clinton's body language in key television appearances (D. Morris 1999).

Third, political campaigns are increasingly treated as forms of marketing. This tendency is only strengthened in first-past-the-post systems where the outcome of any election is disproportionately influenced by a few swing voters whom it is important to locate and communicate with, against a background of increasing speed that I noted above. Thus, polling techniques have become a key to many political campaigns, techniques that can gauge intensity of feelings and the general quality of mood. Parties and other pressure groups have adopted a series of these practices: all manner of polls, focus groups,[41] voter databases, geographical information systems, customer relations management software, targeted mail and e-mail, and so on, especially to target particularly passionate constituencies (Reynolds 2006).[42] In the USA, since the 1970s these techniques have become far-advanced. In each case, the goal is to identify a susceptible constituency as accurately as possible through continuous polling[43] and to boost affective gain by making voters feel differently, for example by finding wedge issues. But, more than this, increasingly it is about rapidly identifying individuals and their interests and concerns as exactly as possible, thereby turning them into 'intimate strangers', celebrities for the passing moment.

Fourth, a whole array of corporate internet-related techniques, from websites to blogs have been used to tap in to and work with voters' concerns. The idea is to maintain constant contact with voters and to mobilize their concerns to political ends.

Fifth, the political process, in an odd simulation of the original ambitions of democracy, becomes a continuous one, based on a model of permanent tracking, which can be used outside elections as well as in, according to the play of events. In the 'permanent campaign', a term first used by Pat Caddell in 1976, media time and election time begin to merge, and techniques for campaigning and governing gradually coalesce. The aim, it might be hypothesized, is to produce a semi-conscious onflow of political imitation-suggestion that is unstoppable and which can be played into in order to produce affective firestorms which can be modulated by the new technical means now available, against a general background of increasing lack of formal political engagement in the population as a whole. Free won't rather than free will, if you like (Nunn 2005).

Political life in democracies is a life constantly stirred by the media. It is increasingly characterized, therefore, by individual-level cultivation of anxiety, obsession, and compulsion, against what may – and I emphasize, may[44] – be a general increase in the level of political anxiety brought about by these developments, stemming especially, from the sheer ability to keep various anxieties, compulsions and obsessions in play, paralleled by an increased speed of response (Connolly 2002); 'all speed, no direction. If this heaviness mixed with speediness were analogised to a mental state, the diagnosis would be profound depressive anxiety' (W. Brown 2005: 11). Accordingly, political time is reshaped. It becomes an increasingly anxious business, burrowing into more and more of the 'biological' determinants of affect for sustenance and 'contentless content'.

The technologies I have outlined were undoubtedly born in the USA but they are now diffusing to all democracies at greater or lesser speeds, following the increasingly insistent media logic. The case of Italy is the most extreme. There, Silvio Berlusconi was able to turn a potent mixture of marketing and celebrity into a politics. Stille is worth quoting at length on Berlusconi as a model of where a mediatized and heavily affective politics could go *in extremis*: often described as more American than America, Berlusconi built his political career on importing American political techniques – from focus groups to targeted polling – and then accentuating them.

[In 1994] Berlusconi undertook what has to be one of the most extraordinarily innovative election campaigns of our age. All the divisions of Berlusconi's vast empire – from television stations and newspapers to department stores and an insurance and financial services company – were fused almost overnight into an enormous political machine. The ad executives contacted the companies that bought advertising on the Berlusconi channels. The stockbrokers and insurance agents working for Berlusconi's financial services company became campaign workers and set about turning the hundreds of thousands, possibly millions, of financial clients into voters and party supporters. The candidates took screen tests at the television studios, were given lessons in politics, and were cross-examined to see how they would hold up under the fire of an election campaign. The candidates all were obliged to buy a special kit that included a thirty-five page booklet and eleven videotapes explaining the party's program as well as lessons on how to speak in public and on TV. The company's media experts, with expertise in testing TV programs, conducted focus groups to hone Berlusconi's message to appeal to the largest possible audience. The party/company set up pay-per-call phone numbers . . . that allowed people to listen to the latest comments of Berlusconi, and earned money for the movement at the same time.

(Stille 2006: 1–2)

But the case of the UK is also instructive. Since about 1992, something like a permanent campaign has been in operation there, the result of its adoption from US sources by New Labour. Whilst it does not run at quite the intensity of its North American counterpart, the result of a slightly longer electoral cycle, still nearly all of the techniques found in the US permanent campaign have gradually made their way across the Atlantic (Norris *et al.* 1999), fuelled by the hiring of US-based consultants at various times.[45] For example, all the main parties now use regular opinion polls and volume direct marketing techniques, including customer relations management software, which calls on the large commercial lifestyle databases that are now available. According to Webber (2005: 4), there is common agreement amongst the main political parties that 'the skills needed to operate a campaign were becoming closer to those needed to operate effectively in the commercial sector'. So, all the parties use geodemographic systems, especially to cluster constituencies and to tailor campaigns and to choose the kinds of candidates who would be most likely to win. But it is still a halting process to join prospects to actual political allegiances. For example, the construction of integrated databases has proved a challenge. A key variable is age and this is usually inferred simply from first names. Additionally, all parties are experimenting with internet-related techniques. As one instance, the Conservative Party has become interested in building or tapping into internet communities, though with the difficulty that there are no easy correlates for the affective issues that arouse the passions of so many US citizens (such as gun-owning, gay marriage, and the like). Finally, all parties are using party conferences as explicit machines for manipulating public mood by importing various US means of presenting affective messages that convey a 'mass intimacy' (Faucher-King 2005).

Conclusions: towards new ecologies of belonging

I have tried to begin to show that the challenge of affect is, at least in part, a challenge to what we regard as the social because it involves thinking about waves of influence which depend upon biology to an extent that is rarely recognized or theorized in the social sciences. Whether that means that we need to discard the notion of the social, moving into a world of constantly multiplying collectives, as in actor-network theory – which is now claimed as Tarde's direct descendant – or whether it means reversing the usual direction of causality and claiming that biology can have dominion over the social or whether it means that the social is seen as determining the biological seems less important at this point than the simple move to acknowledge that the biological cannot be set to one side as though it somehow inhabited another background realm rather than being a key moment of the invention of performance and the performance of invention. Of course, it could be argued that such a move has already been discovered in certain areas of theory and practice, and most notably in parts of performance studies and environmental discourse. If that is true, it is a point that still seems to be doggedly resisted in many parts of the social sciences and humanities where the biological is rarely pulled through into the frame.

But, as I have tried to show, the political stakes are too high to continue on such a course of neglect. In particular, understanding affect as imitation-suggestion cannot be laid to one side. Of course, politics has always involved deploying affect. But I think it can be argued – as I certainly have – that the suite of practically formulated political technologies developed recently for deploying affect have never been so powerful, never so likely to bite, because in a highly mediated world imitation-suggestion is so much easier to trigger and diffuse, and is so much more likely to have grip at a distance. If that is indeed so, we need to start formulating new kinds of counter-politics that can combat the increasingly toxic post-liberal forms that are proliferating around the world. The elements of that counter-politics are becoming clearer over time – an emphasis on a politics of small things which is neither apologetic nor cramped (Goldfarb 2006), on hope and also on a certain kind of aggression (Anderson 2006; Elliott and Lemert 2006), on the forms of struggle and organization as important in their own right (and especially new forms of media communication (Gillmor 2004)), on understanding diversity as a strength in composing will, on the importance of political timeliness (W. Brown 2005), on new forms of piety (Goodchild 2002; Braidotti 2006), and on a thoroughly healthy anxiety about losing the future – but it would be difficult to argue that they form a definitive political resource as yet. Yet, taken collectively, these different ingredients seem to me to be building towards new forms of sympathy – new affective recognitions, new psychic opportunity structures, untoward reanimations, call them what you like (Cruz 2005) – forms of sympathy which are more than just a selective cultural performance[46] and which will allow different, more expansive political forms to be built (and equally new forms of sympathy, of course).[47] When that resource finally crystallizes as contrary motion, however, one thing will be clear. It will have to take affect, imitation-suggestion and entrancement in to its workings as more than incidental to what the political is and how the political is conducted.

That insight, in turn, suggests that much more thought needs to be given to a biopolitics of imitation. And it also suggests that the outlook is not necessarily as gloomy as often painted. Whilst the forces ranged against democratic expression are many they do not all run one way. New technologies allow highly performative aggregations at a distance that were not possible before and that can actually be used in local ways too. Many of these techniques were originally used to aggregate and mobilize the passions of 'long tails' of consumers (Anderson 2006) but they have now moved over into the political arena.

Take the example of the new net politics that is currently the subject of much comment. In the USA, organizations like MoveOn.org[48] and Redeem the Vote and United for Peace and Justice, all organized around web sites, have shown that it is possible to produce a politics of political imitation which is effective and can have real political bite. In particular, using web tools it is possible to produce highly disaggregated political performances, like vigils, quickly and with very little infrastructure: for example, in March 2003 a wave of anti-war candlelight vigils involving one million people in more than six thousand ceremonies was organized in six days by just five staff people. It is possible to produce constant and rapid monitoring of media content: political blogs like Daily Kos and Instapundit.com have more than a million visitors a day and themselves represent a kind of permanent political campaign. And it is possible to raise finance fast, for example through large-scale political mapping projects like Fundrace which not only allowed ordinary people to draw on geocoded information heretofore only available to consultants but also allowed them to check on each others' political proclivities and who was donating what to which party (Abrams and Hall 2006). What we see here is a new kind of political domain in which political issues can take light very quickly, a distributed intelligence fuelled by an excitement born out of the direct translation of conception into action and a constant impassioned debate. Both left and right have laid claim to this domain of heightened enthusiasm but the point I want to make most strongly is that it is a passionate domain, dripping with affect. Its speed and imitative capacity allow it to simulate the kinds of expressive interchanges that populate everyday life and provide a political form which in some ways is as important as content (Goldfarb 2006). It is not, as some have claimed, a reformation or a transformation or a new kind of magic but it is, I think, a significant addition to the affective cartography of the world, not least because it allows biological fields to take shape at-a-distance in new ways.[49]

And, as I have pointed out above, this is about cartography. But the problem is that we have only a limited range of models that capture spaces of imitation and invention (Thrift 2006a) and which will allow us too think about how we might ventilate politics, to use Sloterdijk's term. But I think a new and fertile ground is now emerging in which the practices of affect might be better understood and worked with, and that ground lies at the intersection of performance and technology in the reinvention of various spatial crafts (Gough and Wallis 2005). But that is for another book.

Notes

Preface

1 But I do not want to be misunderstood. Though rationality has become a difficult value to adhere to, not least because it is becoming clear from much recent research (e.g. Hurley and Nudds 2006) that what counts as rationality is up for grabs, this does not mean that I want to cast that value aside. Quite the reverse.

2 In particular, they believe that we need to work on those transindividual aspects of human being that operate before understanding in a realm which is not just about subjectivity. These transindividual aspects are themselves open to manipulation, the result of 'mobilizing and modulating the pre-individual, pre-cognitive and pre-verbal components of subjectivity, causing affects, perceptions, and sensations as yet unindividuated or unassigned to a subject, etc. to function like cogs in a machine' (Lazzarato 2006: 4). In turn, understanding this transindividual mobilization and modulation must mean thinking through matter and materiality again and according it a sensibility of its own. This is a way of thinking which holds the natural and fabricated world to be structured by a non-propositional intelligence shared with the human mind.

1 Life, but not as we know it

1 I had originally considered calling this introductory chapter 'Sacraments of expression' after Whitehead but Whitehead means something rather different and there seems no point in confusing the issue. The reference to the superfluous intentionally echoes Voltaire's famous dictum.

2 I agree with Connolly (2005: 166) that 'running the experiment may be the best way to test the claims'.

3 I understand social theory as an art of controlled speculation, not as a faithful rendition of what may be going on, as if that were indeed possible.

4 Throughout the introduction, I use the plural term 'the worlds' in preference to the 'the world' in order to signify that I am trying to describe a set of different but attuned worlds rather than just one order of being, a move prompted by traditions as diverse as von Uexkull's discussion of *umwelten* and contemporary discussions of postcolonialism.

5 It follows that I do not believe that experience has in some way been radically downgraded or made problematic in the contemporary world, in the style of Benjamin or Agamben (see Docherty 2006). There is, in my opinion, no general crisis of modernity: there are plenty of crises to be going on with.

6 Most especially, because publics, as peoples to come, are a conjunction of forces which will always exceed any given human intention.

7 I am uncomfortably aware of the complicated theoretical apparatus that I have myself used to reach these conclusions.

8 It is worth recalling that, according to the *Oxford English Dictionary*, 'vocation'

originated in the Latin noun of action, *vocare*, meaning to call or summon. This meaning fits my purposes well.

9 Lotringer is reproaching Hardt and Negri, justifiably so far as I am concerned.

10 This phrase has become associated with the work of Ernst Bloch and I would want to affirm Bloch's general direction whilst dissociating it from his theory of history.

11 As in rhythm, play, and kinetic markers such as running, chasing, fleeing, jumping, falling, and so on (Sheets-Johnstone 2005).

12 That is, following being in its genesis, by accomplishing the genesis of thought in parallel with the object. So far as I am aware, the term was first used by Simondon.

13 I have not used the word experience because so many philosophical traditions associate that word with interpretation, that is with acts of the attribution of meaning.

14 In particular, I would point to the important work being done in human geography by Ben Anderson, J.D. Dewsbury, Paul Harrison, Eric Laurier, Derek McCormack, John Wylie, and others.

15 Pred's is a useful term because it does not presuppose a specific spatial location (such as the biological body) or any necessary sensory modalities.

16 For a very clear introduction to this line of thought and its implications, see Middleton and Brown (2006).

17 This is one of my main objections to actor-network theory: its curiously flat tone arises from the filters it puts up on what can be included in the world, in a way that, for example, Whitehead's philosophy – which includes feelings as 'concrete elements in the nature of actual entities' – does not.

18 This is a word that needs to be used with care, given its history (Wegner 2002). But I also think that the word's brutal edge is important in pointing to the way in which instinct is laid down. I take the unconscious as normally understood to be one part of bare or creaturely life, a specific mode of expressivity.

19 Though I am extremely sceptical of the current tendency to mark out pretty well anything with a bio prefix.

20 Donald (2001) suggests that the analogy of computation as a means of describing cognition is inaccurate. A better analogy would be digestion.

21 In other words, being human involves the evolution of the capacity to have beliefs about beliefs, the evolution, in other words, from behaviour readers to mind readers (Sterelny 2003).

22 The crucial role of language as affect should be noted here; see Riley (2005).

23 Echoing Wittgenstein's observation that what underlies a number of features of language-games, including the following of rules, is the brute 'natural' fact that people just do continue in certain ways in certain situations.

24 Objects are often thought of as interpretable, in that they demand an unreciprocated affection which is a part of person-making. In other words, 'there are no interpretable objects or intentional objects, only what counts as an interpretable object or, better, groups of people who count as interpretable and who, accordingly, deal with certain objects in recognizable ways' (Tamen 2001: 3).

25 This is actor-network theory's presupposition of symmetry formalized.

26 Which still implies intensive corporeal organization.

27 But there is another feminist tradition, of course; see, for example, Parisi (2004).

28 A point that Donna Haraway makes well in her critique of actor-network theory.

29 In any case, flesh, under the imperatives of bioscience, is itself rapidly becoming the subject and object of numerous technological ensembles which are rapidly making it portable, and which, in certain accounts, are extending the imperatives of farming to the human world (Sloterdijk 2006).

30 This is why I am suspicious of making too easy links between labour and existence, a point often made by Lévinas.

31 Many of the same points can apply to occasions of humour or embarrassment; see Billig (2005).

32 See, especially, the book by Soden (2003) on falling.

33 Kwinter stresses the tool-less nature of this activity but this aesthetic is relative, to put it mildly.

34 We should not make too much of this, of course. At different times in history, various means of producing continuously bounded sites have been invented that have stabilized sites over long periods of time. A good example is barbed wire (see Netz 2004).

35 What exactly I mean by this is outlined in some detail in Chapter 6 of this book.

36 And not in some naïve way in which the history of dance as complicit with social structuring.

37   Most particularly, dance provides an understanding of style as a particular way of doing body; 'dance would be the style not as that which is added on to a body in creation itself: style not as that technique through which creation takes place but as pure creativity with no end or ground outside itself' (Colebrook 2005b: 8). The body is neither a norm towards which bodies ought to strive nor a mere existing that expresses some prior norm of human creativity. However, I retain some scepticism about the residual romanticism I find in this quasi-Deleuzian point of view which is why I finally prefer Deleuze and Guattari's later work on territorialization.

38 See McNeil (2005). I have tried to take in the whole spectrum of senses since my early work. See, for example, my writing on smell and on vision. I am particularly impressed by the histories of the senses currently coming out of North America (See Rath 2003).

39 Thus I have become very interested in the possibilities of transposing imitative theories like that of Tarde with the kinds of conflictual mimesis championed by Girard (cf. Fleming 2004).

40 I should add that I start out from the assumption that

> there is no essence, no historical or spiritual vocation, no biological destiny that humans must enact or realize. That is the only reason why something like an ethics can exist because it is clear that if humans were or had to be this or that substance, this or that destiny, no ethical experience would be possible there would only be tasks to be done.
>
> (Agamben 1993: 43)

41 Thus, 'God is above all the name for the pressure to be alive in the world, to open to the too much of pressure generated in large measure by the uncanny presence of my neighbour' (Santner 2001: 9). Or, as Latour (2002: 7) puts it, in a thoroughly Whiteheadian vein, 'God is the feeling for positive, instead of negative prehensions'.

42 In Aristotelian terms, as *energeia*. It is worth remembering that in past times art and craft were much more closely bound together: indeed the word for craft used to be 'art'. This is an occlusion that I want to see revived as a politics. Additionally I would want to see the meaning of craft broadened out to cover activities such as teaching and the like, which are too often excluded from its orbit.

43 The metaphor of craftsmanship has other benefits too, for example, a willingness to explore ambiguity, a commitment to the task for its own sake, and its often tacit nature.

44 That does not just mean the spatialization of experience as an always having been possible (see Middleton and Brown 2006) but also the way in which spaces feel.

45 This very perception may itself be historically specific, of course. See Wall (2006).

46 Given the size of the gut – its surface area would cover a small room if laid out flat – this really would be a geography.

47   As in the work of Emmanuel Lévinas.

48 As in the work of Michel Henry.

49 A restatement of the classic point that thought cannot be divorced from its object, understood now as meaning that 'the ontology of the sensible is not separable from the constitution of material assemblages and processes themselves' (Toscano 2004a: xxi).

50 See, in particular, work on the spaces of sound and especially the efforts to reconstruct historical soundscapes (e.g. B.R. Smith 1999; Rath 2003; Sterne 2003).

51 For example, I believe that Deleuze and Guattari's work suffers from a residual structuralism (see Schatzki 2002) and too great an emphasis on an unalloyed 'bliss of action' (Deleuze 1988b: 28).

52 Indeed, I am highly sceptical that the history of Western thought could ever be written as if it were simply the history of a set of philosophical excursions.

53 'In fact, a philosophical theory is an elaborately developed question, and nothing else; by itself and in itself, it is not the resolution to a problem, but the elaboration, to the very end, of the necessary implications of a formulated question' (Deleuze 1991: 116)

54 I should add that I think this manuscript is amongst the last that will take on such a dreary form. It seems clear to me that to do justice to the ambitions of much of what I am writing about requires a new cursive register, one that mixes all manner of media and presentational styles in order to achieve its goals, that can roll out at different speeds, and that, as a result, can really perform.

55 Conceived of as if by Malebranche, as the natural prayer of the soul, an attentiveness to all living creatures.

56 It is, of course, possible to take the theoretical technology wielded in this book too seriously. As Gombrowicz put it with reference to existentialism:

> It seems impossible to meet the demands of Dasein and simultaneously have coffee and croissants for an evening snack. To fear nothingness but to fear the dentist more. To be consciousness, which walks around in pants and talks on the telephone. To be responsibility, which runs little shopping errands downtown. To bear the weight of significant being, to install the world with meaning and then return the change from ten pesos.
>
> (cited in Simic 2006: 22)

57 Eagleton (2006: 26) puts it nicely in describing Jameson's style: 'it rolls its way across an intellectual landscape which it levels beneath it, emulsifying everything until connections become more insistent than conflicts'.

58 The evolution of new protocols carries on apace. Thus, since I wrote the first chapter, co-production with the consumer has become a new orthodoxy, signalled by its arrival in the pages of *Harvard Business Review*.

59 The reference to atmospheres consciously summons up the work of Peter Sloterdijk, whose work on spaces is, I think, the closest to what I am trying to achieve (see Sloterdijk 2005a, 2005b).

2   Re-inventing invention

1 Importantly, this is not meant to function as a vanguardism of the kind found in, for example, some variants of Italian Marxism (Wright 2002). It is imperative to understand that the economy is a radical heterogeneity that is always diverse, and cannot therefore be captured in precisely this way, as though everything will eventually follow on.

2 However, as I will make clear, this is not just a case of opening up new 'fishing grounds', to use market research parlance. It is a change in how the commodity itself is conceived.

3 The speed of this onset is almost certainly the result of the cultural circuit of capital which is able to circulate theories at an accelerated rate showing, once again, that theory has increasingly transmuted into method, a method of producing maximum connectivity with the minimum of material. What we see is theory becoming a second nature but that theory is of an attenuated, instrumental kind.

4 It is important to note that I am trying to provide a diagram of a new set of tendencies that are now infesting the business of innovation and which together form a functioning process. *This does not, of course, preclude all kinds of other models of innovation from*

continuing to exist. Rather it points to the construction of a novel overlay. The economy is heterogeneous and there is no reason to think that there is just one model of innovation.

5   It is not at all clear that this new world is restricted to the traditional Western economic core, not just because parts of countries like China and India are booming but because, in the light of considerable information and communications technology take-up, they are seeing some of the same phenomena. For example, consumer communities are booming in China, based around websites like AliBaba (or at least its e-Bay like subsidiary, TaoBao) and EasyReach. Significantly, both of these have recently been subject to Western equity buy-ins.

6   It is a profitable exaggeration at this moment in time, since it can be retailed as a problem to which consultants can find solutions.

7   The two not being exactly the same. For a long period of time writing was a limited skill in the same way that touch typing is today.

8   This is not to say that capitalism has not attempted to use the structure of forethought. One thinks just of Packard's (1960) *The Hidden Persuaders* and the general panic in the 1950s and 1960s about the subliminal powers of advertising.

9   This work often focused on various kinds of practical organizational knowledge, for example, influencing and co-operating with others.

10 The resort to neuroscience may be partly to do with the need of management writers to seek out credibility by associating themselves with science but it is not just rhetorical (Hill 2003).

11 See, for example, D. Miller's (1998) exposition of love as a key element of shopping.

12 For example, see the various emotional instruments used by the advertising, market research and human resources industries, as in, for example, Goleman's Emotional Competence Inventory, widely retailed by the Hay Group as a means of evaluating individuals and organizations.

13 Indeed, Kellogg's has patented its cornflake crunch.

14 As in the Stefan Floridian Waters aroma used by Singapore Airlines, a scent formerly used in flight attendants' perfume that has now been extended right across the airline experience, from the hot towels before take-off to the cabin air freshener (Lindstrom 2005).

15 Brands are probably the arena of the economy in which this kind of thinking and practice has gone farthest. The practice of constructing 'multisensory', experiential brands that function across all the senses has become more and more common (Lindstrom 2005). Brands must be 'five-dimensional', appealing to all five senses. Why? Because in a world in which there is a profits squeeze which demands more commodity performance for less, and in which traditional means of advertising are becoming less and less effective, and in which consumers are becoming more interactive, the fight for brand definition demands more and more tapping of sensory potential. To put it another way, brands are attempting to build a certain kind of authenticity, based on co-creation, on acknowledging context and on passions, both in the sense of tapping into the passions of consumers and in the sense of becoming more passionate, through appeals to the full range of the senses. 'Emotional positioning' becomes vital.

16 Of affects, concepts and percepts all built into particular environments.

17 A factor that has become much more important as the speed of production processes has increased.

18 See the comments by Callon and Muniesa (2005) concerning new forms of calculation brought into being by devices like information technology.

19 The use of the diminutive here is no doubt suspect, given that three decades of research on consumption have shown just how rich a field of cultural practice it is.

20 Though by no means all: many products have become simpler or so difficult to operate on that they require professional intervention (e.g. many repairs of automobile electronics).

21 What is interesting has been the way in which information technology has so rapidly become a pervasive feature of the design and presence of commodities as societies have become incorporated in an information culture so that increasingly information has a *feel* to it generated by the interface (Liu 2004).

22 These building forms are not restricted to the biosciences, of course. For example, the Isaac Newton Centre at Cambridge is dependent on the same idea of high interaction.

23 Although, at none of them could I find systems that go as far as some commercial organizations. For example, some IT firms search the hard drives and e-mails of their researchers for evidence of ideas and interests that can be sent on to others in the organization.

24 Notice the similarity to what is found now in a number of organizations (see Storey and Salaman 2005).

25 Though it is taken from Marx, I am not myself keen on this terminology which nowadays has too many associations with the idea of some immaterial, virtual realm conjured up by information and communications technology.

26 The analogy with the media is a good one. Not only does play back involve media models but more and more of experience is mediatized.

27 This does not mean that all kinds of perception are not outside consciousness: perception is a wide-ranging faculty.

28 These conceptual determinations assume a variety of *capacities* which trace out what matters: in turn, they therefore assume a particular materiality which reciprocally confirms those determinations. And, in part, they bring that materiality into existence by arranging time and space so that they produce the requisite followings-on (percepts) which themselves confirm that particular existence. They also assume a particular self-efficacy, a belief in the abilities of what counts as a person which depends precisely on what those abilities are supposed to be and what their supposed consequences are (Bandura 1997).

29 Ways which are closer to a musical score than an old-fashioned calculating machine. As I have pointed out elsewhere (Thrift 2005b), these latter functions are now so widespread that they have simply become part of the background.

30 See Virno (2004) on opportunism as a technical virtue.

31 Hill (2003: 42). Business can do Bloch too.

32 Hence, for example, multinationals' increasing interaction with non-governmental organizations. They need to know what criticisms are coming up.

33 Indeed, it is possible to argue that theory is itself becoming a source of affect.

3   Still life in nearly present time

1 I use the word 'instincts' here to signal my intention to try to transcend humanist approaches to nature, though many of these 'instincts' are complex biological–cultural constructions.

2 Then when we say 'information' in everyday life, we spontaneously think of information as the result of a discarding of information. We do not consider the fact that there is more information in an experience than in an account of it. It is the account that we consider to be information. But the whole basis of such an account is information that is discarded. Only after information has been discarded can a situation become an event people can talk about. The total situation we find ourselves in at any given time is precisely one we cannot provide an account of: we can give an account of it only when it has 'collapsed' into an event through the discarding of information (Norretranders 1998: 109).

3 Many of these bodily practices necessarily contain improvisational elements, since they are always performative instantiated in the capacities of particular bodies and content-specific (see Hayles 1999; Thrift 2000a). Think only of the face with its potent muscular geography (cf. Brothers 1997; McNeil 1998; Taussig 1998).

4 This is a very different notion of metaphor from that employed by Lakoff and Johnson (1998) which seems to me to over-determine both the idea of metaphor and the process of metaphorization.

5 In other words, the notion of speed is part of the rhetoric of how Euro-American societies go on,

6 There are interesting connections here with all kinds of earlier body practices from drill to dance which could be brought out and which are brought together in the twentieth-century city in the work of writers like Laban (see Thrift 2000a).

7 The practice of photography, in other words, is as important for its process of doing as for its results (photographs which are normally rarely looked at).

8 Aided, in certain cases, by stimulants like drugs.

9 All these practices are heightened by the growing sense, stimulated by the media, of audience (see Abercrombie and Longhurst 1998); we now constantly see and take in other body practices: ways of walking and the like. This mundane anthropology is becoming more and more important.

10 Thus, for example:

> when we approach a great fir on the crest of a mountain, we stand tall or our eyes travel upward to the clouds and eagles, when we approach a willow our gaze sweeps in languid arcs across the backs of lime branches rippling over the lake. When we come upon a fallen tree, we have difficulty seeing it is a willow or a pine or a tree; it appears as a thicket about a log, in a confused lay out inviting closer scrutiny.
>
> (Lingis 1998: 53)

11 Note also Derrida's thoughts on nature as a form of writing (see Kirby 1997).

12 Ancient Christian prayer cited in de Certeau (1992: 1).

13 The main marketing slogan of the American Wilderness Experience.

14 See think of the following quotation as a business proposition.

> To recognise a person is to recognise a typical way of addressing tasks, of envisaging landscapes, of advancing hesitantly and cautiously or ironically, of playing exuberantly down the paths to us. Someone we know is someone we relate to posturally, someone we walk in step with, someone who maintains a certain style of positioning himself or herself and gesticulating in conversation and with whom we take up a compromising position as we talk.
>
> (Lingis 1998: 53)

15 I realize that this section might he read as a Baudrillardian account of the rise of simulacra. This is not, however the way I would want it read. Baudrillard's accounts are far too sweeping for me and lack any but a stylized historical sense.

4 *Driving* in the city

1 In what follows, I have generally used the translation by Blonsky (de Certeau 1987) retitled 'Practices of space' which generally strikes me as clearer than the Rendall translation (de Certeau 1984).

2 Hence, the original French title of *The Practice of Everyday Life*, namely *L'Invention du quotidien*.

3 De Certeau's humanism is not one that proceeds from a fully formed human subject but is based in practices, and the tension between humans to be found in the encounters that take place within them. According to Conley (2001: 485), it combines a residue of Hegelianism or existentialism with Christian ethics.

4 This distinction between anthropological space and the geometrical space of grids and networks is taken from Merleau-Ponty (Conley 2001).

5 In any case, to take the UK as an example, journeys on foot now account for only between a quarter and a third of all journeys, and are still declining as a proportion of all journeys. However, this proportion is higher in inner urban areas (Hillman 2001).

6 From the vast scriptural apparatus of the travel industry to the evolution of videos on power walking (Morris 1998).

7 I make no value judgements about automobility here because these judgements seem to me to have too often stood in the way of an understanding of the attractions of the phenomenon. This is certainly not to say, however, that I am some kind of fan of automobility, and for all the usual reasons (see Rajan 1996).

8 There may, of course, be a simple, if rather glib, explanation for this elision: in 1967, driving with his parents from his brother's house to a restaurant, de Certeau was involved in a serious automobile collision in which his mother was killed and he lost the sight of one eye. Miraculously his father, the driver, was hardly injured at all. Apparently, according to Dosse (2002), the accident caused de Certeau considerable guilt because he felt he had been responsible for the delay which caused his father to drive so fast. I am indebted to Tom Conley for this information. As Stuart Elden has noted in a personal communication, this lack of the presence of the automobile is in marked contrast to a writer like Henri Lefebvre, who mentions cars at various points in his works. Lefebvre was, of course, a cab driver for two years of his life.

9 Some other traversiste authors like Paul Virilio and, latterly, Marc Auge do tackle the automobile but in a high-handed and, more often than not, hyperbolic tone which I want to get away from.

10 These techniques of wholesale landscape design have existed since at least the 1930s. The work of Merriman (2001) shows how important they were in, for example, the construction of the British motorway system. I am indebted to Geof Bowker for pointing me to viewshed analysis.

11 I am indebted to Michael Curry for this information.

12 This statistic includes a good number of homes in trailer parks and custom-designed 'estates' that are only nominally mobile, it should be added. Some of these homes now have to comply with local building codes but, even so, even the most immobile mobile homes are still sold, financed, regulated and taxed as vehicles.

13 Thus, there is a whole 'manipulatory area', as Mead put it, of sensing objects which cannot be understood as just the incarnation of symbolic systems but relies on various kinaesthetic dispositions held in the bodily memory. In turn, we can speak of objects pushing back.

14 As Katz (2000: 46) rightly points out, the location of this hybrid is not exactly locatable: 'The driver operates from a moving point in a terrain for interaction, and that terrain is defined in part by the driver's current style of driving'.

15 Drivers often seem to assume that other forms of road user embodiment (e.g. cyclists) should conform to the same rules of the road as they do and become irate when such users follow what seem to be, in some sense, unfair tactics.

16 Thus, by one account, automobile electronics now account for more than 80 per cent of all innovation in automobile technology. On average, modern cars now have some four kilometres of wiring in total. In some higher-end vehicles, electronics components account for 20 to 23 per cent of total manufacturing cost. By 2005, by one estimate, higher-end vehicles will require an average power supply of 2.5 KW and consequently there are moves towards 36 volt batteries and 42 volt systems (Leen and Heffernan 2002).

17 Such a viewpoint is, of course, congruent with many intellectual developments of late, such as actor-network theory and other developments originating from the sociology of science (cf. Schatzki 2002), and is taken to its farthest extreme by Rouse (1996: 149) who denotes 'practice' in such a way that it can embrace the actions of both humans

and nonhumans as 'the field within which both the determinations of objects and the doings and respondings of agents are intelligible'. Clearly, such a development can itself be taken to be historically specific.

18 A number of cars now have speed limiters. More impressively, one car manufacturer has now introduced so-called active cruise control which senses the traffic ahead and throttles back or even brakes if the driver gets too close to the car ahead.

19 I have always puzzled about how de Certeau would interpret speech recognition systems: as yet another blow for the binary logic of an informationalized capitalism, as a new form of machinic enunciation, and so on.

20 To some extent, this process is already happening in a muted form. As one referee pointed out, software is already a means by which manufacturers tie their purchasers to a service relationship. For example, if a boot lock fails on some models, the onboard systems fail, and the solution – which in the past was mechanical – now requires the application of specialist software and technical know-how.

21 The two terms are nearly interchangeable but ergonomics is often reserved for a narrower aspect of human factors dealing with anthropometry, biomechanics, and body kinematics whereas human factors is reserved for wider applications. Terms like cognitive engineering have also come into vogue.

22 The sheer number of switches and instruments on modern cars has become an ergonomic problem in its own right, since 'dashboard clutter' is thought to have significant safety risks. All manner of solutions are being tried, such as rotating dials.

23 One referee pointed out that such developments may change the nature of 'driving' as a skill, rather in the way that a new driving skill has become spotting speed cameras and taking appropriate action. Certainly, developments like in-car satellite navigation are already transferring wayfinding skills into software. Presumably, other skills will follow as cars and cities increasingly drive drivers.

24 Indeed, one of the key technological frontiers is currently artificial ethology and there is every reason to believe that innovations from this field will make their way into automobility (Holland and McFarland 2001).

25 The quotation is from a 1930s text by Saint-Paul Roux called *Vitesse*.

26 The recent science fiction novel by Clarke and Baxter (2002) can, I think, be seen as a meditation on this state of affairs.

27 'Anachoristic', presumably. However, it is important to note, as V.A. Conley (2001) has pointed out, that de Certeau had some hopes for the liberatory potential of new computer technology.

5 Movement-space

1 In so doing, I am attempting to move just a little way ahead of the past, and produce what Manovich (2001) calls, not simply following Foucault, a theory of the present. See also Thrift (2004a). Necessarily, the paper is therefore speculative in parts but I do not apologise for this. Rather, through this speculation, I want to show the possibility of new properties emerging in the world.

2 As Irigaray puts it

> When Heidegger questions the danger of a modern physico-technological project for man's inhabitation of space, isn't this questioning still posed through a Greek perspective? The opening that is brought about by the modern prospecting of space is closed up again by a topo-logic that is still Aristotelian, and, to some extent, pre-Socratic.
>
> (1999: 20)

3 Authors like Wolfram (2002) argue that the world should be described in algorithmic terms.

4 'Now we have finally found [the Greek mathematician]: thinking aloud, in a few formulae, made up of a small set of words, staring at a diagram, lettering it' (Netz 1999: 167).

5 To use Newton's well-worn phrase in *Principiae*.

6 For an elaboration of these points, see Thrift (2004a) and Fraser (2002).

7 Perhaps the best example of this is a number of modern fighter planes which are inherently unstable and are able to fly only because of the numerous calculations and recalculations made by on-board computers which keep the plane in trim.

8 Interestingly, Anlo seem more concerned with stabilizing the internal state than the external environment.

9 So, for example, the interoceptive and proprioceptive sensations get comparatively short shrift as formal categories of the senses in Euro-American societies, even though their importance can hardly be denied.

10 At the same time, the hand allows humans to think of tools as separate from themselves in a way which animals would find difficult to do.

11 In the Anlo world, for example, touching something soft and touching something hard are regarded as two quite distinct phenomena, two separate ways of touching and experiencing.

12 Activities like geocaching seem to me to be the first of many attempts to make new kinds of way in a world where co-ordinates are easily established. In a sense, they are new rounds of exploration of an already explored world.

6 Afterwords

1 Of course, in this chapter, as elsewhere, I am trying to avoid Wittgenstein's extreme ethical individualism, and his lack of historical sense.

2 As will become clear, my perspective is what Deleuze (1997a) calls cartographic rather than psychoanalytic, but I think there are some clear and obvious connections between these two approaches. See, for example, Billig's recent (1999) work on the 'dialogical unconscious'.

3 These affinities date from an attempt (Thrift 1983) to produce a 'science of the particular', a phrase often deployed in actor-network theory (see, for example, Law and Benschop 1997: 179).

4 A whole paper could be written on this issue. Suffice it to say, for now, that this chapter is, in a sense, an attempt to write/not-write the human in nonhumanist, distributed ways which can avoid the myth of self-presence. I am not trying to create a new humanism: 'the hideous anthropomorphic colonialism of a wholesale making conscious' (McClure 1998: 11). But, on the other hand, I do not want to go as far as Deleuze, for whom there is only matter-energy and the human is 'merely the eventual sediment of the continual process of desiring-production; they are neither its means nor its ends' (McClure 1998: 181). I want, in other words, to retain the tension of the in-between that has produced certain human capacities to produce.

Glendinning puts it well when he writes that

> What is needed, then, is a conception of human existence which eschews bald naturalism but which does not simply affirm a new humanism. Achieving this, I am suggesting, will perforce require a new account of human behaviour in general; an account which explains how something manifest in that behaviour might be (pace humanism) 'immanent to the behaviour as such' and yet (pace bald naturalism) 'transcendent in relation to the anatomical apparatus' (Merleau-Ponty).
>
> (1998: 4)

5 As Gell puts it,

> the point I want to emphasise here is that the means we generally have to form a notion of the disposition and intentions of 'social others' is via a large number of

abductions from indexes which are neither 'semiotic conventions' or 'laws of nature' but something in between.

(1998: 15)

It is this something in-between which I try to lay out in this paper.

6 I am well aware that this description of the world can be seen as resting on an assumption of restless change that is built into many current Euro-American practices (Strathern 1996). However, as I hope will become clear, this assumption is not a correct one.

7 This said, I would not want to go along with all Deleuze's thoughts on the event, which seem to me to move perilously close to a kind of vitalist mysticism.

8 In particular,

Because embodiment has both a material and a sentient aspect to it, we do more than know a ready-made physical reality through our separate bodies; we transform it through the actions we make together. In the case of something like flirtation, what is conveyed is not simply an emotion but an invitation, a call to the other to participate. The material aspect of the body then takes on a greater significance, because the physical world is now detained in relation to social projects, shared and contested meanings. What we are capable of showing through our embodied actions, therefore, are matters concerning our social condition. While this includes face-to-face relationships between individuals, such as those involving flirtation or play, it also extends to all kinds of groupings and crowds in which matters of collective feeling are nurtured and conveyed by virtue of the physical presence of those concerned.

(Radley 1996: 560–561)

9 In other words, personal agency is not just human agency.

10 Peirce was, of course, a major influence on both Deleuze and Derrida. There are some fascinating connections to be drawn between Deleuze and Derrida and North American pragmatism. See, for example, Eldridge (1998).

11 In particular, in Simmel's later work, which views 'human freedom as lying precisely not in humankind's capacity for purposive action but rather in our capacity to break with purpose' (Joas 1996: 156).

12 Or as Gordon puts it:

A different way of knowing and working about the social world, an entirely different mode of production still awaits our invention. Such a mode of production would not reject the value of empirical observation per se, but might, to use Taussig's words be more 'surprised' by social construction, the making and making up of social worlds, thereby giving it the respect it deserves.

(1997: 21)

13 In turn, academic practice would have to change to something rather like Albright's description of 'witnessing', an observant participation in which

to witness something implies a responsiveness, the response/ability of the viewer towards the performer. It is radically different from what we might call the 'consuming' gaze that says 'here, you entertain me, I bought a ticket, and I'm going to sit back and watch'. This consuming gaze doesn't want to get involved, doesn't want to give anything back. In contrast, what I call witnessing is much more interactive, a kind of perceiving (with one's whole body) that is committed to a process of mutual dialogue. These are precedents for this responsive watching in Quaker Meetings, African–American notions of being witness, the responsive dynamic of many evangelistic religions, as well as the aesthetic theory of rasa in

> Classical Indian Dance, to mention only a few such examples. The act of witnessing, however, raises the stakes of audience engagement, sometimes making the audience members uncomfortable, sometimes providing highly charged responses to the work. This is particularly true of dances that foreground issues of social, political and sexual difference in ways that make the spectator aware of the performer's cultural identity as well as his or her own cultural positioning.
>
> (Albright 1997: xxii)

14 Goffman was also much influenced in his early career by Simmel.

15 Issues of vision and visuality are clearly important, but I have set an extended treatment aside in this chapter for reasons of space (see Phelan 1993; Thrift 1998).

16 Thus 'the modern faculty of daydreaming means that people are able to imagine themselves performing in front of other people and also imagine the reactions that others will have' (Abercrombie and Longhurst 1998: 103).

17 This is in line with Deleuze's chief principle that his work is a 'logic of multiplicities' but the multiple is never given in itself, it must be made. Thus works of art, for example, are machines for producing nonpreexistent relations (cf. Rodowick 1997).

18 Though I am drawn to Deleuze and Guattari's work, it does have significant problems. Five of these seem important. First, Deleuze and Guattari tend to evacuate the social.

> Robert Castel says that Freud had two 'lines' on the question of cathexis. Sometimes he placed it in a social structure; but elsewhere, he reduces institutions to forms of psychic cathexis, and explains social organisations in terms of psychological conflict. The second direction leads to a dead-end, but the first shows the importance of individual investment in social and political structures. Deleuze and Guattari have taken more from Freud than they think. They obviously believe in collective desire and social-historical desire, but they also adopt the second line, albeit in a less crude form. They interpret history from the point of view of desire, and therefore miss the social qua social. The non-metaphors of machine, flow and coding end up having a reductive effect, desire eats society away.
>
> (Lecercle 1990: 192–198)

Second, on one reading, they insist on singularities, on individual arrangements of desire, rather than mediate generalizations, on particular historical situations rather than a global class analysis.

> But even when they assert the value of singularities, they are bound to use general concepts, such as fascism. Even if schizo-analysis makes no claim to be a science in the ordinary sense of the term, it has to conform to certain general rules, and the rule which forbids rise to general rules of interpretation is itself a form of interpretation. A familiar paradox.
>
> (Lecercle 1990: 142)

Third, Deleuze and Guattari's attitude to history is similarly paradoxical. They want to be both more and less historical. For example,

> the critique of those unhistorical concepts used by Freud (the unconscious, the family . . .) is a powerful one. But . . . their own critique ultimately takes back an unhistorical concept: like ideology, fascism is both historical and unhistorical. Nomadic trides, we are told, forever fight the state, and their war machine eventually captures it. Which tribe? and which desert? The price for such sweeping generalities is high: the disappearance of concrete historical analysis.
>
> (Lecercle 1990: 143)

Fourth, there is a further paradox. Though Deleuze and Guattari work through a logic of multiplicity they proceed through careful dichotomies: paranoia versus schizophrenia, molar versus molecular, deterritorialization versus reterritorialization, smooth versus striated, and so on. Implicitly, they respect certain boundaries. Lecercle for example, writes of their critique of language that

> They opt for parole against language, style against grammar, dialects or idiolects against standard languages, fragments against syntax, the minor against the general, the material (speech acts are material in so far as they are acts) against the abstract. This is the methology of the professional smuggler: give me a frontier, and I shall cross it; give me a rule, and I shall break it. But . . . the crossing of a linguistic frontier is an ambiguous act, since it acknowledges the rule which it breaks.
>
> (Lecercle 1990: 143)

Fifthly, the body tends to disappear into the flow of desiring-production:

> while the poststructuralist commitment to fluidity and flow, after centuries of dualist thought, is indeed refreshing, Deleuze and Guattari's own particular treatment of these issues; especially their emphasis on the process of 'becoming', not only results in a radical reconfiguration of materiality itself, but also, as we have seen, an 'acidic dissolution' or disintegration of the body and the subject (i.e. the process of 'becoming-imperceptible'); a position which, quite simply, loses too much in the 'process'. A similar fate, in other words, befalls both the Deleuzo-Guattarian and the Foucaldian body; first it becomes elusive and eventually it 'disappears' altogether.
>
> (S.T. Williams 1998: 74)

19 And

> the relation between performance and practice turns on this moment of improvisation. Performance embodies the expressive dimension of the strategic articulation of practice. The italicized expression here could stand as our definition of performativity itself. It is manifest in the expression as part of the 'way' something is done on a particular occasion: the particular orchestration of the pacing, tension, evocation, emphasis, mode of participation, etc. in the way a practice (at the moment), is 'practised', that is, 'brought off'. It gives the particular improvisation of a practice in a particular situation its particular turn of significance and efficiency for oneself and others at the time and in the moment where habitude becomes action. This performativity is located at the creative, improvisatory edge of practice in the moment it is carried out, though everything that comes across is not necessarily intended.
>
> (Schieffelin 1998: 199)

20 Although many performances are bound up with text, often very consciously, as in the case of geometrical dance (see Franko 1993) which then elicited a counterreaction: 'antitextual or burlesque dance was an attempt to establish a legibility for dance independent of verbal means. Such aesthetic autonomy had political significance when a body, independent of language, could mean something "more" or other than what language said it did' (Franko 1993: 5). Franko goes on to point out that in dance text is often a metaphor for autocratic power.

21 As Turner noted in his discussion of liminality, in turning the world upside down for an instant, the power of the dominant order could be reinforced. I am indebted to Derek Gregory for this point.

22 But it cannot be reduced to it, not least because text itself tends to convey a dominant ideology of textualism. For example, in philosophy, textualist ideology insists that

> language exhausts the scope of experience, since whatever lies outside of language cannot be thought or given context. Hence Sellars claims that 'all awareness . . . is a linguistic affair'. Gadamer stresses 'the essential logisticallity of all human experience in the world'; Rorty asserts that we humans are 'nothing more than sentential attitudes'; and Derrida declares that there cannot be a 'hors-texte'; a reality whose content could take place, could have taken place outside of language.
>
> Textualist ideology has been extremely helpful in dissuading philosophy from misguided quests for absolute foundations outside of contingent linguistic and social practices. But in making this therapeutic point by stressing what Rorty terms 'the ubiquity of language', textualization also encourages an unhealthy idealism that identifies human being-in-the world with linguistic activity and so tends to neglect or overly textualise nondiscursive somatic experience. As 'the contemporary counterpart of [nineteenth century] idealism', textualism displays idealism's disdain for materiality, hence for the corporeal. Seeking to secure a realm of spirituality after natural science, science had displaced religion's authority and despiritualised the world, idealism focused on mental consciousness and inherited, by and large, the dominant Christian impulse to deprecate the body. After Freud's disenchantment of consciousness, language has become the new representative of the spiritual in contrast to corporeal nondiscursivity.
>
> (Shusterman 1997: 173–174)

In performance studies, there has been a move to performative writing, intended to simulate the twists and turns of practice (see, for example, Phelan 1998). I am not overly convinced by this move which often seems like a series of modernist experiments.

23 Clearly there is a problem of locating performance in the historical record, with which I cannot deal here. The signs and traces of the archive become crucial. But I suspect there are more signs and traces than have been looked for until quite recently.

24 In particular, the literature on dance is part of a growing awareness in feminist theory that bodies are not just moulded, reiterative objects that have an excess arising out of embodiment. For example,

> the bodies of ballet dancers are clearly cultural bodies. In other words, female and male take up the culture definitions of feminity and masculinity through ballet, with its Western aesthetics, offers them. In order to render these representations on stage, what is required is 'a sculpting of the original body into a culture form'. Put in Butler's terminology, the physical practices of dancers are 'reiterative and citational practices'.
>
> But a discourse that views female dancers as nothing more than the passive recipients and unquestioning transmitters of the culture meanings of femininity is too limited. While the world of classical ballet is clearly permeated with gender stereotypes and power inequalities, if the life of a female dancer is as unbearable as society suggested, why would any woman ever aspire to become a professional dancer? And how is it possible that I have met many dancers who, while suffering from the body demands made of them, clearly enjoyed their profession? Are these demands experienced as oppressive or maybe as a continual challenge?
>
> To enable the answering of questions like these, one has to abandon the woman-as-victim model and devote more attention to the stories of female dancers.
>
> (Aalten 1997: 55–56)

Maybe this is one of the reasons why many of the great choreographers have been women, especially of late. Dance calls for a language that is often 'fragments rather than whole, ambiguous rather than clear, and interrupted rather than complete' and it may be that here the feminine form is 'without a sense of formal closure [and] without closure the sense of beginning, middle and end as a central form, it abandons the hierarchical organising principles . . . that served to elide women from discourse' (Case 1998: 129).

25 Thus Lefebvre argued that 'Western philosophy had abandoned the living body as the store of non-formal knowledge (non-savoir) which constitutes a source of potential knowledge (connaissance)' (Kofman and Lebas 1995: 32), in part because it had split time from space:

> in social practice, scientific knowledge and philosophical speculation, an ancient tradition separates time and space like two entities or clearly distinct substances. This in spite of contemporary themes which show a relationship between time and space, or more precisely, express how they are relating to each other. Despite these theories, in the social sciences one continues to split time between lived time, measured time, historical time, work and leisure time and daily time, etc., which usually are studied outside their spatial framework. Now concrete theories have rhythms, or rather, are rhythms and every rhythm implies the relation of time with a space, a localised time, or if one wishes, a temporalised place. Rhythm is always linked to such and such a place, to its place, whether it be the heart, the fluttering of the eyelids, the movement of a street, or the tempo of a waltz. This does not prevent it from being a time, that is an aspect of a moment and a becoming.
>
> (Lefebvre 1995: 230)

As Gregory (1997) points out, Lefebvre's thoughts on psychoanalysis were in part stimulated by a desire to stand against Lacan's psychoanalytic theory through the deployment of a cartographic sensibility (and subjectivity) which could detect those rhythms 'whose existence is signalled only through mediations, through indirect effects of manifestations' (Lefebvre 1991: 205).

26 Though Gane (1993) quite rightly notes the gender imbalance of so many of these partnerships what surprises Chadwick and de Courtivron (1993: 7) is that they often generate 'multiple creativities' which can 'provide us with a renewed sense of wonder at the endless complexities of partnership itself'.

27

> Dewey wanted philosophers to see that nondiscursive experience could be used to enrich knowledge, not just the 'felt' quality of living. That such experience had no value for philosophy's favourite cognitive goal of epistemological justification did not mean that it had no other cognitive value. A better measured sense of breathing could provide a calmer, better measured process of thought; an ineffable flush of energetic evaluation could spur one to think beyond habitual limits.
>
> (Shusterman 1997: 167)

28 Such views as Foucault professes are not so far removed, as Shusterman (1997) notes, from those of Emerson and Thoreau for which 'intellectual tasting of life will not supersede muscular activity' (Emerson 1942: 236).

29 One of the remarkable ironies of contemporary life is that these kinds of thoughts are best recognized by modern business theorists, and are beginning to be applied (cf. Krogh and Roos 1995; see also George 1998). For example, Krogh and Roos (1995) take what they call an 'anti-representationist' perspective which is more relevant to practice by rejecting some of the assumptions of the cognitivist perspective and instead emphasizing the embodied, autopoetic perspective of Maturana and Varela.

8   Spatialities of feeling

1 This paper was occasioned by a challenge from Doreen Massey to think more seriously about the politics of affect. That I have tried to do!

2 This emotional labour can turn up in unexpected places. Take the example of the trading floors of large investment banks: 'traders frequently and consistently speak of the need to manage emotions, they develop routines for dealing with these emotions, and they consider emotion management part of the expertise and savvy of professional trading' (Knorr Cetina and Bruegger 2002: 400). The last three examples are all taken from Katz's (2000) seminal book.

3 Why, for example, are there no studies of cities of tears or laughter which do not approach these subjects as other things?

4 Virtues like courage, stamina and bravery arise from restraing one's immediate desires. Another good illustration of this point is Sophocles' *Antigone*, in which, in a medium that Plato deplores, similar criticisms arise (Butler 2002). Antigone's claim to a right to grieve and bury her traitorous brother corrupts the state from within as the spectacle erodes public judgement.

5 Of course, there are emotions through the history of philosophy which have been considered politically virtuous. Love for wisdom was an affect that even Plato (in *The Symposium*) wanted to separate from the dangerous madness of love and other such waywardnesses. Hegel mentioned love and generosity as desirable emotions. And so on.

6 A good review of both areas is provided by Reddy (2001). It seems likely that there are, in fact, some emotional states which are common to all societies at all times (e.g. shame) but, equally, there are some states which are massively at variance.

7 For example, Ekman's work was strongly influenced by that of Tomkins on the face, and the ghosts of Gregory Bateson and Charles Darwin lurk in the background fairly constantly.

8 These bodily resources are manifold and many of them have not been fully considered. For example, one of the most potent means of bodily communication is clearly touch. It can, according to the type of encounter, produce feelings of affection and joy and equally feelings of insecurity and inhibition (Montagu 1986; Field 2001). Touch in turn leads on to consideration of the hand as the chief touching organ, a haptic extension which has great biological-cultural complexity (think only of the handshake or the salute or clapping, the various means of writing or the lover's touch) (see Tallis 2003). In turn development of the hand seems to have been a crucial factor in the development of our brain. Similar chains of affect/intelligence/development can be found, for example, for smell and balance.

9 Thus, for Tomkins, affects *are* the correlated responses (involving the facial muscles, the viscera, the respiratory system, the skeleton, changes in blood flow, vocalizations, and so on) that an organism makes to a situation, which produce an analogue of the particular gradient or intensity of stimulation impinging on it

10 Sedgwick (2003) gives the example of enjoyment of a piece of music leading to wanting to hear it over and over again, listen to other music or even training to become a musician oneself.

11 Tomkins also thought voice and breathing were crucial.

12 In a famous passage from the *Ethics* Spinoza puts this proposition baldly:

> The mind and body are one and the same thing, which is conceived now under the attribute of thought, now under the attribute of extension. Whence it comes about that the order of the concatenation of things is one, or, nature is conceived now under this, now under that attribute, and consequently that the order of actions and passions of our body is simultaneous in nature with the order of actions and passions of our mind.
>
> (*Ethics* III prop. 2, note)

13 Other emotions we might identify like shame and embarrassment do not seem to have common facial expressions.

14 Ekman (1998: 387) goes on to write 'I believe that much of the initial emotion-specific physiological activity in the first few milliseconds of an emotional experience is also not penetrable by social experience', a statement which I am sure is not correct as can be inferred from what comes later in the paper but this does not mean that I would want to deny the influence of biology.

15 For example, interpreting sadness as a sickness.

16 A term that refers to the thesis that we now live in a 'postsocial' world in which social principles and relations are 'emptying out' and being replaced by other cultural elements and relationships, and most notably objects.

   Postsocial theory analyses the phenomenon of a disintegrating 'traditional' social universe, the reasons for this disintegration and the direction of changes. It attempts to conceptualize postsocial relations as forms of sociality which challenge core concepts of human interaction and solidarity, but which nonetheless constitute forms of binding self and other. The changes also affect human sociality in ways which warrant a detailed analysis in their own right (Knorr Cetina 2001: 520).

17 For example, it is relatively easy to generate emotions like fear by dint of this kind of detail (see Altheide 2002).

18 Thus, increasingly, modern educational and training systems stress the need for adaptability and creativity – but within very narrowly defined parameters. They often utilize performance knowledges to inculcate these values.

19 Of course, none of this brief explication of the so-called 'half-second delay' is meant to suggest that conscious awareness is just along for the ride. Rather, we might say that the pre-conscious comes to be more highly valued and, at the same time, conscious awareness is repositioned as a means of focusing and sanctioning action.

20 I will take up this phrase again in considering the work of Bill Viola.

21 I think here about the way in which the work of choreographers like Wigman and Laban was put to the service of mass political events during the Nazi period in Germany.

22 For example, what does it mean to argue for the emancipation of emotional labour? (P. Smith 2002)

23 It is no accident that so many authors have turned to Buddhism for inspiration (cf. Varela 1999; Sedgwick 2003).

24 Subheading taken from a video disk made by Bill Viola in 1986 (see Viola 1995).

25 A good example here is the rise of morphing which provides a visible flux of becoming. Significantly for affect, much of the work in this area has concentrated on the face (see Sobchack 2000).

26 There are obvious forebears for this project apart from Fourier, such as Teilhard de Chardin, James Lovelock and Gregory Bateson.

27 As Sobchack puts it:

> A human face . . . can be seen with a clarity and dimension impossible in 'ordinary' unmediated, lived-body vision. If I get too physically close to another, the other's face loses its precise visible presence as a figure in my visual field even as it increases its haptic presence. The visible face partially blurs as it fills my visual field, thus becoming, in part, its ground. Indeed some of the face flows into indeterminacy and the final invisibility that marks the horizon of my perceptive act. An extreme close-up of a human mediated for me by the projector . . . is given to the experience transformed. It is centered in my visual field.[. . .] Its entirety is the figure of my perception, not its ground, and thus does not flow into indeterminacy in my vision.
> (Sobchack 2000: 185)

28 Viola's work has been heavily criticized by some, for example, for its hackneyed aesthetic, its parasitism of great works of art, its attraction to a narrow spectrum of affects, and so

on. These may or may not be valid criticisms but I am more interested in why Viola's work can elicit strong emotional reactions in the first place.

29 Often extreme slow motion. For example, film is often shot at 300 fps and played back at 30 fps.

30 It is worth remembering that in its original Greek form *mimesis* meant performance (understood as enactment and re-enactment rather than imitation) and, of course, mimesis is still very rarely the production of an exact copy (Rush 1999).

31 Slow-motion film of the face has been a constant in artwork for some time, but I think Viola has managed to get the right speed, unlike some earlier, interminable experiments.

32

> It effectively assists us in discovering the material world with its psychophysical correspondences. We literally redeem this world from its dormant state, its state of virtual non-existence, by endeavouring to experience it through the camera. And we are free to experience it because we are fragmented.
>
> (Kracauer 1960: 300)

33 In using this term , I mean to imply the way in which engineering is always born out of concrete encounters which allow the world to speak back. I am not trying to imply that engineering is just make-it-up-on-the-spot.

9   But malice aforethought

1 As well as gleefully adding more such representations to the stock, I might add.

2 As in the recent conference on metropolitan catastrophes held at the Institute of Historical Research by the Centre for Metropolitan History, which featured a series of historians who were moving their attention from the battlefield to the city as battlefield.

3 I hope that my intention in these papers is clear. I want to begin to place side-by-side a series of themes in my work which have remained relatively separate, notably the articulation of non-representational theory, and especially the exploration of affect, with the changes now taking place in the nature of technologies and the technical. I have consistently tried to bring themes like these (and others, like time) back to the living fabric of the city, but what the juxtaposition of these themes has pushed me to do, in turn, has been to challenge what is meant by the 'living' in the city. In making this rapprochement, I wanted to take particular account of a criticism sometimes made of non-representational theory – and the politics of performance that flows from it – that it is entirely too optimistic. As I hope is clear from what follows, I think that this is both a valid criticism and at the same time names an important political task: to construct a positive politics of affect in what is an increasingly 'intimate public sphere', to use Berlant's phrase (cf. Cvetkovich 2003)

4 This is, of course, a classical Freudian point, as is the point made later that destructiveness is very close to love. Freud's work acts, fittingly perhaps, as a perpetual undertow in this paper.

5 Mouffe's work has, of course, been much influenced by Schmitt.

6 None of this, of course, is to suggest that no attempt should be made to rid the world of all manner of horrors: wars, genocides, tortures, famines, and so forth. Rather, as will become clear, it may be better to attempt to institute lower-level forms of kindness, as a first step at least.

7 In other words, and importantly, I want to stay faithful to Tarde's micrometaphysics which refuses to make a distinction between the complexity of 'large' and 'small', nor necessarily therefore their transformative powers. Following Tarde's reading of Spinoza, everything can be a society.

8 It also points to the fact, often forgotten, that *demolition* is as much a part of the history of cities as construction. But I know of remarkably little work on this aspect of cities,

even after recent traumatic events, except that centred around sense of loss (e.g. of the byways of pre-boulevard Paris).

9 There is beginning to be some work on these companies and their workforces. See, especially, Allen and Pryke (1994).

10 For the record, I have used this pragmatic classification in preference to other such classifications because it seems to me to get closer to the sheer diversity of this sector than other attempts. However, it is worth noting that the labour force statistics of many countries do include some kind of relevant statistics. For example, the US Bureau of Labor Statistics includes 'Installation, maintenance and repair occupations', subdivided into electrical and electronic equipment, vehicle and mobile equipment, and other.

11 See, in particular, Gershuny (1978) on the self-service economy. I do not make much of it here but there is also an obvious connection to the second-hand market which requires repair and maintenance as a matter of course.

12 For example, when Broadband was first introduced, telecommunications engineers would tell each other of the different solutions and shortcuts they had discovered. Later, their telecommunications companies provided them with electronic bulletin boards so that this information could be more widely circulated.

13 Indeed, the standard devices of novels and films often include repair and maintenance workers as quintessential minor characters (Woloch 2003), iconic urban non-icons, from chimney sweeps to plumbers to car mechanics to window cleaners.

14 This is to ignore the plethora of major incident and disaster recovery plans which are periodically rehearsed.

15 Of course, this is a highly debatable statement. In many such cities, it may be that there is *more* repair and maintenance infrastructure oriented to the much greater problems of simply reproducing everyday life. I know of no evidence that would resolve this debate. I am indebted to Stuart Corbridge for this point.

16 Indeed, we might see the expectation of danger as constituting a kind of contract with the future (cf. Salecl 2004). Or perhaps the past. As Robin (2004) points out, the contemporary 'liberalism of fear' that infects too many polities argues that it is fear that motivates public life and structures its exertions. The memories of cruelties past and the threat of cruelties present can be used as justification for liberal norms to colonize the future. As Ignatieff puts it

> In the twentieth century, the idea of human universality rests less on hope than on fear, less on optimism about the human capacity for good than on dread of human capacity for evil, less on a vision of man as maker of his history than of man the wolf toward his own kind.
>
> (Ignatieff 1997: 18)

Needless to say, I want to argue against this tendency.

17 As Dalrymple (2004) points out, some of this may even be excusable, given how few people have any control over their lives. But certainly, once one starts looking, it is possible to see small acts of cruelty everywhere.

18 The fact that small rural communities are often shot through with feuds and vendettas is conveniently forgotten, yet alone the fact that cities are shot through with eaves-dropping and general nosiness: sometimes I wish that cities were a bit more alienated!

19 Thus Schopenhauer argued in *On Human Nature* that 'to the boundless egoism of our nature there is joined more or less in every human breast a fund of hatred, anger, envy, rancour and malice, accumulated like the venom in a serpent's tooth, and waiting only for an opportunity to vent itself' while Stirner wrote of 'surplus rage' and of the value of 'repelling the world' (cited in Lane 2004: 27).

20 And, it might be added, to Elias's argument in *The Civilizing Process*.

21 Notice here that I am not arguing for a reductionist notion of the biological which could simply read off behaviour rigidly from (say) genetic and/or evolutionary

predispositions, as if there were a fixed relation of logical or empirical necessity (Oyama 2000).

22 There are obvious gender connotations in this paper which I am leaving to a later paper.

23 This military art began to migrate into civil society sometime in the nineteenth century but made more specific and extensive inroads after the Second World War when a whole series of logistical practices which had been invented in or just after that war became general means of planning and operationalizing urban movement (Thrift 2004b).

24 There is, of course, a rich urban literature founded on the mixing of the practices of adultery with the contours of the city, all the way from the urban passions of *Madame Bovary* to the suburban angst to be found in the novels of Richard Ford. Much the same point can be made with regard to film.

25 Though I do not attempt it here, it would be possible to situate misanthropy and romantic love in a grid which takes passion as one axis and affect as the other. In turn, such a mapping would allow other kinds of passion (e.g. the revolutionary passion of the early Marx) to be mapped. See Sørenson (2004).

26 Comte coined the noun from the Italian *altrui* ('to or of others') and a phrase in French law, *le bien, le droit d'autrui* ('the well-being and right of the other').

27 I could no doubt have fixed on other authors than Bloch. For example, there is Levinas's extended commentary on war and peace in *Totality and Infinity*, and especially his explorations of exteriority and enjoyment which stresses the constitutive role of the future (see Caygill 2002). But I prefer Bloch's more concrete approach.

28 Though it has to be said that this work is prefigured in numerous ways in Bloch (2000 [1923]).

29 Though I am aware that Diprose is intent on exposing a more general debt to life in a way that is reminiscent of both Bergson and Bloch.

30 I want to understand the city as an organization that exceeds the human, conventionally defined, at every juncture. My sense of kindness therefore exceeds the human, in part because the human has become bogged down in precisely the kinds of stay-at-home ethics that I am most concerned to avoid. In particular, in what is by now a familiar move, I will be stressing the importance of 'thingness' as a determinant of human relationality.

31 Perhaps, indeed, the two are linked in much the same way as loneliness and communication.

32 Yet, it can be said that it is being pursued by a whole series of authors interested in the politics of singularity, from Agamben through Deleuze to Žižek, though often in radically different ways.

33 Which, in a number of its emphases, seems to me to show just how misanthropy can bubble up as a formal government policy. Even as many indicators of such behaviour (e.g. vandalism) seem to be in decline, this policy is forging ahead.

34 Though it is important to point to the more positive contributions of Benjamin and Kracauer.

35 Though I do not go into it here, there is a whole literature on the profusion of 'familiar strangers' dating from the work of Milgram which shows up a similar kind of shadow presence.

36 Although this is often very difficult to know. For example, a recent UK survey showed that 94 per cent of white Britons said that most or all of their friends were of the same race, while 47 per cent of ethnic minority Britons said white people form all or most of their friends. Fifty four per cent of white Britons did not have a single black or Asian person that they considered as a close friend while 46 per cent had at least one such friend (*Guardian* 2004). But debate then raged about whether these results were actually a bad or a good indicator, given the overall ethnic make-up of the population and its spatial distribution.

37 Indeed, love may be part of the problem, insofar as it provides us with a vision of the world which we cannot possibly live up to.

10 Turbulent passions

1 So, to take one just example:

> A disposition to irascibility does not just mean low tolerance for frustration, a reaction or reactivity, but it also involves seeking frustrating situations in the environment and perceiving them as frustrating. Who is not familiar with that? I take a bus but I am in a bad mood, close to feeling like doing something terrible. The bus is packed and the people in it are all in a bad mood as well, which only makes mine worse. I reach the point of wanting to be elbowed and maybe putting myself in a position where I might be elbowed, which would then allow me to let all my anger and frustration of the day loose on some innocent bystander, who in my mind is redefined as an ill-mannered jerk.
>
> (Despret 2004: 94–95)

2 It is worth remembering that many classical social theorists did at the very least wrestle with affect but then let it go by. Weber is a good example. Affect counts as one of his forms of rationality but it is the least developed.

3 In other words, scale is not the issue. A 'small' node like a body, can, in certain circumstances, exert as much agency as a much 'larger' entity.

4 This is a different claim from the one that these programmes are part of a universal human nature which Despret (2004) and others have rightly criticized. Rather, the claim being made is the same as the claim that brown eyes are found in all or most human populations and are a product of human evolution but are not thereby part of a universal human nature: affect programmes display similar heritable variation within populations (Griffiths 1997). It would, in any case be difficult to argue that certain affects can be found in all human cultures when the ethnographic evidence suggests that such a viewpoint cannot be sustained. For example, anger does not seem to be universal: thus both Tahitians and Utku Eskimos appear not to possess this quality (though they recognize it well enough in other peoples).

5 Including, incidentally, a challenge to an assumed centre of a constituting consciousness or a single body from which relations emerge, and by implication an attempt to move beyond investment in a body which could be that of any subject whatsoever (and thus beyond the differing intensities of affect); the striving to think space beyond its human territory, and by implication an attempt to think a world with all kinds of actors' powers, and the project of sensing concepts and percepts beyond one's own purview because all other perceivers are no longer included in one's own space and time, and by implication an attempt to think different folds which play upon the intrinsic differences of possible conceptions and perceptions.

6 A realization that has also underlined that the use of genetics is not necessarily genetic determinism (cf. McKinnon and Silverman 2005).

7 For example, a few hundred generations are easily sufficient to bring a rare mutant allele to dominance in a population, as in the case of lactose intolerance.

8 About 40 per cent of the energy of the human body is expended on digestion, compared with about 10 per cent on locomotion. Thus cooking indirectly provides an enormous extra reservoir of energy. Indeed the biological adaptation to cooking has been so great that if humans consume only raw food they will suffer a major loss of energy with substantial physiological consequences (e.g. in women, menstruation is halted). See, for example, the recent work of Richard Wrangham (cf. Sterelny 2003: 110–112).

9 Pheromone: from the Greek *pherein*, meaning to carry or transfer, and *hormōn*, meaning to excite or stimulate.

10 Although they can often be 'eavesdropped' by other species.

11 This is not far from one common definition of intelligence – a system is intelligent if its behaviour furthers its uninterrupted existence.

12 The problem, of course, is that so little of Tarde's mainstream work is available in English, most notably *Social Laws* and *Underground*, and some edited collections.

13 Such a viewpoint has some obvious disadvantages, of course, which I will have to lay aside for now. In particular, it tends to privilege change when one of the most striking things about cultural systems is their resistance to change, without which a 'ratchet culture' could not exist. 'If the meme was the full story of culture, cultural change as a whole would be as rapid as fashions in clothes or pop songs' (Levinson 2005: 34). It patently is not.

14 Thus, for example, the market becomes an imprint of the passions, not a rational, calculative plane.

15 These models all bear a resemblance to Law's (2004b) model of 'fire'.

16 We need to do this not just on theoretical but also on political grounds as a means of understanding how the envelope of understanding develops as a series of choices about what makes a collective.

17 This is a theme I have taken up in a number of papers (e.g. Thrift 2001).

18 In so doing, Sloterdijk follows an increasingly common argument that an engagement with place, explicit in Heidegger's later work, informs Heidegger's thought as a whole. What guides Heidegger's thinking, in this interpretation, is a conception of philosophy's starting point as our finding ourselves already 'there', situated in the world, in 'place'. Heidegger's concepts of being and place are therefore inextricably bound together.

19 Thus Sloterdijk retains Heidegger's radical emphasis on the recently discovered notion of the environment, as circumstances being adjusted to accommodate the entity in their midst.

20 In bringing forward this formulation, Sloterdijk is making a similar move to those approaches based on joint action that have become increasingly common, as well as the renewed emphasis by Heideggerian scholars on *Mitsein* and *Mitwelt*.

21 It is important to note that in this paper I will be taking embodiment to be a linked, hybrid field of flesh and accompanying objects, rather than a series of individual bodies, intersubjectively linked. I take the presence of objects to be particularly important because they provide new means of linkage (Zielinski 2005) – new folds, if you like.

22 In turn, it is worth remembering that the dynamic range of sensory nerves is startlingly poor: for example, they usually fire at no more than about 200 impulses per second, compared with, say, the 15 log units of variation of intensity of light that the eye can deal with. So consciousness of whatever kind always comes heavily pre-treated (although all manner of tricks of information compression help to overcome some of the limited channel capacity of the sensory nerves to the brain).

23 For example, it is possible to write about the history of facial expressions like the smile (Trumble 2003) because media have been invented which can transmit these expressions.

24 Thus, imitation has proved to be the rarer and cognitively more demanding ability in animals than trial and error.

25 There is, of course, a lively debate in the cognitive sciences and primatology about what exactly is meant by mind-reading (so, for example, some would have it that it requires the construction of full-blown beliefs about others' cognitive states, for example, something I think unlikely). And equally how far it stretches (so, for example, some apparent mind-reading might consist of sophisticated behaviour programmes). But, as Sterelny (2003: 65) puts it, though imitation may not always be a 'theory of mind task . . . it is a cognitively sophisticated one'.

26 It may even be, following Tarde, that memory and habit are forms of imitation: 'engaged in either, we in fact imitate ourselves, instead of another person: memory recalls a mental image, much as habit repeats an action' (Potolsky 2006: 116).

27 This is fairly easily disproved. See Göncli and Perone (2005).

28 For Girard, although mimetic desire is distinctly human it arises out of non-human capacities for imitation.

29 In other words, intentionality does not have to be conscious (Brennan 2004).

30 After all, there are hundreds of mental states that we achieve every day of which we are no longer conscious of having tried to or wanted to achieve that state. Thus critics of Western society (e.g. Castoriadis 2003) who charge it with entering into a 'big sleep' may, in part, simply be describing how the imaginary is instituted.

31 Given the very great difficulty of identifying affective states, still there do seem to be increasing rates of psychiatric morbidity in Western populations. For example, in the UK it is estimated that 11 per cent of the population are suffering from some kind of mixed anxiety order, while in the USA a recent National Comorbidity Survey estimated the prevalence of depression to be 17.1 per cent of the population (Wilkinson 2005). Other surveys have produced even higher figures, though these have often been conducted by organizations with an interest in high proportions.

32 Notice, however, that I am not concentrating on here on the individualized self-evaluative model of creativity and innovation that cross-cuts this model (cf. McKenzie 2001)

33 Notice here that I resist the temptation to link anxiety, obsession and compulsion to affects like fear, anger or rage that can all too easily shade off into violence. This is not because there is no link and it is not to deny that violent fantasies and more general hostile thought about others do seem to be a staple of many cultures (Thrift 2005b). Thus, both men and women in Western cultures seem to routinely have homicidal fantasies while men seem to be particularly prone to practices like stalking. Violence seems to be a key part of human culture although whether human beings have 'homicidal circuits' of the kind described by evolutionary psychologists like Buss (2005: 244) for whom 'killing is a marvellously effective solution to an astonishing array of human social conflicts', is not an argument I wish to become involved in but, at the same time, the world clearly does not lack for contexts – being fired from a job, humiliated by peers, beaten up by a rival, betrayed or dumped by a partner, encroached upon by an interloper – which can generate violence. However, I want to concentrate on affects which are part of the general hum of judgement.

34 Over 1,000 people are killed in Britain each year simply by falling down stairs. The number of sprains and more serious injuries from pavement falls currently goes unrecorded.

35 Although the number of formal news outlets existing outside conglomerate ownership may be declining, news can now be obtained from many other outlets (e.g. the internat, quasi-entertainment media, cable news, radio call-in shows, talk shows, etc.).

36 Though it is important to point out that the traffic is not all one way. For example, certain kinds of polling techniques were originally invented to service the political sphere but were then adapted for corporate clients, mainly as a result of political consultants trying to find greater sources of income (see Klein 2006).

37 Though one needs to be careful here. Such a judgement often follows from under-standing emotion as a weakness, and fear as necessarily bad, whereas fear can serve a number of positive functions, such as promoting vigilance (Brader 2006).

38 Though I make little of it here, they are also the arts of not swaying constituencies too. Sometimes what is needed is to 'reduce the juice' by inducing apathy in its many forms (Eliasoph 1998). But apathy, as Eliasoph shows, can involve a whole series of denials, omissions, suppressions and evasions which add up to much more than a simple absence of thought and action.

39 But it is important to be careful. There is also motivated reasoning and conviction to consider, both of which are based in affect.

40 There are an estimated 7,000 political consultants in the USA.

41 Used differently by different politicians. Bill Clinton hardly used them whilst John Kerry was addicted to them.

42 Thus Karl Rove started out as a direct mail expert.

43 Thus Dick Morris used not just weekly but daily polls for Bill Clinton. At one point in

1995, at the urging of Clinton, he instituted the 'mother of all polls', using a 259 question-long telephone questionnaire which had to be divided into five parts since no one would willingly stay on the phone for the hours it would take to answer every question (D. Morris 1999). Famously Morris used polling data to send the president on a cowboy vacation in Wyoming rather than having him indulge in his and Hillary's preferred vacation on Martha's Vineyard (Klein 2006).

44 One should not go too far: anxiety levels have historically risen and fallen in populations and, in any case, as G.E. Marcus (2002) has argued, anxiety can play a vital and rational role in the political process, serving to promote vigilance as well as servility. The danger is that too many commentators make general statements based on very specific historical circumstances.

45 For example, most recently Gordon Brown has reportedly been being advised by Bob Shrum while Howard Dean is advising the Labour Party more generally on how to conduct viral politics.

46 Such as multiculturalism.

47 For example, Cruz (2005) points to the growth of pathos, compassion and commiseration – what he collectively calls 'ethnosympathy' – at the turn of the century as providing a valuable resource in ethnic struggles.

48 MoveOn produced the highly effective meeting tool which made it possible to produce instant anti-war vigils and was also key in developing support for the Howard Dean campaign.

49 And indeed one of the most interesting outcomes of these developments is the attempt to map them (see Abrams and Hall 2006).

Bibliography

Aalten A. (1997) 'Performing the body, creating culture' in Davis, K. (ed.), *Embodied Practices, Feminist Perspectives on the Body*, London: Sage, pp. 41–58.

Abbott, A. (2001) *Time Matters*, Chicago: University of Chicago Press.

Abercrombie, N. and Longhurst, B. (1998) *Audiences: A Sociological Theory of Performance and Imagination*, London: Sage.

Abrahams, R.D. (2005) *Everyday Life: A Poetics of Vernacular Practices*, Philadelphia: University of Pennsylvania Press.

Abrams, J. and Hall, P. (eds) (2006) *Else/Where: Mapping New Cartographies of Networks and Territories*, Minneapolis: University of Minnesota Press.

Abu-Lughod, L. (1999) *Veiled Sentiments: Honor and Poetry in a Bedouin Society*, Berkeley: University of California Press.

Abu-Lughod, L. (2002) 'Egyptian melodrama – technology of the modern subject?' in Ginsburg, F.D., Abu-Lughod, L. and Larkin, B. (eds) *Media Worlds. Anthropology on New Terrain*, Berkeley: University of California Press, pp. 115–133.

Adkins, L. (2005) 'The new economy, property and personhood' *Theory Culture and Society*, 22: 111–130.

Agamben, G. (1993) *The Coming Community. Minneapolis*, Minneapolis: University of Minnesota Press.

Agamben, G. (1998) *Homo Sacer: Sovereign Power and Bare Life*, Stanford, CA: Stanford University Press.

Agamben, G. (2001) *Potentialities*, Stanford, CA: Stanford University Press.

Agamben, G. (2004) *The Open: Man and Animal*, Stanford, CA: Stanford University Press.

Ahearne, J. (1995) *Michel de Certeau. Interpretation and its Other*, Cambridge: Polity Press.

Ahmed, S. (2004) *The Cultural Politics of Emotion*, Edinburgh: Edinburgh University Press.

Albright, A.C. (1989) 'Mining the dance field: spectacle, moving subjects and feminist theory' *Contact Quarterly* 12: 23–47.

Albright A.C. (1997) *Choreographing Difference: The Body and Identity in Contemporary Dance*, Hanover, NH: Wesleyan University Press.

Allen, J. and Pryke, M. (1994) 'The production of service space' *Environment and Planning D: Society and Space*, 12: 453–476.

Alliez, E. (2004a) 'Remarks on Whitehead', available online at http://www.goldsmiths.ac.uk/csisp/papers/Alliez_Remarks_on_Whitehead.pdf.

Alliez, E. (2004b) *The Signature of the World: What is Deleuze and Guattari's Philosophy?* London: Continuum.

Alliez, E. and Negri, A. (2003) 'Peace and war' *Theory Culture and Society*, 20: 109–118.

Altheide, D.L. (2002) *Creating Fear: News and the Construction of Crisis*, New York: Aldine de Gruyter.

Alvarez, A. (1971) *The Savage God: A Study of Suicide*, New York: Norton.

Amato, J.A. (2004) *On Foot: A History of Walking*, New York: New York University Press.

Amin, A. (2004) 'Regulating economic glabolization' *Transactions of the Institiute of British Geographers*, NS 29: 217–233.

Amin, A. and Thrift, N.J. (2002) *Cities: Re-Imagining Urban Theory*, Cambridge: Polity Press.

Amin, A. and Thrift, N.J. (2005a) 'What's left? Just the future' *Antipode*, 37: 220–238.

Amin, A. and Thrift, N.J. (2005b) 'Citizens of the world. Seeing the city as a site of international influence' *Harvard International Review* 27 (3).

Anderson, C. (2006) *The Long Tail: How Endless Choice is Creating Unlimited Demand*, London: Random House.

Ang, I. (1982) *Watching Dallas: Soap Opera and the Melodramatic Imagination*, London: Routledge.

Ansell Pearson, K. (1997) *Viroid Life: Perspectives on Nietzsche and the Transhuman Condition*, London: Routledge.

Ansell Pearson, K. (1999) *Germinal Life: The Difference and Repetition of Deleuze*, London: Routledge.

Appadurai, A. (1993) 'Number in the colonial imagination' in Breckenridge, C. and van der Veer, P. (eds) *Orientalism and the Postcolonial Predicament: Perspectives on South Asia*, Philadelphia: University of Pennsylvania Press.

Appadurai, A. (2006) *Fear of Small Numbers. An Essay on the Geography of Anger*, Durham, NC: Duke University Press.

Arendt, H. (1970) *On Violence*, San Diego, New York, London: Harcourt Brace.

Arendt, H. (1990) *On Revolution*, Harmondsworth: Penguin.

Armitage, J. (ed.) (2003) Special Issue on Militarized Bodies, *Body and Society* 9: 1–227.

Armstrong, T. (1998) *Modernism, Technology and the Body: A Cultural Study*, Cambridge: Cambridge University Press.

Armstrong, J. and Zúniga, M.M. (2006) *Crashing the Gate. Netroots, Grassroots, and the Rise of People-Powered Politics*, White River, VT: Chelsea Green.

Arsic, B. (2003) Review of Warren Montag: *Bodies, Masses, Power, Spinoza and his Contemporaries, The Review of Metaphysics*, 56 (4): 892–907.

Asad, T (1993) *Genealogy of Religion*, Baltimore, MD: Johns Hopkins University Press.

Ascher, M. (2002) *Mathematics Elsewhere: An Exploration of Ideas Across Cultures*, Princeton, NJ: Princeton University Press.

Ascott, R. (2003) *Telematic Embrace. Visionary Theories of Art, Technology, and Consciousness*, Berkeley: University of California Press.

Atkin, D. (2004) *The Culting of Brands: When Customers Become True Believers*, New York: Portfolio.

Attfield, J. (2000) *Wild Things: The Material Culture of Everyday Life*, Oxford: Berg.

Auslander, P. (1999) *Liveness*, London: Routledge.

Axell, A. (2002) *Kamikaze: Japan's Suicide Gods*, London: Longman.

Badiou, A. (2003) 'Beyond formalization: an interview' *Angelaki*, 8: 111–126.

Baillie, G. (1995) *Violence Unveiled: Humanity at the Crossroads*, New York: Crossroad Publishing Company.

Balázs, B. (1970) *Theory of the Film: Character and Growth of a New Art*, New York: Dover.

Balibar, E. (2002) *Politics and the Other Scene*, London: Verso.

Balint, M. (1959) *Thrills and Regressions*, London: Maresfield Press.

Barad, K. (2003) 'Posthumanist performativity: Toward an understanding of how matter comes to matter', *Signs*, 28: 802–831.

Barletta, M. (2002) *Marketing to Women*, New York: Dearborn.

Barnett, C., Cloke, P., Clarke, N. and Malpass, A. (2004) 'Consuming ethics: articulating the subjects and spaces of ethical consumption' *Antipode* 31 (1): 23–45.

Barrows, S. (1981) *Distorting Mirrors: Visions of the Crowd in Late Nineteenth-Century France*, New Haven, CT: Yale University Press.

Barry. A. (2000) 'Air' in Pile, S. and Thrift, N.J. (eds) *City A–Z*, London: Routledge.

Barry, A. (2005) 'Pharmaceutical matters: the invention of informed materials' *Theory, Culture and Society*, 22: 93–110.

Bataille, G. (1988) *The Accursed Share*, New York: Zone Books.

Batchen, G. (2001) *Each Wild Idea: Writing, Photography, History*, Cambridge, MA: MIT Press.

Bateson, G. (1973) *Steps to an Ecology of Mind*, London: Paladin Books.

Battersby, C. (1999) *The Phenomenal Woman*, Cambridge: Polity Press.

Bayart, J. (2001) 'The paradoxical invention of economic modernity' in Appadurai, A. (ed.) *Globalization*, Durham, NC: Duke Press, pp. 307–334.

Bayer, B. (1998) 'Between apparatus and apparitions: phantoms of the laboratory' in Bayer, B. and Shotter, J. (eds) *Reconstructing the Psychological Subject: Bodies, Practices and Technologies*, London: Sage, pp. 187–213.

Bayer, B. and Shotter, J. (eds) *Bodies, Practices and Technologies*, London: Sage, pp. 68–93.

Beckmann, J. (2001) 'Automobilization – a social problem and a theoretical concept' *Environment and Planning D. Society and Space*, 19: 593–607.

Bekoff, M. (2002) *Minding Animals: Awareness, Emotions and Heart*, Oxford: Oxford University Press.

Beirne, P. (1987) 'Between classicism and positivism. Crime and penality in the writings of Gabriel Tarde' *Criminology*, 25: 785–817.

Bell, V. (2005) 'The scenography of suicide: Terror, politics and the humiliated witness' *Economy and Society*, 34 (2): 241–260.

Benjamin, W. (1977 [1938]) 'The Paris of the Second Empire' in *Charles Baudelaire: A Lyric Poet in the Second Empire*, London: New Left Books.

Bennett, J. (2001) *The Enchantment of Modern Life: Attachments, Crossings, and Ethics*, Princeton, NJ: Princeton University Press.

Bennett, J. (2004) 'The force of things: steps toward an ecology of matter' *Political Theory*, 32: 347–372.

Bennett, J. and Shapiro, M.J. (eds) (2002) *The Politics of Moralizing*, New York: Routledge.

Bennett, W.L. and Entman, R.M. (eds) (2001) *Mediated Politics: Communication in the Future of Democracy*, Cambridge: Cambridge University Press.

Berardi, F. (2005) 'Biopolotics and connective mutation', available online at http://cultutemachine.tees.ac.uk/Articles/bifo.htm.

Bergson, H. (1889) *Time and Free Will*, New York: Dover.

Bergson, H. (1998 [1911]) *Creative Evolution*, New York: Dover.

Berlant, L. (2003) 'Uncle Sam needs a wife: citizenship and denegation' in Castronovo, R. and Nelson, D. (eds) *Materializing Democracy: Toward a Revitalised Cultural Politics*, Princeton, NJ: Princeton University Press, pp.144–174.

Berlant, L. (2004a) 'Affirmative culture' *Critical Inquiry* 30 (2): 445–451.

Berlant, L. (ed.) (2004b) *Compassion: The Culture and Politics of an Emotion*, New York: Routledge.

Berlant, L. (ed.) (2000) *Intimacy*, Chicago: University of Chicago Press.

Bernstein, M.A. (1994) *Foregone Conclusions: Against Apocalyptic History*, Berkeley, CA: University of California Press.

Bertman, S. (1998) *Hyperculture: The Human Cost of Speed*, New York: Praeger.

Best, J. (2005) *The Limits of Transparency. Ambiguity and the History of International Finance*, Ithaca, NY: Cornell University Press.

Biller, P. (2000) *The Measure of Multitude: Population in Medieval Thought*, Oxford: Oxford University Press.

Billig, M. (1999) *Freudian Repression: Conversation Creating the Unconscious*, Cambridge: Cambridge University Press.

Billig, M. (2005) *Laughter and Ridicule: Towards a Social Critique of Humour*, London: Sage.

Blackman, L. (2001) *Hearing Voices: Contesting the Voice of Reason*, London: Free Association Books.

Blakemore, C. (2005) *In Celebration of Cerebration. The Harveian Oration of 2005*, London: Royal College of Physicians.

Blank, J. (2001) *Mullahs on the Mainframe: Islam and Modernity amongst the Daudi Bohras*, Chicago: University of Chicago Press.

Bloch, E. (1986 [1959]) *The Politics of Hope* (3 vols), Oxford: Blackwell.

Bloch, E. (1998 [1929]) *The Anxiety of the Engineer in Literary Essays*, Stanford, CA: Stanford University Press, pp. 304–313.

Bloch, E. (2000 [1923]) *The Spirit of Utopia*, Stanford, CA: Stanford University Press.

Blum, V. (2005) *Flesh Wounds. The Culture of Cosmetic Surgery*, Berkeley: University of California Press.

Boal, F. (1998) *Legislative Theatre*, London: Routledge.

Boltanski, L. (1999) *Distant Suffering: Morality, Media and Politics*, Cambridge: Cambridge University Press.

Boltanski, L. (2002) 'The fetus and the image war' in Latour, B. and Weibel, P. (eds) *Iconoclash: Beyond the Image Wars*, Cambridge, MA: MIT Press, pp. 78–81.

Boon, J.C.W. and Sheridan, L. (eds) (2002) *Stalking and Psychosexual Obsession. Psychological Perspectives for Prevention, Policing and Treatment*, London: John Wiley.

Bottjer, D.J. (2005) 'The early evolution of animals' *Scientific American*, August: 30–35.

Bourdieu, P. (1991) *The Logic of Practice*, Cambridge: Polity Press.

Bourke, J. (2000) *An Intimate History of Killing*, London: Granta.

Bourriaud, N. (2002) *Relational Aesthetics*, Dijon: Les Presses du Réel.

Bowker, G. (2003) 'The past and the internet' *SSRC Items and Issues*, 4 (4): 28–30.

Brace, P. and Hinckley, B. (1992) *Follow the Leader: Opinion Polls and the Modern Presidents*, New York: Basic Books.

Brader, T. (2006) *Campaigning for Hearts and Minds. How Emotional Appeals in Political Ads Work*, Chicago: University of Chicago Press.

Bradley, B. (1998) 'Two ways to talk about change' in Bayer, B. and Shotter, J. (eds) *Reconstructing the Psychological Subject: Bodies, Practices and Technologies*, London: Sage, pp. 68–93.

Braidotti, R. (2006) *Transpositions*, Cambridge: Polity Press.

Brand, S. (1999) *The Clock of the Long Now*, London: Phoenix.

Brandon, R. (2002) *Automobile: How the Car Changed Life*, London: Macmillan.

Braudel, F. (1977) *Afterthoughts on Material Civilization and Capitalsim*, Baltimore, MD: Johns Hopkins University Press.

Bray, A. (2004) *The Friend*, Chicago: University of Chicago Press.

Brennan, T. (2004) *The Transmission of Affect*, London: Continuum.

Brenner, S. (2000) 'The end of the beginning' *Science*, 287 (5461): 2173.

Brenner, R. (2003a) 'Towards the precipice' *London Review of Books*, 6 February.

Brenner, R. (2003b) *The Boom and the Bubble. The US in the World Economy*, London: Verso.

Brentano, A. (1994) *Performance*, Durham, NC: Duke University Press.

Bromell, N. (2000) *Tomorrow Never Knows: Rock and Psychedelics in the 1960s*, Chicago: University of Chicago Press.

Brontë, C. (1993 [1847]) *Jane Eyre*, Oxford: Oxford University Press.

Brooks, P. (1976) *The Melodramatic Imagination*, New Haven, CT: Yale University Press.

Brooks, R (1991) 'Intelligence without representation' in *Artificial Intelligence Journal*, 47: 139–160; reprinted in Brooks, R. (1999) *Cambrian Intelligence*, Cambridge, MA: MIT Press, pp. 79–101.

Brothers, L. (1997) *Friday's Footprint: Flow Society Shapes the Human Mind*, New York: Oxford University Press.

Brown, B. (2003) *A Sense of Things: The Object Matter of American Literature*, Chicago: University of Chicago Press.

Brown, D. (2002) 'Martyrdom in Sunni revivalist thought' in Cormack, M. (ed.) *Sacrificing the Self: Perspectives on Martyrdom and Religion*, New York: Oxford University Press, pp. 107–117.

Brown, N. and Webster, A. (2004) *New Medical Technologies and Society: Reordering Life*, Cambridge: Polity Press.

Brown, S.D. and Stenner, P. (2001) 'Being affected: Spinoza and the psychology of emotion' *International Journal of Group Tensions*, 30 (1) 81–105.

Brown, W. (2005) *Edgework. Critical Essays on Knowledge and Politics*, Princeton, NJ: Princeton University Press.

Bruno, G. (2002) *Atlas of Emotion: Journeys in Art, Architecture and Film*, New York: Verso.

Brynjolfsson, E., Hu, Y. and Smith, M.D. (2003) 'Consumer surplus in the digital economy: estimating the value of increase product variety at online bestsellers' *Management Science* 49: 1580–1596.

Buchanan, I. (2000) *Michel de Certeau: Cultural Theorist*, London: Sage.

Buchanan, I. (ed.) (2001) 'Michel de Certeau in the *Plural*' *South Atlantic Quarterly*, 100 (2): 323–329.

Buchanan, I. and Lambert, G. (eds) (2005) *Deleuze and Space*, Edinburgh: Edinburgh University Press.

Buchli, V. and Lucas, G. (2001) *Archaeologies of the Contemporary Past*, London: Routledge.

Bullivant, L. (ed.) (2005) Special Issue on 4d space: interactive architecture, *Architectural Design*.

Burnett, D.G. (2003) 'Mapping time: chronometry on top of the world' *Daedalus*, Spring: 5–19.

Burt, R. (2005) *Trust, Reputation and Competitive Advantage*, New York: Oxford University Press.

Buss, D.M. (2005) *The Murderer Next Door. Why the Mind is Designed to Kill*, New York: Penguin Press.

Burns, T. (1992) *Erving Goffman*, London: Routledge.

Butler, J. (1990a) *Gender Trouble: Feminism and the Subversion of Identity*, New York: Routledge.

Butler, J. (1990b) 'Performative acts and gender constitution: an essay in phenomenology and feminist theory' in Case, S. (ed.) *Performing Feminisms: Feminist Critical Theory and Theatre*, Baltimore, MD: Johns Hopkins University Press, pp. 26–35.

Butler, J. (1997) *Excitable Speech*, New York: Routledge.

Butler, J. (2002) *Antigone's Claim: Kinship Between Life and Death*, New York: Columbia University Press.

Butler, J. (2005) *Giving an Account of Oneself*, New York: Fordham University Press.

Cache, B. (1995) *Earth Moves: The Furnishing of Territories*, Cambridge, MA: MIT Press.

Callon, M. and Law, J. (2004) 'Introduction: absence, presence, circulation, and encountering in complex social space' *Environment and Planning D. Society and Space*, 22: 3–11.

Callon, M. and Muniesa, F. (2005) 'Economic markets as calculative collective devices' *Organization Studies* 26: 1229–150.

Callon, M. and Rabeharisoa, V. (2004) 'Gino's lesson on humanity: genetics, mutual entanglements and the sociologist's role' *Economy and Society*, 33: 1–27.

Callon, M., Meadal, C. and Rabeharisoa, V. (2002) 'The economy of qualities' *Economy and Society*, 31: 194–217.

Calvino, L. (1979) *Invisible Cities*, London: Minerva Press.

Campbell, D. and Shapiro, M.J. (eds) (1999) *Moral Spaces. Rethinking Ethics and World Politics*, Minneapolis: University of Minnesota Press.

Campbell. P. (2003) 'On video' *London Review of Books*, 11 September, p. 14.

Carter, P. (1992) *The Sound In Between: Voice, Space, Performance*, Kensington: New South Wales University Press.

Carter, P. (2002) *Repressed Spaces: The Poetics of Agoraphobia*, London: Reaktion.

Casciaro, T. and Lobo, M.S. (2005) 'Competent jerks, lovable fools, and the formation of social networks' *Harvard Business Review*, 1 June.

Case, S. (1998) 'Tracking the vampire' *Differences*, 3: 1–17.

Castoriadis C. (1997) *World in Fragments: Writings on Politics, Society, Psychoanalysis and the Imagination*, Stanford, CA: Stanford University Press.

Castoriadis, C. (2003) *The Rising Tide of Insignificancy: The Big Sleep*, available online at http//:www.notbored.org/RTI.html.

Castronovo, R. and Nelson, D.D. (eds) (2003) *Materializing Democracy. Towards a Revitalised Cultural Politics*, Durham, NC: Duke University Press.

Caygill, H. (1998) *Walter Benjamin: The Colour of Experience*, London: Routledge.

Caygill, H. (2002) *Levinas and the Political*, London: Routledge.

Chadwick, W. and de Courtivron, L. (1993) *Significant Others: Creativity and Intimate Partnership*, London: Thames and Hudson.

Chakrabarty, D. (2002) *Habitations of Modernity: Essays in the Wake of Subaltern Studies*, Chicago: University of Chicago Press.

Changeux, J.P. and Ricoeur, P. (2002) *What Makes Us Think?* Princeton, NJ: Princeton University Press.

Chatterjee, P. (2004) *The Politics of the Goverened. Reflections on Popular Politics in Most of the World*, New York: Columbia University Press.

Chesborough, H. (2003) *Open Innovation. The New Imperative for Creating and Profiting from Technology*, Boston, MA: Harvard Business School Press.

Chilton, P. (2003) *Analyzing Political Discourse. Theory and Practice*, London: Routledge.

Clanchy, M.T. (1992) *From Memory to Written Record: England 1066–1307*, Oxford: Blackwell.

Clark, A. (1997) *Being There: Putting Brain, Body, and World Together Again*, Cambridge, MA: MIT Press.

Clark, T.J. (1999) *Farewell to an Idea: Episodes from a History of Modernism*, New Haven, CT: Yale University Press.

Clarke, A.C. and Baxter, S. (2002) *The Light of Other Days*, London: HarperCollins.

Claxton, G. (2000) *Wise Up, The Challenge of Lifelong Learning*, London: Bloomsbury

Clough, P.T. (2000) *Autoaffection: Unconscious Thought in the Age of Teletechnology*, Minneapolis: University of Minnesota Press.

Clubb, R. and Mason, G. (2003) 'Captivity effects on wide-ranging carnivores' *Nature*, 131: 425–434.

Cohen, S. (2001) *States of Denial. Knowing about Atrocities and Suffering*, Cambridge: Polity Press.

Cohen-Cruz, J.(ed.) (1998) *Radical Street Performance*, London: Routledge.

Colebrook, C. (2005a) 'On the specificity of affect' in Buchanan, I. and Lambert, G. (eds) *Deleuze and Space*, Edinburgh: Edinburgh University Press, pp. 189–206.

Colebrook, C. (2005b) 'How can we tell the dancer from the dance? The subject of dance and the subject of philosophy' *Topoi*, 25: 5–14.

Comte, A. (1877) *System of Positive Polity, Vol 1*, London: Longmans, Green and Co.

Conley, T. (1992) *The Graphic Unconscious in Early Modern French Writing*, Cambridge: Cambridge University Press.

Conley, T. (1996) *The Self-Made Map: Cartographic Writing in Early Modern France*, Minneapolis: University of Minnesota Press.

Conley, V.A. (2001) 'Processual practices' *South Atlantic Quarterly*, 100: 483–500.

Connolly, W.E. (1999) 'Brain wars, transcendental fields and techniques of thought' *Radical Philosophy*, 94: 19–28.

Connolly, W.E. (2002) *Neuropolitics*, Minneapolis: University of Minnesota Press.

Connolly, W.E. (2005) *Pluralism*, Durham, NC: Duke University Press.

Connor, S. (1996) 'Postmodern performance' in Campbell, P. (ed.) *Analysing Performance: A Critical Reader*, Manchester: Manchester University Press.

Cormack, M. (ed.) (2002) *Sacrificing the Self: Perspectives on Martyrdom and Religion*, New York: Oxford University Press.

Crang, P. (1997) 'Performing the tourist product' in Rojek, C. and Urry, J. (eds) *Touring Cultures*, London: Routledge, pp. 137–154.

Crary, J. (1999) *Suspensions of Perception: Attention, Spectacle and Modern Culture*, Cambridge, MA: MIT Press.

Crary, J. (2004) 'Foreword' in Oliveira, N., Oxley, N. and Petry, M. (eds) *Installation Art in the New Millenium. The Empire of the Senses*, London: Thames and Hudson, pp. 6–9.

Crawshaw, C. and Urry, J. (1997) 'Tourism and the photographic eye' in Rojek, C. and Urry, J. (eds) *Touring Cultures: Transformations of Travel and Theory*, London: Routledge, pp. 176–95.

Critchley, S. (2002) 'Introduction' in Critchley, S. and Bernasconi, R. (eds) *The Cambridge Companion to Levinas*, Cambridge: Cambridge University Press, pp. 1–32.

Critchley, S. (2005) *Things Merely Are. Philosophy in the Poetry of Wallace Stevens*, London: Routledge.

Cruz, J.D. (2005) 'Ethnosympathy: reflections on an American dilemma' in Friedland, J. and Mohr, J. (eds) *Matters of Culture: Cultural Sociology in Practice*, Cambridge: Cambridge University Press, pp. 378–399.

Csányi, V. (2005) *If Dogs Could Talk. Exploring the Canine Mind*, New York: North Point Press.

Curtis, K. (1999) *Our Sense of the Real: Aesthetic Experience and Arendtian Politics*, Ithaca, NY: Cornell University Press.

Cvetkovich, A. (2003) *An Archive of Feelings: Trauma, Sexuality and Lesbian Public Cultures*, Durham, NC: Duke University Press.

Czarniawska, B. and Sevon, G. (eds) (2005) *Global Ideas. How Ideas, Objects and Practices Travel in the Global Economy*, Malmö: Liber AB.

Dagognet, E (1992) *Etienne-Jules Marey: A Passion for the Trace*, New York: Zone Books.

Dalrymple, T. (2004) 'Lynndie England was acting out the fantasies of frustrated people everywhere' *The Times*, 7 August, p. 24.

Damasio, A. (1999) *The Feeling of What Happens*, London: Vintage.

Damasio, A. (2003) *Looking for Spinoza: Joy, Sorrow and the Feeling Brain*, London: Heinemann.

Dant, T. (2004) *Materiality and Society*, Maidenhead: Open University Press.

Dant, T. and Martin, P. (2001) 'By car: carrying modern society' in Warde, A. and Grunow, J. (eds) *Ordinary Consumption*, London: Routledge.

Darwin, C. (1998 [1872]) *The Expression of the Emotions in Man and Animals*, London: Fontana.

Daston, L. (ed.) (2004) *Things That Talk: Object Lessons from Art and Science*, New York: Zone Books.

Daston, L. (2005) 'Intelligences: angelic, animal, human' in Daston, L. and Mitman, G. (eds) *Thinking with Animals: New Perspectives on Anthropomorphism*, New York: Columbia University Press, pp. 37–58.

Davidson, R.J., Scherer, K.R. and Goldsmith, H.H. (eds) (2003) *Handbook of Affective Sciences*, New York: Oxford University Press.

Davis, J.M. (2003) *Martyrs: Innocence, Vengeance and Despair in the Middle East*, London: Palgrave Macmillan.

Davis, M. (2002) *Dead Cities and Other Tales*, New York: New Press.

Dawkins, R. (2002) 'Thoughts of Deleuze, Spinoza and the cinema' *Contretemps*, 3: 66–74.

De Certeau, M. (1984) *The Practice of Everyday Life*, trans. S. Rendall, Berkeley: University of California Press.

De Certeau, M. (1987) 'Practices of space' in Blonsky, M. (ed.) *On Signs*, Oxford: Blackwell.

De Certeau, M. (1992) *The Mystic Fable*, vol. 1, *The Sixteenth and Seventeenth Centuries*, Chicago: University of Chicago Press.

De Certeau, M. (1998) *Culture in the Plural*, Minneapolis: University of Minnesota Press.

De Certeau, M. (2000) *The Possession at Loudon*, Chicago: Chicago University Press.

De Waal, F. (2005) *Our Inner Ape*, New York: Riverhead Books.

De Waal, F. and Tyack, P. (eds) (2003) *Animal Social Complexity: Intelligence, Culture and Individualized Societies*, Cambridge, MA: Harvard University Press.

De Landa, M. (2002) *Intensive Science and Virtual Philosophy*, London: Continuum.

Deleuze G. (1986) *The Movement Image*, Minneapolis: University of Minnesota Press.

Deleuze, G. (1988a) *Bergsonism*, New York: Zone Books.

Deleuze, G. (1988b) *Spinoza: Practical Philosophy*, San Francisco: City Lights Books.

Deleuze, G. (1991) *Empiricism and Subjectivity: An Essay on Hume's Theory of Human Nature*, New York: Columbia University Press.

Deleuze G. (1994) *Difference and Repetition*, London: Athlone Press.

Deleuze, G. (1995) *Negotiations, 1972–1990*, New York: Columbia University Press.

Deleuze, G. (1997a) *Essays Critical and Clinical*, Minneapolis: University of Minnesota Press.

Deleuze, G. (1997b) 'One less manifesto' in Murray, T. (ed.) *Mimesis, Masochism, Mime. The Politics of Theatricality in Contemporary French Thought*, Ann Arbor: University of Michigan Press, pp. 239–258.

Deleuze, G. and Guattari, F. (1987) *A Thousand Plateaus: Capitalism and Schizophrenia*, London: Athlone.

Deleuze, G. and Guattari, F. (1994) *What is Philosophy?* London: Verso.

Demos, E.V. (ed.) (1995) *Exploring Affect: The Selected Writings of Silvan S. Tomkins*, Cambridge: Cambridge University Press.

Dening, C. (1996) *Performances*, Chicago: University of Chicago Press.

Depraz, N., Varela, F. and Vermersch, P. (2000) 'The gesture of awareness: an account of its structural dynamics' in Velmans, M. (ed.) *Investigating Phenomenal Consciousness*, Amsterdam: John Benjamins, pp.121–137.

Derrida, J. (2002) 'The animal that I am (more to follow)' *Critical Inquiry*, 28: 369–418.

Desmond, J.C. (ed.) (1997) *Meaning in Motion: New Cultural Studies of Dance*, Durham, NC: Duke University Press.

Despret, V. (2004) *Our Emotional Make-Up: Ethnopsychology and Selfhood*, New York: Other Press.

Desrosières, J. (1998) *The Politics of Large Numbers: A History of Statistical Reasoning*, Cambridge, MA: Harvard University Press.

Diprose, R. (2002) *Corporeal Generosity: On Giving with Nietzsche, Merleau-Ponty and Levinas*, Albany: State University Press of New York.

Doane, M.A. (2002) *The Emergence of Cinematic Time: Modernity, Contingency, The Archive*, Cambridge, MA: MIT Press.

Docherty, T. (2006) *Aesthetic Democracy*, Stanford, CA: Stanford University Press.

Dolan, J. (ed.) (1993) *Presence and Desire: Essays on Gender, Sexuality and Performance*, Ann Arbor, MI: University of Michigan Press.

Donald, M. (2001) *A Mind So Rare. The Evolution of Human Consciousness*, New York: W.W. Norton.

Dosse, J.F. (2002) *Michel de Certeau. Le Marcheur Blessé*, Paris: La Découverte.

Dourish, P. (2001) *Where the Action is. The Foundations of Embodied Interation*, Cambridge, MA: MIT Press.

Dreyfus, H. (2005) 'Merleau-Ponty and cognitive science' in Carman, T. and Hansen, M.B.N. (eds) *The Cambridge Companion to Merleau-Ponty*, Cambridge: Cambridge University Press, pp. 129–150.

Duffy, F. (1997) *The New Office*, London: Conran Octopus.

Dumit, J. (2004) *Picturing Personhood: Brain Scans and Biomedical Identity*, Princeton, NJ: Princeton University Press.

Dunagan, C. (2005) 'Dance, knowledge, and power' *Topoi*, 24: 29–41.

Dupuy, J. (2002) *Pour un Catastrophisme éclairé*, Paris: Editions du Seuil.

Duster, T. (1990) *Backdoor to Eugenics*, New York: Routledge.

Eagleton, T. (2006) 'Making a break' *London Review of Books*, 9 March: 25–26.

Eco, U. (1989) *The Aesthetics of Chaosmos*, Cambridge, MA: Harvard University Press.

Economist, The (2005a) 'Better than people' *The Economist*, 24 December: 84–85.

Economist, The (2005b) 'In search of stealth' *The Economist*, 21 April: 56–57.

Economist, The (2005c) 'Overdue and over budget, again and again' *The Economist*, 11 June: 65–66.

Edwards, J. (1995) *Discursive Psychology*, London: Sage.

Eglash, R. (1999) *African Fractals: Modern Computing and Indigenous Design*, New York: Rutgers University Press.

Ekman, P. (1972) *Emotion in the Human Face: Guidelines for Research and Integration of Findings*, Oxford: Pergamon.

Ekman, P. (1995) *Telling Lies: Clues to Deceit in the Marketplace, Marriage and Politics*, New York: Norton.

Ekman, P. (2003) *Emotions Revealed: Understanding Faces and Feelings*, London: Weidenfeld and Nicolson.

Ekman, P. and Rosenberg, E. (eds) (1997) *What the Face Reveals*, New York: Oxford University Press.

Eldridge J. (1998) *Transforming Experience: John Dewey's Cultural Instrumentalism*, Nashville, TN: Vanderbilt University Press.

Elias, N, (2000) *The Civilizing Process*, Oxford: Blackwell.

Eliasoph, N. (1998) *Avoiding Politics. How Americans Produce Apathy in Everyday Life*, Cambridge: Cambridge University Press.

Elkins, J. (1999) *Pictures of the Body. Pain and Metamorphosis*, Stanford, CA: Stanford University Press.

Elliott, A. and Lemert, C. (2006) *The New Individualism: The Emotional Costs of Globalization*, London: Routledge.

Emerson, R.W. (1942) 'Experience' in *Essays*, London: Everyman, pp. 26–43.

Enge, P. (2004) 'Retooling the global positioning system' *Scientific American*, 290 (5): 90–97.

Englemann, P. (1967) *Letters from Ludwig Wittgenstein, with a Memoir*, Oxford: Blackwell.

Farnell, B. (1994) 'Ethnographics and the moving body' *Man, New Series* 29: 929–974.

Faucher-King, F. (2005) *Changing Parties: An Anthropology of British Political Conferences*, London: Palgrave Macmillan.

Fawcett-Tang, R. (2005) *Mapping. An Illustrated Guide to Graphical Navigational Systems*, Mies, Switzerland: Rotovision.

Feldenkrais, M. (1972) *Awareness through Movement: Health Exercises for Personal Growth*, New York: Harper and Row.

Fellous, J. and Arbib, M.A. (eds) (2005) *Who Needs Emotions? The Brain Meets the Robot*, Oxford: Oxford University Press.

Fenves, P. (1993) 'Chatter' in *Language and History in Kierkegaard*, Stanford, CA: Stanford University Press.

Ferguson, H. (2004) 'The sublime and the subliminal: modern identities and the aesthetics of combat' *Theory in Culture and Society* 21: 1–34.

Field, T. (2001) *Touch*, Cambridge, MA: MIT Press.

Fields, R.M. (2004) *Martyrdom. The Psychology, Theology and Politics of Self-Sacrifice*, New York: Praeger.

Finnegan, R. (1989) *The Hidden Musicians*, Cambridge: Cambridge University Press.

Finnegan, R. (2002) *Communicating: The Multiple Modes of Human Interaction*, London: Routledge.

Fischer, M.J. (2003) *Emergent Forms of Life and the Anthropological Voice*, Durham, NC: Duke University Press.

Fisher, M. (2002) *The Vehement Passions*, Princeton, NJ: Princeton University Press.

Flaherty, M.G. (1998) *A Watched Pot: How We Experience Time*, New York: New York University Press.

Fleming, C. (2004) *René Girard: Violence and Mimesis*, Cambridge: Polity Press.

Foray, D. (2004) *The Economics of Knowledge*, Cambridge, MA: MIT Press.

Forbes, N. (2004) *Imitation of Life: How Biology is Inspiring Computing*, Cambridge, MA: MIT Press.

Fortun, K. (2001) *Advocacy After Bhopal: Environmentalism, Disaster and Global Orders*, Chicago: University of Chicago Press.

Foster, S.L. (ed.) (1995) *Choreographing History*, Bloomington: Indiana University Press.

Foster, S.L. (2005) 'Choreographing empathy' *Topoi*, 24: 81–91.

Foucault, M. (1984) 'On the genealogy of ethics: an overview of work in progress', in Rabinow, P. (ed.) *The Foucault Reader*, New York: Pantheon.

Foucault M. (1984) 'Collège de France lecture', 14 March 1984, cited in Shusterman, R. *Practising Philosophy. Pragmatism and the Philosophical Life*, New York: Routledge, pp. 176–177.

Foucault, M. (1986) *The Care of the Self: The History of Sexuality*, Vol. 3, New York: Pantheon Books.

Fraleigh, S.H. (1987) *Dance and the Lived Body: A Descriptive Aesthetics*, Philadelphia: University of Pennsylvania Press.

France, A. (2002 [1909]) *Penguin Island*, trans. A.W. Evans, Rockville, MD: Wildside Press.

Franklin, B. (2004) *Packaging Politics. Political Communications in Britain's Media Democracy*, 2nd edn, London: Arnold.

Franko, M. (1993) *Dance as Text: Ideologies of the Baroque Body*, Cambridge: Cambridge University Press.

Franz, K. (2005) *Tinkering. Consumers Reinvent the Early Automobile*, Philadelphia: University of Pennsylvania Press.

Fraser, M. (2002) 'What is the matter of feminist criticism?' *Economy and Society*, 31: 606–625.

Fraser, M. (2003) 'Material theory: duration and the serotonin hypothesis of depression' *Theory Culture and Society*, 20: 1–26.

Freud, S. (2002 [1930]) *Civilization and its Discontents*, London: Penguin.

Frith, S. (1997) *Performing Rites*, Oxford: Oxford University Press.

Frow, J. (1997) *Time and Commodity Culture. Essays in Cultural Theory and Postmodernity*, Oxford: Oxford University Press.

Fuller, M. (2005) *Media Ecologies: Materialist Energies in Art and Technoculture*, Cambridge, MA: MIT Press.

Funcke, B. (2005) 'Against gravity. Bettina Funcke talks with Peter Sloterdijk' *Bookforum*, February/March.

Galison, P. (2003) *Einstein's Clocks, Poincaré's Maps: Empires of Time*, New York: Norton.

Galison, P. and Thompson, P. (eds) (1999) *The Architecture of Science*, Cambridge, MA: MIT Press.

Gamble, J. (1977) 'On contact improvisation' *The Painted Bride Quarterly*, 4: 17–28.

Gane, M. (1993) *Harmless Lovers? Gender Theory and Personal Relationships*, London: Routledge.

Gardiner, M.E. (2000) *Critiques of Everyday Life*, London: Routledge.

Garfinkel, H. (2002) *Ethnomethodology's Program. Working Out Durkheim's Aphorism*, Lanham, MD: Rowman and Littlefield.

Gay, P. (2002) *Savage Reprisals: Bleak House, Madame Bovary, Buddenbrooks*, New York: Norton.

Gee, H. (2004) *Jacob's Ladder: The History of the Human Genome*, London: Fourth Estate.

Gell, A. (1998) *Art and Agency*, Oxford: Blackwell.

Gehlen, A. (1988) *Man: His Nature and Place in the World*, New York: Columbia Press.

George, L. (1998) 'Artists incorporating: business savvy meets creative experimentation' in Marcus, G.E. (ed.) *Corporate Futures: The Diffusion of the Culturally Sensitive Corporate Form*, Chicago: University of Chicago Press, pp. 311–336.

Gerhardt, S. (2004) *Why Love Matters. How Affection Shapes a Baby's Brain*, Hove: Brunner-Routledge.

Gershuny, J. (1978) *After Industrial Society? The Emerging Self-Service Economy*, London: Macmillan.

Geurts, K.L. (2002) *Culture and the Senses. Bodily Ways of Knowing in an African Community*, Berkeley: University of California Press.

Giard, L. (1997) 'Introduction: opening the possible' in de Certeau, M. *Culture in the Plural*, Minneapolis: University of Minnesota Press, pp. ix–xv.

Gibbons, F. (2003) 'Display of passion which will end in tears' *The Guardian*, 5 July, p. 11.

Gibson, A. (1996) *Towards a Postmodern Theory of Narrative*, Edinburgh: Edinburgh University Press.

Gibson, J.T. (1966) *The Senses Considered as Perceptual Systems*, Boston, MA: Houghton Mifflin.

Gibson, W. and Sterling, B. (1992) *The Difference Engine*, London: Gollancz.

Giddens, A. (1991) *Modernity and Self-Identity*, Cambridge: Polity Press.

Gil, J. (1998) *Metamorphoses of the Body*, Minneapolis: University of Minnesota Press.

Gillham, N.W. (2002) *A Life of Sir Francis Galton: From African Exploration to the Birth of Eugenics*, Oxford: Oxford University Press.

Gillmor, D. (2004) *We the Media: Grassroots Journalism by the People, for the People*, Sebastopol, CA: O'Reilly.

Gilroy, P. (2004) *After Empire: Melancholia or Convivial Culture?* London: Routledge.

Ginsborg, P. (2005) *The Politics of Everyday Life: Making Choices, Changing Lives*, New Haven, CT: Yale University Press.

Ginsburg, F.D., Abu-Lughod, L. and Larkin, B. (eds) *Media Worlds. Anthropology on New Terrain*, Berkeley: University of California Press.

Ginzburg, C. (2001a) 'Your country needs you: a case study in political iconography' *History Workshop Journal*, Autumn: 1–22.

Ginzburg, C. (2001b) *Wooden Eyes. Nine Reflections on Distance*, New York: Columbia University Press.

Girard, R. (1987) *Things Hidden Since the Foundation of the World*, Stanford, CA: Stanford University Press.

Gladwell, M. (2005) *Blink: The Power of Thinking without Thinking*, London: Allen Lane.

Glendinning, S. (1998) *On Being with Others, Heidegger, Derrida, Wittgenstein*, London: Routledge.

Globus, G. (1995) *The Postmodern Brain*, Amsterdam: John Benjamins.

Goffey, A. (2002) 'Naturalizing phenomenology: cognitive science and the bestowal of sense' *Radical Philosophy*, 114: 20–28.

Goffman, E. (1971) *The Presentation of Self in Everyday Life*, Harmondsworth: Penguin Books.

Goffman, E. (1974) *Frame Analysis*, London: Peregrine Books.

Goldfarb, J.C. (2006) *The Politics of Small Things: The Power of the Powerless in Dark Times*, Chicago: University of Chicago Press.

Göncli, A. and Perone, A. (2005) 'Pretend play as lifetime activity' *Topoi*, 24: 137–147.

Goodchild, P. (2002) *Capitalism and Religion*, London: Routledge.

Goody, J. (1986) *The Logic of Writing and the Organization of Society*, Cambridge: Cambridge University Press.

Goon, P. (2003) 'Keyboard resistance. The construction of presence as power in computer-mediated communication and mobile texting' *Southern Review*, 36 (2): 40–51.

Gordon, A. (1997) *Ghostly Matters: Haunting and the Sociological Imagination*, Minneapolis: University of Minnesota Press.

Gordon, S.P. (2002) *The Power of the Passive Self in English Literature, 1640–1770*, Cambridge: Cambridge University Press.

Gottdiener, M. (1997) *The Theming of America: Dreams, Visions and Commercial Spaces*, Boulder, CO: Westview Press.

Gough, R. and Wallis, M. (eds) (2005) 'On Techne' *Performance Research*, 10 (4).

Graham, S. (2003) 'Lessons in urbicide' *New Left Review* 19: 63–77.

Grandin, T. and Johnson, C. (2005) *Animals in Translation. Using the Mysteries of Autism to Decode Animal Behaviour*, London: Bloomsbury.

Gray, J. (2002) *Straw Dogs: Thoughts on Humans and Animals*, London: Granta.

Gregory D. (1997) 'Lacan and geography: the *Production of Space* revisited' in Benko, G. and Strohmayer, U. (eds) *Space and Social Theory: Interpreting Modernity and Postmodernity*, Oxford: Blackwell, pp. 203–234.

Greis, N.P. (2004) 'Integrated infrastructures for moving goods in the digital age' in Hanley, R. (ed.) *Moving Goods, People and Information in the 21st Century: The Cutting-Edge Infrastructures of Networked Cities*, London: Routledge, pp. 31–45.

Grene, M. and Depew, D. (2004) *The Philosophy of Biology: An Episodic History*, Cambridge: Cambridge University Press.

Griffiths, P. (1997) *What Emotions Really Are. The Problems of Psychological Categories*, Chicago: University of Chicago Press.

Gross, D. (2006) *The Secret History of Emotion, From Aristotle's Rhetoric to Modern Brain Science*, Chicago: University of Chicago Press.

Grossman, D. (1996) *On Killing: The Psychological Cost of Learning to Kill in War and Society*, Boston, MA: Little Brown.

Grosz, E. (2004) *The Nick of Time: Politics, Evolution, and the Untimely*, Durham, NC: Duke University Press.

Grosz, E.A. (2005) *Time Travels: Feminism, Nature, Power*, Durham, NC: Duke University Press.

Grosz, F. (ed.) (1999) *Becomings: Explorations in Time, Memory and Futures*, Ithaca, NY: Cornell University Press.

Guardian (2004) '90% of whites have few or no black friends' *The Guardian* 19 July, p. 1.

Gumbrecht, H.U. (2004) *Production of Presence: What Meaning Cannot Convey*, Stanford, CA: Stanford University Press.

Gunn, T. (1965) 'The Nature of an Action' in Michael Roberts (ed.) *The Faber Book of Modern Verse*, London: Faber & Faber, p. 392.

Habermas, J. (2003) *The Future of Human Nature*, Cambridge: Polity.

Hacking, I. (1998) *Mad Travellers: Reflections on the Reality of Transient Mental Diseases*, Cambridge, MA: Harvard University Press.

Hage, G. (2003) "Comes a time we are all enthusiasm': understanding Palestinian suicide bombers in times of exighophobia' *Public Culture*, 15: 65–89.

Halewood, M. (2005) 'A.N.Whitehead, information and social theory' *Theory Culture and Society*, 22: 73–94.

Hall, F.T. (1990) *The Hidden Dimension*, New York: Anchor Doubleday.

Hampshire, S. (2005) *Spinoza and Spinozism*, Oxford: Clarendon Press.

Haraway, D.J. (1991) *Simians, Cyborgs and Women: The Reinvention of Nature*, New York: Routledge.

Harman, G. (2002) *Tool-Being: Heidegger and the Metaphysics of Objects*, Chicago: Open Court.

Harrison, P. (2007) 'Corporeal remains: vulnerability, proximity, and living after the end of the world' *Environment and Planning A* (forthcoming).

Hart, J.F., Rhodes, M.J. and Morgan, J.T. (2002) *The Unknown World of the Mobile Home*, Baltimore, MD: Johns Hopkins University Press.

Hartley, L. (1995) *Wisdom of the Body Moving: An Introduction to Body-Mind Centring*, Berkeley, CA: North Atlantic Books.

Harvey, D. (2003) *The New Imperialism*, Oxford: Oxford University Press.

Hatfield, G. (1990) *The Natural and the Normative: Theories of Spatial Perception from Kant to Helmholtz*, Cambridge, MA: MIT Press.

Hauser, M. (2000) *Wild Minds: What Animals Really Think*, New York: Henry Holt.

Hayles, N.K. (1999) *How We Became Posthuman: Virtual Bodies in Cybernetics, Literature and Informatics*, Chicago: University of Chicago Press.

Heinrich, J., Boyd, R., Bowles, S., Camerer, C., Fehr, E. and Gintis, H. (eds) (2004) *Foundations of Human Sociality*, Oxford: Oxford University Press.

Hemmings, C. (2005) 'Invoking affect: cultural theory and the ontological turn' *Cultural Studies*, 15: 548–567.

Henalf, A. (1997) 'Actor-network' *Common Knowledge* 6: 69–83.

Henry, M. (1993) *The Genealogy of Psychoanalysis*, Stanford, CA: Stanford University Press.

Henry, M. (2003a) 'Phenomenology of life' *Angelaki*, 8: 100–110.

Henry, M. (2003b) *I Am the Truth: Toward a Philosophy of Christianity*, Stanford, CA: Stanford University Press.

Hetherington, K. (1997) 'In place of geometry: the materiality of place' in Hetherington, K. and Munro, R. (eds) *Ideas of Difference: Social Spaces and The Labour of Division*, Oxford: Blackwell, pp. 183–199.

Hewitt, A. (2005) *Social Choreography: Ideology as Performance in Dance and Everyday Movement*, Durham, NC: Duke University Press.

Highmore, B. (2002) *Everyday Life and Cultural Theory: An Introduction*, London: Routledge.

Hill, D. (2003) *The Body of Truth. Leveraging What Consumers Can't or Won't Say*, Hoboken, NJ: John Wiley.

Hillman, D. and Massio, D. (1997) *The Body in Parts: Fantasies of Corporeality in Early Modern Europe*, New York: Routledge.

Hillman, M. (2001) 'Prioritising policy and practice to favour walking' *World Transport Policy and Practice*, 7: 39–43.

Hinchliffe, S., Kearnes, M., Degen, M. and Whatmore, S. (2005) 'Urban wild things: a cosmopolitical experiment' *Environment and Planning D. Society and Space* 23: 643–658.

Hirsh, D. (2003) *Law Against Genocide: Cosmopolitan Trials*, London: Glasshouse Press.

Hofstadter, R. (1964) 'The paranoid style in American politics' *Harper's Magazine*, November: 77–86.

Holland, O. and McFarland, D. (2001) *Artificial Ethology*, Oxford: Oxford University Press.

Holmes, B. (2004) 'Barcode me' *New Scientist*, 26 June, 32–35.

Holmes, R. (2003) *Acts of War*, London: Weidenfeld and Nicolson.

Howes, D. (2003) *Sensual Relations: Engaging the Senses in Cultural Theory*, Ann Arbor: University of Michigan Press.

Huddy, L., Feldman, S., Taber, C. and Lahav, G. (2005) ' Threat, anxiety and support of antiterrorism policies' *American Journal of Political Science*, 49: 593–607.

Huffington, C., Armstrong, D., Halton, W., Hoyle, L. and Pooley, J. (eds) (2005) *Working Below the Surface. The Emotional Life of Organizations*, London: Karnac Books.

Hughes-Freeland, F. (ed.) (1998) *Ritual, Performance Media*, London: Routledge.

Hurley, S. and Chater, N. (eds) (2005) *Perspectives on Imitation*, 2 vols, Cambridge, MA: MIT Press.

Hurley, S. and Nudds, M. (2006) *Rational Animals?* Oxford: Oxford University Press.

Hutchby, I. (2001) *Conversation and Technology: From the Telephone to the Internet*, Cambridge: Polity Press.

Hutchins, F. (1995) *Cognition in the Wild*, Cambridge, MA: MIT Press.

Ignatieff, M. (1997) *The Warrior's Honor. Ethnic War and the Modern Conscience*, New York: Henry Holt.

Ind, N. (ed.) (2003) *Beyond Branding*, London: Kogan Page.

Ingold, T. (2002) *The Perception of the Environment. Essays on Livelihood, Dwelling and Skill*, London: Routledge.

Ingold, T. (2004) 'Culture on the ground: the world perceived through the feet' *Journal of Material Culture*, 9: 315–340.

Ingold, T. (2006) 'Rethinking the animate, re-animating thought' *Ethos*, 71, 9–20.

Irigaray, L. (1999) *The Forgetting of Air in Martin Heidegger*, London: Athlone.

Israeli, R. (2003) *Islamiskaze. Manifestations of Islamic Martyrology*, London: Frank Cass.

Jablonka, E. and Lamb, M.J. (2005) *Evolution in Four Dimensions: Genetic, Epigenetic, Behavioral, and Symbolic Variation in the History of Life*, Cambridge, MA: MIT Press.

Jackson, K. (1999) *Invisible Forms. A Guide to Literary Curiosities*, New York: St Martin's Press.

Jacobs, J. and Nash, C. (2003) 'Too little, too much: cultural feminist geographies' *Gender Place and Culture*, 10: 265–279.

Jain, S.L. (2002) 'Urban errands: the means of mobility' *Journal of Consumer Research*, 2: 385–404.

Jakle, J.A. (2001) *City Lights. Illuminating the American Night*, Baltimore, MD: Johns Hopkins University Press.

Jakle, J.A. and Sculle, K.A. (2002) *Fast Food: Roadside Restaurants in the Automobile Age*, Baltimore, MD: Johns Hopkins University Press.

James, W. (1960 [1890]) *The Principles of Psychology*, 2 vols, New York: Dover.

James, W. (1999 [1911]) *Some Problems of Philosophy*, Cambridge, MA: Harvard University Press.

Jameson, F. (2005) *Archaeologies of the Future: The Desire Called Utopia and Other Science Fictions*, London: Verso.

Janik, A. and Toulmin, S. (1973) *Wittgenstein's Vienna*, New York: Touchstone.

Jaques, E. (1995) 'Why the psychoanalytic approach to organizations is dysfunctional' *Human Relations*, 48: 343–349.

Jay, M. (2003) *Refractions of Violence*, New York: Routledge.

Joas, H. (1996) *The Creativity of Action*, Cambridge: Polity Press.

Jones, A. and Stephenson, A. (eds) (1999) *Performing the Body, Performing the Text*, London: Routledge.

Jordanova, L. (1994) 'The hand' in Taylor, L. (ed.) *Visualizing Theory*, New York: Routledge, pp. 252–259.

Joyce, P. (2003) *The Rule of Freedom: Liberalism and the Modern City*, London: Verso.

Jullien, F. (1995) *The Propensity of Things: Towards a History of Efficacy in China*, New York: Zone Books.

Jullien, F. (2004) *In Praise of Blandness: Proceeding from Chinese Thought and Aesthetics*, New York: Zone Books.

Kafka, F. (1988) 'My neighbor' in Glatzer, N.N. (ed.) *The Complete Short Stories of Franz Kafka*, London: Minerva, pp. 424–425.

Katz, J. (2000) *How Emotions Work*, Chicago: University of Chicago Press.

Keane, J. (1996) *Reflections on Violence*, London: Verso.

Kelly, S. (2006) *Customer Intelligence: From Data to Dialogue*, Chichester: John Wiley.

Kemp, S. (1996) 'Reading difficulties' in Campbell, P. (ed.) *Analysing Performance: A Critical Reader*, Manchester: Manchester University Press, pp. 153–174.

Kern, S. (1983) *The Culture of Space and Time, 1880–1914*, Berkeley: University of California Press.

Kern, S. (2004) *A Cultural History of Casuality. Science, Murder Novels, and Systems of Thought*, Princeton, NJ: Princeton University Press.

Kershaw, B. (1994) 'Framing the audience for theatre' in Keat, R., Whiteley, N. and Abercrombie, N. (eds) *The Authority of the Consumer*, London: Routledge, pp. 120–136.

Kershaw, B. (2005) 'Performance studies and Po-chang's Ox: Steps to a paradoxology of performance' *New Theatre Quarterly*, 30–53.

Khaitovich, P., Hellmann, I., Enard, W., Nowick, K., Leinweber, M., Franz, H., Weiss, G., Lachmann, M. and Pääbo, S. (2005) 'Parallel patterns of evolution in the genomes and transcriptomes of humans and chimpanzees' *Science Express*, 1 September.

Khosrokhavar, F. (2002) *Les Nouveaux Martyrs d'Allah*, Paris: Flammarion.

Killen, M. and Hart, D. (eds) (1995) *Morality in Everyday Life: Developmental Perspectives*, Cambridge: Cambridge University Press.

Kimbell, L. (2002) *Audit*, London: Book Works.

Kipnis, L. (2003) *Against Love: A Polemic*, New York: Pantheon.

Kirby, V. (1997a) *Forgetting Flesh*, London: Routledge.

Kirby, V (1997b) *Thinking Flesh*, London: Routledge.

Klein, J. (2002) *Greek Mathematical Thought and the Origin of Algebra*, New York: Dover.

Klein, J. (2006) *Politics Lost. How American Politics Was Trivialized by People Who Think You're Stupid*, New York: Doubleday.

Klinenberg, E. (2003) *Heat Wave: A Social Autopsy of Disaster*, Chicago: Chicago University of Chicago Press.

Kluth, A. (2004) 'Make it simple. A survey of information technology' *The Economist* 30 October: 1–26.

Knorr Cetina, K. (2001) 'Postsocial relations: Theorizing sociality in a postsocial environment' in Ritzer, G. and Smart, B. (eds) *Handbook of Social Theory*, London: Sage, pp. 520–537.

Knorr Cetina, K. (2003) 'How are global markets global? The architecture of a flow world', Paper presented to the Economies at Large Conference, New York, November.

Knorr Cetina, K. (2005) 'Complex global microstructures: the new terrorist micro-structures' *Theory, Culture and Society*, 22: 213–234.

Knorr Cetina, K. and Bruegger, U. (2002) 'Inhabiting technology: the global life form of financial markets' *Current Sociology*, 50: 389–405.

Kofman, E. and Lebas, E. (1995) 'Lost in transposition-time, space and the city' in *Writings on Cities: H. Lefebvre*, Oxford: Blackwell, pp. 3–100.

Konvitz, J. (1990) 'Why cities don't die' *American Heritage of Invention and Technology*, Winter: 58–63.

Koolhaas, R. (2003) *Lagos: How it Works*, Harvard Project on the City, Baden: Lars Müller.

Kovach, B. and Rosenstiel, T. (1999) 'Warp Speed' in *America in the Age of Mixed Media*, New York: Century Press.

Koziak, B. (2000) *Retrieving Political Emotion: Thumos, Aristotle, and Gender*, University Park: Pennsylvania State University Press.

Kracauer, S. (1960) *Theory of Film: The Redemption of Physical Reality*, New York: Oxford University Press.

Krell, D.F. (1992) *Daimon Life: Heidegger and Life-Philosophy*, Bloomington: Indiana: University Press.

Krogh, G. and Roos, J. (1995) *Managing Knowledge*, London: Sage.

Küchler, S. (1988) 'Malanggan: objects, sacrifice and the production of memory' *American Ethnologist*, 15: 625–637.

Küchler, S. (1992) 'Making skins: Malanggan and the idiom of kinship in Northern New Ireland' in Coote, J. and Shelton, A. (eds) *Anthropology, Art and Aesthetics*, Oxford: Clarendon Press, pp. 94–112.

Küchler, S. (2002) *Malanggan. Art, Memory, and Sacrifice*, Oxford: Berg.

Kuwabara, K. (2004) 'Affective attachment in electronic markets. A sociological study of eBay' in Nee, V. and Swedberg, R. (eds) *The Economic Sociology of Capitalism*, Princeton, NJ: Princeton University Press, pp. 268–288.

Kwinter, S. (2001) *Architiectures of Time: Toward a Theory of the Event in Modernist Culture*, Cambridge, MA: MIT Press.

Kwon, M.P. (2004) *One Place After Another: Site-Specific Art and Locational Identity*, Cambridge, MA: MIT Press.

Lachterman, D.R. (1989) *The Ethics of Geometry: A Genealogy of Modernity*, London: Routledge.

Lakoff, G. and Johnson, M. (1998) *Philosophy in the Flesh: The Embodied Mind and its Challenge to Western Thought*, New York: Basic Books.

Lamont-Brown, R. (1997) *Kamikaze. Japan's Suicide Samurai*, London: Weidenfeld and Nicolson.

Lane, C. (2004) *Hatred and Civility: The Antisocial Life in Victorian England*, New York: Columbia University Press.

Langbauer, L. (1999) *Novels of Everyday Life: The Series in English Fiction, 1850–1930*, Ithaca, NY: Cornell University Press.

Langer, S.K. (1953) *Feeling and Form: A Theory of Art Developed from Philosophy in a New Key*, London: Routledge and Kegan Paul.

Latour, B. (1992) 'Where are the missing masses? The sociology of a few mundane artifacts' in Bijker, W., Hughes, T. and Pinch, T. (eds) *The Social Construction of Technical Systems*, Cambridge, MA: MIT Press, pp. 225–258.

Latour, B. (1996) *Aramis: Or the Love of Technology*, Cambridge, MA and London: Harvard University Press.

Latour, B. (1997) 'Trains of thought: Piaget, formalism and the fifth dimension' *Common Knowledge*, 6: 170–191.

Latour, B. (2000) 'A well-articulated primatology: reflections of a fellow traveller' in Strum, S.C. and Fedigan, L.M. (eds) (2000) *Primate Encounters: Models of Science, Gender and Society*, Chicago: University of Chicago Press, pp. 358–381.

Latour, B. (2002a) 'Gabriel Tarde and the question of the social' in Joyce, P. (ed.) *The Social in Question: New Bearings in History and the Social Sciences*, London: Routledge, pp. 117–132.

Latour, B. (2002b) 'What is given in experience?' *Boundary* 2, 32 (1): 209–222.

Latour, B. (2004a) 'Why has critique run out of steam? From matters of fact to matters of concern' *Critical Inquiry*, 30: 225–248.

Latour, B. (2004b) *Politics of Nature: How to Bring the Sciences into Democracy*, Cambridge, MA: Harvard University Press.

Latour, B. (2005) *Reassembling the Social: An Introduction to Actor-Network Theory*, Oxford: Oxford University Press.

Latour, B. (2006) 'Air' in Jones, C.A. (ed.) *Sensorium: Embodied Experience, Technology, and Contemporary Art*, Cambridge, MA: MIT Press, pp. 104–107.

Latour, B. and Hermant, B. (1998) *Paris Ville Invisible*, Paris: La Decouverte/Institut Synthelabo.

Latour, B. and Weibel, P. (2002) *Iconoclash: Beyond the Image Wars*, Cambridge, MA: MIT Press.

Lave, J. (1996) 'Teaching as learning, in practice' *Mind, Culture and Activity*, 3 (3): 149–64.

Law J. (1998) 'After ANT: complexity, naming and technology' in Law, J. and Hassard, J. (eds) *Actor Network Theory and After*, Oxford: Blackwell, pp. 1–14.

Law, J. (2004a) 'Mattering – or how might STS contribute?' available online at http://www.comp.lancs.ac.uk/sociology/staff/law/law.htm.

Law, J. (2004b) *After Method: Mess in Social Science Research*, London: Routledge.

Law, J. and Benschop, R. (1997) 'Resisting pictures: representation, distribution and autological politics' in Hetherington, K. and Munro, R. *Ideas of Difference*, Oxford: Blackwell.

Lazzarato, M. (2002a) 'From biopower to biopolitics' *Pli: Warwick Journal of Philosophy*, 13: 100–111.

Lazzarato, M. (2002b) *Videophilosophie. Zeitwahrnehmung im Postfordismus*, Berlin: B. Books.

Lazzarato, M. (2002c) *Puissances de l'invention: la psychologie économique de Gabriel Trade contre l'économie politique*, Paris: Seuil.

Lazzarato, M. (2004) 'From capital-labour to capital-life' *Ephemera*, 4: 187–208.

Lazzarato, M. (2005a) 'Introduction' in Tarde, G. *Underground: Fragments of Future Histories*, Brussels: Les Maîtres de Formes Contemporains.

Lazzarato, M. (2005b) 'Struggle, event, media', Department of Sociology, Goldsmiths College.

Lazzarato, M. (2005c) 'Invention et travail dans la coopération entre cervaux', Department of Sociology, Goldsmiths College.

Lazzarato, M. (2006) 'European cultural tradition and the new forms of production and circulation of knowledge' *Multitudes: une revue trimestrielle, politique, artistique, artistique et culturelle*, 16 January.

Lazzarato, M. (2006) 'The machine' available online at http://transform.eipcp.net/.

Lecercle, J.J. (1990) *Philosophy Through the Looking Glass: Language, Nonsense, Desire*, La Salle, IL: Open Court.

Lee, B. and Lipuma, E (2000) 'Cultures of circulation: the imaginations of modernity' *Public Culture*, 14: 191–213.

Leen, G. and Heffernan, D. (2002) 'Expanding automotive electronic systems' *IEEE*, January: 8.

Lefebvre, G. (1973) *The Great Fear of 1789*, London: New Left Books.

Lefebvre, H. (1939) *Morceaux Choisis de Marx*, Paris: NRF.

Lefebvre, H. (1991) *The Production of Space*, Oxford: Blackwell.

Lefebvre, H. (1995) *Writings on Cities*, Oxford: Blackwell.

Lentricchia, F. and McAuliffe, J. (2003) *Crimes of Art and Terror*, Chicago: Chicago University Press.

Lessig, L. (2005) 'Do you floss?' *London Review of Books*, 18 August, pp. 24–25.

Levinson, S.C. (1995) 'Interactional biases in human thinking' in Goody, E.N. (ed.) *Social Intelligence and Interaction*, Cambridge: Cambridge University Press, pp. 221–260.

Levinson, S.C. (2003) *Space in Language and Cognition: Explorations in Cognitive Diversity*, Cambridge: Cambridge University Press.

Levinson, S.C. (2005) 'Introduction: the evolution of culture in a microcosm' in Levinson, S.C. and Jaisson, P. (eds) *Evolution and Culture*, Cambridge, MA: MIT Press, pp. 1–43.

Leys, R. (1993) 'Mead's voices: imitation as foundation, or, the struggle against mimesis' *Critical Inquiry*, 19: 277–307.

Leys, R. (2000) *Trauma. A Genealogy*, Chicago: University of Chicago Press.

Libet, B. (2004) *Mind Time: The Temporal Factor in Consciousness*, Cambridge, MA: Harvard University Press.

Lindstrom, M. (2005) *Brand Sense: How to Build Powerful Brands through Touch, Taste, Smell, Sight and Sound*, London: Kogan Page.

Lingis, A. (1998) *The Imperative*, Bloomington: Indiana University Press.

Liu, A. (2004) *The Laws of the Cool: Knowledge Work and the Culture of Information*, Chicago: University of Chicago Press.

Livingstone, D. (2003) *Spaces of Knowledge*, Chicago: University of Chicago Press.

Llobera, J.R. (2003) *The Making of Totalitarian Thought*, Oxford: Berg.

Loos, A. (1982 [1898]) Plumbers in *Spoken into the Void Collected Essays 1897–1900*, Cambridge MA: MIT Press.

Lorimer, H. (2006) 'Herding memories of animals and humans' *Environment and Planning D: Society and Space* 24(4): 497–518.

Lotringer, S. (2004) 'Foreword: We, the multitude' in Virno, P., *A Grammar of the Multitude*, New York: Semiotext(e), pp. 7–19.

Lowen, A. (1975) *Biotnergetics*, Harmondsworth: Penguin/Arkana.

Lukács, G. (1980) *The Destruction of Reason*, London: Merlin Press.

Lulka, D. (2004) 'Stabilizing the herd: fixing the identity of nonhumans' *Environment and Planning D: Society and Space*, 22: 439–464.

Lupton, D. (1999) 'Monsters in metal cocoons: road rage and cyborgs' *Body and Society*, 51: 57–72.

Lury, C. (2004) *Brands: The Logos of the Global Economy*, London: Routledge.

Lury, C. (2005) 'Contemplating a self-portrait as a pharmacist: a trade mark style of doing art and science' *Theory Culture and Society*, 22: 93–110.

Mabey, R. (2006) 'God and me' *Granta*, 93: 195–199.

McAloon, J.J. (1995) 'Interval training' in Foster, S.L. (ed.) *Choreographing History*, Bloomington: Indiana University Press, pp. pp. 32–53.

McCarthy, A. (2001) *Ambient Television*, Durham, NC: Duke University Press.

McClure, B. (1998) 'Machinic philosophy' *Theory, Culture and Society*, 15: 175–185.

McCrone, J. (1999) *Going Inside: A Tour Round a Single Moment of Consciousness*, London: Faber and Faber.

McCullough, M. (2004) *Digital Ground: Architecture, Pervasive Computing, and Environmental Knowing*, Cambridge, MA: MIT Press.

MacDonald, C. (1998) *The Complete Illustrated Guide to the Alexander Technique*, Shaftesbury, Dorset: Element Books.

McGowan, D. (1997a) *Alexander Technique: Original Writings of F.M. Alexander*, Burdett, NY: Larsons.

McGowan, D. (1997b) *Constructive Awareness: Alexander Technique and the Spiritual Quest*, Burdett, NY: Larsons.

Mackenzie, A. (2002) *Transductions. Bodies and Machines at Speed*, London: Continuum.

McKenzie, J. (1997) 'Genre trouble: (the) Butler did it' in Phelan, P. and Lane, J. *The Ends of Performance*, New York: New York University Press, pp. pp. 217–235.

McKenzie, J. (2001) *Perform or Else: From Discipline to Performance*, New York: Routledge.

McKibben, B. (2003) *Enough: Genetic Engineering and the End of Human Nature*, London: Bloomsbury.

McKinnon, S. and Silverman, S. (eds) (2005) *Complexities: Beyond Nature and Nurture*, Chicago: University of Chicago Press.

McNamee, S. and Gergen, K. (eds) (1998) *Relational Responsibility: Resources for Sustainable Dialogue*, Thousand Oaks, CA: Sage.

McNeill, D. (1998) *The Face: A Guided Tour*, London: Hamish Hamilton.

McNeill, D. (2005) *Gesture and Thought*, Chicago: University of Chicago Press.

McRobbie, A. (1991) *Feminism and Youth Culture*, London: Macmillan.

Malbon, B. (1999) *Clubbing*, London: Routledge.

Malnar, J.M. and Vodvarka, F. (2004) *Sensory Design*, Minneapolis: University of Minnesota Press.

Manovich, L. (2001) *The Language of New Media*, Cambridge, MA: MIT Press.

Marcus, G. (2002) *The Manchurian Candidate*, London: British Film Institute.

Marcus, G. (2005) *Like a Rolling Stone: Bob Dylan at the Crossroads*, London: Faber and Faber.

Marcus, G.E. (2002) *The Sentimental Citizen: Emotion in Democratic Politics*, University Park: Pennsylvania State University Press.

Marcus, G.E., Neuman, R. and Mackuen, M. (2000) *Affective Intelligence and Political Judgement*, Chicago: University of Chicago Press.

Margulis, L. (1998) *The Symbiotic Planet*, London: Weidenfeld and Nicolson.

Margulis, L. and Sagan, D. (2002) *Acquiring Genomes: A Theory of the Origins of the Species*, New York: Basic Books.

Margulis, L., Sagan, D. and Schwartz, W. (1999) *Slanted Truths: Essays on Gaia, Symbiosis and Evolution*, Berlin: Springer Verlag.

Marks, J. (1998) *Gilles Deleuze: Vitalism and Multiplicity*, London: Pluto Press.

Marks, L. (2002) *Touch: Sensuous Theory and Multisensory Media*, Minneapolis: University of Minnesota Press.

Marr, A. (2004) *My Trade: A Short History of British Journalism*, London: Macmillan.

Martin, R. (1997) 'Staging crisis: twin tales in moving performance', in Phelan, P. and Lane, J. (eds) *Ends of Performance*, New York: New York University Press, pp. 186–196.

Massard, C. Guilbaud, G. Platt, H. and Schott, D. (eds) (2002) *Cities and Catastrophes*, Frankfurt: Peter Lang.

Massey, D. (1991) 'A global sense of place' *Marxism Today*, June, 24–29.

Massumi, B. (1997a) 'The political economy of belonging and the logic of relation' in Davidson, C. (ed.) *Anybody*, Cambridge, MA: MIT Press, pp. 224–238.

Massumi, B. (1997b) 'The autonomy of affect' in Patton, P. (ed.) *Deleuze: A Critical Reader*, Oxford: Blackwell, pp. 217–39.

Massumi, B. (2002) *Parables for the Virtual: Movement, Affect, Sensation*, Durham, NC: Duke University Press.

Massumi, B. (2004) 'Building experience' in Spuybroek, L., *Machining Architiecture*, London: Thames and Hudson, pp. 322–331.

Mattelart, A. (1996) *The Invention of Communication*, Minneapolis: University of Minnesota Press.

Mauss, M. (1992) *Techniques of the Body*, Cambridge: Cambridge University Press.

Merleau-Ponty, M. (1962) *The Phenomenology of Perception*, London: Routledge and Kegan Paul.

Mbembe, A. (2003) 'Necropolitics' *Public Culture*, 15: 11–40.

Medin, D.L. (ed.) (1999) *Folkbiology*, Cambridge, MA: MIT Press.

Meister, D. (1999) *The History of Human Factors and Ergonomics*, Mahwah, NJ: Lawrence Erlbaum Associates.

Merriman, P. (2001) 'M1: a cultural geography of an English motorway, 1946–1965', PhD Thesis, University of Nottingham.

Meyer, R. (2003) *Representing the Passions: Histories, Bodies, Visions*, Los Angeles: Getty Research Institute.

Middleton, D. and Brown, S.D. (2006) *The Social Psychology of Experience. Studies in Remembering and Forgetting*, London: Sage.

Miller, D. (1998) *A Theory of Shopping*, Cambridge: Polity Press.

Miller, D. (ed.) (2001) *Car Cultures*, Oxford: Berg.

Miller, J. (1983) 'Crowds and power: some English ideas on the state of primitive personality' *International Review of Psychoanalysis*, 10: 253–264.

Milton, K. and Svašek, M. (eds) (2005) *Mixed Emotions. Anthropological Studies of Feeling*, Oxford: Berg.

Milutis, J. (2006) *Ether: The Nothing That Connects Everything*, Minneapolis: University of Minnesota Press.

Mimica, J. (1992) *Intimations of Infinity: Cultural Meanings of the Iqwaye*, Oxford: Berg.

Mindich, D.T.Z. (2004) *Tuned Out: Why Americans Under 40 Don't Follow the News*, New York: Oxford University Press.

Mirowski, P. (2002) *Machine Dreams: Economics Becomes a Cyborg Science*, Cambridge: Cambridge University Press.

Mitchell, T. (2002) *Rule of Experts. Egypt, Techno-Poltics and Modernity*, Berkeley: University of California Press.

Mitchell, W.J. (2003) *Me++. The Cyborg Self and the Networked City*, Cambridge, MA: MIT Press.

Mitchell, W.J. (2005) *Placing Words: Symbols, Space and the City*, Cambridge, MA: MIT Press.

Miyazaki, H. (2004) *The Method of Hope. Anthropology, Philosophy, and Fijian Knowledge*, Stanford, CA: Stanford University Press.

Miyazaki, H. (2006) 'Economy of dreams: hope in global capitalism and its critiques' *Cultural Anthropology*, 21: 147–172.

Mokyr, J. (2003) *The Gifts of Athena*, Princeton, NJ: Princeton University Press.

Molotch, H. (2003) *Where Stuff Comes From*, New York: Routledge.

Montagu, A. (1986) *Touching: The Human Significance of the Skin*, New York: Harper and Row.

Moore, H. (2004) 'Global anxieties: concept-metaphors and pre-theoretical commitments in anthropology' *Anthropolgical Theory*, 4: 71–88.

Moore, J. and Slater, W. (2003) *Bush's Brain: How Karl Rove Made George W. Bush Presidential*, Hoboken, NJ: John Wiley.

Moore, R.O. (2000) *Savage Theory: Cinema as Modern Magic*, Durham, NC: Duke University Press.

Morris, D. (1999) *Behind the Oval Office: Getting Re-elected Against All Odds*, Los Angeles: Renaissance Books.

Morris, M. (1998) *Too Soon Too Late: History in Popular Culture*, Bloomington: Indiana University Press.

Morson, G.S. (1994) *Narrative and Freedom: The Shadows of Time*, New Haven, CT: Yale University Press.

Moscovici, S. (1985) 'Social influence and conformity' in Lindzey, G. and Aronson, E. (eds) *Handbook of Social Psychology*, Vol. 2, 3rd edn, New York: Random House, pp. 347–412.

Mouffe, C. (2002) 'Which public sphere for a democratic society' *Theoria*, June: 55–65.

Mulvey, L. (2005) *Death 24x a Second. Stillness and the Moving Image*, London: Reaktion.

Muecke, S. (1999) 'Travelling the subterranean river of blood: philosophy and magic in cultural studies' *Cultural Studies* 13: 1–17.

Myers, D.G. (2002) *Intuition: Its Powers and Perils*, New Haven, CT: Yale University Press.

Nancy, J.L. (2003) *A Finite Thinking*, Stanford, CA: Stanford University Press.

Nash, C. (2004) 'Genetic kinship' *Cultural Studies*, 18: 1–34.

Nee, V. and Swedberg, R. (eds) (2005) *The Economic Sociology of Capitalism*, Princeton, NJ: Princeton University Press.

Neff, G. and Stark, D. (2003) 'Permanently beta: responsive organization in the internet era', in Howard, P.E.N and Jones, S.(eds) *The Internet and American Life*, Thousand Oaks, CA: Sage.

Negri, A. (1988) *Revolution Retrieved: Writings on Marx, Keynes, Capitalist Crisis and New Social Subjects (1967–83)*, London: Rednotes.

Negri, A. (1991) *Marxism after Marx*, London: Pluto Press.

Nelson, D. (2006) 'The president and presidentialism' *South Atlantic Quarterly*, 105: 1–17.

NEST (2005) *What it Means to be Human: Origin and Evolution of Human Higher Cognitive Faculties*, Brussels: Directorate General for Research.

Netz, R. (1999) *The Shaping of Deduction in Greek Mathematics*, Cambridge: Cambridge University Press.

Netz, R. (2004) *Barbed Wire: An Ecology of Modernity*, Middletown, CT: Wesleyan University Press.

Newman, F. and Holzman, L. (1997) *The End of Knowing: A New Developmental Way of Learning*, New York: Routledge.

Newman, P. and Tarassenko, L. (eds) (2005) *Robotics: London, Cognitive Systems Foresight Project*, Project Review, November 2004.

Nietzsche, F. (1968) *The Will to Power*, New York: Vintage.

Nolan, J.L. (1998) *The Theurapeutic State. Justifying Government at Century's End*, Albany: New York University Press.

Nordstrom, C. (2004) *Shadows of War. Violence, Power and International Profiteering in the Twenty-First Century*, Berkeley: University of California Press.

Nordstrom, C. and Martin, J. (1992) *The Paths to Domination, Resistance and Terror*, Berkeley: University of California Press.

Nordstrom, C. and Robben, A.C.G.M. (1995) *Fieldwork under Fire*, Berkeley: University of California Press.

Norman, D.A. (2004) *Emotional Design: Why We Love (or Hate) Everyday Things*, New York: Basic Books.

Norretranders, T. (1998) *The User Illusion: Cutting Consciousness Down to Size*, New York: Viking.

Norris, P. (2002) *Democratic Phoenix. Reinventing Political Activism*, Cambridge: Cambridge University Press.

Norris, P., Curtice, J., Sanders, D., Scammell, M. and Semetko, H.A. (1999) *On Message. Communicating the Campaign*, London: Sage.

Norris, P., Kern, M. and Just, M. (eds) *Framing Terrorism: The News Media, the Government and the Public*, New York: Routledge.

Novack, C.J. (1990) *Sharing the Dance: Contact Improvisation and American Culture*, Madison, WI: University of Wisconsin Press.

Nunn, C. (2005) *De La Mettrie's Ghost : The Story of Decisions*, London: Macmillan.

Nussbaum, M.C. (2001) *Upheavals of Thought: The Intelligence of Emotions*, Cambridge: Cambridge University Press.

Ohnuki-Tierney, E. (2002) *Kamikaze, Cherry Blossoms and Nationalisms. The Militarization of Aesthetics in Japanese History*, Chicago: University of Chicago Press.

Orlie, M. (2002) 'The desire for freedom and the consumption of politics' *Philosophy and Social Criticism*, 28: 397–412.

Osborne, T. (2003) 'Against creativity. A philistine rant' *Economy and Society*, 32 (4): 507–525.

Oyama, S. (2000) *Evolution's Eye. A Systems View of the Biology–Culture Divide*, Durham, NC: Duke University Press.

Packard, V. (1960) *The Hidden Persuaders*, Harmondsworth: Penguin.

Pahl, R. (2000) *On Friendship*, Cambridge: Polity.

Parisi, L. (2004) *Abstract Sex. Philosophy, Bio-Technology and the Mutations of Desire*, London: Continuum.

Parkes, D.N. and Thrift, N.J. (1980) *Times, Spaces and Places. A Chronogeographic Perspective*, Chichester: John Wiley.

Parkin, D. (ed.) (1987) *The Anthropology of Evil*, Oxford: Blackwell.

Parks, L. (2003) 'Kinetic screens' in Couldry, N. and McCarthy, A. (eds) *Place, Scale and Culture in a Media Age*, London: Routledge, pp. 37–57.

Parry, B. (2004) *Trading the Genome*, New York: Columbia University Press.

Peek, P.M. (1991) *African Divination Systems*, Bloomington, IN: Indiana University Press.

Peluso, N. and Watts, M. (eds) (2001) *Violent Environments*, Ithaca, NY: Cornell University Press.

Pepperburg, M.I. (2002) *The Alex Studies. Cognitive and Communicative Abilities of Grey Parrots*, Cambridge, MA: Harvard University Press.

Perloff, M. (1996) *Wittgenstein's Ladder*, Chicago: Chicago University Press.

Perniola, M. (2004) *Sex Appeal of the Inorganic*, London: Continuum.

Peters, J.D. (1999) *Speaking into the Air: A History of the Idea of Communication*, Chicago: University of Chicago Press.

Petersen, A. (1996) *Martyrdom and the Politics of Religion*, Albany: State University Press of New York.

Petitot, J., Varela, F.J., Pachoud, B. and Roy, J. (eds) (1999) *Naturalizing Phenomenology. Issues in Contemporary Phenomenology and Cognitive Science*, Stanford, CA: Stanford University Press.

Phelan, P. (1993) *Unmarked: The Politics of Performance*, New York: Routledge.

Phelan, P. (1998) 'Introduction: the ends of performance' in *The Ends of Performance*, New York: New York University Press, pp. 1–19.

Phillips, A. (1999) *Darwin's Worms*, London: Faber and Faber.

Phillips, T. (2005 [1980]) *A Humument: A Treated Victorian Novel*, London: Thames and Hudson.

Pickering, A. (2003) 'On becoming: imagination, metaphysics and the mangle' in Ihde, D. and Selinger, E. (eds) *Chasing Technoscience: Matrix for Materiality*, Bloomington: Indiana University Press, pp. 96–116.

Pignarre, P. and Stengers, I. (2005) *La Sorcellerie capitaliste. Pratiques de désenvoûtement*, Paris: Editions de la Découverte.

Pine, J. and Gilmore, J.H (1999) *The Experience Economy*, Boston, MA: Harvard Business School Press.

Pini, M. (1996) 'Dance classes-dancing between classifications' *Feminism and Psychology*, 6: 411–426.

Pixley, J. (2004) *Emotions in Finance*, Cambridge: Cambridge University Press.

Pollock, G. (ed.) (1998) *Exceptional Spaces: Essays in Performance and History*, Chapel Hill, NC: University of North Carolina Press.

Poovey, M. (1998) *The History of the Modern Fact*, Chicago: University of Chicago Press.

Popkin, S.L. (1991) *The Reasoning Voter: Communication and Persuasion and Presidential Campaigns*, Chicago: University of Chicago Press.

Porter, T.M. (1992) *Trust in Numbers: The Pursuit of Objectivity in Science and Public Life*, Princeton, NJ: Princeton University Press.

Potolsky, M. (2006) *Mimesis*, New York: Routledge.

Povinelli, D.J. (2000) *Folk Physics for Apes: The Chimpanzee's Theory of How the World Works*, Oxford: Oxford University Press.

Prahalad, C.K. and Ramaswamy, V. (2004) *The Future of Competition*, Boston, MA: Harvard Business School Press.

Pred, R. (2005) *Onflow: Dynamics of Consciousness of Experience*, Cambridge, MA: MIT Press.

Probyn, E. (2005) *Blush: Faces of Shame*, Minneapolis: University of Minnesota Press.

Protevi, J. (2001) *Political Physics: Deleuze, Derrida and the Body Politic*, London: Athlone.

Rabinow, P. (1995) *Making PC: A Study of Biotechnology*, Chicago: University of Chicago Press.

Rabinow, P. (1996) *Essays on the Anthropology of Reason*, Princeton, NJ: Princeton University Press.

Rabinow, P. (2003) *Anthropos Today: Reflections on Modern Equipment*, Princeton, NJ: Princeton University Press.

Rabinow, P. (2004) 'Life sciences: discontents and consolations' in Baillie, H.W. and

Casey, T.K. (eds) *Is Human Nature Obsolete? Genetics, Bioengineering, and the Future of the Human Condition*, Cambridge, MA: MIT Press, pp. 99–122.

Rabinow, P. (2006) 'Steps toward an anthropological laboratory' *Discussion Paper*, 2 February 2006.

Radley, A. (1996) 'Displays and fragments: embodiment and the configuration of social worlds' *Theory and Psychology*, 6: 559–576.

Rajan, C.S. (1996) *The Enigma of Automobility*, Pittsburgh, PA: University of Pittsburgh Press.

Rajchman, J. (1998) *Constructions*, Cambridge, MA: MIT Press.

Rancière, J. (1999) *Disagreement: Politics and Philosophy*, Minneapolis: University of Minnesota Press.

Rath, R.C. (2003) *How Early America Sounded*, New York and London: Cornell University Press.

Rawls, A.M. (2002) 'Editor's introduction' in Garfinkel, H. *Ethnomethodology's Program. Working Out Durkheim's Aphorism*, Lanham, MD: Rowman and Littlefield, pp. 1–64.

Reason, J.T. (1982) 'Sensory Processes' in A. Taylor (ed.) *Introducing Psychology*, Harmondsworth: Penguin, pp. 218–52.

Redding, P. (1999) *The Logic of Affect*, Ithaca, NY: Cornell University Press.

Reddy, W. (2001) *The Navigation of Feeling. A Framework for the History of the Emotions*, Cambridge: Cambridge University Press.

Reginster, B. (2006) *The Affirmation of Life. Nietzsche on Overcoming Nihilism*, Cambridge, MA: Harvard University Press.

Rehm, R. (2002) *The Play of Space: Spatial Transformation in Greek Tragedy*, Princeton, NJ: Princeton University Press.

Retort (2005) *Afflicted Powers. Capital and Spectacle in a New Age of War*, London: Verso.

Reuter, C. (2004) *My Life is a Weapon: A Modern History of Suicide Bombing*, Princeton, NJ: Princeton University Press.

Reynolds, G. (2006) *An Army of Davids*, Nashville, TN: Nelson.

Rhoten, D. (2003) *A Multi-Method Analysis of the Social and Technical Conditions for Scientific Collaboration*, San Francisco: Hybrid Vigor Institute.

Richerson, P.J. and Boyd, R. (2005) *Not By Genes Alone. How Culture Transformed Evolution*, Chicago: University of Chicago Press.

Riley, D. (2005) *Impersonal Passion: Language as Affect*, Durham, NC.: Duke University Press.

Ritzer, G. (2003) *The Globalization of Nothing*, London: Sage.

Rival, L. (ed.) (1998) *The Social Life of Trees: Anthropological Perspectives on Tree Symbolism*, Oxford: Berg.

Roach, J. (1995) 'Culture and performance in the circum-Atlantic world' in Parker, A. and Sedgwick, E.K. (eds) *Performativity and Performance*, London: Routledge, pp. 63–78.

Roach, J. (1996) *Cities of the Dead: Circum-Atlantic Performance*, New York: Columbia University Press.

Roberts, J. (2004) *The Modern Firm. Organizational Design for Performance and Growth*, Oxford: Oxford University Press.

Robin, C. (2004) *Fear: The History of a Political Idea*, Oxford: Oxford University Press.

Robson, J. (2003) *Natural History*, London: Macmillan.

Rodowick, D.N. (1997) *Gilles Deleuze's Time Machine*, Durham, NC: Duke University Press.

Rogers, E. (2003) *Diffusion of Innovations*, New York: Free Press.

Roughgarden, J. (2004) *Evolution's Rainbow: Diversity, Gender, and Sexuality in Nature and People*, Berkeley: University of California Press.

Rubin, J. (1970) *Do It!* New York: Simon and Schuster.

Rose, J. (2004) 'Deadly embrace' *London Review of Books*, 26: 21–24.

Ross, C. (2006) *The Aesthetics of Disengagement. Contemporary Art and Depression*, Minneapolis: University of Minnesota Press.

Ross, K. (1996) *Fast Cars, Clean Bodies: De-colonization and the Re-ordering of France*, Cambridge, MA: MIT Press.

Ross, K. (2002) *May '68 and its Afterlives*, Chicago: University of Chicago Press.

Roth, G. (1989) *Maps to Ecstasy*, London: HarperCollins.

Roth, G. (1998) *Sweat Your Prayers: Movement as Spiritual Practice*, London: HarperCollins.

Rotman, B. (1993) *Ad Infinitum. The Ghost in Turing's Machine: Taking God out of Mathematics and Putting the Body Back In*, Stanford, CA: Stanford University Press.

Rotman, B. (2000) *Mathematics as Sign: Writing, Imagining Counting*, Stanford, CA: Stanford University Press

Rouse, J. (1996) *Engaging Science: How to Understand its Practices Philosophically*, Ithaca, NY: Cornell University Press.

Runciman, D. (2006) *The Politics of Good Intentions. History, Fear and Hypocrisy in the New World Order*, Princeton, NJ: Princeton University Press.

Rush, M. (1999) *New Media in Late Twentieth Century Art*, London: Thames and Hudson.

Ryan, A. (1995) *John Dewey and the High Tide of American Liberalism*, Ithaca, NY: Cornell University Press.

Sachs, W. (2002) *For Love of the Automobile. Looking Back into the History of Our Desires*, Berkeley: University of California Press.

Said, E.W. (1996) *Covering Islam: How the Media and Experts Determine How We See the Rest of the World*, New York: Vintage.

Salecl, R. (2004) *On Anxiety*, London: Routledge.

Salisbury, J. (2004) *The Blood of Martyrs: Unintended Consequences of Ancient Violence*, New York: Routledge.

Sandford, M.R. (ed.) (1995) *Happenings and Other Acts*, London: Routledge.

Santner, E.L. (2001) *On the Psychotheology of Everyday Life*, Chicago: University of Chicago Press.

Santner, E.L. (2006) *On Creaturely Life. Rilke, Benjamin, Sebald*, Chicago: University of Chicago Press.

Scarry, E. (1985) *The Body in Pain: The Making and Unmaking of the World*, New York: Oxford University Press.

Schatzki, T.R. (2002) *The Site of the Social: A Philosophical Account of the Constitution of Social Life and Change*, University Park: Pennsylvania State University Press.

Schechner, R. (1993) *The Future of Ritual: Writings on Culture and Performance*, London: Routledge.

Schechner, R. (1998) 'What is performance studies anyway?' in Phelan, P. and Lane, J. (eds) *The Ends of Performance*, New York: New York University Press, pp. 357–362.

Schechner, R. (2002) *Performance Studies: An Introduction*, London: Routledge.

Schieffelin, E.L. (1998) 'Problematising performance' in Hughes Freeland, R. (ed.) *Ritual, Performance, Media*, London: Routledge, pp. 194–207.

Schivelsbuch, W. (1986) *The Railway Journey: The Industrialization of Time and Space in the 19th Century*, Berkeley: University of California Press.

Schneider, J. and Susser, I. (eds) (2003) *Wounded Cities. Destruction and Reconstruction in a Globalized World*, Oxford: Berg.

Schoolman, M. (2001) *Reason and Horror: Critical Theory, Democracy and Aesthetic Individuality*, New York: Routledge.

Schrödinger, E. (1954) *Nature and the Greeks*, Cambridge: Cambridge University Press.

Schwartzman, B. (1978) *Transformations: The Anthropology of Children's Play*, New York: Plenum.

Schwenger, P. (2006) *The Tears of Things: Melancholy and Physical Objects*, Minneapolis: University of Minnesota Press.

Scott, C.E. (2002) *The Lives of Things*, Bloomington: Indiana University Press.

Scott, J. (1998) *Seeing Like a State: How Certain Schemes to Improve the Human Condition Have Failed*, New Haven, CT: Yale University Press.

Seabright, J. (2004) *The Company of Strangers: A Natural History of Economic Life*, Princeton, NJ: Princeton University Press.

Sears, D.O., Huddy, L. and Jervis, R. (eds) (2003) *The Oxford Handbook of Political Psychology*, Oxford: Oxford University Press.

Sedgwick, E.K. (2003) *Touching Feeling: Affect, Pedagogy, Performativity*, Durham, NC: Duke University Press.

Sedgwick, E.K. and Frank, A. (eds) (1995) *Shame and its Sisters: A Silvan Tomkins Reader*, Durham, NC: Duke University Press.

Seel, M. (2004) *Aesthetics of Appearing*, Stanford, CA: Stanford University Press.

Segel, H.B. (1998) *Modernism and the Physical Imperative*, Baltimore, MD: Johns Hopkins University Press.

Sennett, R. (1973) *The Hidden Injuries of Class*, New York: Vintage Books.

Sennett, R. (1994) *Flesh and Stone: The Body and the City in Western Civilization*, London: Faber and Faber.

Sennett, R. (2003) *Respect in an Age of Inequality*, New York: Norton.

Serres, M. (1980) *Le Parasite*, Paris: Bernard Grasset.

Serres, M. (1995) *Angels: A Modern Myth*, Paris: Flammarion.

Shanken, E.A. (2003) *Telematic Embrace: Visionary Theories of Art, Technology, and Consciousness*, Berkeley, CA: University of California Press.

Sharpe, W. (2003) *Cognitive Systems Project: Applications and Impact*, London: DTI/Foresight.

Sheets-Johnston, M. (1966) *The Phenomenology of Dance*, Madison: University of Wisconsin Press.

Sheets-Johnston, M. (2005) 'Man has always danced: forays into an art largely forgotten by philosophers' *Contemporary Aesthetics*, vol. 3; available online at http://www.contempaesthetics.org/newvolume/pages/article.php?articleID=273.

Sheller, M. and Urry, J. (2000) 'The city and the car' *International Journal of Urban and Regional Research*, 24: 737–757.

Sheridan, T.B. (2002) *Humans and Automation: Systems Design and Research Issues*, New York: John Wiley.

Sheringham, M. (1996) 'City space, mental space, poetic space: Paris in Breton, Benjamin and Reda' in Sheringham, M. (ed.) *Parisian Fields*, London: Reaktion, pp. 85–114.

Shotter, J. (1993) *Cultural Politics of Everyday Life*, Milton Keynes: Open University Press.

Shotter, J. (1995) *Conversational Realities*, London: Sage.

Shotter, J. (1998) 'Social construction as social politics: Oliver Sacks and the case of Dr P' in Bayer, B. and Shotter, J. (eds) *Reconstructing the Psychological Subject: Bodies, Practices and Technologies,* London: Sage, pp. 33–51.

Shotter, J. (2004) 'Responsive expression in living bodies' *Cultural Studies,* 18: 443–460.

Shusterman, R. (1997) *Practising Philosophy: Pragmatism and the Philosophical Life,* New York: Routledge.

Shusterman, R. (1999) 'Somaesrhetics: a disciplinary proposal' *Journal of Aesthetics and Art Criticism* 57: 299–313.

Siegert, B. (1999) *Relays: Literature as an Epoch of the Postal System,* Stanford, CA: Stanford University Press.

Simic, C. (2006) 'Salvation through laughter' *New York Review of Books,* 12 January: 22–25.

Simmel, G. (1990 [1900]) *The Philosophy of Money,* London: Routledge.

Simondon, G. (1989) *Du mode d'existence des objects techniques,* Paris: Aubier.

Sloterdijk, P. (1998) *Sphären I. Blasen,* Frankfurt: Suhrkamp Verlag.

Sloterdijk, P. (1999) *Sphären II. Globen,* Frankfurt: Suhrkamp Verlag.

Sloterdijk, P. (2004) *Sphären III. Schaume,* Frankfurt: Suhrkamp Verlag.

Sloterdijk, P. (2005a) 'Against gravity. Bettina Funcke talks with Peter *Sloterdijk'* *Bookforum,* February/March.

Sloterdijk, P. (2005b) *Im Weltinnenraum des Kapitals,* Frankfurt: Suhrkamp Verlag.

Sloterdijk, P. (2005c) 'Atmospheric politics' in Latour, B. and Weibel, P. (eds) *Making Things Public. Atmospheres of Democracy,* Cambridge, MA: MIT Press, pp. 944–951.

Sloterdijk, P. (2005d) 'Foreword to the theory of spheres' in Ohanian, M. and Royaux, J.C. (eds) *Cosmograms,* pp. 223–240. New York: Lukas and Sternberg.

Sloterdijk, P. (2006) 'War on latency: on some relations between surrealism and terror' *Radical Philosophy,* 137: 14–19.

Smith, B.R. (1999) *The Acoustic World of Early Modern England: Attending to the O-Factor,* Chicago: University of Chicago Press.

Smith, D.V. (2003) *The Arts of Possession: The Middle English Household Imaginary,* Minneapolis: University of Minnesota Press.

Smith, D.W. (1997) 'A life of pure immanence: Deleuze's "Critique et Clinique" project' in Deleuze, G., *Essays Critical and Clinical,* Minneapolis, MN: University of Minnesota Press, pp. xi–liii.

Smith, M. and Morra, J. (eds) (2006) *The Prosthetic Impulse. From a Posthuman Present to a Biocultural Future,* Cambridge, MA: MIT Press.

Smith, N. (1982) 'Dance in translation: the hieroglyphs' *Contact Quarterly,* 7: 43–46.

Smith, P. (ed.) (2002) 'Regimes of emotion' Special Issue of *Soundings,* 20: 98–217.

Sobchack, V. (ed.) (2000) *Metamorphing. Visual Transformation and the Culture of Quick Change,* Minneapolis: University of Minnesota Press.

Soden, G. (2003) *Defying Gravity: Land Divers, Roller Coasters, Gravity Bums, and the Human Obsession with Falling,* New York: Norton.

Soete, L. (2005) *Activating Knowledge,* Discussion Paper for the UK Presidency.

Solnit, R. (2000) *Wanderlust: A History of Walking,* London: Viking.

Solnit, R. (2005) *Hope in the Dark: The Untold History of People Power,* revised edn, Edinburgh: Canongate Books.

Solomon, R.C. (ed.) (2003) *What Is An Emotion? Classic and Contemporary Readings,* 2nd edn, Oxford: Oxford University Press.

Sorel, G. (1906/1999) *Reflections on Violence,* Cambridge: Cambridge University Press.

Sørenson, B. (2004) *Making Events Work: Or, How to Multiply a Crisis*, Frederiksburg: Samsfundlitteratur.

Sosky, W. (2002) *Violence: Terrorism, Genocide, War*, London: Granta.

Speak, D. (1999) *The End of Patience*, Bloomington: Indiana University Press.

Spinks, T. (2001) 'Thinking the posthuman: literature, affect and the politics of style' *Textual Practice*, 15: 23–46.

Spinosa, C., Flores, F. and Dreyfus, H. (1997) *Disclosing New Worlds: Entrepreneurship, Democratic Action and the Culturalisation of Solidarity*, Cambridge, MA: MIT Press.

Spivey, N. (2001) *Enduring Creation: Art, Pain and Fortitude*, London: Thames and Hudson.

Squier, S.M. (2004) *Liminal Lives: Imagining the Human at the Frontiers of Bioscience*, Durham, NC: Duke University Press.

Stark, R. (2001) *One True God: Historical Consequences of Monotheism*, Princeton, NJ: Princeton University Press.

Steedman, C. (1998) 'What a rag rug means' *Journal of Material Culture*, 3: 23–64.

Steiger, B. (1998) *Technics and Time: Vol. 1. The Fault of Epimetheus*, Stanford, CA: Stanford University Press.

Steinberg, M. (2005) *The Fiction of a Thinkable World. Body, Meaning and the Culture of Capitalism*, New York: Monthly Review Press.

Stengers, I. (1997) *Power and Invention: Situating Science*, Minneapolis: University of Minnesota Press.

Stengers, I. (2002a) 'A "cosmo-politics" – risk, hope, change' in Zournazi, M. (ed.) *Hope: New Philosophies for Change*, London: Routledge.

Stengers, I. (2002b) *Penser Avec Whitehead: Une Libre et Sauvage Création de Concepts*, Paris: Gallimard.

Stengers, I. (2004) *A Constructivist Reading of Process and Reality*, London: Goldsmiths.

Stengers, I. (2005) 'Whitehead and science: from philosophy of nature to speculative cosmology', Seminar Paper, available online at http://www.mcgill.ca/files/hpsc/Whitmontreal.pdf.

Stengers, I. (2006) 'Gilles Deleuze's last message' *The Virgin and the Neutrino: Which Future for Science*, Paris.

Sterne, J. (2003) *The Audible Past: Cultural Origins of Sound Reproduction*, Durham, NC: Duke University Press.

Sterelny, K. (2003) *Thought in a Hostile World: The Evolution of Human Cognition*, Oxford: Blackwell.

Stevens, W. (1960) *The Necessary Angel. Essays on Reality and the Imagination*, London: Faber.

Steventon, A. and Wright, S. (eds) (2005) *Intelligent Spaces. The Application of Pervasive ICT*, Berlin: Springer Verlag.

Stewart, N. (1998) 'Relanguaging the body: phenomenological descriptions and the body image' *Performance Research*, 3: 42–58.

Stille, A. (2006) *The Sack of Rome*, New York: Penguin Press.

Stivers, R. (1999) *Technology as Magic: The Triumph of the Irrational*, New York: Continuum.

Storey, J. and Salaman, G. (eds) (2005) *Managers of Innovation. Insights into Making Innovation Happen*, Oxford: Blackwell.

Storper, M. and Venables, A.J. (2004) 'Buzz: face-to-face contact and the urban economy' *Journal of Economic Geography*, 4: 351–370.

Strathern, M. (1996) 'Cutting the network' *Journal of the Royal Anthropological Institute*, 2: 517–535.

Strathern, M. (1999) *Property, Substance, and Effect*, London: Athlone Press.

Strathern, M. (2004) *Commons and Borderlands*, Wantage: Sean Kingston Publishing.

Sudnow, D. (1993) *Ways of the Hand*, Cambridge, MA: MIT Press.

Sutton-Smith, B. (1997) *The Ambiguity of Play*, Cambridge, MA: Harvard University Press.

Swearingen, J. and Cutting-Gray, J. (eds) (2002) *Extreme Beauty: Aesthetics, Politics, Death*, London: Continuum.

Tallis, R. (2003) *The Hand: A Philosophical Inquiry into Human Being*, Edinburgh: Edinburgh University Press.

Tamen, M. (2001) *Friends of Interpretable Objects*, Cambridge, MA: Harvard University Press.

Tarde, G. (1902) *Psychologie Economique*, Paris: Félix Alcan.

Tarde, G. (1962) *The Laws of Imitation*, Gloucester, MA: Peter Smith.

Tarde, G. (2000) *Social Laws: An Outline of Sociology*, Kitchener: Batoche Books.

Tarde, G. (2005) *Underground (Fragments of Future Histories)*, Brussels: Les Maîtres de Formes Contemporains.

Taussig, M. (1992) *The Nervous System*, New York: Routledge.

Taussig, M. (1993) *Mimesis and Alterity: A Particular History of the Senses*, New York: Routledge.

Taussig, M. (1994) 'Physiognomic aspects of visual words' in Taylor, L. (ed.) *Visualizing Theory*, New York: Routledge, pp. 205–212.

Taussig, M. (1997) *The Magic of the State*, London: Routledge.

Taussig, M. (1998) 'Crossing the Face' in Spyer, P. (ed.) *Border Fetishisms: Material Objects in Unstable Spaces*, New York: Routeldge, pp. 224–43.

Taussig, M. (1999) *Defacement: Public Secrecy and the Labor of the Negative*, Stanford, CA: Stanford University Press.

Taylor, C. (2004) *Modern Social Imaginaries*, Durham NC: Duke University Press.

Ten Bos, R. and Kaulingfreks, R. (2002) 'Life between faces' *Ephemera*, 2: 6–27.

Thackara, J. (2005) *In the Bubble. Designing in a Complex World*, Cambridge, MA: MIT Press.

Thomas, H. (ed.) (1998) *Dance in the City*, London: Macmillan.

Thomke, S.H. (2003) *Experimentation Matters. Unlocking thePotentioal of New Technologies for Innovation*, Boston, MA: Harvard Business School Press.

Thompson, C. (2002) 'When elephants stand for competing philosophies of nature: Amboseli National Park, Kenya' in Law, J. and Mol, A. (eds) *Complexities: Social Studies of Knowledge Practices*, Durham, NC: Duke University Press, pp. 166–190.

Threadgold, T. (1997) *Feminist Poetics: Poiesis, Performance, Histories*, London: Routledge.

Thrift, N.J. (1983) 'On the determination of social action in space and time' *Environment and Planning D: Society and Space*, 1: 22–57.

Thrift, N.J. (1990) 'Transport and communication 1770–1914' in Dodgshon, R.J. and Butlin, R. (eds) *A New Historical Geography of England and Wales*, 2nd edn, London: Academic Press, pp. 453–486.

Thrift, N.J. (1995) 'A hyperactive world' in Johnston, R.J. Taylor, P.J. and Watts, M. (eds) *Geographies of Global Transformation*, Oxford: Blackwell.

Thrift, N.J. (1996) *Spatial Formations*, London: Sage.

Thrift, N.J. (1997) 'The still point: resistance, expressive embodiment and dance' in Pile, S. and Keith, M. (eds) *Geographies of Resistance*, London: Routledge, pp. 124–151.

Thrift, N.J. (1998) 'Steps to an ecology of place' in Massey, D., Allen, J. and Sarre, P. (eds) *Human Geography Today*, Cambridge: Policy, pp. 220–243.

Thrift, N.J. (1999) 'Entanglements of power: shadows?' in Sharp, J., Routledge, P., Philo, C. and Paddison, R. (eds) *Geographies of Domination/Resistance*, London: Routledge, pp. 269–277.

Thrift, N.J. (2000a) 'Afterwords' *Environment and Planning D. Society and Space*, 18: 213–255.

Thrift, N.J. (2000b) 'Still life in nearly present time: the object of Nature' *Body and Society*, 6 (3–4): 34–57.

Thrift, N.J. (2001) 'Summoning life' in Cloke, P., Crang, P. and Goodwin, P.B. (eds) *Envisioning Geography*, London: Arnold.

Thrift, N.J. (2003a) 'Bare life' in Thomas, H. and Ahmed, J. (eds) *Cultural Bodies*, Oxford: Blackwell.

Thrift, N.J. (2003b) 'Closer to the machine? Intelligent environments, new forms of possession and the rise of the supertoy' *Cultural Geographies*, 10: 389–407.

Thrift, N.J. (2004a) 'Remembering the technological unconscious by foregrounding knowledges of position' *Environment and Planning D. Society and Space*, 22: 175–190.

Thrift, N.J. (2004b) 'Intensities of feeling: towards a spatial politics of affect' *Geografiska Annaler*, 86: 57–78.

Thrift, N.J. (2004c) 'Remembering the technological unconscious by foregrounding knowledges of position' *Environment and Planning D. Society and Space*, 22: 175–190.

Thrift, N.J. (2004d) 'Electric animals. New models of everyday life?' *Cultural Studies*, 18: 461–482.

Thrift, N.J. (2004e) 'Radio' in Harrison, S., Pile, S. and Thrift, N.J. (eds) *Patterned Ground. Entanglements of Nature and Culture*, London: Reaktion, pp. 269–270.

Thrift, N.J. (2004f) 'A geography of unknown lands' in Duncan, J.S. and Johnson, N. (eds) *The Companion to Cultural Geography*, Oxford: Blackwell.

Thrift, N.J. (2004g) 'Beyond mediation' in Miller, D. (ed.) *Materiality*, Durham, NC: Duke University Press.

Thrift, N.J. (2005a) *Knowing Capitalism*, London: Sage.

Thrift, N.J. (2005b) 'Movement space: the changing domain of thinking resulting from the development of new kinds of spatial awareness' *Economy and Society*, 33: 582–604.

Thrift, N.J. (2005c) 'But malice aforethought: cities and the natural history of hatred' *Transactions of the Institute of British Geographers*, NS30: 133–150.

Thrift, N.J. (2005d) 'From born to made: technology, biology and space' *Transactions of the Institute of British Geographers*, NS30: 463–476.

Thrift, N.J. (2006a) 'Re-inventing invention: the generalization of outsourcing and other new forms of efficacy under globalization' *Economy and Society*, 35: 279–306.

Thrift, N.J. (2006b) 'Space' *Theory Culture and Society*, 23, 139–146.

Thrift, N.J. (2007) 'Immaculate warfare? The spatial politics of extreme violence' in Gregory, D. and Pred, A.R. (eds) *Violent Geographies: Fear, Terror and Political Violence*, New York, London: Routledge.

Thrift, N.J. and Forbes, D.K. (1986) *The Price of War*, London: George Allen and Unwin.

Thrift, N.J. and French, S. (2002) 'The automatic production of space' *Transactions of the Institute of British Geographers*, NS27: 309–325.

Tilly, C. (2003) *The Politics of Collective Violence*, Cambridge: Cambridge University Press.

Todes, S. (2001) *Body and World*, Cambridge, MA: MIT Press.

Tomasello, M. (1999) *The Cultural Origins of Human Cognition*, Cambridge, MA: Harvard University Press.

Todorov, A. and Willis, J. (2006) 'First impressions: making up your mind after a 100–Ms exposure to a face' *Psychological Science*, 17 (7): 592–598.

Todorov, A., Mandisodza, A.N., Goren, A. and Hall, C.C. (2005) 'Inferences of competence from faces predict election outcomes' *Science*, 308: 1623–1626.

Toscano, A. (2004a) 'Preface: the coloured thickness of a problem' in Alliez, E. *The Signature of the World: What is Deleuze and Guattari's Philosophy?* London: Continuum, pp. ix–xxv.

Toscano, A. (2004b) 'Factory, territory, metropolis, empire' *Angelaki*, 9: 197–216.

Traub, V. (2002) *The Renaissance of Lesbianism in Early Modern England*, Cambridge: Cambridge University Press.

Trumble, A. (2003) *A Brief History of the Smile*, New York: Basic Books.

Tsing, A. (2005) *Friction. An Ethnography of Global Connections*, Princeton, NJ: Princeton University Press.

Tufnell, M. and Crickmay, C. (1990) *Body Space Image: Notes Towards Improvisation and Performance*, London: Dance Books.

Tufte, E.R. (2003) *The Cognitive Style of Powerpoint*, New York: Graphics Press.

Tulloch, J. (1999) *Performing Culture*, London: Sage.

Turner, G. (2004) *Understanding Celebrity*, London: Sage.

Turner, J.S. (2000) *The Extended Organism: The Physiology of Animal-Built Structures*, Cambridge, MA: Harvard University Press.

Turner, S.P. (2002) *Brains/Practices/Relativism: Social Theory after Cognitive Science*, Chicago: University of Chicago Press.

Urry, J. (2000) *Sociology Beyond Societies*, London: Routledge.

Ury, W. (ed.) (2002) *Must We Fight?* San Francisco: Jossey Bass.

Vallega, A.A. (2003) *Heidegger and the Issue of Space: Thinking on Exilic Grounds*, University Park: Pennsylvania State University Press.

Van Gennep, A. (1961) *The Rites of Passage*, Chicago: University of Chicago Press.

Van Henten, J.W. and Avemarie, F. (eds) (2002) *Martyrdom and Noble Death*, London and New York: Routledge.

Varela, F. (1999) *The Psychology of Awakening: Buddhism, Science and Our Day to Day Lives*, London: Rider/Random House.

Vendler, H. (1995) *The Breaking of Style*, Cambridge, MA: Harvard University Press.

Verbeek, P.-P. (2005) *What Things Do. Philosophical Relations on Technology, Agency and Design*, University Park: Pennsylvania State University Press.

Verran, H. (2001) *Science and an African Logic*, Chicago: University of Chicago Press.

Vesely, D. (2004) *Architecture in an Age of Divided Representation*, Cambridge, MA: MIT Press.

Vicinus, M. (2004) *Intimate Friends: Women Who Loved Women*, Chicago: University of Chicago Press.

Victor, B. (2003) *Army of Roses. Inside the World of Palestinian Suicide Bombers*, New York: Rodale.

Vidler, A. (2000) *Warped Space: Art, Architecture, and Anxiety in Modern Culture*, Cambridge, MA: MIT Press.

Viola, B. (1995) *Reasons for Knocking at an Empty House: Writings 1973–1994*, London: Thames and Hudson.

Viola, B. (2003) *The Passions*, Los Angeles: Getty Research Institute.

Vincent-Buffault, A. (1991) *The History of Tears: Sensibility and Sentimentality in France*, New York: St Martin's Press.

Virilio, P. (1995) *The Art of the Motor*, Minneapolis: University Of Minnesota Press.

Virilio, P. (1997) *Open Sky*, London: Verso.

Virno, P. (2004) *A Grammar of the Multitude*, New York: Semiotext(e).

Virno, P. (2005) 'Interview with Paolo Virno', *Grey Room*, 21: 26–37.

Virno, P. (2006) 'Reading Gilbert Simondon. Transindividuality, technical activity and reification' *Radical Philosophy*, 136: 34–43.

Viveiros de Castro, E. (2005) 'From multiculturalism to multi-naturalism' in Chanian, M. and Royoux, J.C. (eds) *Cosmograms*, New York: Lukas and Sternberg, pp. 137–156.

Vogel, S. (2001) *Prime Mover. A Natural History of Muscle*, New York, W.W. Norton.

Vollmann, W.T. (2004) *Rising Up and Rising Down: Some Thoughts on Violence, Freedom and Urgent Means*, London: Ecco.

Von Hippel, E. (2005) *Democratising Innovation*, Cambridge, MA: MIT Press.

Wacquant, L. (2004) *Body and Soul. Notebooks of an Apprentice Boxer*, Oxford: Oxford University Press.

Wagner, R. (2001) *An Anthropology of the Subject: Holographic Worldview in New Guinea and Its Meaning and Significance for the World of Anthropology*, Berkeley: University of California Press.

Walkerdine, V. and Blackman, L. (2003) *Mass Hysteria*, London: Macmillan Palgrave.

Wall, C.S. (2006) *The Prose of Things. Transformations of Desription in the Eighteenth Century*, Chicago: University of Chicago Press.

Wall, T.C. (1999) *Radical Passivity: Levinas, Blanchot and Agamben*, Albany: State University of New York Press.

Wallace, A.C. (1993) *Walking, Literature, and English Culture: The Origins and Uses of Peripatetic in the Nineteenth Century*, Oxford: Clarendon Press.

Walton, K.L. (1990) *Mimesis as Make-Believe: On the Foundations of the Representational Arts*, Cambridge, MA: Harvard University Press.

Ward, G. (ed.) (2000) *The Certeau Reader*, Oxford: Blackwell.

Warner, M. (2002) *Publics and Counterpublics*, New York: Zone Books.

Watson, S. (1998a) 'The neurobiology of sorcery: Deleuze and Guattari's brain' *Biology and Society*, 4 (4): 23–45.

Watson, S. (1998b) 'The New Bergsonism' *Radical Philosophy*, 92: 1–23.

We Are What We Do (2004) *Change the World for a Fiver*, London: Short Books.

Webber, R. (2005) 'The 2005 General Election campaign: how effectively did the parties apply segmentation to their direct marketing strategies?' (forthcoming).

Webbon, C, Baker, P.J. and Harris, S. (2004) 'Faecal density counts for monitoring changes in red fox numbers in rural Britain' *Journal of Applied Ecology*, 41: 768–779.

Wegner, D.M. (2002) *The Illusion of Conscious Will*, Cambridge, MA: MIT Press.

Weinstein, P. (2005) *Unknowing: The Work of Modernist Fiction*, Ithaca, NY: Cornell University Press.

Weinstein, M. (ed.) (2005) *Globalisation. What's New?* New York: Columbia University Press.

Weir, A., Chappell, J. and Kacelnik, A. (2002) 'Shaping of hooks in New Caledonian crows' *Science*, 297: 981.

Weiss, B. (1996) *The Making and Unmaking of the Maya Lived World: Consumption, Commodification and Everyday Practice*, Durham, NC: Duke University Press.

Weiss, M.J. (2000) *The Clustered World*, Boston, MA: Little, Brown.

Weitz, E.D. (2003) *A Century of Genocide: Utopias of Race and Nation*, Princeton, NJ: Princeton University Press.

West, H.G. and Sanders, T. (eds) (2003) *Transparency and Conspiracy: Ethnograpics and Suspicion in the New World Order*, Durham, NC: Duke University Press.

Whatmore, S.J. (2002) *Hybrid Geographies*, London: Sage.

Wheeler, W. (2006) *The Whole Creature: Complexity, Biosemiotics and the Evolution of Culture*, London: Lawrence and Wishart.

White, M. (2005) 'The liberal character of ethological governance' *Economy and Society*, 34: 474–94.

White, S.K. (2000) *Sustaining Affirmation: The Strengths of Weak Ontology in Political Theory*, Princeton, NJ: Princeton University Press.

Whitehead, A.N. (1920) *The Concept of Nature*, Cambridge: Cambridge University Press.

Whitehead, A.N. (1968) *Modes of Thought*, New York: Free Press.

Whitehead, A.N. (1978) *Process and Reality*, New York: Macmillan.

Whitehead, N.L. (2002) *Dark Shamans: Kanaimà and the Poetics of Violent Death*, Durham, NC: Duke University Press.

Whitehead, N.L. (2004a) 'Rethinking anthropology of violence' *Anthropology Today*, 20 (5): 1–2.

Whitehead, N.L. (ed.) (2004b) *Violence: Poetics, Performance, Expression*, London: James Currey Publishers.

Whitfield, D. and Langford, J. (2001) 'Ergonomics' in Blakemore, C. and Jennett, S. (eds) *The Oxford Companion to the Body*, Oxford: Oxford University Press.

Wilkinson, I. (2005) *Suffering: A Sociological Introduction*, Cambridge: Polity Press.

Williams, R. (1972) *Marxism and Literature*, New York: Oxford University Press.

Williams, S.J. (2001) *Emotion and Social Theory*, London: Sage.

Williams, S.T. (1998) 'Bodily dys-order: desire, excess and the transgression of corporeal boundaries' *Body and Society* 4: 54–82.

Wilson, E. (2004) *Psychosomatic. Feminism and the Neurobiological Body*, Durham, NC: Duke University Press.

Wilson, E.R. (1998) *The Hand: How its Use Shapes the Brain, Language and Culture*, New York: Pantheon.

Wilson, T. (1993 [1553]) *The Art of Rhetoric*, University Park: Pennsylvania State University Press.

Wilson, T.D. (2002) *Strangers to Ourselves. Discovering the Adaptive Unconscious*, Cambridge, MA: Belknap Press.

Wittgenstein, L. (1953) *Philosophical Investigations*, Oxford: Basil Blackwell.

Wittgenstein, L. (1969) *On Certainty*, Oxford: Basil Blackwell.

Wittgenstein, L. (1980) *Remarks on the Philosophy of Psychology*, 2 vols, Oxford: Blackwell.

Woese, C.R. (2004) 'A new biology for a new century' *Microbiology and Molecular Biology Reviews*, 68: 173–186.

Wolfe, C. (ed.) (2003) *Zoontologies: The Question of the Animal*, Minneapolis: University of Minnesota Press.

Wolff, E. (2002) 'Digital cathedral' *Millimeter*, 1 February.

Wolfram, S. (2002) *A New Kind of Science*, Champaign, IL: Wolfram Media Incorporated.

Wolin, S. (2000) 'Political theory: from vocation to invocation' in Frank, J.A. and Tamborino, J. (eds) *Vocations of Political Theory*, Minneapolis: University of Minnesota Press, pp. 3–22.

Wollheim, R. (1999) *On the Emotions*, New Haven, CT: Yale University Press.

Woloch, A. (2003) *The One vs the Many. Minor Characters and the Space of the Protagonist in the Novel*, Princeton, NJ: Princeton University Press.

Woodward, R. (2004) *Military Geographies*, Oxford: Blackwell.

Wright, S. (2002) *Storming Heaven: Class Composition and Struggle in Italian Autonomist Marxism*, London: Pluto Press.

Wyatt, T. (2003) *Pheromones and Animal Behaviour: Communication by Smell and Taste*, Cambridge: Cambridge University Press.

Wynne, C.D.L. (2004) *Do Animals Think?* Princeton, NJ: Princeton University Press.

Yates, J. (1994) 'Evolving information use in firms, 1850–1920: ideology and information technologies' in Bud-Frierman, L. (ed.) *Information Acumen: The Understanding and Use of Business Knowledge in Modern Business*, London: Routledge, pp. 26–50.

Yates, J. (ed.) (2001) *Information Technology and Organizational Transformation*, London: Sage.

Zielinski, S. (2005) *Deep Time of the Media: Toward an Archaeology of Hearing and Seeing by Technical Means*, Cambridge, MA: MIT Press.

Zizek, S. (2003) *The Puppet and the Dwarf: The Perverse Core of Christianity*, Cambridge, MA: MIT Press.

Zizek, S. (2004) *Organs without Bodies: Deleuze and Consequences*, New York: Routledge.

Zubiri, X., trans. Caponigri, A.R. (2000) *On Essence*, Washington, DC: Catholic University Press of America.

Zubiri, X., trans. Orringer, R. (2003) *Dynamic Structure of Reality*, Champaign: University of Illinois Press.

Zumthor, P. (2006) *Atmospheres. Architectural Environments. Surrounding Objects*, Basel: Birkhäuser Verlag.

Index

Note: page numbers in italics denote tables or figures